December 3, 2006

To ~~Beth~~ Beynen,

On this day when you join into membership with Germantown Mennonite Church, we commit ourselves to walking together on Jesus' path of peace.

PEACE IS THE WAY

GMC Peace + Social Concerns Committee

PEACE IS THE WAY

Writings on Nonviolence
from the Fellowship of Reconciliation

Edited by Walter Wink

ORBIS BOOKS

Maryknoll, New York 10545

Eighth Printing, February 2006

The Catholic Foreign Mission Society of America (Maryknoll) recruits and trains people for overseas missionary service. Through Orbis Books, Maryknoll aims to foster the international dialogue that is essential to mission. The books published, however, reflect the opinions of their authors and are not meant to represent the official position of the society.

To obtain more information about Maryknoll and Orbis Books, please visit our website at www.maryknoll.org.

Manufactured in the United States of America.
Manuscript editing and typesetting by Joan Weber Laflamme.

About the F.O.R.
The Fellowship of Reconciliation is the largest, oldest, interfaith peace organization in the United States. With thousands of individual members, local groups, and religious peace fellowships, FOR pursues its mission of promoting peace and justice through the way of active nonviolence. For more information about FOR, to join FOR, or to subscribe to *Fellowship* magazine, contact:
FOR, Box 271, Nyack, New York 10960. Phone: (845) 358-1601. Fax: (845) 358-4924.
E-mail: for@forusa.org
Web: www.forusa.org

Library of Congress Cataloging-in-Publication Data

Peace is the way : writings on nonviolence from the Fellowship of Reconciliation / edited by Walter Wink.
    p.cm.
  ISBN 1-57075-315-6 (pbk.)
    1. Peace—Religious aspects. 2. Religion and justice. I. Wink, Walter. II. Fellowship of Reconciliation (U.S.)

BL65.P4 P4315 2000
291.1'7873—dc21

                                                        00-022077

For all members of the Fellowship of Reconciliation
past, present, and future
with gratitude and hope

There is no way to peace.
Peace is the way.
A. J. Muste

Contents

Preface xi
    WALTER WINK

Introduction: The Rebel Passion xv
Eighty-five Years of the Fellowship of Reconciliation
    RICHARD DEATS

Part One
THE VISION OF PEACE

1 Nonviolence—The Greatest Force 2
    M. K. GANDHI

2 Pacifism and Class War 4
    A. J. MUSTE

3 Has Pacifism Become Impossible? 8
    JOHN HAYNES HOLMES

4 The Relevance of an Impossible Ideal 17
    G. H. C. MACGREGOR

5 The Pacifist Way of Life 30
    A. J. MUSTE

6 A Post-liberal Pacifism 37
    JOHN M. SWOMLEY JR.

7 Blessed Are the Meek 41
  The Roots of Christian Nonviolence
    THOMAS MERTON

8 Nonviolence and Feminism 46
    SHELLEY DOUGLASS

9 The Pacifist Vision 49
    MARY EVELYN JEGEN

10 How Nonviolence Works 54
    GLENN SMILEY

Part Two
WITNESSES FOR PEACE

11 The Way of Peace 60
    MARTIN NIEMOELLER

12 My Pilgrimage to Nonviolence 64
    MARTIN LUTHER KING JR.

13 Martin Buber and the Covenant of Peace 72
    MAURICE S. FRIEDMAN

14 The Principle Is the Unity of Life 76
    A CONVERSATION WITH LANZA DEL VASTO

15 An Aspiration, Not an Achievement 82
    AN INTERVIEW WITH ALFRED HASSLER

16 Thomas Merton 89
    A Friend Remembered
    JIM FOREST

17 Connecting the Altar to the Pentagon 93
    DANIEL BERRIGAN

18 Adolfo Perez Esquivel 98
    Behind the Man and the Prize
    RICHARD CHARTIER

19 Remembering Dorothy Day 104
    JIM FOREST

20 Peace Pilgrim 109
    ANN AND JOHN RUSH

21 The Experiments of Gandhi 112
    Nonviolence in the Nuclear Age
    JOHN DEAR

Part Three
SPIRIT OF PEACE

22 Hasidism and the Love of Enemies 118
    MAURICE S. FRIEDMAN

23 Social Action and the Need for Prayer 124
    DOROTHY FRIESEN

24 Envisioning the Peaceable Kingdom 129
    ELISE BOULDING

25 Taking Heart 135
    Spiritual Exercises from Social Activists
    JOANNA MACY

26 Saying No to Death 143
    Henri J. M. Nouwen

27 Civil Disobedience as Prayer 149
    Jim Douglass

28 Being Peace 153
    Thich Nhat Hanh

29 Gandhi and the Ancient Wisdom of Nonviolence 159
    Mairead Corrigan Maguire

Part Four
INTERRACIAL JUSTICE

30 The Will to Segregation 164
    Howard Thurman

31 The Coming Revolt against Jim Crow 170
    James Farmer

32 Walk for Freedom 175
    Martin Luther King Jr.

33 Facing the Challenge of a New Age 178
    Martin Luther King Jr.

34 Behind the Sit-ins 187
    Lillian Smith

35 We Must Keep Going 193
    Martin Luther King Jr. and the Future of America
    Vincent Harding

36 Growing up Black 204
    Charles Alphin

Part Five
NONVIOLENCE IN ACTION

37 Disarmament and Defense 210
    John Nevin Sayre

38 How to Stop Aggressors 216
    M. K. Gandhi

39 The Stages of Nonviolence 218
    André Trocmé

40 On Nonviolent Revolution 224
    Danilo Dolci

41 "People Are Willing to Sacrifice Themselves . . . " 227
    An Interview with Cesar Chavez

x • Contents

42 Disregarded History 231
    The Power of Nonviolent Action
    GENE SHARP

43 Awakening from a Dream of Kings and Wizards 236
    DANIEL ELLSBERG

44 The Violence in Ourselves 240
    DOROTHY T. SAMUEL

45 Justice and Military Madness 244
    THE CASE OF THE SPERRY SOFTWARE PAIR

46 When Prayer and Revolution Become People Power 248
    HILDEGARD GOSS-MAYR

47 Shine on in Montana 255
    JO CLARE HARTSIG

Part Six
THE PATH OF RECONCILIATION

48 Daring to Be Human 258
    MAGDA YOORS-PEETERS

49 Tale from Vienna 260
    MURIEL LESTER

50 The Préfet's Dirty Job 262
    MAGDA TROCMÉ

51 We Are All Part of One Another 265
    BARBARA DEMING

52 The Road to Transformation 269
    A CONVERSATION WITH BRIAN WILLSON

53 Baghdad after the War 273
    DON MOSLEY

54 God Makes the Crooked Places Straight 278
    JOSEPH E. LOWERY

CONCLUSION

55 The Global Spread of Active Nonviolence 283
    RICHARD DEATS

Preface

Walter Wink

Nonviolence is the human future. As Martin Luther King Jr. said on the night before he was killed, "The choice is no longer between violence and nonviolence. It's nonviolence or nonexistence."

One of the leading groups that has worked year in and year out to foster nonviolence in America is the Fellowship of Reconciliation (FOR). Founded in 1915, FOR is the largest, oldest, interfaith peace organization in this country. It has spawned a whole raft of other organizations, such as the Congress of Racial Equality (CORE), the American Civil Liberties Union (ACLU), the National Congress of Christians and Jews, the National Council against Conscription, the Worker's Defense League, the Committee for Social Responsibility in Science, the Committee on Militarism in Education, and the American Committee on Africa. In 1970 FOR began Dai Dong, a transnational project linking war, environmental problems, poverty, and other social issues. In the 1980s, it helped spark the antinuclear Freeze Campaign, and in the 1990s, it helped form national coalitions against U.S. bombings of Iraq and Serbia.

Throughout those years FOR produced the oldest, continuously published peace journal in the United States. This book is a collection of articles on nonviolence published in its journal, originally called *The New World* for its first five issues, then *The World Tomorrow*, and from 1935 to the present, *Fellowship*.

Reading through all the back issues of these magazines has been a fascinating and instructive experience for me. I am struck by how right the instincts and commitments of FOR have often been. They lobbied (and are still lobbying around the world) for recognition of the status of conscientious objectors (COs) and their right to refuse to go to war. They inveighed repeatedly against the futility of the First World War and the folly of the Versailles treaty that treated Germany as the sole perpetrator. They campaigned for cancellation of war debts. They championed Gandhi's efforts to create a nonviolent movement in India's struggle for independence from Britain. They opposed the postwar blockade of German ports by the British, which was causing starvation. They began interracial work in the American South as early as 1923, challenging the Jim Crow laws. They helped build world sentiment for the removal of U.S.

occupation troops from Nicaragua and Haiti. They opposed compulsory military drill in schools and an end to universal military training. And one of FOR's foremost leaders, A. J. Muste, personally led the successful textile strike at Lawrence, Massachusetts, in 1919.

Even as Nazism and the Second World War bore down on Europe, FOR representatives like A. J. Muste were right in most of their antiwar proposals: that the United States should join the League of Nations; that all forms of anti-Semitism and racism should be resisted; that Congress should revise immigration laws so as to offer haven to all victims of Nazism; that the North American/South American "alliance in defense of democracy against fascism" should be called by its real name: U.S. imperialism; that the economic boycott against Germany should be lifted; that the Treaty of Versailles should be abrogated and a just peace be negotiated by a world conference of nations; that the churches of the world should utterly and unequivocally renounce war.

What few saw was the demonic in Hitler. Even Reinhold Niebuhr, then president of FOR, initially overlooked the Nazi menace. Writing as an editor, Niebuhr urged in the March 15, 1934, issue that America should observe "strict neutrality under any and all circumstances" in case of a new war. The periodical said remarkably little about Hitler in 1937–38, and was still pleading for disarmament and neutrality.

But by then Niebuhr had seen the Nazi threat and bolted from FOR, convinced that pacifism was inadequate to deal with the evil incarnate in Hitler. He faulted FOR's idealism, its naïveté about the innate goodness of humanity, its blind faith in progress, its superficial understanding of evil and sin, and its perfectionistic preoccupation with the pacifist's own purity rather than concern for those who suffer. Many pacifists today would agree with much of Niebuhr's critique. The problem was theological liberalism, however, not the inadequacies of nonviolence (see the essay by G. H. C. Macgregor). Niebuhr had himself suggested trying nonviolent direct action against racial segregation in his *Moral Man and Immoral Society* (1934).

The onset of World War II was a time of virtual eclipse for FOR and the peace effort generally. As Lawrence S. Wittner observes in *Rebels against War: The American Peace Movement, 1933–1983*, "Not only had public support for the cause of peace largely evaporated after 1941, but the tiny peace movement itself was showing marked signs of caution and conservatism." Peace groups were unable to make any significant impact on war policy. Organized nonviolence was still in its infancy, and the sheer numbers of people necessary to make it work simply had not been recruited and trained in the industrial West. So there was little for FOR faithful to do but simply hunker down and hang on until the war ended. Surprisingly, as the broad front of non-pacifist peace organizations crumbled with American participation in World War II, the small pacifist groups mushroomed. By the end of the war the membership and income of FOR had reached a new high.

Even during the war, FOR began new initiatives. It was in 1943 that FOR staff member James Farmer began organizing against racism. And when Japanese-Americans were interned, FOR responded instantly and actively intervened to protect homes and property abandoned when they were rounded up. A. J. Muste, "Mr. FOR," had learned from bitter experience in the 1930s that Communists could not be trusted, and he reiterated his views in the June 1944 issue, while the Soviet Union was still our putative ally.

FOR had lionized Gandhi, but it had almost never tried active nonviolence in the United States, apart from a few union strikes. Now the beginnings of new, more confrontative nonviolence can be seen in the refusal by people like Dorothy Day of the Catholic Worker and A. J. Muste of FOR to go underground during nuclear bomb drills in the 1950s. Some people demonstrated against nuclear testing. But these tended to be the actions of a few individuals. It was Martin Luther King Jr., who for the first time launched a concerted nonviolent movement in the United States. One could even go so far as to say that King saved FOR by showing it and the world that nonviolence could be used effectively to win equal rights for African Americans. King himself, at the onset of the Montgomery bus boycott, had called on FOR to send someone who knew about Gandhian nonviolence firsthand. Staffer Glenn Smiley answered the call for FOR, and Bayard Rustin did the same for the War Resisters League. Together they provided King a depth of experience with nonviolence sorely needed in the early days of the civil rights struggle.

It was the example of King that made the nonviolent opposition to the Vietnam War possible, and after that, the struggle against nuclear weapons and reactors. Over the expanse of the 1960s and 1970s a major shift began to take place, however. FOR no longer focused its efforts on converting the churches and synagogues to the nonviolent way. Instead, it worked in coalitions to build political support for changes in U.S. foreign and domestic policy. Its allies in that endeavor certainly included large numbers of people of faith, but now its allies included secular and religious peace groups, not congregations or church bureaucracies. Whereas the top religious leaders of the 1920s and 1930s virtually all belonged to FOR, as Albert G. Watson observed, by the 1980s almost none of them did. Nevertheless, FOR maintained its religious orientation, broadened to include not only Jews, but Muslims, Hindus, Buddhists, Baha'is, and persons of other faiths.

Today the Fellowship of Reconciliation is stronger than ever. It has trainers in nonviolence in almost every state in the Union. It actively promotes nuclear disarmament and racial and economic justice, and it opposes U.S. war-making in Iraq and Yugoslavia. *Fellowship* continues, under the editorial direction of Richard Deats, to be the same excellent journal that it has been since the founding of *The New World* back in 1918. Staff members are dedicated to propagating nonviolence in season and out, regardless of its popularity in the general culture, because they are convinced, with Martin Luther King Jr., that nonviolence is not only the human future, it is the only future.

•

The list of contributors to this volume is a veritable Who's Who of nonviolent philosophy and action in the twentieth century. Yet they are but a fraction of the total. Deciding which articles should go into this volume was excruciating. My first pass through the entire collection of back issues from *The World*

Tomorrow and *Fellowship* resulted in three hundred absolutely essential articles. With great difficulty I pared that number down to sixty-seven. Richard Deats and John Dear of the Fellowship of Reconciliation added another dozen. We then handed the ensemble over to Robert Ellsberg of Orbis Books, who cut some pieces, added more, and finally cut again to achieve the present volume. The result: over fifty invaluable, brilliant, and indispensable essays on a whole spectrum of nonviolent themes.

Many, if not most, of these pieces have been edited from their original length—in some cases, quite drastically. I have not used ellipses to indicate where the cuts have been made because they are so intrusive. And while I have endeavored to revise sexist language somewhat, in the belief that these authors would have done so had the issue been alive in their time, the reader is reminded that these pieces were written before present sensitivities to inclusive language were established.

•

Special thanks go to Mary Jo Lichard and Geri Dilauro for their assistance in typing, formatting, and editing the manuscript, and to Rebecca Pickard for scanning the articles for our use.

Introduction

THE REBEL PASSION

Eighty-five Years
of the Fellowship of Reconciliation

Richard Deats

The history of FOR is tantamount to the history of nonviolence in America. Whether in opposition to war, or the struggle for racial justice and reconciliation, or the defense of human rights, FOR has been in the thick of it, usually on the cutting edge. Knowing the context of these struggles is crucial to the effort to adapt nonviolence to each new crisis and each new cause. To that end, Richard Deats's retrospective, updated for this volume, is an important contribution (Fellowship, *January-February 1990*).

In his introduction to Euripides' *The Trojan Women,* Gilbert Murray writes of pity as the "rebel passion. Its hand is against the strong, against the organized force of society, against conventional sanctions and accepted gods. It is the Kingdom of Heaven within us fighting against the brute powers of the world." From this idea Vera Brittain took the title for her history of FOR at the time of its fiftieth anniversary: *The Rebel Passion* (1965).

It was such a passion that brought the Fellowship of Reconciliation into being in 1914. Convinced that war was near, some 150 Christians came together at an international conference in Germany, seeking desperately to find a way to head off the outbreak of hostilities. The conference ended in failure; indeed, the war broke out while the meeting was being held. The participants hurried to catch trains back to their respective homelands.

At the Cologne rail station two of the participants—Henry Hodgkin, British Quaker, and Friedrich Siegmund-Schultze, pacifist chaplain to the German Kaiser—believing that the bonds of Christian love transcended all national boundaries, vowed that they would refuse to sanction war or violence and that they would sow the seeds of peace and love no matter what the future might bring. As they shook hands in farewell, they agreed that they were "one in Christ and can never be at war."

Out of this vow the Fellowship of Reconciliation was born. The formal beginning came four months later at Trinity College, Cambridge, where 128 English members elected Hodgkin as their first chairperson. The founding of the German branch, Versohnungsbund, came later. Schultze was arrested twenty-seven times during World War I and was forced to live in exile during the Nazi period.

In 1915 Hodgkin came to the United States to meet with sixty-eight men and women at Garden City, New York, where the American FOR was founded on November 11, with Gilbert A. Beaver as its first chairperson. Leaders during those early years included Edward Evans, Norman Thomas, Bishop Paul Jones (who had been removed from the Episcopal Diocese of Utah because of his pacifism), and Grace Hutchins. John Haynes Holmes, Unitarian minister and one of the early FOR members, pointed out that most people believe war is wrong in general but nonetheless go on to justify each particular war. Placing the claims of the nation-state below that of religious faith, Holmes wrote: "No one is wise enough, no nation is important enough, no human interest is precious enough, to justify the wholesale destruction and murder which constitute the science of war."

Members of the Fellowship bore gallant witness to the insanity of war and the belief that truth is stronger than falsehood, that love overcomes hate, and that nonviolence is more enduring than violence. For them, religious faith broke down the barriers of nation and race, class and tradition. Spreading this vision, even in wartime, has remained the central witness of the Fellowship.

A major focus has been working for the rights of conscientious objectors, who were treated harshly during World War I. Except for those from the historic peace churches (who usually were granted CO status), many were imprisoned, left without clothes in cold cells, fire-hosed, and manacled in their cells.

Prison sentences ranged from twenty-five years to life!

John Nevin Sayre, American churchman and early chair of FOR, went directly to President Wilson to protest the inhumane treatment and the torture was ended. After extensive lobbying by FOR and others, concessions were made that led finally to legal recognition of conscientious objection during World War II. In that war more than sixteen thousand men performed "work of national importance" in public service camps. Some, however, still went to prison when their beliefs clashed with Selective Service rules. These included five FOR staff members: Roger Axford, Caleb Foote, Alfred Hassler, Bayard Rustin, and Glenn Smiley.

While war has been the central social evil FOR has sought to eradicate, an expanding social vision has moved the Fellowship into other critical areas needing the work of reconciliation and the establishment of justice. In 1918 it helped found Brookwood Labor College. In 1919 A. J. Muste, who was then head of the Boston FOR, rose to prominence during the textile strike in Lawrence,

Massachusetts, where the power of nonviolent action was effectively demonstrated.

Another area of enduring FOR concern has been to eradicate the evil of racism and to build what Martin Luther King Jr. called "the Beloved Community." Years before there was a civil rights movement, FOR was active in this effort. With the Congress of Racial Equality (CORE), FOR sponsored the first interracial sit-in, in 1943. As a consequence of its interracial Journey of Reconciliation through the South in 1947, FOR race relations secretaries received the Jefferson Award of the Council against Intolerance. FOR was instrumental in ending segregation in public facilities in such cities as Denver and Washington, D.C., and in 1957 staff member Glenn Smiley worked beside Martin Luther King Jr. in the decisive Montgomery bus boycott. Staff member James Lawson, based in Nashville, led nonviolence training sessions throughout the South that were of seminal importance to the civil rights movement. FOR provided speakers in churches, synagogues, and schools; held workshops; raised money for bombed churches; and produced films and literature (including the film "Walk to Freedom" and the Martin Luther King Jr. comic book in English and Spanish) that were widely distributed across the country.

Alongside such efforts of FOR in the United States, the work of the Fellowship was growing worldwide. The International FOR was established in 1919 to coordinate the new national chapters that were being formed. Its first secretary was Pierre Ceresole, the Swiss pacifist who was jailed time and again for his peace witness, and from whose vision and labors came the modern work-camp movement. It first brought together volunteers from former enemy nations to undertake reconstruction projects in war-ravaged Europe. Relief for the victims of war was carried out, and international conferences and meetings spread the work of peace to many other parts of the globe. In 1932 IFOR led a Youth Crusade across Europe in support of the Geneva World Disarmament Conference. Protestants and Catholics from all over converged on Geneva by various routes, reaching over fifty thousand people and presenting to the conference a petition calling for total disarmament among the nations. As the clouds of war gathered across Europe later in that decade, IFOR established Embassies of Reconciliation that initiated peace efforts not only in Europe but in Japan and China as well. "Ambassadors of Reconciliation," such as George Lansbury, Muriel Lester, and Anne Seesholtz, visited many world leaders, including Hitler, Mussolini, Leon Blum, and Roosevelt. Muriel Lester, English social worker, served as IFOR traveling secretary throughout the world, helping to establish its work in many countries. A stirring speaker and writer, she was a practical mystic who was equally at home holding a School of Prayer in Uruguay, working with Gandhi for India's independence, or fighting the drug trade in China. When World War II erupted, many European members of FOR were in the front ranks of nonviolent resistance to totalitarianism and to all the dehumanizing aspects of the war. Many were imprisoned and scores were executed. Heroic efforts were undertaken to aid the victims of war. Thousands of Jews and other refugees were successfully hidden and smuggled to safety, as in the south of France, where André and Magda Trocmé led the villagers of Le Chambon to establish a haven in the midst of Nazi and Vichy terror. Even in Germany itself, members of the Versohnungsbund, like Heinz Kloppenburg, Irmgard Schuchardt, and Martin Niemoeller, were active in the nonviolent resistance to fascism.

In the United States, FOR took action when the U.S. government ordered Japanese-Americans into internment camps in 1942. FOR held public protests of the action and extended concrete help to the victims (such as caring for the property of those forcibly evacuated). A FOR member, Gordon Hirabayashi, was the only Nisei to refuse to register for evacuation; his case went to the Supreme Court. FOR provided for visits to the camps and set up a travel loan fund to help resettle people after they were released from the relocation centers. The national office added a young Japanese-American to its staff to interpret to schools, churches, and FOR groups what was happening to people of Japanese ancestry. In 1944 FOR published Vera Brittain's "Massacre by Bombing," a carefully documented study of the saturation bombing of Germany by the Allies. Signed by twenty-eight prominent American church leaders, the publication aroused international concern over the effects of obliteration bombing and heightened public awareness of the savagery of modern warfare.

Bringing such information to the public has been one of FOR's main functions. Its first magazine, *The World Tomorrow*, was begun in 1918. By 1934 its circulation had risen to forty thousand. Editors over the years included Norman Thomas, Devere Allen, Kirby Page, and Reinhold Niebuhr. *The World Tomorrow* was succeeded in 1935 by *Fellowship*, edited by Harold Fey; later editors included John Nevin Sayre, Alfred Hassler, William Miller, James Forest, and Virginia Baron.

After World War II there was a major effort to establish a year of permanent military training for all young men in the United States, to be followed by seven years of reserve service. Under the leadership of John Swomley, FOR worked with a large coalition to form the National Council against Conscription, which waged a successful campaign to defeat the proposal for universal military training.

The end of World War II brought in its wake a new and unprecedented moral issue: nuclear weapons. From the dropping of the first atomic bombs on Hiroshima and Nagasaki, FOR condemned nuclear weapons. In the 1950s FOR opposed atomic testing and sent a public statement to Japan expressing sorrow over the tragedy of fishermen who were radioactively burned by the Pacific bomb tests. It also spoke out against the civil-defense program that conditioned people to be ready for still another war. Members such as Dorothy Day and A. J. Muste refused to take shelter in New York City during air raid drills. Their repeated arrests for civil disobedience helped to build public awareness that there is no shelter from nuclear war. In 1995 FOR executive secretary Jo Becker led a delegation to Japan with a message of repentance for the atomic bombing of Hiroshima and Nagasaki that helped challenge anew the official U.S. view of the necessity of those bombings.

FOR responded creatively to the fad for fallout shelters with its Shelters for the Shelterless campaign, which built dwellings for homeless people in India. It also made the first proposal that American surplus food be sent to communist China. In 1954 FOR launched a six-year Food for China Program in response to Chinese famine. Tens of thousands of miniature bags of grain were sent to President Eisenhower with the inscription, "If thine enemy hunger, feed him."

During this period the witch-hunts of Senator Joseph McCarthy intimidated many leaders. Communists and blacklisted persons were denied access to speaking platforms. FOR sponsored a public forum in which A. J. Muste and Norman Thomas debated two Communist leaders in a forceful and daring affirmation of free speech at Carnegie Hall in New York. In the 1960s FOR formed the International Committee of Conscience on Vietnam, with ten thousand clergy in forty countries. Contact with the Vietnamese Buddhist pacifist movement was established, spearheaded by the untiring efforts of the U.S. executive secretary, Alfred Hassler. In 1968, at the height of the suffering in Vietnam, FOR sponsored a world tour by Buddhist monk Thich Nhat Hanh, whose poetry and other writings, as well as his speeches and presence, made a profound impact wherever he went. FOR's "Meals of Reconciliation" raised money for medical aid for all areas of Vietnam. In 1969 the FOR Study Team on Religious and Political Freedom documented Saigon's reliance on torture and initiated a prodigious effort to gain the release of Vietnamese political prisoners, some of whom had been crippled for life. These various missions to Vietnam continued a tradition of FOR since its inception, in which missions of reconciliation and friendship have been sent to such places as the Philippines (1925), Haiti (1926), Central America (in the 1920s, 1980s, and 1990s), the U.S.S.R. throughout the 1980s, Libya in 1989, and Iraq and Israel/Palestine in the 1990s. After the Vietnamese war ended, a campaign for amnesty for U.S. war resisters was launched, as well as a program to help support Vietnamese orphans.

In 1970 Dai Dong was founded as a ground-breaking transnational project linking war, environmental problems, poverty, and other social issues. Thousands of scientists around the world were reached through this program, as evidenced by the Menton Statement, signed by twenty-two hundred biologists (including four Nobel Prize laureates). The full statement, "A Message to Our 3½ Billion Neighbors on Planet Earth," was published in the *UNESCO Courier* and received worldwide attention. In 1972, in an effort to move public opinion beyond the constraints of national self-interest, Dai Dong sponsored an alternative environmental conference in Stockholm at the time of the UN Environmental Conference.

With the end of the Vietnam War, FOR placed major emphasis on ending the Cold War, reversing the arms race, meeting human needs, and building global solidarity. FOR was part of a growing number of groups—peace, environmental, minority rights, women, anti-intervention—that worked for a more compassionate domestic and foreign policy. It joined in campaigns, marches, educational projects, and civil disobedience. At sessions of the World Council of Churches and the United Nations, FOR sponsored Plowshares Coffee Houses to provide an alternative forum for critical issues facing the world community.

In the 1980s, as the Cold War deepened, FOR launched a major emphasis on U.S.-U.S.S.R. reconciliation to undergird its disarmament efforts and to root out the enemy image that had so poisoned East-West relations. Through people-to-people projects and exchanges, FOR made a significant contribution to the dramatic turnaround in U.S.-Soviet relations that occurred in the late 1980s. FOR also pioneered in bringing nonviolence education and training to Russia and Lithuania as the Soviet Union broke up.

Recent years have seen the growth of IFOR branches and affiliates in Latin America, Asia, Africa, and the Middle East. The seeds planted earlier by traveling secretaries like Muriel Lester and John Nevin Sayre bore fruit, along with the decades of seminars in active nonviolence carried out by Jean and Hildegard Goss-Mayr of Paris and Vienna, three times nominated for the Nobel Peace Prize. From such labors arose Servicio Paz y Justicia (SERPAJ) throughout Latin America. SERPAJ's Adolfo Perez Esquivel of Argentina was awarded the Nobel Peace Prize in 1980. IFOR training in active nonviolence contributed significantly to the people-power overthrow of the Marcos dictatorship in the Philippines in 1986, as well as the growth of nonviolent movements in Asia and Africa. The Goss-Mayrs, IFOR honorary presidents, were central to the global spread of active nonviolence.

FOR, under the work of executive secretary Doug Hostetter, made valiant efforts to stop the Gulf War through repeated delegations to Iraq that sought to keep open possibilities of a peaceful resolution of the crisis brought on by Iraq's invasion of Kuwait. After the war one million dollars in medical supplies were taken to victims of the war. Efforts to build peace with Iraq and to stop the sanctions that killed so many innocent Iraqis have continued through the 1990s.

In response to ethnic cleansing in the former Yugoslavia, FOR initiated the Bosnian Student Project to bring Bosnian students to the United States for study due to the disruption of their lives by the war. This effort was matched by work camps for reconstruction and reconciliation in Bosnia.

Despite the end of the Cold War, the U.S. military budget remained obscenely high, leading FOR to issue an Interfaith Call to Restore Sanity and Compassion to the National Agenda. FOR has also joined with other religious peace groups to foster a New Abolitionist Covenant to get rid of all nuclear weapons. FOR has placed special emphasis on youth through its Peacemaker Training Institute and its peace internships.

Also in this period FOR worked for racial and economic justice, especially for women of color who so often work under dangerous and degrading conditions. There has also been a healing emphasis on racial dialogue and reconciliation in the United States.

FOR's vigorous work in Latin America has been highlighted by its national leadership to ensure that the United States fulfill its historic promise to decolonize and demilitarize the U.S. presence in Panama and to comply faithfully with the Panama Canal Treaties. FOR joined with other groups to organize SIPAZ (International Service for Peace) to support a just and lasting peace in Chiapas.

With the assistance of FOR and its members, over the years a wide variety of parallel groups have come into existence: the American Civil Liberties Union, the National Conference of Christians and Jews, the Congress of Racial Equality, the Workers Defense League, the Committee for Social Responsibility in Science, the Committee on Militarism in Education, and the American Committee on Africa. Such organizations have taken up tasks in such specific fields as civil liberties or the support of African independence movements. FOR has sought to remain on the cutting edge of nonviolent witness in each generation.

While the Fellowship has been religious in inspiration and outlook since its inception, the nature and dimensions of this commitment have broadened over the years. Founded by Christians, the Fellowship was at first centered in the ethic of love that Jesus taught, and this remains the faith of many FOR members. At the same time, the remarkable growth of nonviolent thought and life in the twentieth century has had a profound impact on the Fellowship. It was deeply affected by Gandhi and the freedom struggle in India, with its roots in the ancient teachings of Hinduism. Jews have brought to the FOR a commitment to nonviolence that grows out of Judaism's allegiance to universalism, justice, and love. The powerful pacifist movement in Vietnam brought to the world's attention the great tradition of nonviolence that derives from Buddhism. One of IFOR's new Asian branches, in Bangladesh, includes many Muslims, as well as Hindus and Christians. Out of FOR's work against the Gulf War and the continuing sanctions in Iraq, FOR has joined increasingly with Muslims in peacemaking. The Muslim Peace Fellowship has become one of FOR's vital affiliates.

FOR has seen these and other expressions of nonviolence as indications of an unfolding understanding of the meaning of truth and the way of love. As a result, FOR has become interfaith, and as such is a religious pioneer, pushing beyond contemporary ecumenism. It encourages people to live out the full dimensions of their beliefs, even as they are enriched and strengthened by traditions other than their own.

FOR has fostered and encouraged peace fellowships within the various religious traditions, and with these fellowships has often led the way in challenging (and assisting) established religious bodies to take up the peacemaking task, from combating homophobia and anti-Muslim prejudice to witnessing against handgun violence at home and support of dictatorial and exploitative regimes abroad.

As we enter the twenty-first century, the challenge to peacemakers continues, not only to rid the world of nuclear weapons and all weapons of mass destruction, but to remove the occasion for war, oppression, and hostility between and within nations, and to build a just peace and to save the earth. Under the vigorous leadership of executive secretary John Dear (the first priest in that position) and its national chairperson, James Lawson, FOR called for a forty-day People's Campaign for peace and justice in the summer of 2000 in Washington, D.C.

Throughout the world people are showing their determination to be free and to be treated justly; they are learning the great power of nonviolent struggle, compassion, and reconciliation, even in the face of seemingly overwhelming odds. The UN declaration of the first decade of the new millennium as a decade for a culture of peace and nonviolence is evidence of this hope.

The Fellowship of Reconciliation, with its message of peace and active nonviolence, grounded in faith and tested over many years, is uniquely equipped to speak to the present age and the universal longing for peace and justice.

Part One

THE VISION OF PEACE

Activists sometimes exhibit impatience with theory—often for good reason. They have seen nonviolence caught in an ideological net in which the purity of ideology eclipsed activity and the nonviolent effort was undermined by a deflection of energy. But nonviolent theory is absolutely necessary. It introduces to the world a new strategy for resisting evil without creating new evils and becoming evil ourselves. But more important, it articulates a new way of being that yields a vision of peace more powerful than all the armies of all the nations in the world.

That is no exaggeration. In the past two decades the world has seen nonviolence used in an escalating number of situations. In 1989-90 alone, thirteen nations underwent nonviolent revolutions, all of them successful but one (China), and all of them nonviolent on the part of the revolutionaries except one (Romania, and there it was largely the secret police fighting the army, with the public maintaining nonviolent demonstrations throughout). Those nonviolent struggles affected 1.7 billion people—one-third of the population of the world. If we add all the nonviolent efforts of this century, we get the astonishing figure of 3.3 billion—over half of the human race! No one can ever again say that nonviolence doesn't work. But it is true that we don't always know how to make it work.

Part One offers us visions of nonviolence that can help us make it work. That we have not yet caught up with these visions in no way invalidates them. It is one of the characteristics of nonviolence that its proponents not only theorize but engage in the struggles about which they write. It is their struggles, in fact, that provide them with the insights that go to make up their theories. Here, then, are some of their visions of peace.

1

1

NONVIOLENCE— THE GREATEST FORCE

M. K. Gandhi

Mohandas K. Gandhi was one of the towering figures, not just of the twentieth century, but of all time. The nonviolent struggle that he led for Indian independence provided peace groups around the world with a practical model for achieving their aims. Others before him had articulated and even used nonviolent tactics in opposition to oppression. But no one had been able to make nonviolence the basis of an ongoing movement and at the same time the basis of a philosophical and spiritual way of living. FOR revered Gandhi, publishing many of his articles and devoting whole issues of its magazine to his cause (The World Tomorrow, *October 1926*).

Nonviolence is the greatest force humanity has been endowed with. Truth is the only goal we have. For God is none other than Truth. But Truth cannot be, never will be reached except through nonviolence.

That which distinguishes us from all other animals is our capacity to be nonviolent. And we fulfill our mission only to the extent that we are nonviolent and no more. We have no doubt many other gifts. But if they do not serve the main purpose—the development of the spirit of nonviolence in us—they but drag us down lower than the brute, a status from which we have only just emerged.

The cry for peace will be a cry in the wilderness, so long as the spirit of nonviolence does not dominate millions of men and women.

An armed conflict between nations horrifies us. But the economic war is no better than an armed conflict. This is like a surgical operation. An economic war is prolonged torture. And its ravages are no less terrible than those depicted in the literature on war properly so called. We think nothing of the other because we are used to its deadly effects.

Many of us in India shudder to see blood spilled. Many of us resent cow slaughter, but we think nothing of the slow torture through which by our greed we put our people and cattle. But because we are used to this lingering death, we think no more about it.

The movement against war is sound. I pray for its success. But I cannot help the gnawing fear that the movement will fail if it does not touch the root of all evil—human greed.

Will America, England, and the other great nations of the West continue to exploit the so-called weaker or uncivilized races and hope to attain peace that the whole world is pining for? Or will Americans continue to prey upon one another, have commercial rivalries, and yet expect to dictate peace to the world?

Not till the spirit is changed can the form be altered. The form is merely an expression of the spirit within. We may succeed in seemingly altering the form, but the alteration will be a mere make-believe if the spirit within remains unalterable. A whited sepulcher still conceals beneath it the rotting flesh and bone.

Far be it from me to discount or underrate the great effort that is being made in the West to kill the war spirit. Mine is merely a word of caution as from a fellow seeker who has been striving in his own humble manner after the same thing, maybe in a different way, no doubt on a much smaller scale. But if the experiment demonstrably succeeds on the smaller field and, if those who are working on the larger field have not overtaken me, it will at least pave the way for a similar experiment on a large field.

I observe, in the limited field in which I find myself, that unless I can reach the hearts of men and women, I am able to do nothing. I observe further that so long as the spirit of hate persists in some shape or other, it is impossible to establish peace or to gain our freedom by peaceful effort. We cannot love one another if we hate Englishmen. We cannot love the Japanese and hate Englishmen. We must either let the law of love rule us through and through or not at all. Love among ourselves based on hatred of others breaks down under the slightest pressure. The fact is, such love is never real love. It is an armed peace. And so it will be in this great movement in the West against war. War will only be stopped when the conscience of humankind has become sufficiently elevated to recognize the undisputed supremacy of the Law of Love in all the walks of life. Some say this will never come to pass. I shall retain the faith till the end of my earthly existence that it shall come to pass.

2

PACIFISM AND CLASS WAR

A. J. Muste

Over a long and productive life, much of it associated with the FOR, A. J. Muste blew the trumpet for nonviolent direct action as a religious commitment and a political lifestyle. One of the truly great figures of the twentieth century, Muste was trusted by the whole spectrum of socialists, anarchists, unionists, and peace groups, and was thus able to put together coalitions that otherwise would have simply sniped at each other. In this essay he drew on wisdom gleaned from his early work as a radical trade union-ist (The World Tomorrow, *September 1928*).

It is expected perhaps that the article in the present series dealing with paci-fism in relation to class war should consist of an exhortation to labor organiza-tions and radicals to eschew violent methods in the pursuit of their ends, to-gether with an exposition of the use of pacifistic methods in labor disputes and social revolutions. If there is such an expectation, this article will be in large measure disappointing. Chiefly, because in my opinion much more time must be spent than has yet been given to clearing away some exceedingly mischie-vous misconceptions before we can think fruitfully about concrete nonviolent methods of social change, and because there are very, very few individuals in the world, including the pacifist groups and churches, who are in a moral po-sition to preach nonresistance to the labor or radical movement.

Practically all our thinking about pacifism in connection with class war starts out at the wrong point. The question raised is how the oppressed in struggling for freedom and the good life may be dissuaded from employing "the revolu-tionary method of violence" and won over to "the peaceful process of evolu-tion." Two erroneous assumptions are concealed in the question put that way. The first is that the oppressed, the radicals, are the ones who are creating the disturbance. To the leaders of Jesus' day—Pharisees, Sadducees, Roman gov-ernor—it was Jesus who was upsetting the people, turning the world upside down. In the same way we speak of the Kuomintang "making a revolution" in China today, seldom of the Powers having made the revolution by almost a hundred years of trickery, oppression, and inhumanity. Similarly, society may permit an utterly impossible situation to develop in an industry like coal, but the workers who finally in desperation put down tools and fold their arms, are "the strikers," the cause of the breach of the peace. We need to get our thinking focused right and to see the selfish employers or a negligent society, not striking workers, as the cause of disturbance in the social order.

A second assumption underlying much of our thinking is that the violence is solely or chiefly committed by the rebels against oppression, and that this violence constitutes the heart of our problem. However, the basic fact is that the economic, social, and political order in which we live was built up largely by violence, is now being extended by violence, and is maintained only by violence. A slight knowledge of history, a glimpse at the armies and navies of the Most Christian Powers, at our police and constabulary, at the militaristic fashion in which practically every attempt of workers to organize is greeted, at Nicaragua or China, will suffice to make the point clear to an unbiased mind.

The foremost task, therefore, of the pacifist in connection with class war is to denounce the violence on which the present system is based and all the evil, material and spiritual, this entails for the masses throughout the world, and to exhort all rulers in social, political, industrial life, all who occupy places of privilege, all who are the beneficiaries of the present state of things, to relinquish every attempt to hold on to wealth, position, and power by force, to give up the instruments of violence on which they annually spend billions of wealth produced by the sweat and anguish of the toilers. So long as we are not dealing honestly and adequately with this 90 percent of our problem, there is something ludicrous, and perhaps hypocritical about our concern over the 10 percent of violence employed by the rebels against oppression. Can we win the rulers of earth to peaceful methods?

The psychological basis for the use of nonviolent methods is the simple rule that like produces like, kindness provokes kindness as surely as injustice produces resentment and evil. It is sometimes forgotten by those whose pacifism is a spurious, namby-pamby thing that if one biblical statement of this rule is "Do good to them that hate you" (an exhortation presumably intended for the capitalist as well as for the laborer), another statement of the same rule is, "They that sow the wind shall reap the whirlwind." You get from the universe what you give, with interest. What if people build a system on violence and injustice, on not doing good to those who hate them or even to those who meekly obey and toil for them? And persist in this course through centuries of Christian history? And if then the oppressed raise the chant:

> Ye who sowed the wind of sorrow,
> Now the whirlwind you must dare,
> As ye face upon the morrow,
> The advancing Proletaire?

In such a day the pacifist is presumably not absolved from preaching to the rebels that they also shall reap what they sow but assuredly not in such wise as to leave the oppressors safely entrenched in their position, not at the cost of preaching to them in all sternness that "the judgments of the Lord are true and righteous altogether."

As we are stayed from preaching nonviolence to the underdog unless and until we have dealt adequately with the dog who is chewing him up, so also are all those who would support a country in war against another country stayed from preaching nonviolence in principle to labor or to radical movements. Much could be said on this point, but it is perhaps unnecessary to dwell on it here. Suffice it to observe in passing that to one who has had any intimate connection with labor the flutter occasioned in certain breasts by the occasional violence in connection with strikes seems utterly ridiculous, and will continue to seem so until the possessors of these fluttering breasts have sacrificed a great deal more than they already have in order to banish from the earth the horrible monster of international war.

We are not, to pursue the matter a little further, in a moral position to advocate nonviolent methods to labor while we continue to be beneficiaries of the existing order. They who profit by violence, though it be indirectly, unwillingly, and only in a small measure, will always be under suspicion and rightly so of seeking to protect their profits, of being selfishly motivated, if they address pious exhortations to those who suffer by that violence.

Nor can anyone really with good conscience advocate abstention from violence to the masses of labor in revolt, unless such a person is identified in spirit with labor and helping it with all his or her might to achieve its rights and to realize its ideals. In a world built on violence one must be a revolutionary before one can be a pacifist: in such a world a non-revolutionary pacifist is a contradiction in terms, a monstrosity. During the war no absolute pacifist in America would have felt justified in exhorting Germany to lay down its arms while saying and doing nothing about America's belligerent activities. We should have recognized instantly the moral absurdity, the implied hypocrisy of such a position. Our duty was to win our own "side" to a "more excellent way." It is a sign of ignorance and lack of realism in our pacifist groups and churches that so many fail to recognize clearly and instantly the same point with regard to the practice of pacifism in social and labor struggles.

Here it may be well to point out that as a matter of fact the amount of violence on the part of workers on strike is usually grossly exaggerated, and that, on the other hand, practically every great strike furnishes inspiring examples of nonresistance under cruel provocation and victory by "soul force" alone, victory through patient endurance of evil and sacrifice even unto death for spiritual ends. I have witnessed these things repeatedly. More than once I have exhorted masses of strikers to fold their arms, not to strike back, to smile at those who beat them and tramp them under their horses' feet, and their response has been instantaneous, unreserved, exalted. I have also appealed to police heads to call off violence-provoking extra forces and to employers to discharge labor spies, and have been laughed at for my pains.

Much of what has already been said bears upon the special problem of Communists with their frank espousal of terrorism, their conviction that no great and salutary social change can be accomplished without violence and that the workers must therefore be prepared for armed revolt. Our whole focus on this problem also is wrong unless we get it clear that violence inheres first in the system against which Communists revolt, that they who suffer from social revolt in the main reap what by positive evil-doing or indifference they have sown, that practically every great revolution begins peacefully and might proceed so to all appearances but for the development of violent counterrevolution, that the degree of terrorism employed in such an upheaval as the French or Russian revolution is always directly proportionate to the pressure of foreign attack, that in general the amount of "red" terrorism in human history is a bagatelle compared to the "white" terrorism of reactionaries. The question is pertinent as to whether the "Lord's will" is done by the servant who talks about terrorism and practices very little, or by the servant who talks about law and order and practices a vast deal of terrorism.

Most discussions assume that on this point of the use of violence there is a fundamental difference between the conservative and radical wings of the labor movement, and between Socialism and Communism. There are important differences between these elements, but the contention that they differ in principle on the use of violence, in the sense that the absolute pacifist attaches to these terms, cannot be sustained. Among the unions in the United States many of the more conservative ones practice violence in industrial disputes more extensively than radical unions. Gangsterism in the American labor world is not an invention of the Communist unions, though the latter have not refrained from employing it. The Socialist parties do not commit themselves in advance to the inevitability of violent revolution, but neither do they promise to refrain from the use of force to defend a Socialist order if they deem that necessary. If Ramsay MacDonald, for example, is to be called a pacifist because he favors the League of Nations and disarmament, though he helps to keep the British navy in trim when he is in power and tells Indian revolutionists he will have the British army shoot them down if they go too far, then it will be difficult to prove that Stalin and Litvinov are not entitled to the same designation.

All this does not mean that the labor movement is not confronted with a serious problem as to the means to which it will resort to advance its aims. Many times employers, on the one hand, and workers, on the other hand, are approached by the most crude and self-defeating psychological methods. Money is spent on gangsters, for example, that might well net a thousandfold better return if devoted to the education of workers and of the public. Violence begets violence by whomever used. War is a dirty business and entails the use of degrading means, whoever wages it.

Those who can bring themselves to renounce wealth, position, and power accruing from a social system based on violence and putting a premium on acquisitiveness, and to identify themselves in some real fashion with the struggle of the masses toward the light, may help in a measure, more doubtless by life than by words, to devise a more excellent way, a technique of social progress less crude, brutal, costly, and slow than humankind has yet evolved.

3

HAS PACIFISM BECOME IMPOSSIBLE?

John Haynes Holmes

John Haynes Holmes was one of the most eloquent and brilliant champions of the pacifist way. The minister of the Community Church in New York City, he was associated with FOR for most of his life, engaging in peace missions to heads of state and serving as a contributing editor of Fellowship. *In this essay he faces straight on the kinds of objections to pacifism that had increasingly led former stalwarts to abandon the pacifist cause as war seemed increasingly inevitable and Hitler's atrocities began to become known. Holmes's strongest point is that without moral absolutes every act becomes morally relative regardless of what side one takes* (Fellowship, *June 1936*).

Out of the Great War of 1914 there emerged a pacifism which promised to be one of the few compensations of that vast calamity. Thousands of persons in every belligerent country refused to take any part in the war for reasons which have become an impressive part of the history of our times. They were persuaded that the war was a struggle between sordid and greedy imperialisms, and thus involved no issues which were worth an expenditure of blood. They felt as well that, even though there were some issues of genuine significance involved, the resort to arms was not only unwise but fatal, since war never settles anything. In the last analysis they were convinced that the price of war is so heavy—its waste and destruction, its agony and death, so uncontrollable and irreparable—that its evil is altogether out of proportion to any conceivable good it may achieve. War is "the sum of all villainies," the complete act of social and racial suicide, and nothing can justify its use as an instrument for the settlement of international disputes. This was the conception out of which modern pacifism was born.

Everything that happened during the war, and especially after the war, seemed to justify this conception. In the fight and fury of the combat, and in the utter futility of the peace that followed the combat, people seemed to be discovering anew the ineffectiveness of violence, and in contrast the beneficence and truth of that gospel of love which prophets of religion, from the beginning of the world, have proclaimed as the one great law of life.

8

Then, as though to dramatize the issue and open up what might be a new era in human affairs, there came Gandhi, the Indian Mahatma, the supreme statesman and saint of pacifism. It seemed as though we were finding an answer to the problem of war and of all other uses of violence in human affairs. Perhaps the Great War would vindicate itself as marking an end to the reign of force in society. For a dozen years the day of pacifism seemed to be dawning upon the world.

Now suddenly, yet not so suddenly, darkness is shutting down again. Pacifism is being called into question. Pacifists are falling into doubt, or denial. A movement of idealism and sacrifice, conceived by prophets and consecrated martyrs of every age, is crumbling before our eyes. All the experience of the war, all the truth baptized in these last two decades in torrents of blood and oceans of tears, stand in danger of being lost as a new generation arises to find new excuses for violence.

Such a collapse of what has represented the conviction of many of the noblest souls of our time cannot be without cause. It must be the result of influences which are rushing into our lives like ravaging floods to sweep away the landmarks of our being. As I look abroad in the world today to find out why pacifism is disintegrating so fast I seem to see at least three separate influences at work.

In the first place there is Russia. To many minds, especially to those idealistically inclined, this represents the most amazing and promising phenomenon of modern times. Here is a new experiment in the organization of society—a deliberate attempt to abolish poverty, misery, and death by securing a just and equitable distribution of the world's goods. The Soviets are engaged in an endeavor not only to produce wealth but to distribute it evenly and abundantly, so that, like water in a desert, it may fertilize human lives. If this experiment succeeds, it will mark a new era in human history. This revolution contains the seeds of all justice, brotherhood, and peace of which men have ever dreamed. It is the quest, if not yet fulfillment, of that vision of the prophet who foresaw the coming of the day when men and women

> shall not labor in vain
> Nor bring forth for calamity. . . .
> They shall build houses, and inhabit them;
> They shall plant vineyards, and eat the fruit of them;
> They shall not build, and another inhabit
> They shall not plant, and another eat.

Yet this great adventure in social idealism was launched amid a storm of violence; it was defended, against traitors within and enemies without, by desperate and heroic resort to armed force; and it would be defended again, if capitalism should ever hurl its long-meditated attack upon it, by the superbly organized and disciplined Red Army. What place has pacifism in the history of revolutionary Russia? Would pacifism have been possible in any one of the crises of its life? Does anybody blame Lenin for not being a pacifist yesterday, or Stalin for not being a pacifist today? Does anybody recommend, if Japan should attack Russia from the east, or Germany from the west, or both of them together from west and east, that Soviet Russia should not fight? In such cases as this, where great human interests are at stake, the end obviously justifies the means, does it not? There are occasions when it is not only prudent but right to meet violence with violence. Pacifism, in other words, may become impossible in certain great issues of life and death. There are values so precious that they must be defended—if necessary by force!

A second and much more recent influence making against pacifism today is Germany. The advent of Hitler has brought a shock to the world such as it has not sustained since the Kaiser's legions went smashing through Belgium. It is true that the German dictator is the product of causes set on foot by the Allies, as the Nazis themselves are the armed men sprung from the sowing of the dragon's teeth at Versailles. But the explanation of the fact does not alter the character of the fact. Here suddenly in the heart of Europe has appeared the most formidable and ruthless military power since Napoleon. The National Socialists believe three things. First, to quote Prof. Calvin B. Hoover, "that war is not only an inevitable part of the lives of nations and men, but that it is a desirable institution for their development. The genius of the German race is expressed in the superiority of its warriors on the field of battle." Second, that war is the instrument for the accomplishment of the German nationalistic purpose, which is to gain whatever lands may be necessary for the expansion of German power. "With the German sword," says Hitler, "we must . . . give sod to the German plow." Third, that Germany must be prepared for this inevitable and triumphant war of conquest. To this end the Nazis are at this moment arming the Reich with a speed which will assure them of the military hegemony of the continent within five years.

Now, what are we going to do in the face of a menace of this description? Has pacifism any security to offer? Shall we disarm, or surrender, or "turn the other cheek?" What we must realize is that barbarism has been let loose among us. A type of savagery which we thought had disappeared a thousand years ago has suddenly arisen against us. A vast eruption of brutality and superstition is threatening to engulf everything that is precious in centuries of progress and enlightenment. In such a crisis what has pacifism to say? Is it not impossible as a policy either of weakness or of madness? Now and again, after all, there come evils so terrible that they must be destroyed.

A third influence against pacifism in our time is to be found in what is known as the class struggle—by which we mean the struggle of the workers of the world for the ownership and control of the means of physical subsistence. This struggle is being waged between two classes—the "haves" and the "have-nots." It is in essence a struggle for power. The upper class now holds this power through its possession of the land, machinery, goods, and money. It uses this power, fundamentally economic in character, to maintain and extend its mastery of society. It controls the government, manipulates the courts, utilizes the police, organizes the military—all in the defense and advancement of its own especial interests. In the face of such a massing of social power, the workers are helpless except as they may take advantage of their numbers to mobilize a power of brute force to break down and destroy the tyranny which oppresses them. It is power, in other words, against power. It is a struggle on the level of sheer violence, not because the workers desire it but because the masters determine it.

Now, it is said, to intrude upon such a conflict as this with pacifist pleas for reconciliation and peace is simply to betray the workers. It is to disarm them in a battle which involves all the hope of liberty there is for the great masses of humankind and thus to doom them to perpetual bondage and despair. In such a struggle for the mastery of the world, pacifism it is argued, can have no place. It presents a program which is unreal, and therefore pragmatically impossible. Here is a cause which is being persistently frustrated, and may in the end be defeated, by a preponderance of power which can only be broken by a greater preponderance of power. This cause is a holy cause. In such a situation such a cause must be vindicated and carried through to triumph—if necessary, by force!

Such are the influences and arguments which are washing away the ramparts of pacifism in the days of sweeping storm. Here is Russia, with its plea that there are interests so precious that they may well be defended by force. Here is Germany, with its challenge that there may be evils so monstrous that they may have to be destroyed by force. And here is the class struggle, with its insistence that there exist causes so holy that they must be vindicated by force.

ARE THERE NO ABSOLUTES?

At bottom in their philosophical content these contentions are all the same. They are so many specific expressions of the idea that there are no absolutes in the world of practical affairs. No law, no principal, no ideal, pacifist or any other, can be set up as having infallible application to all problems of human life. Inevitably there must enter into every problem in which human interests are involved especial conditions of time and place. There are circumstances, in other words, which may alter any law or suspend the operation of any principle. To cling fast to an abstract ideal for its own sake, in defiance of the determining factors of a concrete situation, is romantic, unrealistic, quixotic. We cannot make "nonviolence an absolute social ethic," says one of the most influential of the religious teachers of our day, for the reason that "we can find no stable absolute in the shifting situation of a social struggle where everything must be finally decided in pragmatic terms."

What are we to say in answer to this contention? The first thing that impresses me is the significant fact that I have heard all this before. It sounds strangely familiar as an echo of the Great War. Do you say that there are interests, like those of Russia, which must be defended if necessary by force? That is what the French and the Belgians were saying about the interests of their countries when the Germans came crashing into their territory in 1914.

Do you assert that there are evils like those of Nazi Germany which must be destroyed if necessary by resort to arms? That is what millions of people in England and America were saying when they confronted the Germany not of Hitler but of the Kaiser. Do you argue that there may be a cause, like that of the working class, which is so holy that it may specify the use of violence? That is what the world was saying when it rose up with one consent to fight the war to save civilization from destruction.

What has happened since the Great War to persuade us to carry over from that tragic conflict these hoary arguments to justify the new conflicts that threaten in our time? I thought enough had happened to teach us the disastrous character of force and violence when dedicated to any purpose or used for any end. "No prediction of pacifists (in 1914) as to the uselessness of war," says a recent commentator, "was more dire than the actuality has proved after these fifteen years." What I seem to see in this collapse of pacifism is the collapse of the contemporary mind in instinctive reversion to old fallacies and superstitions under the stress and strain of unfamiliar circumstance, and the attempt to rationalize this collapse into a conviction that the new circumstance makes sound and righteous today what was unsound and unrighteous yesterday. All of which means that I am not impressed by this repetition in 1934 of the slogans of 1914! I have seen enough of violence and the consequences of violence in these twenty years to last me for the remainder of my life.

What is peculiarly tragic in this revamping of the philosophy of force is the absence of standards, the abandonment of principles and ideals. For what is appealed to in these contentions but personal interest, partisanship, or prejudice? Here is a man who is concerned today about Russia, and who believes that the welfare of the Soviets is so precious a thing that it must be defended if necessary by violence. But here is another man who was concerned in 1914 about Austria, and who believed that the safety of the Dual Monarchy, his native land, was so precious to himself and to the integrity of Europe that it had to be defended by appeal to arms when Serbia loosed its assassins upon the Archduke.

The same thing holds true not only of interests to be defended but of causes to be advanced. My radical friend is devoted to the proletarian side of the class struggle. He thinks this cause is a crusade for the recapture of the holy places of humanity and therefore does not hesitate to draw the sword in its behalf. But my conservative friend is devoted to the capitalistic side of the class struggle. He thinks that the preservation of the institutions of private property and private profits is so essential to the preservation of civilization itself that any resort to force is amply justified. At the same time across the seas there are the Nazis, who have their own struggle and have organized their storm troops to carry it through to triumph. In the absence of principles or standards how can we judge between them? If we have no ideals, we cannot call any of them wrong. But if any one of them is right, then all of them are right, at least from the standpoint of their own particular interests and ideas. For these interests from this standpoint are the only criterion we have. What each individual thinks and desires and asserts is the all-sufficient justification of his or her acts.

Where such a situation takes us must be obvious. It takes us into a world where individuals may justifiably resort to violence and bloodshed on behalf of any cause which chances for some reason to be dear to them. But many people, many minds! And therefore, many causes! Some of these causes must be mutually inconsistent, antagonistic, hostile. This means that there must be conflict between them; and, if conflict, in terms of violence, then bloodshed and destruction. Which brings us to anarchy, chaos, and death—precisely the predicament predicted by Jesus when he said, "They that take the sword shall perish by the sword!"

Surely there must be some better and truer way of life. We cannot be forever lost in a world of "each man for himself" and "might makes right." Even our recreant pacifists seem to concede that there must be some law, or standard, or ideal, which may deliver us from an eternal battlefield "where ignorant armies clash by night."

Reinhold Niebuhr, who has repudiated his pacifism so far as the class struggle is concerned, agrees that there is at least one "absolute law" which must be recognized—"the law of love . . . an ideal," he says, "which transcends all law." But why does it transcend all law, if not because it completes the law in that one synthesis of high accord which renders conflict, and therefore violence, impossible? This is what St. Paul meant in his immortal statement that "love is the fulfillment of the law." "He that loveth his neighbor," said the Apostle, "hath fulfilled the law"—the law of that kingdom where "violence shall no more be heard in thy land, desolation nor destruction within thy borders."

So obvious is the truth, so elementary this lesson of the spirit, that I am persuaded we have not yet penetrated to the center of disintegration in the modern pacifist movement. What is the influence really at work in the hearts of our retreating pacifists? What is the motive, noble yet perverted, which is moving them?

We find the core of the problem, I believe, in the class struggle, which is dividing the ranks of the pacifists exactly as it is dividing the ranks of society at large. Some of the sincerest and noblest persons I know feel under compulsion to take what they call a realistic attitude toward a struggle which they regard as a kind of final conflict for the mastery of the world and the liberation of humankind. This conflict, they aver, is already with us in many forms of open or hidden violence, and will be determined in the end only by that massing of physical force which will enable one class to overcome the other. In such a crisis, our hearts must be with the proletariat, and our hands as well, for their struggle is a struggle for emancipation from a bondage which has enslaved multitudes. If we refuse to participate in this battle for economic freedom because it must be fought out with violence, this means we shall have to step aside and let the struggle go on without us. If the battle is lost, and the proletariat doomed to a perpetual servitude to wealth and power, it may well be because we have refused that aid which might have been decisive in their interest. We shall have withdrawn our support and consented to defeat in an unworthy desire to preserve our personal purity from pollution with a fantastic conception of sin.

In the imminence of the class struggle, in other words, we are confronted by a vigorous alternative. We must either plunge into this struggle, with all its violence and hate, or else keep out of the struggle to the end of an abstract ideal of individual perfectionism. We must either fight, or run away—and to run away is oftentimes to fight on the other side. "He that is not for us is against us." *The New Republic*, in a recent editorial, summed up the whole difficulty of the situation and pierced straight to the core of the pacifist problem of today in a single remarkable sentence: "To accept absolute pacifism is nowadays at best to retire into an ivory tower . . . with a good chance of finding this tower overturned ere long in the hurricane of social change by violence which is sweeping the world."

If this dilemma is sound, if this alternative of the battlefield and the ivory tower presents the only choice before us, I hope I may be among the first to abandon pacifism, at least of the absolutist type. For we are confronted here with that dichotomy of cowardice and violence, that spectacle of absolute surrender to evil, that horror of saving one's life while the kingdom is lost, which no less a pacifist than Mahatma Gandhi has found so utterly intolerable. You must remember the Mahatma's unforgettable statements on this point. "I believe," he says, "that where there is only a choice between cowardice and violence, I would advise violence." And again in specific reference to the crisis in his own country, "I would rather have India resort to arms in order to defend her honor than that she should in a cowardly manner become or remain a helpless witness to her own dishonor."

But who would say that this alternative is sound— that in the class struggle, or in any other struggle in the field of human affairs, "there is only a choice between cowardice and violence"? Nothing to do, you say, but to fight, or to run away? Gandhi did not find it so, in the terrific dilemma which confronted him when he undertook the leadership of his country's cause of national independence. On the one side, he saw the great masses of the common people sunk in apathy and indifference, abjectly surrendered to the tyranny of British rule. To condone, much less to participate in, this attitude of subjection to the Empire, was impossible for him, as he regarded "cooperation with the government a weakness and a sin." On the other side, the Mahatma saw the heroic leaders of the nationalist cause counseling a violent uprising against the Raj. But this also he could not approve, first because he regarded violence as wrong, and second because, in the Indian situation, he regarded it as impracticable. "Violence," he said, "can never free India." Neither horn of this dilemma, in other words, could Gandhi grasp, for both horns were held by Britain. "The government wants to goad us into violence or abject submission," he declared, "and we must do neither."

"If I can have nothing to do with the organized violence of the Government," said Gandhi, "I can have less to do with the unorganized violence of the people. I would prefer to be crushed between the two." But it is not necessary to be crushed between the two. This alternative of obedience or violence is not a real alternative. There is a third choice, said Gandhi. "It is the way of nonviolence, the only remedy open to us." Not nonviolence in the sense of inaction, passivity, acquiescence, but nonviolence in the sense of noncooperation, civil disobedience, organized spiritual resistance to a political rule which can only function on the basis of popular consent! It is Gandhi's highest claim to creative statesmanship that, rejecting violence as the means of winning liberty, he did not abandon his people to the alternative of slavery but worked out a third policy. *Satyagraha*, as he called it, showed the way to national independence without resort to arms. Out of the genius of the Indian people he wrought a weapon, perfectly adapted to their use, which was mightier and more beneficent than "the drawn sword and the bent bow." Refusing to shed the blood of his enemy in battle, the Mahatma also refused to retreat into an ivory tower but led his people in a warfare of the spirit which is marking at this moment a new and glorious epoch in human history.

It is this achievement of Gandhi, if nothing else, which makes ridiculous the idea that in this momentous issue of the class struggle we have no choice but to fight or to run away. We are bound down to no such alternative as this. We can refuse to condone or to practice violence, and still give aid and comfort to the workers in their heroic endeavor to secure and enjoy that full measure of earthly inheritance which is theirs. Indeed, we can give better and more effective aid than that of violence which must soon or late rebound with deadly effect upon those who use it.

THE PACIFIST MISSION

The mission of the pacifists, at this moment of stormy and convulsive social change, is to my mind perfectly plain. It is made plain, in this country, at least, by the comparative remoteness of the crisis of final conflict. It is true that the class struggle has already begun, but it is also true that it has *only* begun. There are outbreaks on a hundred fronts, but these are sporadic, superficial, inconsequential. The decisive battle, if it comes at all, is still far in the future. The revolution is not yet at hand. Which means that we have ample time *for working out that program of peaceful and yet fundamental change which may bring us all the fruits of revolution with none of its violence and horror!* This is the mission, the unique and noble mission, of the pacifist at this hour—to do in this country what Mahatma Gandhi has done in his. To take the genius of America—its traditions, institutions, and ideals—and work out a policy of creative statesmanship which will repudiate all use of the weapons of force, avoid all hazard of bloodshed and death, and achieve none the less the farthest ends of economic justice and social brotherhood.

Gandhi's task was enormously more difficult than this which is our challenge. He had to work with a primitive people, lost in ignorance and superstition, and long since subdued to the power of alien rule. He confronted conditions of economic misery and dependence which rendered helpless even those of his countrymen who were intelligently aware of their condition. He faced the immediate exigencies of a situation already beset by the stress and strain of open rebellion against the crown. In contrast to this, we have the inestimable advantage of an educated people, equipped with instrumentalities of democracy, trained to the exercise of self-rule, rich in the tradition of culture and liberty, and not yet overwhelmed by the crisis of instant action. Already in the natural functioning of our institutions, under the touch of courageous and devoted leadership, we are moving peacefully toward the attainment of goals which would have seemed incredible a few years ago. What we have already begun, not by violence but by orderly constitutional procedure, we can continue and ultimately complete. If in any country in the world, in other words, humanity should achieve an ideal commonwealth, without the waste and woe of war, it is here where society may be constructively adapted to the process of social change.

This is our opportunity! Failure to use this opportunity cannot justify resort to violence. Inability or unwillingness to summon the patience, courage, and endurance necessary to such an opportunity cannot be charged to the impracticability of pacifism. If the class struggle does not develop a conflict of ideas wherein disciplined men and women direct the action of high intelligence to the orderly triumph of essential justice, but degenerates at last into a ghastly conflict of force and terror, it will not be because pacifism is impossible as a program of life. Rather, it will be because the fierce passions of the jungle are still untamed within human souls. And also because pacifists, cowered with opportunity and charged with duty, are unequal to their task. Not the impossibility of pacifism but the weakness of pacifists is our bane. "Why are ye fearful, O ye of little faith?"

So I am still for pacifism—yes, pacifism in the absolutist sense! Though worse comes to worst in "one death-grapple in the darkness 'twixt old systems and the Word," I shall still be opposed to the use of force, and still strive for the better way. For I believe that the triumph of no cause can be safely bought at the price of humanity's reversion to the brute. If a certain end can be attained only by fighting and destroying and killing for it, then is it not worth attaining, for our very fighting lowers us to levels of existence where this end cannot be served. A war to end war defeats itself. A war to make the world safe for democracy creates conditions in which democracy must perforce perish. A war to save civilization must by its own processes destroy civilization and restore barbarism and savagery. Force, like the tiger, devours its own children. Therefore there can be but one real aim in life, and that is to raise humanity to the stature of its own spirit. Greater than all other causes is this cosmic cause of delivering the human creature, "half akin to brute," to final kinship with the divine. Pacifism, in other words, is the cause supreme. Not merely as means for the attainment of other ends, it is its own sufficient end. For all else is won, if this be won; and all else lost, if this be lost. This is the reason for pacifism, and the reason why I had rather die for this cause than live for any other. "Not by might, not by power, but by my spirit, saith the Lord!"

4

THE RELEVANCE
OF AN IMPOSSIBLE IDEAL

G. H. C. Macgregor

G. H. C. Macgregor was professor of divinity and biblical criticism and dean of the faculty of theology at the University of Glasgow. A native of Scotland, he saw service in World War I, and became vice-chair of the Fellowship of Reconciliation in Great Britain. In these years the most significant challenge to the pacifist position came from Reinhold Niebuhr, who argued in his book Moral Man and Immoral Society *that while the love command in the New Testament is absolute, it cannot be applied to states under the condition of fallen human nature. In the following essay (severely abridged) Macgregor offered a devastating critique of Niebuhr's position, one which remains as timely, and perhaps even more persuasive, than when it first appeared. Unfortunately, at that time Niebuhr's pessimistic theology seemed better able to answer the terrible events surrounding the rise of Nazism. Macgregor's article was not to bear immediate fruit, but it did serve to strengthen pacifists at a time when so many were defecting to the war effort. Today it deserves a respect it never garnered* (Fellowship, June 1941).

In the perennial debate concerning the bearing of the New Testament ethic upon the question of peace and war no one has had more influence recently than Reinhold Niebuhr. To the non-pacifist majority in the churches his writings have come as a veritable godsend, and no one has been so successful in salving the conscience of the non-pacifist, and even in weaning the pacifist from the pure milk of his faith. And no wonder! For Niebuhr is an intensely acute and virile thinker, and his argument has a forcefulness and persuasiveness which set him almost alone among the advocates of Christian non-pacifism. His views concerning pacifism are set forth in his recent booklet, "Why the Christian Church Is Not Pacifist," which must be read in the light of his two books, *Moral Man and Immoral Society* and *An Interpretation of Christian Ethics*. There is, I believe, a convincing Christian pacifist answer to Niebuhr's position, and this I shall attempt. But first we must try thoroughly to understand the formidable case which we have to meet. Niebuhr's indictment of pacifism may be stated under three heads.

First, pacifists are misled by the belief that "man is essentially good at some level of his being," while they have "rejected the Christian doctrine of original sin as an outmoded bit of pessimism." According to Niebuhr, "A theology which thus fails to come to grips with the tragic fact of sin is heretical." Like liberal Christianity in general, pacifism has "adopted the simple expedient of denying, in effect, the reality of evil in order to maintain its hope in the triumph of the ideal of love in the world." Hence the baseless optimism which interprets world history "as a gradual ascent to the Kingdom of God which waits for final triumph only upon the willingness of Christians to take Christ seriously." Hence, too, our naive faith in "simple" solutions for the world's complex ills, our belief that "if only men loved one another, all the . . . horrible realities of the political order could be dispensed with." Indeed, the issue between pacifist and non-pacifist is "between those who have a confidence in human nature which human nature cannot support and those who have looked too deeply into life and their own souls to place their trust in so broken a reed."

Second, this failure to recognize the reality and power of the evil inherent in human nature breeds a childlike confidence in the practicability and efficacy of "nonresistance" as a method of overcoming evil, even in the field of social and political relationships. Such "nonresistance" is for Niebuhr the core of the pacifist ethic. Yet, he argues, in believing that nonresistance, or forgiveness, is a means of overcoming evil in an enemy, the pacifist is reading into the New Testament something that is not there: "Nothing is said about the possibility of transmuting enmity to friendship through the practice of forgiveness." The pacifist, moreover, half conscious that nonresistance can have no immediate relevance to any political situation, construes Jesus' summons to nonresistance as if it were one to "nonviolent resistance." Yet this again is to read back into Jesus' teaching what is in fact the pacifist's own misinterpretation of it: "There is not the slightest support in Scripture for this doctrine of nonviolence. Nothing could be plainer than that the ethic uncompromisingly enjoins nonresistance and not nonviolent resistance."

Third, pacifists with their obsession concerning war unjustifiably isolate one particular moral issue, and demand with reference to it an absolute obedience to Jesus' teaching which they are not prepared to give over the whole range of life. Here Niebuhr is quite merciless: "If pacifists were less anxious to dilute the ethic of Christ to make it conform to their particular type of nonviolent politics, and if they were less obsessed with the obvious contradiction between the ethic of Christ and the fact of war, they might have noticed that the injunction 'resist not evil' is only part and parcel of a total ethic which we violate not only in war-time, but every day of our life."

THE BASIC FACT OF HUMAN SIN

Niebuhr builds his own case for Christian non-pacifism on the basic fact of human sin. "Christianity is a religion which measures the total dimension of human existence not only in terms of the final norm of human conduct, which is expressed in the law of love, but also in terms of the fact of sin. . . . The Gospel is something more than the law of love. The Gospel deals with the fact that men violate the law of love." When orthodox doctrine is reinterpreted in the light of modern psychological science we see that original sin "is not an inherited corruption, but it is an inevitable fact of human existence." Thus pacifist perfectionism is so much out of touch with human experience that "there are no historical realities which remotely conform to it." This inherent sinfulness of human nature expresses itself above all in a "will-to-live" which, when it becomes accentuated, develops into a "will-to-power." Both these impulses are diametrically opposed to Jesus' ethic, which finds a person's fullest self-attainment in a willingness to "lose his life," and insists that the way of greatness is the way of humble service. Thus, even though we know that we can become our true selves only by striving for self-realization beyond ourselves, we are inevitably involved in making our own narrow selves the chief end of existence. There is an insuperable contradiction within our own souls: though we know we ought to love our neighbors as ourselves, there is "a law in our members which wars against the law that is in our mind," so that in fact we love first and foremost our own selves.

Thus, even for the most Christlike individual, loyalty to the way of Christ must mean only "realization in intention, but does not actually mean the full realization of the measure of Christ." And if this is true of the Christian individual, much more is it true of social, political, and national groups. For it is one of Niebuhr's postulates that "human collectives are less moral than the individuals which compose them." "Human finiteness and sin are revealed with particular force in collective relationships" and "the full evil of human finitude and sin is most vividly revealed in conflicts between national communities." Who, looking at the world today, would deny that "the evil impulses in men may be compounded in collective actions until they reach diabolical proportions"? What possible relevance can an absolute perfectionist ethic have in such a world?

If we argue that the grace of God in Jesus Christ can make possible what is beyond the power of unregenerate human nature, and that in the church we have a "collective" or social fellowship in which the Holy Spirit should be active and powerful in a measure granted to no one individual, Niebuhr would reply somewhat as follows. Certainly the grace of God is regarded by Christian faith as an actual "power of righteousness" healing the contradiction within our hearts. But "the question is whether the grace of Christ is primarily a power of righteousness which so heals the sinful heart that henceforth it is able to fulfill the law of love; or whether it is primarily the assurance of divine mercy for a persistent sinfulness." Is the emphasis on sanctification or on justification? Niebuhr holds that in the New Testament "grace is conceived as justification, as pardon rather than as power, as the forgiveness of God which is vouchsafed to man despite the fact that he never achieves the full measure of Christ."

Niebuhr then draws his conclusions against Christian pacifism. Pacifists "do not see that sin introduces an element of conflict into the world, and that even the most loving relations are not free of it. . . . It is because we are sinners that justice can be achieved only by a certain degree of coercion on the one hand, and by resistance to coercion and tyranny on the other hand." It is on these grounds that under certain conditions even war may be justified:

> Given the fact of sin, all justice in the realm of man's collective behavior is achieved by securing some kind of decent equilibrium of power. But every such equilibrium stands under the peril of either tyranny or anarchy. Such a war as this one is merely the consequence of, and remedy for, the tyranny which results from irresponsible power. . . . If we are challenged to justify our participation in war in terms of our Christian faith, our answer is quite simply that we do not regard Christianity as a religion which merely preaches the simple moral injunction that we ought to love one another. Rather it is a religion which illumines the tragic fact that though love is the law of life, no man completely lives by that law.

THE TENSION BETWEEN THE HISTORICAL AND THE TRANSCENDENT

To what extent, then, is Jesus' absolute ethic relevant to the practical affairs of life? "The orthodox Church dismissed the immediate relevance of the law of love for politics. The modern Church declared it to be relevant without qualification, and insisted upon the direct application of the Sermon on the Mount to the problems of politics and economics as the only way of salvation for a sick society." Orthodoxy has led to complacency, liberalism to a naive Utopianism. In either case the original and fruitful tension of the Christian ethic has been destroyed; but pacifism is the more guilty because for it "the transcendent impossibilities of the Christian ethic of love" have become "the immanent and imminent possibilities of an historical process." Accordingly, "if the relevance of the love commandment must be asserted against Christian orthodoxy, the impossibility of the ideal must be insisted upon against all those forms of liberalism which generate Utopian illusions and regard the love commandment as ultimately realizable."

What relevance then has this impossible ethical ideal? Clearly it is not immediately applicable to social and international problems. It was framed for the kingdom of God, which is a divine reality and not a human possibility. Probably Jesus himself never thought of it as practicable, even in the world as he knew it; and even if he did, it does not follow that it is practicable for us who are "involved in the relativities of politics, in resistance to tyranny or in social conflict" as Jesus himself never was. Moreover, this ethic of the kingdom is one in which "no concession is made to human sin," and in which "there is no advice on how we may hold the world of sin in check until the coming of the kingdom of God." It demands an absolute obedience to the will of God without consideration of any of the consequences of trying to practice a perfectionist ethic in an imperfect world. And yet this ethic does, within strict limits, have a real relevance to every sphere of life.

First, it provides us with an ideal standard against which we may measure the magnitude of our failure. Christianity demands the impossible, and by that very demand it emphasizes the impotence of human nature. People are saved not by achieving perfection, but by the recognition of their inability to do so.

Second, the ideal law of love provides us with the absolute standard, the ultimate criterion by which every attempt to create a new and better world must be judged. Though as a transcendent ideal the ethic of Jesus can itself provide no practicable way of life for a sinful world, nevertheless it "may offer valuable insights to and sources of criticism for a prudential social ethic which deals with present realities." Faith "sees history as a realm of infinite possibilities. No limit can be placed upon the higher possibilities of justice which may be achieved in any given historic situation." If Jesus' ethic can never become the way of life for a sinful humanity, it can at least help us to set all our poor tentative experiments under the criticism of the ultimate ideal.

Third, and for Niebuhr this is of paramount importance, "the ideal of love is not merely a principle of indiscriminate criticism upon all approximations of justice. It is also a principle of discriminate criticism between forms of justice." That is to say, when there are two or more alternatives, both admittedly falling short of the ideal, the law of love provides the criterion by which we may determine which of these several "second bests" approximates more closely to the ideal. It may even lay upon us the duty of accepting what, in the light of the ideal, is obviously the lesser of *two evils*—for example, according to Niebuhr, war rather than submission to tyranny. Niebuhr's charge against Christian pacifism is that, in its mistaken striving after the absolute ideal, it refuses to make such discriminate judgments and face up to such discriminate choices. "Pacifism either tempts us to make no judgments at all, or to give an undue preference to tyranny in comparison with the momentary anarchy which is necessary to overcome tyranny."

There follow from all this several very important practical conclusions:

First, given a sinful world and the impracticability of the way of absolute love, the nearest approximation to the ideal is to be found in "equal justice." It is admitted that such justice is a "second best," which in the kingdom of God would be transcended and "fulfilled" in the law of love. "The principles of equal justice are approximations of the law of love in the kind of imperfect world which we know and not principles which belong to a world of transcendent perfection." Yet these principles are our only practicable "guide to conduct in the common relationships of life."

Second, in order to attain even to this approximation to the ideal we must be prepared to make relative judgments, that is to discriminate between alternative "second bests," to choose "the lesser of two evils," and with a good conscience to act upon such choices.

Third, the ultimate standard of the Christian ideal "ought to persuade us that political controversies are always conflicts between sinners and not between righteous men and sinners." But the fact that we ourselves are sinners, and that our own sin is always partly the cause of the evil by which we are confronted, must not be taken as proof that we have no right to resist that evil. If we imagine that "we have no right to act against an acknowledged evil because we are not ourselves pure, we are delivered into historic futility." For example, "the fact that the evil incarnated in the Nazi state is the culminating expression of forms of cultural and social decay which are rife among ourselves does not absolve us from the task of opposing that evil." The truth is that "the Christian is freed by grace to act in history; to give his devotion to the highest values he knows," even though "he is persuaded by that grace to remember the ambiguity of even his best actions."

THE TRAGIC RESULTS OF PACIFISM

Niebuhr finally insists that a failure to recognize these principles will inevitably result in moral anarchy both for the individual life and also in social and international relationships. "It may yet be proved that the greatest tragedy of the present war is that Nazi tyranny was allowed to grow until it reached unparalleled proportions, precisely because so many citizens of a Christian civilization were prevented by these (pacifist) scruples from resisting the monster when there was yet time. If this should be true it would be 'tragic' in the narrow and exact sense of the word. It would reveal the possibility of evil emerging from our highest good."

NIEBUHR'S CONCESSIONS TO THE PACIFIST POSITION

First, there can be no question that the teaching of Jesus, if taken at its face value, is uncompromisingly pacifist. Niebuhr has no patience with those Christian theologians and ecclesiastics who still seek to discover loopholes through which war may be actually brought within the pale of Christian ethics and blessed in the name of the Prince of Peace: "It is very foolish to deny that the ethic of Jesus is an absolute and uncompromising ethic. . . . The injunctions 'resist not evil,' 'love your enemies,' . . . 'be not anxious for your life,' 'be ye therefore perfect even as your Father in heaven is perfect,' are all of one piece, and they are all uncompromising and absolute." In the world as it is, forces over which we have no control may drive our nation into war as what appears the lesser of two evils; but when Christians take up arms there is not anything in either the teaching or example of Jesus which would justify us in pointing to him as our precedent:

> Nothing is more futile and pathetic than the effort of some Christian theologians who find it necessary to become involved in the relativities of politics, in resistance to tyranny or in social conflict, to justify them-

selves by seeking to prove that Christ was also involved in some of these relativities, that He used whips to drive the money-changers out of the Temple, or that He came "not to bring peace but a sword," or that He asked the disciples to "sell a cloak and buy a sword."

The necessity of making "relative judgments" may drive us to compromise, but that does not alter the essentially uncompromising nature of Jesus' commands. "Those of us who regard the ethic of Jesus as finally and ultimately normative, but as not immediately applicable to the task of securing justice in a sinful world, are very foolish if we try to reduce the ethic so that it will cover and justify our prudential and relative standards and strategies."

In other words, the debate between pacifist and non-pacifist ought to be, not concerning any possible ambiguity in Jesus' teaching, which should be admitted to be unequivocally pacifist, but rather concerning its practicability, its relevance to present circumstances, the extent to which even Jesus himself intended it to be put into effect in an imperfect world. The question is not, "Does Jesus command this?" but rather, "Does he mean us to obey what appears to be a plain command, and will he give us power to do so?" If the question was always as clearly posed as it is by Niebuhr, one feels that for most Christians the debate would be closed.

Second, Niebuhr concedes that "pacifists are quite right in one emphasis. They are right in asserting that love is really the law of life." Niebuhr rightly insists on the "relevance of the ideal of love to the moral experience of mankind on every conceivable level. It is not an ideal magically superimposed upon life by a revelation which has no relation to total human experience." The compulsion of the love-commandment is as all-embracing as the love of God itself for us. "The Christian love-commandment does not demand love of others because they are with us equally divine, or because we ought to have 'respect for personality,' but because God loves them." All pacifists will feel that in writing thus Niebuhr has done much to build the bridge which must ultimately reunite pacifist and non-pacifist Christians.

Finally, while pronouncing much pacifist doctrine to be "heretical," Niebuhr allows that there is a certain value in pacifism and a real place for pacifists in the church. Modern Christian pacifism "expresses a genuine impulse in the heart of Christianity, the impulse to take the law of Christ seriously and not to allow the political strategies, which the sinful character of man makes necessary, to become final norms." Such Christian perfectionism, provided that it limits itself to "the effort to achieve a standard of perfect love in individual life," need not come under the ban: it does so only when it regards the law of love "as an alternative to the political strategies by which the world achieves a precarious justice." But when it relegates itself judiciously to its own sphere, and when "the political problem and task are specifically disavowed," this kind of pacifism is "not a heresy. It is rather a valuable asset for the Christian faith." It may seem here—to use Niebuhr's own criticism of Brunner—that our author touches his cap to pacifism only at the cost of "neatly dismissing the Christian ideal from any immediate relevance to political issues."

On the immediate problem of the church's attitude to war in general and this war in particular Niebuhr utters two warnings to which Christian pacifists will give an emphatic "Amen!" First, there is the peril of compromising with the absolute, particularly in the church's relations with the state. Protestant tradition has given the state "special sanctification as an ordinance of God," and the Lutheran doctrine of the two "domains" has resulted too often in an unwillingness on the part of the church to apply to the state's actions within the sphere of the latter's own domain the critical sanctions of a Christian morality which was held to function only within the "order of grace." Yet, says Niebuhr, "it must also be noted that the Church usually capitulated in the end to the lower standards which it failed to challenge in the State." So today the way of least resistance for the church is to renounce all criticism of the state, so long as it acts strictly within its own domain, and (like the German Confessional Church) to protest in the name of Christ only when the state claims not only "the things that are Caesar's" but also "the things that are God's." Yet, says Niebuhr again, "a Church which refrains from practically every moral criticism of the State and allows itself only an ultimate religious criticism of the spiritual pretensions of the State must logically end in the plight in which the German Church finds itself."

Second, Niebuhr warns us against the tragic results of invoking religion in support of a national war effort. There has never been a war in which it has not been found necessary to buttress national morale by appealing to the religious instinct. "All wars are religious wars, whether fought in the name of historic creeds or not. Men do not fight for causes until they are 'religiously' devoted to them; which means not until the cause seems to them the center of their universe of meaning. This is just as true in a supposedly secular age as in an avowedly religious one." The result has been a vast amount of national hypocrisy and self-deception, as was only too evident in the last war.

Worst of all the constant invocation of religion produces a mood of national self-righteousness which at the moment is perhaps the least admirable feature of our own national temper. The very fact that, at least in our own eyes, our cause is so obviously righteous sorely tempts us to identify our cause with God's and our victory with the triumph of God's kingdom. God grant that it may indeed be so! Yet, warns Niebuhr, in all international disputes "every appeal to moral standards degenerates into a moral justification of the self against the enemy. Parties to a dispute inevitably make themselves judges over it and thus fall into the sin of pretending to be God. . . . The introduction of religious motives into these conflicts is usually no more than the final and most demonic pretension. Religion may be regarded as the last and final effort of the human spirit to escape relativity and gain a vantage point in the eternal."

It is encouraging that so keen an opponent of Christian pacifism as Niebuhr yet finds himself wholly at one with us over so large a portion of the field. Indeed, one is conscious of a growing wonder that, starting from such presuppositions, our author can, on the main issue of pacifism, reach the conclusions set forth in his latest booklet.

THE THEOLOGICAL FOUNDATIONS OF NIEBUHR'S POSITION

I shall try to deal next with the first of the two main theological foundations of Niebuhr's position. One—and that is the starting point of the whole argument—is his doctrine of human depravity; the other is his view that Jesus' teaching envisages a kingdom of God wholly transcendent and future, and his perfectionist ethic therefore has no immediate relevance (save as an ideal standard and a principle of "discriminate criticism") to the practical problems of today. The first, I shall argue, springs from a quite unscriptural view of human nature; the second from a failure to grasp the really characteristic and essential elements in Jesus' teaching concerning the kingdom of God. On purely rational grounds Niebuhr's case appears exceedingly formidable. But when examined in the light of the New Testament it is seen to be quite inconsistent with any but a badly maimed doctrine alike of the Incarnation, the church, the Holy Spirit, the cross, and the kingdom of God.

Niebuhr's View of Human Nature

First then, argues Niebuhr, human beings are so corrupted by sin as to be incapable, even if they would, of the sublimation of their selfish and antisocial instincts which obedience to the ethic of Jesus would demand. Between the "perfect" Father in heaven, to whom Jesus points as our exemplar, and we sinful creatures there is a gulf fixed which no striving after a perfectionist ideal can ever bridge. Humans as slaves of sin are incapacitated from cooperating with God in the building of God's kingdom, a kingdom which cannot be advanced by any human endeavor, but which will come only when human history is wound up by an apocalyptic act of God. Complacency and self-sufficiency is humanity's fundamental sin; the confession that "our righteousnesses are as filthy rags" is the first condition of his forgiveness; the denial of the reality and power of evil is his final apostasy. All that Niebuhr has to say about the nothingness and sinfulness of people before God is true. But is it the whole truth? If the world is indeed a sink of iniquity for which there is no hope of progress within the span of history, if all striving toward the kingdom of God is mere unregenerate arrogance, then clearly the pacifist renunciation of war is little short of blasphemous presumption.

But the gospels give us a very different picture. So far from teaching that God is "wholly other" than his world and his creatures, Jesus saw the world always and everywhere as God's world. He drew his lessons from birds and flowers, from the processes of growth and human handiwork; and when he wished to teach us what God is like he pointed to the Godlike in humankind. Even in the worst sinner he could discover the hidden good and appeal to it, knowing that the good and not the evil is the essential person. He tells us that it is when a sinner "comes to himself" that he arises and goes to his Father: the truly human, our true self, is that within us which responds to God. This faith in an ever-present Father never blinds Jesus to the reality of sin or to the eternal warfare between light and darkness. Yet he believes that, if we will but "lose our lives" in order to "find them," then God's will can "be done in earth as it is in heaven"—even though that will may prove to be a cross.

The estimate of human nature on which Niebuhr's case so largely depends is one of pessimism and gloom entirely out of tune with the joy and hope of the whole New Testament. It seriously distorts the New Testament doctrine of the Incarnation, for it makes Christ's nature exclusive rather than representative, and sees him as a "divine intruder" into an alien world rather than as "the firstborn of all creation." It gives little or no meaning, as we shall see, to the Holy Spirit, and it makes nonsense of Paul's claim that "we are fellow-workers together with God."

But if it is possible for the redeemed Christian individual to cooperate with God in the achievement of God's perfect will, is it any less possible for a redeemed fellowship, in this case, for the Christian church? For it is fair to remind Niebuhr that by his own definition the question at issue is "Why the *Christian church* is not pacifist." It is Niebuhr's thesis that "human collectives are less moral than the individuals which compose them" and that therefore there is a radical difference between personal and collective ethics. Now, the question of war apart, the average Christian would almost certainly repudiate the suggestion that a person may legitimately live by one set of principles as an individual and by another as a citizen. Yet this assumption underlies practically every statement of the Christian non-pacifist position.

But is this thesis of "moral man and immoral society" really tenable on Christian grounds? Surely it is questionable even with respect to ordinary secular society. No doubt there is a superficial truth in the view that the group mind tends to revert toward the primitive and the savage, and that the morality of the crowd falls below that of the individual. But a group can rise above the sum of its members as well as fall below it. There is an inspiration in fellowship which enables comrades to rise to levels impossible to the mere individual. *Esprit de corps* raises and does not lower morale! But the needful condition is inspiration by a common enthusiasm and a common purpose. It is this that distinguishes a fellowship from a mob, and though Niebuhr's thesis may be true of a mob it is emphatically not true of a fellowship. And the classic example of the fulfillment of such a condition is the Christian church "continuing steadfastly of one accord" at Pentecost. Suffice it for the moment to remark that Niebuhr's thesis is flatly irreconcilable with the Christian's faith in the church and his own experience of *koinonia* in that church. Can it really be true that such a body as a whole is so sunk in depravity, and is so nerveless through the ravages of sin, that it cannot cooperate with God in the doing of God's perfect will? Has the absolute ethic of Jesus really no more immediate relevance to such a body than is recognized by the rival leaders of warring states? Again we remind ourselves that our problem is, "Why the *Christian church* is not pacifist."

If Niebuhr's argument does injustice to the New Testament doctrine of the church, he has apparently no doctrine at all of the Holy Spirit—at any rate in the New Testament sense. We have already noted that he regards grace as pardon rather than as power: he appears to have little conception at all of "enabling grace." Yet to remove this doctrine from the New Testament is to tear out its very heart. It is an essential part of Paul's faith; otherwise how can he speak of "his power that worketh in me mightily" (Col 1:29), or pray to be "strengthened with might by his spirit in the inner man" (Eph 1:16), or boast that "I can do all things through Christ which strengtheneth me" (Phil 4:13)? That such is Paul's teaching—however incredible it may seem to our poor faith or in the light of our own experience of failure both as individuals and as a church—there can be no shadow of doubt, and no treatment of Christian ethics can be adequate which does not take account of it.

Niebuhr's View of the Kingdom of God

The second foundation of Professor Niebuhr's case is that Jesus' ethic, framed as it is in view of a wholly transcendent and future kingdom of God, was never intended, possibly even by our Lord himself, to be applicable to the imperfect world in which we live.

Now there are many ways of evading the relevance of Jesus' demands, so that they may not challenge traditional dogma or conflict with the dictates of prudence and expediency. There is the "eschatological" argument, according to which Jesus' teaching is merely an "interim ethic" intended to bridge the brief gap between Jesus' own day and the breaking-in of the quickly expected transcendent kingdom. But Jesus makes his characteristic demands, not in view of an immediate end of the present age, but on the ground that such a way of life is alone consistent with his own conception of God's nature; Jesus' view of God is surely, if anything is, a permanent and unchangeable element in his teaching.

More integral to Niebuhr's case is the argument that Jesus was not to the slightest degree "involved in the relativities of politics," and therefore his teaching has no immediate bearing upon the practical problems with which a Christian society is confronted today. Niebuhr's argument appears to leave quite out of account what are in fact the most essential and characteristic features of Jesus' teaching about the kingdom of God. For Niebuhr, Jesus' "counsels of perfection" have no immediate relevance to "political relativities," because the kingdom of God to which they are related is, even in the thought of Jesus himself, wholly transcendent and wholly future. Now Niebuhr is stating a profound truth when he insists that the fruitfulness of all ethical teaching depends on its ability to maintain "a tension between the historical and the transcendent," the contrast between the imperfect present and the consummation which is God's perfect will.

The kingdom, though transcendent, is yet to be manifested in this world. We are bidden by Jesus to pray "thy kingdom come; thy will be done *in earth,* as it is in heaven." Earth no less than heaven is the sphere of God's kingdom, where his will can and shall be done. That is to say, although this world is a fallen world, it is still God's world, and "his kingdom ruleth over all." In Christ it is God's will to redeem a sinful world order, and not to abolish this world by the coming of his "reign," as was the dream of the apocalyptists. The obedient servants of his kingdom must therefore be in the world, where alone the process of redemption may be carried on. When we pray "thy kingdom come in earth," we are not merely hoping that some day and somewhere God's kingdom will become a reality; we are not regretfully postponing the reign of God either to heaven or to Utopia. We are accepting it here and now; and the obligation laid upon us by that acceptance is binding here and now, even though we know that it cannot be completely fulfilled by people living in this world. Hence the "tension" of which we have spoken. As, according to Niebuhr, the whole of Jesus' ethic is conceived with direct reference to the kingdom, to deny this is to reduce his teaching to so much apocalyptic daydreaming. As G. J. Heering has pungently put it, "There is no more effective way of disabling the Gospel than first to relegate the fulfillment of Christ's commands to the kingdom of God, and then to read His saying, My kingdom is not *of* this world, as if He had said, My kingdom is not *for* this world."

Though the kingdom in its full consummation is still future, in numerous passages Jesus proclaims that with himself that kingdom, the hope of many generations, has at last come. "Many prophets and righteous men desired to see the things which ye see, and saw them not" (Mt 8:17). The kingdom is not merely imminent; it is here.

Particularly characteristic is the idea that it is in Jesus' own person that the kingdom has come, and that it manifests itself in a *divine power* to transform the world—a power which is already in operation. Particularly significant is the work of Rudolph Otto, all the more so because in certain respects his theological outlook is similar to Niebuhr's own. Jesus, as he says, "ranged far beyond (the Jewish apocalyptists) by an idea which was entirely unique and peculiar to Him, that the kingdom—supramundane, future, and belonging to a new era—penetrated from the future into the present, from its place in the beyond into this order, and was operative redemptively as a divine *dynamis*, as an in-breaking realm of salvation." And again, "What distinguished Jesus' own eschatology from previous forms was that He already lived in the miracle of the new age, which was active even in the present; that with clear vision He saw this as something already developing and growing around Himself; that He knew Himself to be supported by powers which were already penetrating the world, and supported and filled by these powers He worked and preached."

THE INFERENCE FOR THE CHURCH TODAY

To grasp this essential element in New Testament teaching does not indeed make any less agonizing the conflict of loyalties and choices in which Christians are involved when they seek to obey the laws of the kingdom amid the moral anarchy of a world at war. But it does sting them into consciousness of the obligation under which they stand. If Jesus really believed and taught that with his coming there had broken through from the transcendent kingdom a new divine power for the redemption and transformation of the present world, then it will not do for Christians to argue that for Jesus himself the kingdom was wholly other-worldly, and that therefore the ethic framed with a view to that kingdom may be safely and honorably discounted in a world in which that kingdom is still a future dream. Whatever the conclusions of a prudential morality, that is clearly to evade both the intention of Jesus' teaching and the interpretation placed upon it by all the New Testament writers. Above all, it is to shut our eyes to the one adequate source of power for the world's salvation.

To some of us the most tragic factor in the present catastrophe has been the church's failure to use the power which, in Jesus Christ, God has placed in her hands, and which through the church's obedience might have been released for the world's redemption. We Christian pacifists have often been warned by our "realist" friends that we cannot bring in the kingdom of God by acting as if it were already here. Yet this is, I believe, precisely what Jesus *did* teach: if only people were prepared to take God at his word, and to order their lives here and now by the laws of a transcendent kingdom, then the power of God would answer the cry of faith, and the kingdom would break in upon them anew and "take them unawares." If Jesus were no more than a great teacher of ethics—possibly the world's greatest—then Niebuhr's case is unanswerable. But if he is indeed the Son of God? If the church is his body, and we "members in particular"? If in his Word we have a unique revelation of God's will? If by his Spirit we are empowered for obedience?

5

THE PACIFIST WAY OF LIFE

A. J. Muste

Under the shadow of World War II, Muste, in this article, lays down the credo of his pacifist beliefs (Fellowship, *December 1941*).

Pacifism is not a tool or an instrument that you can pick up and lay down, use it today but not use it tomorrow, use it in one relationship of life but not in other relationships of life. It is, itself, a way of life that grows out of convictions, attitudes, and habits, which in time become an inseparable part of the pacifist individual. What are some of the elements in this way of life?

To illustrate them, I want to recall an incident that took place a great many years ago in the "prehistoric" days before the last war, when I was a little boy, of about eleven years, in public school. The incident must have made an impression on me, because I have remembered it, from time to time, through the years, though it is only in the past year or two that I have reflected upon it as being particularly significant.

It happened one afternoon that the big boy of the class, who was also something of a bully and who sat in the back row, was called down to the front to be reprimanded by the teacher. On his way down the aisle, as he passed one of the seats toward the front in which sat one of the smaller boys in the class, that smaller boy surreptitiously stuck out his foot into the aisle and the big boy stumbled over it and landed in something of a heap at the teacher's feet. The teacher took for granted, on the basis of past performances, that this was just another antic of the big boy. She hadn't noticed the foot surreptitiously stuck out. "Just another instance of disrespect for the dignity and authority of the teaching profession." So the big boy got an additional reprimand and punishment for his performance.

We all knew intuitively that something very exciting was going to happen when school was over that afternoon. So, with more primness than usual, we walked out of the classroom and down the hall and down the steps, as the teacher stood at the head of those steps watching us march out, and out of the gate, until we got just a foot or so beyond where the teacher's eye could reach

30

us. Then, at that point, the big boy sort of squared off, with his gang gathered around him. Presently the little boy came along, and the rest of us stood around, all ready for the great excitement. Presently the big boy threw his shoulders back and said: "You tripped me."

What, of course, we all expected was that the little boy was either going to whimper and try to get out of it, or run away, or that he would fight back as best he could. But, for some reason the little boy stood there very calmly, with his hands at his side, and said: "Yes, I did it."

With that, the big boy shifted to the other foot; and then shifted over again; and presently he turned around and walked away, with his gang following him, and presently the little boy walked away, and then the rest of us also walked away—much disappointed.

What was it that had happened? I suggest that perhaps five things may have been involved in that incident: *First*, the little boy did the unexpected thing; *second*, he admitted that he was in the wrong; *third*, he told the truth; *fourth*, he was not afraid; and *fifth*, having somehow transferred the conflict to another plane than that of physical force, he became the channel for another kind of force, so that another kind of law became operative in the situation.

Here, at the outset, the little boy did the *unexpected* thing. We all tend to do one of two things in such circumstances: We attempt flight; or we try to defend ourselves by fighting. If I do either one, then the other fellow, the adversary, knows exactly what to do. That's a familiar pattern and he will be able to perform according to that familiar pattern. But if I do something else, he is caught off his guard. As Richard Gregg has suggested, sort of moral *jiu jitsu* has been performed upon him.

There is something here, I'm sure, which goes very deep. Human beings are of an infinite variety. No two of them are alike. Each is a person. Each was meant to be unique—a center of creativeness. But what we find in this world is conformity. People dress and talk and behave alike—as they think other people expect or want them to; not as deep down each wants and needs to act. The effect of conformity is like foot-binding. It deforms the feet, and furthermore, it sets up strains in the whole body so that it cannot function naturally. So, by this process tensions are set up in people all around who also always do the expected thing. Then, as we say, we have to "take it out." We have to get that tension out, and under these circumstances we "take it out on somebody."

Therefore, Christians, the religious pacifists, are, from one point of view, simply those who do what they want to do; who let the creative in them function, and who consequently are not very likely to conform. Instead, they will be and do something fresh, original, spontaneous. I am sure that pacifists, and those who may be on the way to pacifism; Christians and those who may be on the way to being Christians, need to ponder this matter. Often, far from having attained this spontaneity, we behave under pressures from without rather than letting behavior bubble up from within organically. And we can, of course, be the slaves of others, not only by doing as they want us to do, but also by feeling that we have to do what they don't want us to do—a slave of the outward by always battling against it in an embittered way as well as by submitting to it. Power, effectiveness in life, comes into a situation when a person does the fresh, unexpected thing that comes from within, that suddenly rises above the circumstance, that leaves the circumstance that created the tension off there where it doesn't matter.

This means, too, that we all have to use our imaginations a great deal more than we are in the habit of doing, on people and on situations, visualizing how we can keep from behaving in a stereotyped manner. I pass on to you that great line of W. H. Auden in his "Modern Prayer." He prays to God: "Prohibit sharply the rehearsed response."

War, and of course this whole armament business, is an outstanding instance of this lack of imagination, this giving the rehearsed response. A nation gets a gun, and it says: "Naturally I have no idea whatever of attacking anybody with this gun, and neither do I particularly fear anybody, but I just want to be safe. I want to be secure." Then what does the other nation do? Something original? Something different? Something independent? Oh, no! The other nation says: "Naturally, if Nation Number One gets a gun, it must have some dark purpose in its heart. Anyway, some day it might get excited and the gun would go off." So Nation Number Two gets itself a gun.

Next, what does Nation Number One do? Invariably Nation Number One says: "I'm left utterly defenseless again. I've got a gun. He's got a gun. We're just where we were before." So it gets a *second* gun.

And what does Nation Number Two do? It gets a *second* gun. And so you have an armament race going.

After a while one of the guns goes off. What happens then? Something original? Something different? Not at all. All the guns begin to go off. . . . It's so dull! It's so unimaginative!

Now, coming back to the little boy; in the *second* place, he admitted that he was in the wrong. Here, also, we have something that goes deep. The world is full of human beings who, until they are born again, are trying to justify themselves. They have to be able to think well of themselves. But as long as we think of self as something separate, something that we have to hug and not give away, then this business of justifying oneself is always based on comparison with the other person. "When I look at him, I'm not such a bad fellow. Things went wrong, but it wasn't my fault."

When I thus set myself up, am I not pushing the other down, in my mind, spiritually? I am committing spiritual aggression. My spirit is assaulting, killing, the other's spirit. That is what Jesus was talking about: "It has been said 'Thou shalt not kill', but I say unto you, whoever shall say, even in his heart, under his breath, about his brother, 'Thou fool!' is in danger of the hell of fire."

We cannot hide these attitudes from each other, and so others fight back to assert their dignity, to put themselves on the pedestal. They put up their mental

defenses and say: "Huh! He thinks he's quite something, but I'll show him."
Like the Japanese when we passed the Oriental Exclusion Act.

That goes on in the most respectable circles—ladies' aid societies, peace
organizations, church conventions. This inner war, "the war that is in our *members*," breaks out in war in the conventional sense of the term.

How stop it? How bring peace? There is only one way. We have to quit
trying to justify ourselves. Someone has to say: "Why, of course I'm no better
than I ought to be. Of course I'm in the wrong, and I ought to do something
about it."

"Purify the springs of history which are within ourselves," says Jacques
Maritain. What a healing coolness and sweetness comes into a situation when
people quit indulging in the so-pleasant pastime of confessing other people's
sins and begin to confess their own!

So with the nations. The most tragic and by far the most dangerous thing in
the world situation today is that every nation dares to stand up in the temple of
God's universe and say: "God, I thank thee that I am not as others are, and
especially as this publican, these Nazi swine and Fascist dogs and Japanese
devils," or, if the Germans are saying it, "These effete and hypocritical Englishmen or Americans." Not one of them bows his head in that temple and
smites his own breast and says: "God be merciful to me, a sinner."

In the *third* place, the little boy told the truth. That is also a revolutionary
thing to do. We don't do it in personal relations. Some little incident happens
and we say, when we are trying to settle it, "Well, you tell your story and I'll
tell mine." Why not just tell the story?

We don't do it in business. We give a sales talk which is by no means necessarily the truth—often necessarily not the truth.

So in political, in public life. Everybody says: "I believe in democracy," but
most show that what they really believe in is the fruits or benefits of democracy as practiced by somebody else.

Some businessmen whom you meet can get very eloquent about the "dictatorship" of John L. Lewis or even William Green or some local labor leader,
but they show by their actions what they are really concerned about—that
they should continue to be tsars in their own business; they don't want any of
this nonsense about democracy there.

Some labor leaders can get eloquent about Wall Street and big business,
but what they really want is to continue to be tsars in their own unions. They
don't want any of this nonsense about democracy there.

Haven't we all noticed how suddenly a situation clears up, a balm comes
into it, when nobody is holding back anything? The cards are on the table.
Nobody is pretending anymore. It would be so if there were truthfulness between the nations. Did Hitler ever tell the truth in a public crisis? Did the
other statesmen ever tell the whole truth to Hitler, whatever they may have
meant to do? Did Mr. Chamberlain, after Munich, when he went home and
said, "The dawn of peace has come on earth," and then made a speech in

Parliament, the burden of which was, "Now we've got to arm more rapidly than we ever have before"?

Where there is a lie, any lack of frankness in a situation, there is corruption, my friends. The thing will fall apart. Lies and evasions, not bombs and bullets, in the first instance, are killing those whose blood now drenches the earth.

In the *fourth* place, the little boy was not afraid. We are afraid most of the time. That is one of the great causes of war.

If a wild animal encounters a human being who is not afraid, it is much less likely to attack. There is a good physiological, psychological reason for that: the animal is under tension. If the other animal or human is also afraid, then there are two centers of tension in the situation, and once again you have to "take it out" on somebody. But if, in that situation, there is another being who is not afraid, that releases the tension. There is a lightning rod for it to flow out through. There is nothing for it to feed on and to make an explosion necessary.

When there is a fight, that is done to relieve the tension, to expel the fear, the demon; to bring about a sense of security. But it can do so only for a fleeting moment, if at all. To fight against something, someone out there, when there is a fear within, really aggravates the fear. It brings to the vanquished animal the sickening fear of the defeated, the mortally stricken. And fear is in the heart of the victor, too, for how does the present victor know that a stronger one may not be around the corner?

There is only one way to get security. That is to stop being afraid. That is what Jesus was saying all the time: "Let not your heart be troubled."

How are we going to get rid of fear? It is simple in its essentials. Simply stop caring about myself, hugging *me*. The mother who sees her child in danger, in the crowded street, dares anything, because she is not interested in herself. She is absorbed in the situation of her child. So with anyone. Stop loving yourself. Love someone else. Love humankind. You won't be afraid.

So with nations. Oh, America! Stop loving yourself, hanging on to what you have, which is so much more than any other nation has. Let yourself go today. Love humankind. You won't need to be afraid. "Perfect love casteth out fear," and even a little love will cast out a whole lot of fear. Suppose that we were *practically* loving Jews and Negroes in our country today. Do you think we would be as afraid of Hitler as we are? Suppose we were sending armadas of food and clothing and medicine to the starving millions of Europe and of Asia. Do you think we would be as afraid as we are today?

Finally, the little boy having, for some reason, put aside the conventional use of force either to run away or to fight back, another kind of power came into play. Miraculously, the boy who put his hands at his side and stood defenseless was safe. The big boy couldn't touch him.

There are two kinds of power in the universe. To put it crudely, there is the power that is primarily physical, material, and there is the power of spirit love,

God. It is a law of life that we have to choose which of these we are going to use. It has to be one or the other. It cannot be both. One of the great troubles is that here, as in so many other situations, we want to have our cake and eat it, too. The people of this country don't want to be in the war, but they want "like everything" to bring victory to one side and defeat to another. They want to pass guns to the fighters, but they don't want their sons to be shot at.

It won't do. We have to choose the plane on which, and the weapons with which, we are going to fight; and then take the consequences. If we are going to contend on the material plane and with material weapons, we have to have the most and the biggest. If you happen to be a little nation, on this basis you are just out of luck from the beginning. But even if you are a big nation, what is your situation? You may say you have to make yourself "impregnable." What does it mean to be impregnable? It means to have forces or allies enough, to be able to go out and meet any potential enemy, or set of enemies, and to defeat them. That is, it means, at the *very least*, that you have force enough to hold on to such territory of the earth, raw materials, and markets as you judge are necessary for your nation's *lebensraum*. But if you are in a position to do that, then you are in a position, by preponderance of military might, to shut out a number of other nations. That is exactly what Hitler and Japan are trying to do, and that is what we are supposed to be objecting to as their "aggressions." So the result of the effort to make every nation, or its "axis," impregnable is that all the nations are defenseless against the cost of recurrent war.

Perhaps you say, "Yes, but we could have collective security if the peace-loving nations would be willing to pool their collective force against the law-breaking nations." That, however, could only bring security if there were (a) general disarmament, (b) an international authority to which most nations gave voluntary consent, and (c) a new deal in world affairs which redistributed economic and political power on a basis of much greater justice than obtained in the nineteenth century and in those critical decades of the twentieth century after the last war, when we and our victorious allies had undisputed military and economic might. In other words, the foundations of this security would have to be basically moral, not material. Preponderance of material force in the absence of these other conditions inevitably means the old effort to freeze the status quo to the advantage of one group of nations *vs.* another. It would give us no collective security at all. It might come nearer to producing collective suicide. Unfortunately, the nations at present give little evidence that they are prepared to accept the fundamental requirements of this program.

There is another kind of power: the power of the spirit. There is another kind of defense: God. It is hard for us to believe it. The prophet said to the Israelites in a crisis, when a great imperialism with its armies was advancing upon Israel; when they were turning to another imperialism, Egypt, for help: "The Egyptians are men and not God; and their horses are flesh and not spirit." The Israelites said in effect: "Yes, that's just the trouble. The Egyptians are men, big men, strong men, armed men. How can you meet them with just

God? And their horses are flesh, and how can you meet them without more and better horseflesh?"

But the spirit is real, God does exist, and there is no safety like that of those who put their trust in him and in the practice of his will. "In returning and rest shall ye be saved. In quietness and confidence shall be your strength. Then justice shall dwell in the wilderness, and righteousness in the fruitful field. And the work of righteousness shall be peace; and the effect of righteousness, quietness and confidence forever. And my people shall dwell in peaceable habitations and a safe dwelling and quiet resting places."

The permanent forces always are the silent, the persistent, the constructive forces that are always there after the tumult and the shouting die, and the captains and the kings depart—and the tumult and the shouting do always die, and the captains and the kings do always depart.

You can, of course, kill the body of the person who builds on these forces, but that will not be the end. "After three days I will rise again," said Christ, and the world has had to reckon with him more than ever before. "For if a grain of wheat fall into the ground and die, it beareth much fruit."

Deep down in our hearts we all believe that. It is what we were made for. Let us embrace it, live it.

6

A POST-LIBERAL PACIFISM

John M. Swomley Jr.

*John M. Swomley Jr. began working with FOR in 1939, starting as New England student secretary and eventually becoming general secretary. He continued his activism as professor of Christian ethics at St. Paul's School of Theology in Kansas City. A prolific writer, he published the first exposé of the military-industrial complex (*The Military Establishment, *1964). In this essay he shows not only his capacity to learn from neo-orthodoxy about sin and recalcitrance, but also his ability to stretch beyond the generally reformist attitude of most pacifists (see his superb* Liberation Ethics, *1972) (Fellowship, February 1954).*

Christian pacifism has been under attack in the churches and colleges since the beginning of World War II. The attack has been led largely by religious spokesmen who have rejected theological liberalism for neo-orthodoxy.

Even before the outbreak of World War II, liberalism had been questioned by a growing number of religious thinkers. Personal and social change was proceeding at such a pace and with such dire consequences that some theologians no longer could accept the easy optimism of a more or less inevitable progress toward a better society. They saw the depths to which we could sink in our dealings with others. They saw the gathering war clouds, the dictatorship, and oppression. They felt there should be a greater recognition of human sinfulness instead of the emphasis, often glib, on the "God in everyone."

It is not surprising that they should attack the then-dominant theological school of liberalism as providing a superficial analysis of human nature and of social processes. They did not confine themselves, however, to attacking liberalism in general. They singled out pacifism for special attention, identifying liberalism as the soil out of which modern pacifism had grown. Some even placed upon pacifism much of the blame for the rise of Hitler and other dictators as well as for the spread of war.

Their attack centered on the religious pacifists who consciously engaged in political and social action, rather than on vocational pacifists or non-resisters like the Mennonites.

During the war, some pacifists replied to such neo-orthodox charges by suggesting that the theologians who were most vocal in denouncing pacifists were also most active and outspoken in behalf of partisan political interests, including their own variety of nationalism. The implication was that neo-orthodoxy was simply a convenient rationale for churchmen to participate in and support the horrors of war.

Partly as a result of this neo-orthodox analysis and partly as a result of the times in which we live, many pacifists modified or abandoned their liberalism of the twenties and thirties. Pacifism, of course, was never dependent on liberalism, either in Europe or in America, for there have been pacifists identified with many theological schools. Although there is less identification of pacifism with liberalism than in the prewar days, it is not so clear that the neo-orthodox critics of pacifism have renounced liberalism. With rare exceptions, the theologically neo-orthodox are political liberals. They have tended, rather, to provide a theological rationale which at one and the same time permits them to criticize liberalism while continuing to function as liberals.

Political liberalism can be described in the following five ways:

1. It idealizes evolution, instead of revolution, as the method of social change. It therefore tends to think in terms of a program of legal, economic, and political reforms for dealing with the present world scene, even though the present situation is becoming more and more revolutionary. Having rejected in advance a revolutionary program, the non-pacifist political liberal finds himself in a position of supporting war in behalf of the status quo rather than any act of civil disobedience or revolution, however creative or nonviolent it might be.

2. It emphasizes as its goal the greatest happiness of the greatest number. Liberty, which is an important emphasis of liberalism, is impossible without a reasonable degree of security. Social security and stability are, therefore, as much an object of political policy as liberty. This emphasis is the basis for the liberal's advocacy of the welfare state.

3. It is, in a real sense, the culmination of the whole Western political tradition of political democracy and social and economic security for the whole population. It tends, therefore, to identify itself with Western culture. The non-pacifist liberal to all practical purposes tends also to support and promote the warfare state as the protector of Western culture.

4. It is based on the assumption that government exists to protect all essential interests. It does not think of government as functioning in the interests of one class. A primary function of government in the liberal view is to maintain the conditions or the agencies by which conflicts of interest can be adjusted with as little coercion as possible. This seems to be an unrealistic appraisal of modern governments either as they operate domestically or on the world scene.

5. It holds that policy is determined more by the influence of intangibles, such as moral ideas and social influences on politics, as opposed simply to political or class organization. It is significant that many neo-orthodox leaders function within Americans for Democratic Action and, in New York State, in

the Liberal Party, both of which are regarded chiefly as an influence on the Democratic Party rather than as politically responsible groups in their own right.

The political liberal (even though theologically neo-orthodox) is still optimistic about the evolutionary method in a revolutionary world, about the ability of a huge military establishment to serve as a deterrent to war, and about war as a method for preserving Western culture.

Despite the impact of neo-orthodoxy, there is still a considerable emphasis on pacifism. Liberal pacifism is characterized by some or all of the following:

1. A belief in social change by evolution or gradualism. It is reformist rather than revolutionary in nature.

2. A fundamentally optimistic analysis that emphasizes the essential goodness of the opponent, as well as human beings in general.

3. An optimism which tends to make a success story out of the cross, and in so doing underestimates the cost of the changes which are being sought.

4. A tendency to view everyone's goal as the same (no one wants war) and consequently a belief that war can be averted by an accommodation of interests. This has led to an uncritical emphasis on negotiation as a method for solving the present power struggle.

5. A belief in political formulae for achieving more or less inevitable progress. This, together with optimism about legal and political reformism, has led to political faith in world government and universal disarmament.

6. A tendency to be primarily individualistic as well as a tendency to simplify social and political problems. It has largely failed to think in terms of nonviolent action as a social and political strategy.

7. A failure to recognize the class struggle which is taking place in many nations throughout the world today.

8. Liberal pacifism depends for its existence chiefly on the kind of conditions which we find in Western civilization.

There is, however, a post-liberal pacifism which might be described by the following six points:

1. Post-liberal pacifism is revolutionary as opposed to reformist in its political analysis and in its strategy for effecting social change. It recognizes that some change will be evolutionary but believes that in the present world situation drastic and quick social change is necessary and in some cases inevitable. It supports nonviolent movements for social change, as in India and South Africa, and seeks to stimulate such activity. It does not believe in the possibility of saving the present civilization by some slight or easy amelioration.

2. It is therefore more akin to an apocalyptic outlook, for it does not look upon the world scene with unqualified optimism. Insofar as this pacifism does not engage in revolutionary action, it acts on the basis of a witness which refuses to accept or give loyalty to the present culture.

3. It makes a more realistic analysis of Communism, the U.S./U.S.S.R. power struggle and of the world scene generally, than that view which suggests that there can be an easy accommodation of interests between the East and West.

4. It emphasizes the sin in both our opponents and ourselves and repentance as the precondition for God's operating through us. This repentance it also asks of the church and the nation.

5. It puts less trust in political formulae and more on fundamental change of persons and institutions, especially the church. Unless there is a willingness on the part of the people to sacrifice power advantages and special privilege, political formulae such as negotiation and universal disarmament are not likely to mean very much.

6. It holds that the distinctive sociological mission of the church is revolutionary and that the church should not be identified with the existing culture as the liberals and neo-orthodox alike tend to identify it. Although the early church quite possibly did not think in terms of a revolutionary strategy, it was in effect a revolutionary group in the society of which it was a part, rather than a bulwark of the existing structure as it is today.

There are two things that bind all pacifists together. One is the fact that all are conscientious objectors when it comes to participation in war. The second is the fact that all seek to engage in peacemaking activity that will prevent and end war. A third factor ought to characterize us—namely, a constant reexamination both of our faith and the witness by which we seek to function as peacemakers.

7

BLESSED ARE THE MEEK

The Roots of Christian Nonviolence

Thomas Merton

The Trappist monk Thomas Merton brought a special gift to American social struggles: contemplation. Faced with the burnout of so many young people, veterans of the civil rights and then the anti-Vietnam war efforts, people began looking for ways to replenish the supplies of love, passion, and energy. Merton, while not himself an activist, brought an uncanny appreciation of the spiritual hemorrhaging that endless interventions caused. His answer: prayer. From the invidious split between people who pray and people who act, was born a new, integral person, who prays and acts, with a harmonious balance between them. This ground-breaking article was first published as an FOR pamphlet. Merton died a year later in 1968 (Fellowship, *May 1967*).

It would be a serious mistake to regard Christian nonviolence simply as a novel tactic which is at once efficacious and even edifying, and which enables the sensitive person to participate in the struggles of the world without being dirtied with blood. Nonviolence is not simply a way of proving one's point and getting what one wants without being involved in behavior that one considers ugly and evil. Nor is it, for that matter, a means which anyone legitimately can make use of according to his or her fancy for any purpose whatever. To practice nonviolence for a purely selfish or arbitrary end would in fact discredit and distort the truth of nonviolent resistance.

Nonviolence is perhaps the most exacting of all forms of struggle, not only because it demands first of all that one be ready to suffer evil and even face the threat of death without violent retaliation, but because it excludes mere transient self-interest from its considerations. In a very real sense, those who practice nonviolent resistance must commit themselves not to the defense of their own interests or even those of a particular group: they must commit themselves to the defense of objective truth and right and above all of *human beings*.

Their aim is then not simply to *prevail* or to prove that they are right and the adversary wrong, or to make the adversary give in and yield what is demanded.

Nor should nonviolent resisters be content to prove *to themselves* that they are virtuous and right, that *their* hands and heart are pure even though the adversary's may be evil and defiled. Still less should they seek for themselves the psychological gratification of upsetting the adversary's conscience and perhaps driving that person to an act of bad faith and refusal of the truth. We know that our unconscious motives may, at times, make our nonviolence a form of moral aggression and even a subtle provocation designed (without our awareness) to bring out the evil we hope to find in the adversary, and thus to justify ourselves in our own eyes and in the eyes of "decent people."

Christian nonviolence is not built on a presupposed division, but on the basic unity of humankind. It is not out for the conversion of the wicked to the ideas of the good, but for healing and reconciliation.

For this very reason, as Gandhi saw, the fully consistent practice of nonviolence demands a solid metaphysical and religious basis both in being and in God. This comes *before* subjective good intentions and sincerity. For the Hindu this metaphysical basis was provided by the Vedantist doctrine of the Atman, the true transcendent Self which alone is absolutely real, and before which the empirical self of the individual must be effaced in the faithful practice of *dharma*.

Now all these principles are fine and they accord with our Christian faith. But once we view the principles in the light of current *facts*, a practical difficulty confronts us. If the gospel is preached to the poor; if the Christian message is essentially a message of hope and redemption for the poor, the oppressed, the underprivileged and those who have no power humanly speaking, how are we to reconcile ourselves to the fact that Christians belong for the most part to the rich and powerful nations of the earth? Seventeen percent of the world's population control eighty percent of the world's wealth, and most of these seventeen percent are supposedly Christian. Admittedly those Christians who are interested in nonviolence are not ordinarily the wealthy ones. Nevertheless, like it or not, they share in the power and privilege of the most wealthy and mighty society the world has ever known. Even with the best subjective intentions in the world, how can they avoid a certain ambiguity in preaching nonviolence? Is this not a mystification?

We must remember Marx's accusation that "the social principles of Christianity encourage dullness, lack of self-respect, submissiveness, self-abasement, in short all the characteristics of the proletariat." We must frankly face the possibility that the nonviolence of the European or American preaching Christian meekness may conceivably be adulterated by bourgeois feelings and by an unconscious desire to preserve the status quo against violent upheaval.

On the other hand, Marx's view of Christianity is obviously tendentious and distorted. A real understanding of Christian nonviolence (backed up by the evidence of history in the Apostolic Age) shows not only that it is a *power*, but that it remains perhaps the only really effective way of transforming human beings and human society. After nearly fifty years of communist revolution, we find little evidence that the world is improved by violence. Let us, however, seriously consider at least the *conditions* for relative honesty in the practice of Christian nonviolence.

1. Nonviolence must be aimed above all at the transformation of the present state of the world, and it must therefore be free from all occult, unconscious connivance with an unjust use of power. This poses enormous problems, for if nonviolence is too political it becomes drawn into the power struggle and identified with one side or another in that struggle, while if it is totally apolitical it runs the risk of being ineffective or at best merely symbolic.

2. The nonviolent resistance of the Christians who belong to one of the powerful nations and who are *themselves* in some sense privileged members of world society will have to be clearly not *for themselves* but *for others*, that is for the poor and underprivileged. (Obviously in the case of Negroes in the United States, though they may be citizens of a privileged nation, their case is different. They are clearly entitled to wage a nonviolent struggle for their rights, but even for them this struggle should be primarily for *truth itself*—this being the source of their power.)

3. In the case of nonviolent struggle for peace—the threat of nuclear war abolishes all privileges. Under the bomb there is not much distinction between rich and poor. In fact, the richest nations are usually the most threatened. Nonviolence must simply avoid the ambiguity of an unclear and *confusing protest* that hardens the war-makers in their self-righteous blindness. This means that *in this case above all nonviolence must avoid a facile and fanatical self-righteousness*, and refrain from being satisfied with dramatic self-justifying gestures.

4. Perhaps the most insidious temptation to be avoided is one which is characteristic of the power structure itself: this fetishism of immediate visible results. Modern society understands "possibilities" and "results" in terms of a superficial and quantitative idea of efficacy. One of the missions of Christian nonviolence is to restore a different standard of practical judgment in social conflicts. This means that the Christian humility of nonviolent action must establish itself in the minds and memories of modern people not only as *conceivable* and *possible*, but as *a desirable alternative to* what they now consider the only realistic possibility; namely, political technique backed by force. Here the human dignity of nonviolence must manifest itself clearly in terms of a freedom and a nobility which are able to resist political manipulation and brute force and show them up as arbitrary, barbarous, and irrational. This will not be easy. The temptation to get publicity and quick results by spectacular tricks or by forms of protest that are merely odd and provocative but whose human meaning is not clear, may defeat this purpose.

The realism of nonviolence must be made evident by humility and self-restraint which clearly show frankness and open-mindedness and invite the adversary to serious and reasonable discussion.

Instead of trying to use the adversary as leverage for one's own effort to realize an ideal, nonviolence seeks only to enter into a dialogue in order to attain, together with the adversary, the common good of *everyone*. Nonviolence must be realistic and concrete. Like ordinary political action, it is no more than the "art of the possible." But precisely the advantage of nonviolence is that it has a *more Christian and more humane notion of what is possible*. Where the powerful believe that only power is efficacious, the nonviolent resister is persuaded of the superior efficacy of love, openness, peaceful negotiation, and, above all, of truth. For power can guarantee the interests of *some*, but it can never foster the good of all. Power always protects the good of some at the expense of all the others. Only love can attain and preserve the good of all. Any claim to build the security of *all* on force is a manifest imposture.

It is here that genuine humility is of the greatest importance. Such humility, united with true Christian courage (because it is based on trust in God and not in one's own ingenuity and tenacity), is itself a way of communicating the message that one is interested only in truth and in the genuine rights of others. Conversely, our authentic interest in the common good above all will help us to be humble and to distrust our own hidden drive to self-assertion.

5. Christian nonviolence, therefore, is convinced that the manner in which the conflict for truth is waged will itself manifest or obscure the truth. To fight for truth by dishonest, violent, inhuman, or unreasonable means would simply betray the truth one is trying to vindicate. The absolute refusal of evil or suspect means is a necessary element in the witness of nonviolence.

6. A test of our sincerity in the practice of nonviolence is this: are we willing to *learn something from our adversaries?* If a *new truth is* made known to us by them or through them, will we accept it? Are we willing to admit that they are not totally inhuman, wrong, unreasonable, cruel, and so on? This is important. If they see that we are completely incapable of listening to them with an open mind, our nonviolence will have nothing to say to them except that we distrust them and seek to outwit them. Our readiness to see some good in them and to agree with some of their ideas (though tactically this might look like a weakness on our part), actually gives us power: the power of sincerity and of truth. On the other hand, if we are obviously unwilling to accept any truth that we have not first discovered and declared ourselves, we show by that very fact that we are interested not in the truth so much as in "being right." Since adversaries are presumably interested in being right also, and in proving themselves right by what they consider the superior argument of force, we end up where we started. Nonviolence has great power, provided that it really witnesses to truth and not just to self-righteousness.

The dread of being open to the ideas of others generally comes from our hidden insecurity about our own convictions. We fear that we may be "converted"—or perverted—by a pernicious doctrine. On the other hand, if we are mature and objective in our open-mindedness, we may find that viewing things from a basically different perspective—that of our adversary—we discover our own truth in a new light and are able to understand our own ideal more realistically.

Our willingness to take *an alternative approach* to a problem will perhaps relax the obsessive fixation of our adversaries on their view, which they believe is the only reasonable possibility and which they are determined to impose on everyone else by coercion.

It is the refusal of alternatives—a compulsive state of mind which one might call the ultimatum complex—which makes wars in order to force the unconditional acceptance of one oversimplified interpretation of reality. The mission of Christian humility in social life is not merely to edify but to *keep minds open to many alternatives*. The rigidity of a certain type of Christian thought has seriously impaired this capacity, which nonviolence must recover.

Needless to say, Christian humility must not be confused with a mere desire to win approval and to find reassurance by conciliating others superficially.

7. Christian hope and Christian humility are inseparable. The quality of nonviolence is decided largely by the purity of the Christian hope behind it. The Christian knows that there are radically sound possibilities in everyone, and believes that love and grace always have the power to bring out those possibilities at the most unexpected moments. Therefore, if one has hopes that God will grant peace to the world it is because one also trusts that humanity, God's creature, is not basically evil, that there is in us a potentiality for peace and order which can be realized provided the right conditions are there. Christians will do their part in creating these conditions by preferring love and trust to hate and suspiciousness. Obviously, once again, this "hope in humankind" must not be naive. But experience itself has shown, in the last few years, how much an attitude of simplicity and openness can do to break down barriers of suspicion that had divided people for centuries.

8

NONVIOLENCE AND FEMINISM

Shelley Douglass

During the 1970s Shelley Douglass and her husband Jim founded the Pacific Life Community in Vancouver, a binational pacifist community, and the Ground Zero Community for Nonviolent Action in Bremerton, Washington, along the tracks traveled by the White Trains that carried nuclear weapons to the Trident submarine base. In 1989 they moved to Birmingham, Alabama, where they founded a Catholic Worker house of hospitality. Shelley has led countless workshops on active nonviolence, has been arrested frequently for acts of civil disobedience, and is a former chairperson of the FOR national council (Fellowship, *July-August 1975*).

There was a great controversy among antislavery radicals in the 1850s over the "woman question." Women formed a large part of the strength of abolitionist sentiment, supplied many of the most vocal leaders. But women themselves were nonpersons oppressed and subject to ridicule when, infrequently, they took a public stand. Many women saw their cause as bound up with the abolitionist cause: equality for all people, men and women. The reaction of the movement of that time was to tell the women to wait. It was not yet their turn to be heard; by pushing their untimely issue they would likely deprive the black man of his base of support. Women were not important. For women who have come through the civil rights and peace movements over the last fifteen years, there is a kind of ironic familiarity in reading the history of the abolitionist/feminist debate. We've heard the same arguments in our own time!

My experience as a woman in the movement is fairly typical, I think. Since my early college years in 1962, I've been progressively more involved with the movement, living and working as part of it. Our experience as women has been one of awakening to a reality that was often harsh: we were welcomed into the movement in lower-echelon positions, as somebody's woman, girl, old lady, wife, as sex objects, as workhorses. Women were expected to make coffee and provide refreshments while men planned strategy and did resistance actions. Women kept the home-fires burning while men organized, acted, and went to jail. Women bore and raised children and created the homes to which the men returned. Women did leaflets in the thousands, typed letters, licked stamps, marched in demonstrations. We rarely spoke at demonstrations; our actions did not make us celebrities like the men. When women went to jail, they lacked strong community support. They had no knowledge, by and large, of their historic role in the peace movement. With a few exceptions (Dorothy Day, for example), women lost contact with the contributions of others like ourselves.

The reasons for this were many. At the time, most of us believed in women's place, too. We thought we were appointed to certain functions, and that if we were worthy we would eventually become equal. Those times took a heavy toll. In most cities there are women who have been in the peace movement for years. They have been the backbone of the movement, keeping things going when everyone else was too busy or too discouraged. Because they were women, they had the time for peace work; but because they were women, they were never taken seriously. Miraculously, some of these women were strong enough, well-balanced enough, to cope with the pressures and go on. Others, who should not be forgotten, women with good minds and great concern, cracked or warped under the pressure. They are now the proverbial "little old ladies in tennis shoes"; they could have been matriarchs of the movement. Yet this tragic waste of potential and unconscious dehumanization took place in a movement that only wanted the common good.

During the late 1960s women began to share some of their private problems and their maladjustments to the system in which they lived. We realized that our feelings were not just personal problems; they were political, the results of a system that exploited us all. We were not unique; this oppressive mentality pervaded even the movement itself. Insofar as it was patriarchal, the movement was simply part of the system. When this realization hit home, it was an extremely difficult time for many people in the movement. Attempts to share insights with male companions were met (understandably) with fierce resistance. There was a slow groping toward trust among sisters and disillusion with a movement that fought for other people's freedom while standing upon our backs. There was the shuddering realization of our victimization, our status as sex objects. Even worse was the knowledge that we had believed the lie and the rage we felt at again being pushed aside for another, "more important" issue. There was the growing problem of how to deal with oppression within the movement for liberation. How do we resist the resister? For many of us, the answer was simply to break contact, to work only with women on peace or women's issues. For others (less angry? less independent? more hopeful?) there seemed a chance that the peace movement could become a real movement for peace in all its meanings. We have stayed on.

As women concerned with feminism, we still find hostility, lack of comprehension, even ridicule, within the ranks. We also find more understanding, more honesty, more willingness to face the issue. In ourselves, we find the experience of being women a good one, joyful and strong. We are reclaiming our history—remembering all those founding mothers, all those women who kept the movement going without credit for so long, all the contributions we women have made and undervalued. The experience of being a woman is still one of isolation, frustration, anger. It is also one of confidence, strength, support, and pride. We are; we are becoming. I think we often feel impatient with those who lag behind, who don't see the problems or the possibilities. Not rage, just impatience. Women are strong; women will move forward; women have a crucial insight and a life-giving contribution to make.

Having sounded an optimistic note on women's position and contribution to the movement, I would qualify it. With the end of the Vietnam war and the widespread acceptance of the principle of equality for women, both the peace movement and the women's movement face crucial decisions. The peace movement cannot survive or hope for revolution without joining the women's movement—partly because there is no peace and justice to be built upon the backs of any people, partly because the insights of the feminist movement are necessary to the formation of a new, organic worldview, a basis for thought and action which will be more complete and profound, because more inclusive, than any we've had before. Feminist insights into the nature of God, of humankind, of violence and nonviolence, oppression and resistance, and into a whole life are the life-giving gift of women.

However, there are crucial questions also to be raised from the other side. For years we've asked the Catholic church: "How come you're so upset about abortion but say nothing about Vietnam?" As Dan Berrigan has pointed out, that question can legitimately be turned back upon us. We have been concerned about Vietnam, but what about abortion? Simplistic answers—abortion is anti-life, therefore it's wrong; or, women must control their own bodies, therefore it's necessary—are not enough. There must be a way to take seriously all the societal changes, and all the female agony, the male refusal of responsibility, the pain of poverty or of being stretched too thin. No position on abortion is realistic if it does not take these into consideration. The basic question for both movements now is this: Do we want to keep trying to improve a system by disregarding human rights and the sacredness of life, or do we want to struggle to bring to birth a truly new world community in which both war and abortion are unnecessary and unthinkable? Insofar as the peace movement remains patriarchal, it is part of the system of oppression. Insofar as the women's movement accepts the brutal methods and rewards of the current patriarchal society, it joins the oppressors of all peoples. I believe that the insights of feminism and of the nonviolent resistance movement can come together, painfully and honestly, to create a new, organic, human vision. Neither is complete without the other. With both together, we may be able to survive as a world.

9

THE PACIFIST VISION

Mary Evelyn Jegen

Mary Evelyn Jegen, SND, former coordinator of Pax Christi and national chair of FOR, is an author, teacher, and activist. In this piece she reminds us of the difference between a task-oriented organization and an organization held together and ener-gized by a vision. In asking what is the vision of FOR today she raises a challenge for all who are committed to nonviolence, not just as a tactical means, but as an end, a way of being (Fellowship, *March-April 1980*).

"Where there is no vision, the people perish" is a truth recognized across cultural barriers. In our own Western tradition we acknowledge the wisdom of our father Socrates' words that an unexamined life is not worth living. What is true of an individual life is also true of movements. A movement's life needs to be examined. Its vision dies unless it is continually kept alive by seers.

All that acknowledged, in our culture it is at best a doubtful compliment to be called a visionary. People who claim visions are suspected of being less than normal, and sometimes are. What really makes us uneasy about visions is that we cannot find an external test for them. Either we share another's vision, or we do not. A vision is always highly personal. Unlike a picture which hangs on the wall after the viewer departs, a vision exists only in the imagination. For all that, it is no less real. When a great vision calls forth creative talent in a person of discipline, the result is a work of art. It may be a symphony or a drama. It may also be a work of politics or a social movement.

At the heart of every social movement is a shared vision, held in commun-ion across distance and time. A social movement's vision always has to do with the possibility of a better world. It exists to change the status quo. The vision of a better world gives a movement coherence and keeps it alive, despite the human weakness of the members and the external obstacles that press against it. In contrast to an organization which is only task oriented—a group of people agreeing to follow certain procedures to get something done—a movement is value oriented, a people on the move, bent less on getting some particular thing done than on changing the context for doing things. A movement is at once more fragile, less clearly defined, and, paradoxically, infinitely stronger than an organization—as long as it keeps its vision.

How long an organization lasts depends on how long the material means are at hand to get a job done. An organization gone bankrupt is finished. A movement, on the other hand, can go underground, and even flourish in adversity, as long as its vision is kept bright, and is shared. A classic example is Christianity, impelled in its early days by the visionary apostle, Paul. Flogged, shipwrecked, run out of town, he once wrote in a kind of desperate boast that he was "knocked down, but not knocked out."

THE VISION OF THE FELLOWSHIP OF RECONCILIATION

What lies at the heart of the vision of the Fellowship of Reconciliation? What has held its members in communion, on the move, across national boundaries and religious and ecclesiastical differences for over sixty-five years? It seems to me that it is a hunch, an intuition of goodness, of sheer human goodness. My own faith convinces me that goodness is grounded in God, by whatever name we call God. This goodness can be perceived as a kind of latent aspiration in the heart of each person, an aspiration that needs to be affirmed in order to be set free. This hunch about goodness recognizes it as highly developed in some persons, clear and winning, visible and tangible. Integral to the vision, however, is that goodness is present, though often hidden and unrecognized, in all with whom we share our planet and our common destiny. The Fellowship of Reconciliation has a remarkable ability to sense kindred spirits who share its vision, whether it be a Gandhi, a Cesar Chavez, a Catholic monk, a Buddhist poet, a college student struggling to take a position on conscientious objection, or a prison inmate, reaching out in trust through the pages of *Fellowship* magazine.

Those who know the life and writings of Gandhi will recognize that this notion of goodness is closely akin to his understanding of *sat*, or truth. The doomed Jewish adolescent Ann Frank knew this same reality when she wrote one of the most luminous passages in our literature, that despite all she had experienced she believed people were good. Jesus knew it when, dying, he begged forgiveness for his executioners who, he said, did not know what they were doing. The church came into being by clinging in faith to this man who made us his friends by laying down his life for the very persons who named him enemy.

This intuition of goodness is something much more fundamental than a sunny temperament, and has nothing to do with unreflecting optimism. The people who radiate goodness most clearly, and who lead us to examine its possibility are, in every case I can think of, well acquainted with suffering. An insight into goodness is born in pain.

In the Fellowship of Reconciliation, the experience of human goodness is expressed in a moral imperative: *Do not kill.* It is this that makes FOR one of the small number of religious-social movements that is radically and explicitly pacifist. Like Gandhi's *satyagraha*—which is not the absence of engagement in struggle, but rather the power of clinging to truth—*do not kill* is at heart an affirmation of human dignity joined to a response of humble love. To kill, for the pacifist, is arrogance. It is to play God, who alone gives life, and who entrusts it to us to cherish and develop, as a gift received with grateful love. The pacifist comes to know by experience that God is love, and that when we abide in love and act in the power of love, we abide in God and act in the power of God. This was Dante's great mystical vision of the love that moves the sun and all the stars. It was St. Thomas More's when he told his darling Meg that when all was said and done, it was love that made him the king's good servant, but God's first; a man who struggled, agonized in court and in prison, but who finally could joke at his execution.

Like light refracted through a prism, genuine pacifism shows itself in works of love, trust, and justice, in a profound sense of human dignity and fundamental equality, and in a cloudless, indomitable hope, a hope the German poet Dorothee Soelle expresses in her *Credo:*

> I believe in God
> who did not create an immutable world
> a thing incapable of change
> who does not govern according to eternal laws
> that remain inviolate
> or according to a natural order
> of rich and poor
> of the expert and the ignorant
> of rulers and subjects
> I believe in God
> who willed conflict in life and wanted us to change the
> status quo
> through our work
> through our politics . . .

In the human condition as we experience it, goodness remains elusive, a hallucination, not a vision unless we can face its opposite, taking up a position of conflict in the face of evil. Goodness expresses itself in love, trust, truth, and justice; evil shows itself in deception, injustice, and the reduction of other persons to instruments of self-aggrandizement—three dimensions of violence. When violence takes the form of force which intends to injure, it turns in the direction of killing.

CONTEXT OF THE FELLOWSHIP OF RECONCILIATION

Think of the situation in which the Fellowship of Reconciliation was born, World War I, and in which it has grown: World War II, the Korean War,

Vietnam. Who knows what the present situation may lead to? Wars are seen by the Fellowship not as something to be passively endured, but as events to be confronted actively with love, truth, and justice. Violence and the absence of peace are the dark side of an integral FOR vision. Further, it is not only the major international conflicts that are the context of the Fellowship; there are the domestic violences as well—racism, sexism, and economic exploitation—that FOR must accept as part of its agenda. The Fellowship matures in responding to and engaging in conflict, not in avoiding it. The conflict that is potentially and often actually most devastating is war. The pacifist vision recognizes in war a profound psychological and spiritual sickness, a deep-seated fear, an immature need for security, an inhuman craving for autonomy which is the very absence of fellowship in an attempt to escape the human condition.

In the last analysis, violence springs from arrogance. It lacks a basic modesty, a saving sense of humor, and the trust the psalmist knew when singing

> O Lord, my heart is not proud
> nor are my eyes haughty;
>
> I busy not myself with great things,
> nor with things too sublime for me.
> I have stilled and quieted
> my soul like a weaned child.
> Like a weaned child on its mother's lap,
> so is my soul within me.
> O Israel, hope in the Lord,
> both now and forever.

The peacemaker who acts modestly out of an experience of being held in God's lap resonates with the command given to Moses: "Choose life." Others may see the pacifist's unwillingness to destroy life as squeamishness or downright cowardice. Certainly refusal to act can spring from weakness; but it can also spring from the power of truth. Only those who have experimented with the options know the difference.

A pacifist response to conflict leads to trying actions other than those aimed at victory over an "enemy." The first such action is an attempt to look at all the available data, insisting on this as a condition. This is an effort at reconciliation, a response of love in a situation of enmity, of human weakness and brokenness. Reconciliation means bringing to communion with God as truth, ourselves, each other. Gandhian *satyagraha* is a classic example. It was Gandhi's conviction that every human conflict should be approached not as a win/lose situation but as a win/win situation, and that there could be a way of resolving it that evoked the goodness in all parties. In this way of reconciliation, which honors each person's imperfect hold on truth, a higher truth emerges. This way of reconciliation, however, involves a willingness to bear pain, not to inflict it. Gandhi's conviction and practice of self-suffering is a stumbling block for many, as is Jesus' teaching and example of the mystery of the cross.

OUR NEED

What we need in the present crisis is creative imagination not parity in military force, euphemistically called "peace through strength." We need the Prayer of St. Francis of Assisi raised to the level of a political power, the power of reconciliation. Where there is hatred, we desperately need love, where there is injury, pardon, where there is doubt, faith, where there is despair, hope, and where there is sadness, joy. On the personal level we need to see the links between peacemaking in our homes and in our neighborhoods, and what goes on in the great arenas of decision-making which can impose death or new possibilities of life for millions.

More than ever, the Fellowship of Reconciliation needs to tend its growth as a movement, as a communion of those who share a vision, who see violence as all of a piece, but who see with an even deeper vision the rim of light on the edge of the darkness of violence. A. J. Muste received the gift to express this vision in a single sentence when he said, quoting Gandhi, "There is no way to peace, peace is the way." Peace is not the end result of violent conflict, but the very means of resolving conflict nonviolently. An ancient Christian writer, St. Ignatius of Antioch, anticipated Muste when he wrote, "Peace puts an end to every war." Peace as process, as commitment to love, justice and integrity, peacemaking as style of life: this, it seems to me, is what Jesus meant when he described our human vocation in the words, "Blessed are the peacemakers, for they will be called children of God." Today, perhaps more than ever before, human survival depends upon our saying yes to our calling.

10

HOW NONVIOLENCE WORKS

Glenn Smiley

That genial apostle of nonviolence, Glenn Smiley, was a staff member of FOR for twenty-five years. During World War II he went to prison for refusing to serve in the armed services. He is best remembered for his work with Martin Luther King Jr., beginning with the Montgomery bus boycott. In his late sixties he had forty-four small strokes that affected his memory and speech. For fifteen years he could not make a public address. Then one morning he woke up and was apparently perfectly normal. He immediately embroiled himself in work with FOR and with gangs. Two years before his death in 1993 at the age of 83, he gave 103 major lectures (Fellowship, October-November 1990).

From the beginning of humankind's time on the earth, for about 250,000 years, conflicts between individuals and groups have been settled on the basis of force, or domination or submission. In time, the use of force became more or less institutionalized, and continues to this day in many places.

While in all societies throughout history there must have been men and women who, by reason of superior intelligence, were able to compensate for lack of strength by more innovative means, it has not been until the relatively recent past that an organized third way of addressing conflict has emerged. It is to this third way that we address ourselves, as we seek to develop a method of training in nonviolence. In a world of superpowers armed with unthinkable weapons, the search for alternative means of defense and changing the social structures has become an absolute necessity.

It is important to know at the outset that nonviolence has absolutely nothing to do with passive acceptance or acquiescence to evil done to a person or nation. I, for example, am a pacifist, but it makes me ill to have the word associated with passivity. The fact is that nonviolence can be considered as the art of seeking alternatives to violence in conflict, for conflict is inevitable in life. While history is replete with instances of creative action without violence, there are not many incidents of organized nonviolence on record.

The sort of militant nonviolence I am talking about seems to have more or less begun with Mohandas K. Gandhi, now called the Mahatma (Great Soul), who became the father of Indian independence. The West was interested in the man at times but cared little for his queer ideas, and Winston Churchill spoke of him scornfully as a "half-naked fakir."

In 1939, however, Krishnalal Shidharani wrote a doctoral dissertation while studying at Columbia University that began to change the Western view. Having been a follower of the Mahatma in India, he was well qualified to interpret nonviolence in Indian terms in his book, *War without Violence*. A. Phillip Randolph, head of the Sleeping Car Porters, A. J. Muste, one of the secretaries of the Fellowship of Reconciliation, Dr. John Haynes Holmes of The Community Church of New York, and a few others began to study the book to see if it had relevance to the American racial struggle. They decided that it did, and in time FOR allowed three of its staff members—Jim Farmer, George Houser, and Bayard Rustin—to begin experimentation in Gandhian techniques.

That is how the Congress of Racial Equality was born, with staff and expenses provided by FOR for about eight years. Early experiments attempted to overcome discrimination in restaurants, theaters, and swimming pools in Chicago, Denver, St. Louis, and Los Angeles. It was here that I became interested in Gandhi, a fact that gave major direction to the rest of my professional career. In fact, in time I became one of the few trained and experienced leaders in the growing movement in the United States.

Some of the classic illustrations of nonviolence grew out of Los Angeles and included the Bullock's Tea Room project that lasted three months. It ended in a dramatic victory for what would now be called a sit-in, as the tea room was opened up to African Americans. The success of these early efforts, growing out of the publication of Shidharani's book, were due to the fact that Gandhi had lived and worked long enough to have accumulated an enormous track record of successes. He had left a voluminous literature on the subject, describing in detail the nonviolent efforts in the areas of boycotts and village and community work, as well as the home industries that in time practically emptied the mills of Manchester, England.

Seven years after the assassination of Gandhi in 1948, the Montgomery bus protest took place in Alabama. That event exemplified the various factors and conditions that historically have had revolutionary results. Let me remind you of some of those conditions.

A widespread social evil affecting a large number of people is one requisite. These people must be economically significant, while at the same time they must be outside the existing power structure of the society. They must have an informed and able leadership. All that was lacking in Montgomery was a method. In Montgomery, the wedding of all of these elements came about, largely because of a particular serendipity of leadership in the person of Dr. Martin Luther King Jr., a remarkably well-trained clergyman who had recently become pastor of the Dexter Avenue Baptist Church of that city. The Gandhian method, with its Indian overtones, had been refined in the United States in scores of successful projects in various parts of the country, and this experience was made available to the movement. The movement was church-centered and the entire weight of the [black] local churches was thrown into the battle from the beginning and lasted the 381 days of the campaign, giving the movement time to mature and to perfect its systems of defense and offense.

It should be noted that the earlier nonviolence projects in the '40s and '50s had of necessity been confined to small, more manageable efforts. The Montgomery protest was the first large-scale endeavor. Everything had to begin at the beginning, for one of the "knowns" of nonviolence is that because a method is successful in one place, it does not follow that it is applicable to another. The people of Montgomery developed their own strategies out of their own situation. Imaginative and innovative ideas emerged. The first effort was to persuade the leadership and people of Montgomery of the validity of nonviolence as an alternative to the methods of the opposition. Dr. King said publicly on several occasions that the reason the contribution of the Fellowship of Reconciliation was so crucial was that we were the only organization that came to help without bringing a ready-made solution to their problems.

I spent all of 1956 working in Montgomery and other parts of the South, supported by the Fellowship of Reconciliation. At our first meeting Dr. King had a fair idea of what he wanted me to do for him in the form of a four-part portfolio. He and I agreed on the following: (1) I would teach him everything I knew about nonviolence, since, by his own admission, he had only been casually acquainted with Gandhi and his methods; (2) we would work with the churches and the leadership of Montgomery on the subject of nonviolence, and in support of the bus protest; (3) we would seek out other leadership in black communities in the South and build a support system, as well as service their protests and demonstrations (I had already been doing this in the South, but prior to Montgomery there had not been a mass movement anywhere to relate them all); and (4) I would try to build bridges and connections with the white community in Montgomery, as well as serve as an open and above-board intelligence by which Dr. King could be kept informed about white thinking and, where possible, keep watch on the White Citizens Council, and even the KKK.

There are principles upon which classic nonviolence is based, and these are the most important ones, but not necessarily in order of their importance.

Nonviolence recognizes the essential humanity of every person and in its struggles aims at the conscience of the evil-doer and not at the person. Gandhi and Jesus both called this attitude love, and both of them used the word *love* as a synonym for God. Dr. King said, "My religion requires that I love all men, even my enemies or him who would do me harm, but it does not require that I like him, nor his evil deeds."

In nonviolent action, one must be willing to compromise on tactics but not on principle.

While it is not necessary for every participant to be totally committed to nonviolence, it is necessary for the leadership to be well informed and dedicated to the method in order to prevent the movement from resorting to violence in the middle of what might otherwise be a successful endeavor.

The first training programs for a group should usually be small, with easily identified goals that are achievable within a reasonable period of time.

Nonviolence has its long-term goals and its short-term goals. Even though you have long-term goals with certain definite items on your agenda, you should not ask for everything at the beginning. A long list of grievances has a tendency to make the opposition draw the wagons in a circle and hold out.

In seeking alternatives to violence in a case of conflict, there is never just one alternative to a problem. Nonviolence seeks to clear the mind of the delusion of rightness. Sometimes there may not be one right way. Gandhi said something to the effect that you must have convictions and you must act on those convictions, even though new evidence may cause you to change your mind the next day. You have to act on the convictions you have today, or you will never act at all.

Massive movements of nonviolence take time to mature, although small projects can often be accomplished in a short time with little training. Nonviolence, like violence, can lose its skirmishes or even its battles, as long as it wins the war. The Montgomery boycott was fortunate in that it lasted 381 days, and although they lost some of the smaller battles, there was a constantly growing process that in time made the final victory inevitable.

While nonviolence can bring down a government, as in the case of Czechoslovakia in 1989, I don't believe that in the present world of superpowers a nation can be ruled by nonviolence; the very nature of the modern state is to be violent. But nonviolence can bring a people to a state of awareness, or a will to resist. I can envision a day in which the citizens of a country would become so aware as to force the state to leave its primitive ways, to such a degree that even offenders against society would be dealt with in a healing and redemptive fashion. But I speak here from my faith.

Nonviolence is not a new, untried, pie-in-the-sky, tilting-at-windmills idea, held by a bunch of pietistic do-gooders.

Nonviolence is not a quick-fix, nor a panacea for all the ills of the world.

Nonviolence is not a weapon without cost, but has its price that its users must pay. As in the case of India, where unarmed people resisted the military, sometimes the price is equivalent to the price that is expected in instances of violence, because the privileged do not give up their privileges without a struggle.

The veneer of civilization is often very thin on today's people, and while there is good in every person, human beings are not innately nonviolent. But nonviolence can be taught and it can be learned, thereby taking the next great step in human evolution to the place where "each shall dwell under his own vine and fig tree, and none shall be afraid."

It is not possible to use nonviolence, in the true sense, to accomplish an evil end.

Part Two

WITNESSES FOR PEACE

Truth is not simply a content waiting to be known. It must become incarnate. People must manifest it not only in the way they think, but in the way they act. But it is not enough simply to act. One must be the truth. How is that to be done? We can will to be truth all we want, but it won't happen. We need models, people who have dared to shoulder God into existence. They confirm the possibility of living truth. As we see how they lived their lives, we begin to believe it possible for ourselves. As we emulate them, we begin to get a taste of that authenticity that is the homing beam of our becoming. How do we live the truth? By learning from others how they lived the truth.

But even that is not enough. Just when we feel that we have a fix on becoming truth, it becomes, for us, falsehood. For these models were mere starters, it turns out. They showed us a way, but not our way. We are permitted to imitate them only until we begin to catch intimations of who we really are, or who we might actually become. Then the Spirit withdraws from our models and leads us into the wilderness, where we must wrestle with the demons of the night. Surprisingly, they do not tempt us with evil so much as with the conventional. They try to draw us into a life of imitation. Their supreme seduction is to tempt us with yesterday's will of God—what everyone knows is what God wants, but which on examination has simply become a collective habit. And if we are faithful through the darkness, we begin to sense the outline of our own true being and what God wants to happen in the world. As we begin to emerge into our own authenticity, we discover that our models have done their essential work.

Here, then, are some models, eminently worth following, but only as far as the first fork in the road. Then, travel on, wanderer, sustained by the vision of possibilities that these witnesses for peace have left us.

11

THE WAY OF PEACE

Martin Niemoeller

Pastor Martin Niemoeller was one of the first religious leaders arrested by the Nazis. As a founder of the Confessing Church in Germany, he was imprisoned from 1938 to 1945. On his release, this man, arguably one of the least guilty of complicity in Nazi crimes, nevertheless declared, "We are all guilty." Nevertheless, despite his opposition to Hitler, Niemoeller did not embrace a pacifist position until 1954. The catalyst, as he describes in this article, was the explosion of the first H-bomb (Fellowship, November 1954).

A few months ago, the pope, in an Easter address, spoke a good deal about the H-bomb, and of its nature and consequences, and of how Christians ought to think about it anew, and of how Christians were duty bound to do something about it, that the use of such a weapon should be prevented.

The question arose in the Protestant churches in Germany whether or not we also should express ourselves about the H-bomb, and in this connection someone asked whether the pope had not gone too far and had not presented things as certain or very probable that were not certain or very probable.

The question suggested to me the possibility of having a talk on the subject with Germany's three leading nuclear physicists, Professor Otto Hahn, who split the atom in the Kaiser Wilhelm Institute in 1937, Professor Heisenberg, and Professor von Weiszacker.

I found the three physicists very much inclined to have such a talk, and so it was arranged, with Bishop Dibelius, Professor Gollwitzer, whose book about Russia some of you may know, and myself. In the course of the resulting conversation we raised the question of whether or not the pope had exaggerated in his Easter address.

Professor Hahn's answer was simple and to the point. "He has not exaggerated. It is no real problem today to build a bomb which on going off will make the whole surface of our planet uninhabitable for any human being."

We have known this before. It has been in the papers. But we read the papers without comprehending or taking to heart what we read. In that moment it really came to my heart and to my senses that what these scientists had said meant that war is finished. I put the question to Professor Hahn: "What do you think Hitler would have done if he had had this bomb when at last he sat in the cellar of the Reich's Chancellery in Berlin, and his fate had overtaken him and nothing was left but to surrender or to commit suicide?"

And he answered what anyone must, that Hitler would have exploded this bomb and would have said, "If I am not to survive with my ideas, the whole world is no longer worthy to exist. If I am to go, they may all go."

I doubt whether any government or person who relies on power or force, in the same situation, would act in a different way. That ends the whole discussion about "banning the hydrogen bomb."

"BANNING" THE BOMB

It may be possible to have a full-fledged world war fought with "classic" or conventional weapons and use no poison gas, refrain from the bombing of cities, use no atom bombs and no hydrogen bombs, and no warfare of "mass destruction" of any kind such as the big powers have at their command by now. Yet in the end, when one of the two great opponents is cornered and called to unconditional surrender—and unconditional surrender is the objective in modern war—then rather than accept what it regards as "ultimate" evil and betrayal, this nation will resort to the weapon that can obliterate all life. That cannot but mean the end of humankind on the surface of our planet!

So it is no longer possible for any power, by resorting to warfare, to overcome the adversary and so enter into the enemy's heritage. The conqueror will not be the heir, but in the last minute of that war he will perish with his opponent who was the defeated one.

That means we can no longer debate the question whether war is good or bad, whether there is such a thing as a just war or an unjust war. War—at least between powers that are able to build this bomb as their last resort—has ceased to be a means at all. War is no longer good or bad, just or unjust. However you look at it, war under these circumstances is madness. Madness cannot be characterized by "good" or "bad" or "just" or "unjust." There is no "just madness" and no "unjust madness," no "good madness" and no "bad madness." Madness is simply madness.

That is the point that I want to make very clearly and definitely. We have only two choices left, and these choices were put before us by Professor von Weiszacker.

"I have," he said, "a very good friend of long standing, Professor Teller, who built the H-bomb in the United States. He has undergone all the pricking of conscience which our nuclear physicists are undergoing in our day, but he said to me, 'The Russians will build this bomb anyway, so we must do the same. That is the one way open to us.' But there's another way," Dr. Weiszacker added. "The other way is to become pacifists—on principle."

Faced with this one alternative to choose between those two courses, I prefer to become and meanwhile I have become a pacifist—on principle. It was after this conversation with these physicists that I wrote to my friend Professor Siegmund Schultze of Dortmund that I was now at last joining the Fellowship of Reconciliation as a member.

War is no longer a means of settling any disputes. War is heading for destruction and heading headlong for destruction. Reason, therefore, says there must not be any war. Unfortunately, while we are reasoning creatures, we are not always reasonable ones, and so war can happen by itself, if we don't watch out.

We have to work for peace if we want to prevent war. There is a religious meaning here, you see. People will not go to heaven because of their good deeds, but certainly they will go to hell because of their omissions. I don't find the New Testament elaborating that it is a dangerous thing to do bad, but I find very clearly that it is a very dangerous thing to omit the good deeds that we ought to do. "Inasmuch as you have not done it to one of these least among my brethren, you have not done it unto me."

PROPHET OF GOD

A year and a half ago in India I took part in a so-called Gandhi Seminar in New Delhi. There I learned something about the Beatitudes of the Sermon on the Mount. When Jesus said, "Blessed are the peacemakers," I have come to see he really meant it. It is not just a pious and nice-sounding phrase. He meant that the peacemakers are the blessed ones in this world under the blessing of God. When the Christian church and Christian world did not do something effective and efficient about peacemaking, God found a prophet of nonviolence in Mahatma Gandhi.

Gandhi became a blessing for his nation and I believe God means that he should become a blessing for the Christian world by causing us to examine ourselves. God calls us to ask ourselves today whether we really are Christians or whether we are using the words of Jesus Christ written on a banner to lead the Christian army in exactly the opposite direction from the one he pointed out: hearing the words and hearing not the meaning of the words, and certainly not acting according to these words. Christianity is not the hope of the world; Christ is the hope of the world. We may even say that Christianity has been a doom to the world for the last two thousand years, not because of Christ but because of the so-called Christian people who quoted Christ but did not follow him.

Christ has said clearly that the only means of overcoming enmity is by friendliness, that the bad can be overcome only by good and not by retaliation. That was Gandhi's way of renunciation of force. He has demonstrated that in a "hopeless" situation other means than violence can be devised to achieve something for the bettering of this world of ours.

I do not see in the New Testament any encouragement for the use of force. But that seems to be forgotten in the Christian community all over the world, and there are only small groups, such as the Fellowship of Reconciliation, that have tried to live up to what our Lord is expecting from those who bear his name. Their efforts never have been widely successful, though a little more so in this part of the world than in the old countries of Europe. There, being a pacifist meant at the same time to be a bad Christian. To be called a fellow traveler was the mildest of the bad words used of Christian pacifists.

You must not say that you want or demand peace from everybody, for the way of Christ is not to demand but to offer peace. I think that is also the way of his church—it has to be the way of his church—to offer peace. If God had waited with his reconciliation and his reconciliatory action until we were prepared to become reconciled we would still be waiting today and we would wait till Judgment Day. He offered his peace in Christ Jesus, and the way to put into action the love of Christ is to love our enemies. That is not just a sentimental matter but that is the way God brings about good things in his world and development for the better among the human beings on this globe. Certainly that is a difficult thing, and certainly it is not according to our natural inclinations.

OUR ONLY HOPE

There is no such thing as a holy war. The Crusades of the medieval times were not Christian actions at all. They were answering the attack of Islam in Europe with the same means with which Islam tried to expand. I think very highly of St. Bernard, but his cry, "God wills it," calling men to war on Muslims, was anything but Christian. At that moment he was the most unholy "Holy Bernard." A crusade is unholy even if you put a cross on the banner and put a cross on your breast and put on your belt the words, "God with us," as was done in the time of Adolf Hitler as well as in the time of the Prussian kings.

Today we are getting a second lesson on this point, and I pray that we really learn this lesson once and for all. There is only one "crusade," and that is the way of Jesus from Gethsemane to the palace of Pilate and Herod and to the court of the high priest, and from there to Calvary, carrying his cross. That is the crusade. We Christians are called upon to follow in this crusade and in no other, because every other crusade is not of him but is from a different source. We may think we do good in making these "crusades," but we don't.

Christians met in Evanston last summer to think of Christian hope. There is no Christian hope in a crusade. There is no Christian hope in retaliation or in inflicting force on other people. There is no promise of God for doing this, there is no hope in doing this, but there is a hope in following Christ. That means in offering peace even by means of your own suffering. In our days Gandhi has shown this to a great part of the world, and I wish that Christians would not be the last group of men and women in the world to learn this lesson that God is teaching us through this prophet.

MY PILGRIMAGE TO NONVIOLENCE

Martin Luther King Jr.

This brief autobiographical statement by one of the greatest souls of the twentieth century gives us a window into King's development into a practitioner of nonviolent direct action. Here he makes clear his debt to and his criticism of Reinhold Niebuhr. The latter worked from an inadequate or even faulty view of nonviolence as nonresistance, repeating the mistake of his theological mentor, St. Augustine. In this article, King, freed from the constraints of addressing a mass audience, is able to give free rein to his own theological reflections (Fellowship, *September 1958*).

Often the question has arisen concerning my own intellectual pilgrimage to nonviolence. In order to get at this question it is necessary to go back to my early teens in Atlanta. I had grown up abhorring not only segregation but also the oppressive and barbarous acts that grew out of it. I had passed spots where Negroes had been savagely lynched, and had watched the Ku Klux Klan on its rides at night. I had seen police brutality with my own eyes, and watched Negroes receive the most tragic injustice in the courts. All of these things had done something to my growing personality. I had come perilously close to resenting all white people.

I had also learned that the inseparable twin of racial injustice was economic injustice. Although I came from a home of economic security and relative comfort, I could never get out of my mind the economic insecurity of many of my playmates and the tragic poverty of those living around me. During my late teens I worked two summers, against my father's wishes—he never wanted my brother and me to work around white people because of the oppressive conditions—in a plant that hired both Negroes and whites. Here I saw economic injustice firsthand, and realized that the poor white was exploited just as much as the Negro. Through these early experiences I grew up deeply conscious of the varieties of injustice in our society.

So when I went to Atlanta's Morehouse College as a freshman in 1944, my concern for racial and economic justice was already substantial. During my student days at Morehouse I read Thoreau's *Essay on Civil Disobedience* for the first time. Fascinated by the idea of refusing to cooperate with an evil system, I was so deeply moved that I reread the work several times. This was my first intellectual contact with the theory of nonviolent resistance.

Not until I entered Crozer Theological Seminary in 1948, however, did I begin a serious intellectual quest for a method to eliminate social evil. Although my major interest was in the fields of theology and philosophy, I spent a great deal of time reading the works of the great social philosophers. I came early to Walter Rauschenbusch's *Christianity and the Social Crisis*, which left an indelible imprint on my thinking by giving me a theological basis for the social concern which had already grown up in me as a result of my early experiences. Of course there were points at which I differed with Rauschenbusch. I felt that he had fallen victim to the nineteenth-century "cult of inevitable progress," which led him to a superficial optimism concerning man's nature. Moreover, he came perilously close to identifying the kingdom of God with a particular social and economic system—a tendency that should never befall the church. But in spite of these shortcomings Rauschenbusch had done a great service for the Christian church by insisting that the gospel deals with the whole man, not only his soul but his body; not only his spiritual well-being but his material well-being. It has been my conviction ever since reading Rauschenbusch that any religion which professes to be concerned about the souls of men and is not concerned about the social and economic conditions that scar the soul, is a spiritually moribund religion only waiting for the day to be buried. It well has been said: "A religion that ends with the individual, ends."

After reading Rauschenbusch, I turned to a serious study of the social and ethical theories of the great philosophers, from Plato and Aristotle down to Rousseau, Hobbes, Bentham, Mill, and Locke. All of these masters stimulated my thinking—such as it was—and, while finding things to question in each of them, I nevertheless learned a great deal from their study.

During the Christmas holidays of 1949 I decided to spend my spare time reading Karl Marx to try to understand the appeal of communism for many people. For the first time I carefully scrutinized *Das Kapital* and *The Communist Manifesto*. I also read some interpretive works on the thinking of Marx and Lenin. In reading such Communist writings I drew certain conclusions that have remained with me to this day.

First I rejected their materialistic interpretation of history. Communism, avowedly secularistic and materialistic, has no place for God. This I could never accept, for as a Christian I believe that there is a creative personal power in this universe who is the ground and essence of all reality—a power that cannot be explained in materialistic terms. History is ultimately guided by spirit, not matter.

Second, I strongly disagreed with communism's ethical relativism. Since for the communist there is no divine government, no absolute moral order, there are no fixed, immutable principles; consequently almost anything—force, violence, murder, lying—is a justifiable means to the "millennial" end. This type of relativism was abhorrent to me. Constructive ends can never give absolute moral justification to destructive means, because in the final analysis the end is pre-existent in the mean.

Third, I opposed communism's political totalitarianism. In communism the individual ends up in subjection to the state. True, the Marxist would argue that the state is an "interim" reality which is to be eliminated when the classless society emerges; but the state is the end while it lasts, and man only a means to that end. And if any man's so-called rights or liberties stand in the way of that end, they are simply swept aside. His liberties of expression, his freedom to vote, his freedom to listen to what news he likes or to choose his books are all restricted. Man becomes hardly more, in communism, than a depersonalized cog in the turning wheel of the state.

This deprecation of individual freedom was objectionable to me. I am convinced now, as I was then, that man is an end because he is a child of God. Man is not made for the state; the state is made for man. To deprive man of freedom is to relegate him to the status of a thing, rather than elevate him to the status of a person. Man must never be treated as a means to the end of the state, but always as an end within himself.

Yet, in spite of the fact that my response to communism was and is negative, and I considered it basically evil, there were points at which I found it challenging. The late archbishop of Canterbury, William Temple, referred to communism as a Christian heresy. By this he meant that communism had laid hold of certain truths which are essential parts of the Christian view of things, but that it had bound up with them concepts and practices which no Christian could ever accept or profess. Communism challenged the late archbishop and it should challenge every Christian—as it challenged me—to a growing concern about social justice. With all of its false assumptions and evil methods, communism grew as a protest against the hardships of the underprivileged. Communism in theory emphasized a classless society, and a concern for social justice, though the world knows from sad experience that in practice it created new classes and a new lexicon of injustice. The Christian ought always to be challenged by any protest against unfair treatment of the poor, for Christianity is itself such a protest, nowhere expressed more eloquently than in Jesus' words: "The Spirit of the Lord is upon me, because he hath anointed me to preach the gospel to the poor; he hath sent me to heal the brokenhearted, to preach deliverance to the captives, and recovering of sight to the blind, to set at liberty them that are bruised, to preach the acceptable year of the Lord."

I also sought systematic answers to Marx's critique of modern bourgeois culture. He presented capitalism as essentially a struggle between the owners of the productive resources and the workers, whom Marx regarded as the real producers. Marx interpreted economic forces as the dialectical process by which society moved from feudalism through capitalism to socialism, with the primary mechanism of this historical movement being the struggle between economic classes whose interests were irreconcilable. Obviously this theory left out of account the numerous and significant complexities—political, economic moral, religious, and psychological—which played a vital role in shaping the constellation of institutions and ideas known today as Western civilization. Moreover, it was dated in the sense that the capitalism Marx wrote about bore only a partial resemblance to the capitalism we know in this country today.

But in spite of the shortcomings of his analysis, Marx had raised some basic questions. I was deeply concerned from my early teen days about the gulf between superfluous wealth and abject poverty, and my reading of Marx made me ever more conscious of this gulf. Although modern American capitalism had greatly reduced the gap through social reforms, there was still need for a better distribution of wealth. Moreover, Marx had revealed the danger of the profit motive as the sole basis of an economic system; capitalism is always in danger of inspiring us to be more concerned about making a living than making a life. We are prone to judge success by the index of our salaries or the size of our automobiles, rather than by the quality of our service and relationship to humanity—thus capitalism can lead to a practical materialism that is as pernicious as the materialism taught by communism.

In short, I read Marx as I read all of the influential historical thinkers—from a dialectical point of view, combining a partial "yes" and a partial "no." Insofar as Marx posited a metaphysical materialism, an ethical relativism, and a strangulating totalitarianism, I responded with an unambiguous "no"; but insofar as he pointed to weaknesses of traditional capitalism, contributed to the growth of a definite self-consciousness in the masses, and challenged the social conscience of the Christian churches, I responded with a definite "yes."

My reading of Marx also convinced me that truth is found neither in Marxism nor in traditional capitalism. Each represents a partial truth. Historically capitalism failed to see the truth in collective enterprise, and Marxism failed to see the truth in individual enterprise. Nineteenth-century capitalism failed to see that life is social, and Marxism failed and still fails to see that life is individual and personal. The kingdom of God is neither the thesis of individual enterprise nor the antithesis of collective enterprise, but a synthesis which reconciles the truths of both.

During my stay at Crozer, I was also exposed for the first time to the pacifist position in a lecture by A. J. Muste. I was deeply moved by Mr. Muste's talk, but far from convinced of the practicability of his position. Like most of the students of Crozer, I felt that while war could never be a positive or absolute good, it could serve as a negative good in the sense of preventing the spread and growth of an evil force. War, horrible as it is, might be preferable to surrender to a totalitarian system—Nazi, Fascist, or Communist.

During this period I had about despaired of the power of love in solving social problems. Perhaps my faith in love was temporarily shaken by the philosophy of Nietzsche. I had been reading parts of *The Genealogy of Morals* and the whole of *The Will to Power*. Nietzsche's glorification of power—in his theory all life expressed the will to power—was an outgrowth of his contempt for ordinary morals. He attacked the whole of the Hebraic-Christian morality—with its virtues of piety and humility, its other-worldliness and its attitude toward suffering—as the glorification of weakness, as making virtues out of necessity and impotence. He looked to the development of a superman who would surpass man as man surpassed the ape.

Then one Sunday afternoon I traveled to Philadelphia to hear a sermon by Dr. Mordecai Johnson, president of Howard University. He was there to preach for the Fellowship House of Philadelphia. Dr. Johnson had just returned from a trip to India, and, to my great interest, he spoke of the life and teachings of Mahatma Gandhi. His message was so profound and electrifying that I left the meeting and bought a half dozen books on Gandhi's life and works.

Like most people, I had heard of Gandhi, but I had never studied him seriously. As I read I became deeply fascinated by his campaigns of nonviolent resistance. I was particularly moved by the Salt March to the Sea and his numerous fasts. The whole concept of *satyagraha* (*satya* is truth which equals love, and *agraha* is force; *satyagraha*, therefore, means truth-force or love-force) was profoundly significant to me. As I delved deeper into the philosophy of Gandhi my skepticism concerning the power of love gradually diminished, and I came to see for the first time its potency in the area of social reform. Prior to reading Gandhi, I had about concluded that the ethics of Jesus were only effective in individual relationship. The "turn the other cheek" philosophy and the "love your enemies" philosophy were only valid, I felt, when individuals were in conflict with other individuals; when racial groups and nations were in conflict a more realistic approach seemed necessary. But after reading Gandhi, I saw how utterly mistaken I was.

Gandhi was probably the first person in history to lift the love ethic of Jesus above mere interaction between individuals to a powerful and effective social force on a large scale. Love, for Gandhi, was a potent instrument for social and collective transformation. It was in this Gandhian emphasis on love and non-violence that I discovered the method for social reform that I had been seeking for so many months. The intellectual and moral satisfaction that I failed to gain from the utilitarianism of Bentham and Mill, the revolutionary methods of Marx and Lenin, the social-contracts theory of Hobbes, the "back to nature" optimism of Rousseau, the superman philosophy of Nietzsche, I found in the nonviolent resistance philosophy of Gandhi. I came to feel that this was the only morally and practically sound method open to oppressed people in their struggle for freedom.

But my intellectual odyssey to nonviolence did not end here. During my last year in theological school, I began to read the works of Reinhold Niebuhr. The prophetic and realistic elements in Niebuhr's passionate style and profound thought were appealing to me, and I became so enamored of his social ethics that I almost fell into the trap of accepting uncritically everything he wrote.

About this time I read Niebuhr's critique of the pacifist position. Niebuhr had himself once been a member of the pacifist ranks.

For several years, he had been national chairman of the Fellowship of Reconciliation. His break with pacifism came in the early thirties, and the first full statement of his criticism of pacifism was in *Moral Man and Immoral Society*.

Here he argued that there was no intrinsic moral difference between violent and nonviolent resistance. The social consequences of the two methods were different, he contended, but the differences were in degree rather than kind. Later Niebuhr began emphasizing the irresponsibility of relying on nonviolent resistance when there was no ground for believing that it would be successful in preventing the spread of totalitarian tyranny. It could only be successful, he argued, if the groups against whom the resistance was taking place had some degree of moral conscience, as was the case in Gandhi's struggle against the British. Niebuhr's ultimate rejection of pacifism was based primarily on the doctrine of man. He argued that pacifism failed to do justice to the reformation doctrine of justification by faith, substituting for it a sectarian perfectionism which believes "that divine grace actually lifts man out of the sinful contradictions of history and establishes him above the sins of the world."

At first, Niebuhr's critique of pacifism left me in a state of confusion. As I continued to read, however, I came to see more and more the shortcomings of his position. For instance, many of his statements revealed that he interpreted pacifism as a sort of passive nonresistance to evil expressing naive trust in the power of love. But this was a serious distortion. My study of Gandhi convinced me that true pacifism is not nonresistance to evil, but nonviolent resistance to evil. Between the two positions, there is a world of difference. Gandhi resisted evil with as much vigor and power as the violent resister, but he resisted with love instead of hate. True pacifism is not unrealistic submission to evil power, as Niebuhr contends. It is rather a courageous confrontation of evil by the power of love, in the faith that it is better to be the recipient of violence than the inflicter of it, since the latter only multiplied the existence of violence and bitterness in the universe, while the former may develop a sense of shame in the opponent and thereby bring about a transformation and change of heart.

In spite of the fact that I found many things to be rejected in Niebuhr's philosophy, there were several points at which he constructively influenced my thinking. Niebuhr's great contribution to contemporary theology is that he has refuted the false optimism characteristic of a great segment of Protestant liberalism, without falling into the anti-rationalism of the continental theologian Karl Barth, or the semi-fundamentalism of other dialectical theologians. Moreover, Niebuhr has extraordinary insight into human nature, especially the behavior of nations and social groups. He is keenly aware of the complexity of human motives and of the relation between morality and power. His theology is a persistent reminder of the reality of sin on every level of humanity's existence. These elements in Niebuhr's thinking helped me to recognize the illusions of a superficial optimism concerning human nature and the dangers of a false idealism. While I still believed in the human potential for good, Niebuhr made me realize its potential for evil as well. Moreover, Niebuhr helped me to recognize the complexity of people's social involvement and the glaring reality of collective evil.

Many pacifists, I felt, failed to see this. All too many had an unwarranted optimism concerning man and leaned unconsciously toward self-righteousness.

It was my revolt against these attitudes under the influence of Niebuhr that accounts for the fact that in spite of my strong leaning toward pacifism, I never joined a pacifist organization. After reading Niebuhr, I tried to arrive at a realistic pacifism. In other words, I came to see the pacifist position not as sinless but as the lesser evil in the circumstances. I felt then, and I feel now, that the pacifist would have a greater appeal if he did not claim to be free from the moral dilemmas that the Christian non-pacifist confronts.

The next stage of my intellectual pilgrimage to nonviolence came during my doctoral studies at Boston University. Here I had the opportunity to talk to many exponents of nonviolence, both students and visitors to the campus. Boston University School of Theology under the influence of Dean Walter Muelder and Professor Allan Knight Chalmers had a deep sympathy for pacifism. Both Dean Muelder and Dr. Chalmers had a passion for social justice that stemmed, not from a superficial optimism, but from a deep faith in the possibilities of human beings when they allowed themselves to become co-workers with God. It was at Boston University that I came to see that Niebuhr had overemphasized the corruption of human nature. His pessimism concerning human nature was not balanced by an optimism concerning divine nature. He was so involved in diagnosing man's sickness of sin that he overlooked the cure of grace.

I studied philosophy and theology at Boston University under Edgar S. Brightman and L. Harold DeWolf. Both men greatly stimulated my thinking. It was mainly under these teachers that I studied personalistic philosophy—the theory that the clue to the meaning of ultimate reality is found in personality. This personal idealism remains today my basic philosophical position. Personalism's insistence that only personality—finite and infinite—is ultimately real strengthened me in two convictions: it gave me metaphysical and philosophical grounding for the idea of a personal God, and it gave me a metaphysical basis for the dignity and worth of all human personality.

Just before Dr. Brightman's death, I began studying the philosophy of Hegel with him. Although the course was mainly a study of Hegel's monumental work *Phenomenology of Mind*, I spent my spare time reading his *Philosophy of History* and *Philosophy of Right*. There were points in Hegel's philosophy that I strongly disagreed with. For instance, his absolute idealism was rationally unsound to me because it tended to swallow up the many in the one. But there were other aspects of his thinking that I found stimulating. His contention that "truth is the whole" led me to a philosophical method of rational coherence. His analysis of the dialectical process, in spite of its shortcomings, helped me to see that growth comes through struggle.

In 1954 I ended my formal training with all of these relative divergent intellectual forces converging into a positive social philosophy. One of the main tenets of this philosophy was the conviction that nonviolent resistance was one of the most potent weapons available to oppressed people in their quest for social justice. At this time, however, I had merely an intellectual understanding and appreciation of the position, with no firm determination to organize it in a socially effective situation.

When I went to Montgomery as a pastor, I had not the slightest idea that I would later become involved in a crisis in which nonviolent resistance would be applicable. I neither started the protest nor suggested it. I simply responded to the call of the people for a spokesman. When the protest began, my mind, consciously or unconsciously, was driven back to the Sermon on the Mount, with its sublime teachings on love, and the Gandhian method of nonviolent resistance. As the days unfolded, I came to see the power of nonviolence more and more. Living through the actual experience of the protest, nonviolence became more than a method to which I gave intellectual assent; it became a commitment to a way of life. Many of the things that I had not cleared up intellectually concerning nonviolence were now solved in the sphere of practical action.

13

MARTIN BUBER
AND THE COVENANT OF PEACE

Maurice S. Friedman

Martin Buber was one of the preeminent philosophers of the twentieth century. His influence deeply penetrated Christian theology. Best known for his meditations on the I and the Thou with whom we are in relationship, Buber provided an understanding of dialogue that enabled people of different faiths to talk to one another across all the divides thrown up to prevent it. Maurice S. Friedman was Buber's translator and interpreter and a member of FOR (Fellowship, *January 1961*).

Martin Buber is at once, more than any other, the spokesman of Judaism before the world and one of the truly universal men of our time, comparable in this respect only with Mahatma Gandhi and Albert Schweitzer. Although Martin Buber is one of the greatest living philosophers, it is not this alone that has made men such as the Swiss novelist Hermann Hesse and the Protestant theologian Reinhold Niebuhr speak of him as one of the few wise men living on the earth today. Rather it is his concern with the "lived concrete," the everyday reality which he takes up into his imagining and bears as his responsibility.

We live in an age of compounded crises, an age of hot and cold war and the constant threat of total annihilation by the weapons that we ourselves have perfected. It is an age more and more bereft of authentic human existence, and even the image of such existence increasingly deserts us. Those who cannot accept the compromises of our age run to the extremes—the yogi and the commissar, the saint and the political actionist. The one prayer which seems least likely to be answered, the prayer we have almost ceased to pray, is "Dona nobis pacem," "Give us peace." Yet in our age three great figures have emerged, each of whom in his way is a peacemaker—Gandhi, Schweitzer, and Martin Buber. Each in his own way and on his own ground: Gandhi, who found the meeting point of religion and politics in *satyagraha*, a spiritual "soul-force" which proved effective in liberating India; Schweitzer, whose Christian love has expressed itself in a practical "reverence for life" and whose concern for all of life also extends to repeated pleas for outlawing nuclear weapons; Martin Buber, who has found in the biblical covenant, in Isaiah's "covenant of peace," a base for real meeting between peoples and real reconciliation between conflicting claims.

The peacemaker "is God's fellow worker," writes Buber, but we make peace not by conciliatory words and humane projects but through making peace "wherever we are destined and summoned to do so: in the active life of our own community and in that aspect of it which can actively help determine its relationship to another community." The decisive test of brotherhood is not within the community but at the boundary between community and community, people and people, church and church, for this is the place where diversity of kind and mind is felt most strongly. "Every time we stand this test," writes Buber, "a new step is taken toward a true humanity, gathered in the name of God."

The key to Martin Buber as peacemaker is found in his own conception of *dialogue*—the meeting with the other person, the other group, the other people which confirms it in its otherness yet does not deny oneself and the ground on which one stands. The choice is not between oneself and the other, nor is there some objective ground to which one can rise above the facing sides, the conflicting claims. Rather, genuine dialogue is at once a confirmation of otherness and togetherness—the living embodiment of the biblical creation in which man is really free yet remains bound in relation with God. Modern man has lost his trust in existence, writes Buber, and the most acute symptom of it is that a genuine word cannot arise between the conflicting camps in the so-called Cold War. In a genuine dialogue each of the partners, even when standing in opposition to the other, heeds, affirms, and confirms the opponent as an existing other. "Only so can conflict certainly not be eliminated from the world, but be humanly arbitrated and led toward its overcoming." The reason why such genuine dialogue cannot arise is that in our time the ancient mistrust between men has become existential. "The human world," wrote Buber in 1952, "is today, as never before, split into two camps, each of which understands the other as the embodiment of falsehood and itself as the embodiment of truth." Man not only thinks his principle true and the opposing one false, as in earlier epochs, but now believes "that he is concerned with the recognition and realization of right, his opponent with the masking of selfish interest."

The resumption of true dialogue between peoples will only be possible when the existential mistrust which divides the world into two hostile camps is overcome. But in the closed sphere of the exclusively political there is no way to penetrate to the factual life of factual men or to relieve the present situation whose "'natural end' is the technically perfect suicide of the human race." It is just this powerlessness of politics which must be recognized today before it is too late, writes Buber, and it must be recognized by people who will come together out of the camps and will talk with one another, despite their criticism of the opposing system and their loyalty to their own. People such as these will be able to distinguish between the true and the exaggerated needs of their own and other people. There is one front of such people, the representatives of a true humanity who fight together even without knowing it, each in his own place.

What such genuine dialogue means Martin Buber himself showed when he accepted in 1953 the Peace Prize of the German Book Trade which was given two years earlier to Albert Schweitzer. During the time of the Nazi persecution of the Jews, Buber provided educational, spiritual, and personal leadership of a rare quality, saving thousands from spiritual despair and teaching the German Jews to die as Jews down through the ages have died—sanctifying the name of God. Moreover, Buber counts himself among "those who have not got over what happened and will not get over it." Yet in 1953 he accepted the Peace Prize in the face of severe criticism from many parts of the Jewish press. In his acceptance speech Buber pointed out that less than a decade before several thousand Germans killed millions of his people and fellow-believers

in a systematically prepared and executed procedure, the organized cruelty of which cannot be compared with any earlier historical event. With those who took part in this action in *any* capacity, I, one of the survivors, have only in a formal sense a common humanity. They have so radically removed themselves from the human sphere, so transposed themselves into a sphere of monstrous inhumanity inaccessible to my power of conception, that not even hatred, much less the overcoming of hatred, was able to arise in me. And what am I that I could here presume to "forgive"!

At the same time, Buber pointed to other Germans who underwent martyrdom rather than accept or participate in this murder of a whole people. The inner battle of every people between the forces of humanity and the forces of inhumanity, writes Buber, is the deepest issue in the world today, obscured though it is by the Cold War. "The solidarity of all separate groups in the flaming battle for the becoming of one humanity is, in the present hour, the highest duty on earth. To obey this duty is laid on the Jew chosen as symbol"— on Martin Buber who received the confession of the Germans for his people— "even there, indeed just there, where the never-to-be-effaced memory of what has happened stands in opposition to it."

During the last half-century Buber has been one of the foremost Zionist leaders and thinkers and at the same time has been among the leaders of those Jews who have worked for Jewish-Arab cooperation and understanding. Israel's special vocation is not just another nationalism which makes the nation an end in itself. The people need the land and freedom to organize their own life in order to realize the goal of genuine and just community. "Decisive for us is not the promise of the land," wrote Buber in an open letter to Gandhi, "but the command the fulfillment of which is bound up with the land, with the existence of a free Jewish community in this country. . . . It may not be that the soil and the freedom for fulfillment be denied us." The state as such, however, is at best only a means to the goal of Zion, and it may even be an obstacle to it if the true nature of Zion as commission and task is not held uppermost. The essence of the essays that Buber has written on Zionism over a period of fifty years is the teaching that Zion must be built *bmishpat*, with justice. "No way leads to any other goal but to what is like it."

All too often the word *reconciliation* is associated with a sentimental good will that looks away from the very conflict that is to be reconciled, or assumes that, with this or that action or approach, a tragic situation can be transformed into a harmonious one. Martin Buber, in contrast, has pointed again and again to a genuine reconciliation which begins with fully realistic recognition of real differences and points of conflict and then moves to the task of discovering the standpoint from which some real meeting may take place which includes both points of view.

In Arab-Jewish relations, in the relations of the German people to the Jews who were killed and those who survived, in the conflict between the great camps in the Cold War, in his protest against the hydrogen-cobalt bomb and the supremacy of the political principle, in his call for the resumption of genuine dialogue between person and person and between people and people, Martin Buber has been an image of the peacemaker, a peacemaker out of the covenant of peace. "The mountains may depart and the hills be removed," writes Deutero-Isaiah, "but my steadfast love shall not depart from you, and my covenant of peace shall not be removed, says the LORD, who has compassion on you."

14

THE PRINCIPLE IS THE UNITY OF LIFE

A Conversation with Lanza del Vasto

Lanza del Vasto, who died in 1981, was a leader of the nonviolent movement in France, a poet, musician, philosopher, and artist who wrote over twenty books. A descendant of Sicilian nobility, he grew up in Florence and Genoa and studied philosophy at the University of Pisa. Finding the study of philosophy dissatisfying, he eventually went on pilgrimage to the Holy Land and then to India, where he became a friend and co-worker of Gandhi. The chronicle he wrote of that journey, Return to the Source, *has been published in numerous translations, with copies in the hundreds of thousands. During his year in India, Gandhi gave him a new name, Shantidas, meaning "servant of peace," and urged him to found a community of nonviolence in Europe. Just after World War II the endeavor began—the Community of the Ark, an interreligious community of men and women dedicated to nonviolence, simple living, and peacemaking. This interview was conducted by Richard Deats* (Fellowship, *September 1975).*

DEATS: *What did you learn from Gandhi?*

SHANTIDAS: The principle of the unity of life. This was the basis of nonviolence. Not that we don't find the same principle and the way of nonviolence in our own tradition. Indeed, Gandhi himself took it from the gospel. But you know how poorly it was understood in our society. Besides, Gandhi was able to give nonviolence quite another meaning, new applications which only rarely had been thought of in other times. In Gandhi was a unity of life. Here was a man who believed, thought, felt, and acted in the same unity— precisely what is so lacking in our own culture. I tried to bring back this unity of life and to make a framework for it within the communities I founded.

DEATS: *How do you as a Christian relate your faith to that of a Hindu—Gandhi?*

SHANTIDAS: Well, that is an easy answer. There were many clear applications of the gospel teaching with Gandhi that I could find nowhere in

Christendom or in my own life. Both were full of contradictions. Yet I was aware that if I applied precepts of Christ and put them to work, they would be victorious in every field of life. So I had no difficulty with the Hindu aspect of Gandhi—I wasn't searching for Hindu spirituality. I was trying to become a Christian, which isn't easy. And I found it was enough. I was going to India and Gandhi for the solution of our problems, war especially. Yet Hindu spirituality greatly moved me. I was struck by its analogies with Christianity as soon as the sense of the symbols came through. There was the common treasure of tradition as well. Of course, the differences are important and great. But they give the color; they are something that stimulates curiosity and a sense of poetry. And so I had no difficulty with Hindu religion. I think that Gandhi was more Christian than many of us—nearly all of us. And I remember his saying of Jesus Christ, "To me he is the truth."

DEATS: *Do you see nonviolence as more than a technique?*
SHANTIDAS: Yes. It has a technical side, of course, a way of making it work out. But it is a way of acting that derives from a way of being, and the first thing is to try to *be* nonviolent. Nobody was born nonviolent. No one was born charitable. None of us comes to these things by nature but only by conversion. The first duty of the nonviolent community is helping its members work upon themselves and come to conversion. The community provides a system of rules and ways of living that oblige the individual to convert—to turn around, to put the heart inside-out and upside-down.

DEATS: *I know your community has been involved in a number of nonviolent campaigns, especially in France. One of the first, I recall, was a campaign against the atrocities in the Algerian War . . .*
SHANTIDAS: When we learned that torture was going on, we were deeply upset. I personally decided to fast for twenty days in Paris. Because no one wanted to receive us, our search for a place to fast was quite long. If one does a public fast, the place must be open and poor. Public fasting is something that must be worked upon very carefully. For one person fasting, there must be fifty or a hundred persons giving out leaflets, talking to the press, making the thing known—as the whole purpose is to touch public opinion.

Of course the fast was controversial. People pretended that our charges were not true, that all the atrocities were on the other side, that we were cheating, simply trying to get into politics, even though we belong to no political party.

One might say that the fast had little impact—the torture went on until the end of that horrible war. But at least we were able to help in stirring the conscience of the best citizens. We made people begin to recognize that the war was not right. And you know, when people recognize that they are not right, they don't go on fighting. The same happened with the American involvement in Indochina. The question was not resolved on battlefields but on the streets and in the consciences of people.

DEATS: *I also recall the campaign you helped to launch for recognition of conscientious objectors . . .*

SHANTIDAS: That began when we discovered the concentration camps the French had organized for "suspect" Algerians. We responded by going to the camps and very solemnly asking to be put inside ourselves. Of course, they threw us out. They insisted the camps were only for "suspicious persons." "Why," we asked, "should we not be considered suspicious?" They said they weren't concerned with people who were *voluntarily* suspicious—only those who were suspicious involuntarily! They turned us out. But for months, with great patience and stubbornness, we returned again and again.

We chose this strategy because we knew that nonviolent action must have a limited aim. You can't speak simply of war in general. So we tried to attack the war at various points—and thus to begin reshaping public opinion. No matter what their party, people were insensitive about the charges of torture. But—perhaps because of the Nazis—they didn't like to think that there were concentration camps in their own country.

Then came the question of conscientious objection. Of course, for many years there had been conscientious objectors. One by one, they went to prison and little came of it. We tried a different approach—to organize a general movement. We addressed ourselves not only to those civilians who didn't want to go to war, but to the soldiers as well. We urged them not to leave the country but to resist openly, writing those in authority: "I won't fight in this war and these are my reasons. . . . But I want to serve and I shall be at such and such a place working in the service of the poorest." Of course, the poorest at that time invariably were Algerians.

We established special service camps. When the police would come to arrest one of the boys, we would respond, "We know you are looking for him. Tomorrow he will present himself." The police had come to know that whenever we promised something, we would always do it. The things we announce, we do.

The presentation of the young man would occur in a public square—perhaps some magnificently patriotic monument with statues and wings and inscriptions. When the traffic was heaviest, we began handing out leaflets. By the time the police arrived, they would find us chained one to another around the monument. "Where is so-and-so," they would ask. We would all say, "I am he!" That was embarrassing for them. There are no laws to deal with these things. So we all were taken to jail. They didn't know what to do with us, but they had to do something. They thought they were catching us, but actually we were catching them!

Our posters and leaflets always emphasized the positive element—that we volunteer for service—but not for military service. The emphasis is always on what we are volunteering to do rather than on what we are refusing to do.

Power is like a huge shark. He throws himself on the powerless citizen, as weaponless and naked as a worm. But when he has swallowed the worm, he discovers a hook came with it.

In that campaign, many things went well. By the war's end, a statute on conscientious objection had been accepted in France; it is still the law. It's not perfect, but it's there. At last the right to refuse to kill has been acknowledged. Unexpectedly, as soon as it was achieved in France, it was achieved in Belgium as well, where we hadn't even campaigned. Now we are working for the same right in Spain.

DEATS: *There seems to be a growing awareness of the inadequacy of the traditional "just war" theory, but today there are many who advocate what might be called the "just revolution," especially in the Third World . . .*

SHANTIDAS: It seems revolution is being proposed as the solution for everything. Until we have revolution, they say, we cannot be free or happy. But revolution simply means the turning of the wheel. It implies nothing about an end to injustice. In reality, it is a real scourge.

I think that with nonviolent methods we can do without revolution. Not that things mustn't change. They must. But they must change for the better. Violent revolution can only change things for the worse. When you use bad means to get good ends, you ruin the ends. You find the evil in the end that you introduced into the means. Gandhi pointed out that means and end are related as the seed is to the tree. If you plant a bad seed, you will have a bad tree. Good intentions can't change this.

Intentions, of course, are always good anyway. The worse the fight, the higher its justification. "Justified" violence is the worst. Unjustified violence bursts out of a bad character or bad feelings, but it doesn't go very far. But when people feel justified in the use of violence, it becomes systematic and leads to all the horrors of history.

It really is time to stop it. We can't go on acting like clowns on top of a mountain of bombs. If we can't find another way of solving our problems, we are condemned to death, all of us. There is nothing more urgent for us than to study the alternative methods we already have found. They have proved their efficiency and are continuing to prove it. Why do young people study everything else but this? They want to survive, to live, to breathe. Let us find something else, something new.

DEATS: *Could you tell a little about the Community of the Ark?*

SHANTIDAS: Nonviolence, as you know, is a way of being and living. There is a nonviolent solution to every problem and every quarrel. But what is the nonviolent solution to the problem of economics?

Well, Gandhi found it. Remember that the symbol of his movement was the spinning wheel. That is: Work with your hands. Don't force others to work for you. Don't make others into slaves, even if you call them paid workers. Find the shortest, simplest way between the earth, the hands, and the mouth. Don't put anything in between—no money, no heavy machinery. Then you know at once what are the true needs and what are fantasies. When you have to sweat to satisfy your needs, you soon know whether or not it's worth your while. But if it's someone else's sweat, there is no end to our needs. We need cigarettes, cars, soft drinks, appliances, electronic devices, and on and on. Why not go the other way instead? If we want a more fraternal and just world, let's do it! Let's not wait until others do it. Do it yourself. Show that it is possible to live this way.

Tolstoy said it well. You want to have a chair? Make one. But then perhaps you find you don't need it. You can sit on the floor—it's all right. You learn to do a thing and find it's very interesting, very instructive, something they didn't teach you in the university. Or you learn to do without—another thing they didn't teach you!

Let us form ourselves into communities and work on the land and do what is needed. What do we need? To clothe ourselves? That's easily learned. To build a house? That's not very difficult. You can build one, big or small, to keep out the snow, the wind, and the rain. And one can learn to forge tools. Little by little, one finds ways to escape the big machines that squash us and order us about.

It has been working for us for twenty-six years.

At our community near the Larzac, we are more than 130, counting the children—and not counting all the guests. Too many. Even 50 is too many—because of the need to keep in friendly communication with everyone. In that particular community, we are mostly Roman Catholics, but quite open to people of every religion. We do not forget what we owe to the Hindus. And in our community in Morocco, the majority are Muslims. There, for seven years, Christians and Muslims have lived together, though such a thing was considered impossible. In all our communities, each one is faithful to his or her tradition and tries to keep it in purity and beauty, while remaining open to the tradition of others, trying to understand. There is no discussion, but there are shared readings of books considered sacred by the various traditions. We look for the great beauty that is always there.

Of course, we often see young people trying to start communities that fade after a few months or years. Community is impossible without certain prerequisites. There must be a religious or philosophic background. There must be leadership and agreed rules. There must be a profound sense of sacrifice. Nonviolence must be the practice in daily relationships. Of course, there are quarrels, but if we cannot settle them in our own home and our own community, how can we bring peace in the world? Every day we have the chance to work out our frictions and make peace among ourselves.

One necessity for a successful community is a sense of dignity and beauty. In our communities, great care is given to work with stone and wood, to making a door or table a joy to the eye.

In any nonviolent community, one must practice voluntary poverty. If you become attached to goods, you will have to defend them or have others defend them. So poverty is a crucial ornament of the spirit. Have few things, only necessary things, but make them beautifully, taking the necessary time. Get rid of the rubbish produced by machines.

At the end of each year—for us that means the Feast of St. John the Baptist—our rule requires us to give away everything that hasn't been spent. We give it to projects where there is need in different parts of the world. But we would prefer to have no money at all.

And learn how to celebrate. Keep religious ceremonies and feasts. For every day of work, have an hour preparing for the next feast. Make drawings and decorations, poetry and songs for the next feast. In all the workshops and in the fields, prepare for the feast. Let it be magnificent, joyous—and serious, as well.

Keep moments for meditation. Record the reasons for our living together. Work for unity. And enjoy.

15

AN ASPIRATION,
NOT AN ACHIEVEMENT

An Interview with Alfred Hassler

Alfred Hassler (1910-91) was one of the major figures in FOR. Imprisoned during World War II as a conscientious objector, he joined the FOR staff and went on to serve as editor of Fellowship *magazine and later as executive secretary of FOR and general secretary of the International Fellowship of Reconciliation. He was interviewed on his retirement in 1974 by Jim Forest, editor of* Fellowship, *and Diane Leonetti, associate editor* (Fellowship, *September 1974).*

LEONETTI: *Al, perhaps you could start by trying to remember how you became a pacifist.*

HASSLER: It was during the Depression. Everybody was aware that war was coming. In the summer of 1939 I was teaching a course on Christianity and peace at a Baptist summer conference in western Pennsylvania. The war was so imminent that I recall telling the class that we might not ever see one another again.

Somewhere in that period, my thinking turned from antiwar to pacifist. I can't tell just when. My thinking just evolved. I never read anything that did it. No one converted me. There was no flash of light on the road to Damascus. But suddenly I was. And then I was president of the Baptist Pacifist Fellowship—before I ever heard of FOR.

FOREST: *Many people think of themselves as post–World War II pacifists. They imagine that, had they been of military age before Hiroshima, they might have been volunteers in the war against Hitler. World War II, in their minds, was the last "just war." But you became a pacifist before that war, and you remained a pacifist throughout. Wasn't that difficult?*

HASSLER: Being a pacifist during World War II was difficult, and it has been so ever since. Unquestionably, the things that Hitler and the Nazis were doing were evil, unqualifiedly evil. It is still difficult to speak to the question, "What would you do about Hitler?"

But we pacifists were talking about the reasons World War II would happen well before it came. Out of Versailles, out of the inequities, out of the ringing of Germany with steel by the Allies, out of the refusal of the Allies to live up to their treaty agreements, out of the refusal to disarm—out of all that we saw a national paranoia being created in Germany that inevitably would produce a Hitler-like leader there.

We didn't know any way to prevent the war, once Hitler was in power. But the pragmatic evidence is that we pacifists saved more Jews from Hitler than were saved by any army. Remember, the Holocaust began *after* the war started. Jews were being persecuted and driven out of the country. Their property was being taken. But the mass murder didn't begin until the war was underway. Even then, pacifists in Europe continued to be at the core of efforts to hide Jews and smuggle them to safety.

The analysis that pacifists made about the factors driving us toward war proved quite accurate, but we were powerless to put into effect the recommendations, which might have prevented war.

You know, in some ways it was easier being a pacifist then than it was during the Vietnam war. In World II we *knew* we were powerless. We never thought we could end the war once it began. All we could do was argue for a war without victory rather than the unconditional surrender the governments demanded. We were supporting conscientious objectors. We were rescuing the victims of the Nazis. In this country we were bringing in as many Jews as the government would allow—which, tragically, weren't very many. But we were never under the delusion that we had the political power to stop the war.

During the Vietnam war, however, the peace movement thought it *did* have that power, and people in it became infinitely more frustrated.

FOREST: *Are you glad you went to prison?*
HASSLER: Sure. I wouldn't want to do it again, but I'm glad they sent me where they did. COs were sent to Danbury or Sandstone or one of the other "correctional" institutions. But I was appalled at the thought of being locked up for years with a bunch of conscientious objectors! *(Laughter.)* So when they sent me to Lewisburg, a maximum security prison with only thirty COs among a prison population of thirteen hundred, I was delighted. I was a little frightened too. But it was an experience I had practically lusted after and I was very glad to go. I learned a great deal.

I was naive about going to prison. You know, my family were all law and order people. They weren't the kind who wanted to sic cops on people, but they took it for granted that no good person ever went to prison.

It was very contradictory because we were always going on about St. Paul and St. Peter—except we Baptists called them Paul and Peter—and these guys were always in prison. But *not* in the United States! The idea was, I think, that if Paul had been an American, he wouldn't have gone to prison—and Jesus wouldn't have been crucified.

FOREST: *You remind me of a postcard message I received from Nhat Hanh while I was in prison, something very brief: "Do you remember the tangerine we ate when we were together? Your being there is like that tangerine. Eat it and be one with it. Tomorrow it will be no more." It helped me immensely to find some encouragement in approaching prison in a non-confrontational way—to take the experience bite by bite.*

HASSLER: And day by day.

I hadn't thought about it before, but one of the reasons for wanting to be in a maximum security prison rather than with a lot of COs was my own aversion to sitting around talking with people doing time for the same reason. In a maximum security prison, where you are surrounded by conventional offenders and military, we COs became, individually, a kind of core of identity for other prisoners who had no strength to draw on themselves. You would see a CO out on the playing field surrounded by twenty or thirty non-COs, just talking.

We got so involved in other people's problems that we didn't have time to brood on our own problems. And that was a very good thing.

FOREST: *What made you decide to rejoin the FOR staff after you left prison?*

HASSLER: I decided I would work in the peace movement another five years and then go back to advertising and journalism and make a good living for my family. But I never did. There was always something too interesting going on to stop.

What I really wanted to be was a writer. I didn't want to be a peace executive. There were times when I thought I was the only one on the FOR staff who *didn't* want to be executive secretary. *(Laughter.)*

LEONETTI: *I was wondering how the shape of the pacifist movement has changed since you've been in it.*

HASSLER: In some ways it hasn't changed at all, and in other ways it has changed drastically. Both bother me.

It hasn't changed much in its individualism. We lack discipline. We won't focus our collective efforts at one or two or three things at a time. Our members employ a few program people and support staff—and saddle them with the expectation that they can do twenty or thirty major efforts with some effect. Our efforts are too diffuse. There is a touching faith on the part of members that their staff can do anything—and an almost reprehensible feeling on the staff's part that they *should* do everything. There is, as yet, no sense of a coherent program on which we pacifists can unite in the interests of accomplishing a few things, even if not in the order each of us might privately prefer.

The other change in the peace movement is that there is now a great deal more sophistication regarding the complexities that are involved in the search for peace. We no longer assume history is made only in the United States and Europe—we know, in fact, that it is more likely to be made in the poverty-stricken countries which are the breeding grounds of conflict. We know that peace isn't to be achieved with declarations and treaties—it runs much deeper than that.

But there are still a good many people who want simplified answers, who want to find a magic button that will make everything okay again. We get the feeling that if only we did the right thing or worked a little bit harder, we would achieve what is needed.

There is more sophistication now, by and large—but more despair as well.

FOREST: *What about FOR's name?* Fellowship *seems to be an archaic religious term, and* reconciliation *an archaic political goal. If you could, would you change FOR's name, or any part of it?*

HASSLER: No, though I detested the name myself when I first came on. I came out of a religious setting in which they used *fellowship* as a verb. There was always talk about "fellowshipping together." For me, it was like running your fingernails down a blackboard. And *reconciliation* seemed a weak word.

But the words don't bother me anymore. I've become very attached to them.

It seems to me the essence of the pacifist position is not the refusal to kill or to be a part of an army but the very positive concept of a human society that is familial in nature. A human family. We *are* all interrelated. We humans *are* a fellowship.

And reconciliation has become, for me, a very strong word. It doesn't mean tolerating injustice or the status quo. It does mean finding a common denominator between and among people of vastly different backgrounds and natures and possessions and all the rest.

FOREST: *Perhaps nothing has been more important in your work for eight or ten years now than the Vietnamese Buddhists and the nonviolent movement that has come out of their faith and sufferings. You even call yourself a Baptist Buddhist every now and then. Do you mean it?*

HASSLER: There are two things crucial to me about the Buddhists, or perhaps I should say Nhat Hanh's interpretation of Buddhism, which has been my main source of learning. One is the rejection of an arbitrary claim to knowledge of total truth.

The story that Nhat Hanh told which sticks most vividly in memory occurred when a young woman in Santa Barbara asked him what it meant to seek the Buddha and what happened when you found him. Nhat Hanh answered, "I am a Zen master. And, as you know, Zen masters always reply incomprehensibly. So I will say that you only find the Buddha by killing the Buddha whenever you find him."

Then he laughed and said, "But I am a nice Zen master, so I will tell you that the Buddha is truth and the only thing that keeps you from finding truth is your conviction that you have already found it. So whenever you have 'found truth,' you must recognize that it is a lie, 'kill' it, and go on in the search for truth."

This is quite different from the idea that many Christians cling to—that they have a revealed truth, final and eternal, which you can't deviate from.

The other thing about the Buddhists is their openness to ideas and insights of other people, other faiths, whether religious, political, or whatever. They don't think they have a monopoly on truth.

It is this sort of openness that awes me. In the past they took things from Confucianism and Taoism. They took what seemed good into their own faith, as they are now taking things from Christianity.

FOREST: *Earlier you mentioned that there is more sophistication in the peace movement now about the complexity of the problems we face. You added that there is also more despair. I know I sense this very much in this society. We know certain things are happening; we know they are wrong; we know the consequences will be disastrous; we wish to resist; we want to help form constructive alternatives; but we haven't got the hope that makes response and resistance possible.*

HASSLER: I agree, I'm tempted to say it's always been that way, but that's not adequate. When I was chairman of the housing cooperative in which we still live, I used to laugh and say, "During the day I work at writing tracts about how atomic bombs are about to end the world—and then I come home and talk with people about thirty-year mortgages!"

The problem of despair, I think, hits Americans harder than other people because we have been conditioned by two centuries of overcoming physical obstacles and enriching ourselves in the process—never encountering insoluble problems.

Now we encounter problems that can't be solved.

Our situation is vastly different from that of people—in Europe and Indochina—who have experienced defeat upon defeat in recent memory and who have developed what some Europeans have called a "theology of despair," which is just another way of saying a "theology of the cross."

One FOR member in Europe used to say, "You Americans think that the kingdom of God is coming on earth through your work. We know that it is not. We have been through Hitler and the war."

Personally, I can't accept despair as some sort of basis. Despair may well be a self-fulfilling prophecy. You get so despairing about the human prospect that you have no energy to find solutions.

The reason there is so much despair, I think, is because of our inability to find handles for the various problems—ways of grabbing hold of things in order to solve them. They're so complex, so interrelated, so massive. People don't see much relevance in going out and doing *small* things.

Why set up a day-care center . . . or try to improve housing . . . or even have a child . . . if the world is going to blow itself up in the next few years?

Each person has to find a personal answer to that.

A. J. Muste used to say, "All the really great things in history came as a surprise. Nobody ever predicted them."

The grounds for hope are there but terribly hard to see.

Do you remember FOR's campaign in '54 and '55? There's a story we haven't told very often because it was told to us in great confidence—but that was nearly twenty years ago.

There was a famine in China, extremely grave. We urged people to send President Eisenhower small sacks of grain with the message, "If thine enemy hunger, feed him. Send surplus food to China." The surplus food, in fact, was never sent. On the surface, the project was an utter failure.

But then—quite by accident—we learned from someone on Eisenhower's press staff that our campaign was discussed at three separate cabinet meetings. Also discussed at each of these meetings was a recommendation from the Joint Chiefs of Staff that the United States bomb mainland China in response to the Quemoy-Matsu crisis.

At the third meeting the president turned to a cabinet member responsible for the Food for Peace program and asked, "How many of those grain bags have come in?" The answer was forty-five thousand, plus tens of thousands of letters.

Eisenhower's response was that if that many Americans were trying to find a conciliatory solution with China, it wasn't the time to bomb China. The proposal was vetoed.

LEONETTI: *And you learned that only by pure chance?*

HASSLER: Pure chance! That's the point. You do something and seem to fail—but in the process of failure you sometimes accomplish something else quite unexpected. Something of much greater importance.

History is full of esoteric little groups that live by themselves and, regardless of whatever happens outside, carry on with their particular witness and commitment. Pacifists do that in one sense. FOR members are a minute portion of the world's population, and we strengthen and reinforce each other as best we can. But there's another element to it. We really do have massive world problems and by our very best judgment they can wipe out civilization and the human race.

People say this is exaggerated. They say others have said this before all through history. I reply that particular civilizations have been wiped out before, but ours is the first period in history in which a global civilization has existed, as well as the means of global destruction. When this civilization is wiped out, there won't be another to take its place. Not on this planet.

Now we have a handful of people motivated to go on working despite hopelessness. But if we want to motivate a constituency large enough to effect the changes that are necessary, then there has to be hope there, something to see and work toward, a *belief* that it can be achieved.

FOREST: *How do you inspire that?*

HASSLER: I wish I knew.

FOREST: *During the first night of the FOR conference in Wisconsin, you talked briefly about the word* love, *which is almost a brand-name word now, a discredited word to many people. How do you locate that word in the vocabulary of peacemaking?*

HASSLER: For a long time we tried to point out that there were different kinds of love—agape, eros, etc. But that really doesn't come across to most people. When you talk about love, people think of a very intimate sort of relationship. But that is manifestly impossible with each of nearly four billion people—or even with one person who is doing something extraordinarily unpleasant in your view.

It seems to me that the three elements that are essential to an understanding of love as pacifists talk about it are compassion, humility, and understanding.

Compassion in the sense of awareness, sensitivity, understanding of other persons and their weaknesses, even the ones you think are very strong. Their mortality, their limitations—the fact that they suffer in ways we don't know about or understand.

And humility in understanding just how narrow is the gap between the people we regard as morally good—ourselves!—and the people whom we regard as morally bad—the ones who oppose us.

Milton Mayer repeatedly has written about a religious meeting in which A. J. Muste stood up and said, "If I can't love Hitler, I can't love at all." This statement became almost an obsession with Milton as he dug deeper and deeper into it.

You can't get anywhere with it unless you realize that love means understanding and compassion. Then it opens up. Compassion, not in the sense of lessening your opposition to what Hitler was doing, but compassion for a man who clearly had suffered terribly, who was terribly distorted, who had so little real happiness and joy.

The equivalent for us would be to say, "If I cannot love Richard Nixon, I cannot love at all." Again, love means understanding and compassion. You only have to look at any one of a hundred recent pictures of the man to see the suffering that he's gone through, a suffering that he probably doesn't yet understand. A man who doesn't understand himself, his personality, or the reaction of people to him; a man who really feels that he was right, that he has been persecuted. You can only feel sorry for him; and you can only feel compassion.

That's the essence of pacifism for me: the realization that we are, as it's put in the New Testament, all sinners and have fallen short of the glory of God. We have no right to be self-righteous, but only to be pitying, compassionate, helpful.

Of course we fail at this all the time. Pacifism is an aspiration, not an achievement.

As one of the best pacifists I know—Cao Ngoc Phuong—put it, when asked if she were a pacifist: "Not yet."

16

THOMAS MERTON

A Friend Remembered

Jim Forest

The Trappist monk Thomas Merton (1915-68) was widely known for his spiritual writings and for his classic autobiography, The Seven Storey Mountain. *Less known were his many writings on behalf of peace and racial justice. For many years he served as a kind of spiritual counselor to many Catholic peacemakers, including Jim Forest, an editor of* The Catholic Worker *and one of the founders of the Catholic Peace Fellowship. At the time of this writing Forest was coordinator of the International Fellowship of Reconciliation in Holland. He later published a biography of Merton,* Living with Wisdom *(Fellowship, December 1978).*

It is ten years since the death of Thomas Merton. He was quite famous and widely read then, yet there now seems more interest than ever. A look at the list of his books in print is astonishing.

It isn't well known that he was a member of the Fellowship of Reconciliation. As far as I know, it was the only "group" he formally belonged to apart from the Catholic church and his Trappist monastic community in Kentucky. Still more interesting, he became a Fellowship member when the American branch had but a sprinkling of his co-religionists. Later, of course, there were thousands who joined, generally through the Catholic Peace Fellowship, of which Merton was a founder, advisor, and the most prominent sponsor.

Monks can be the most surprising people. We think of them (if we think of them at all or even know they exist) as being hidden away not only in the geographical but historical sense, people intentionally out of touch with "the real world." Then along comes a Thich Nhat Hanh or Thomas Merton, tearing the stereotype to shreds. I had expected someone as solemn and serious as Job—and found a Merton who was more like the Keystone Cops. In my very first encounter, he was laughing so hard as I walked in the door that he was on the floor, face red as a strawberry, laughing with such monsoon intensity that he could hardly breathe. No one has better underlined for me the truth of an observation by Leon Bloy: "Joy is the most infallible sign of the presence of God."

We were friends the last nine years of his life, long enough for me to discover, in Merton, the extraordinary connection that exists between one's capacity for joy and one's ability to sorrow: to make room in oneself for the suffering of the world. I have never known anyone who felt more personally and intensely the human cost of war, the hell of war, and who recognized work to end war as a fundamental religious responsibility. As he put it in his usual plain speech, "The duty of the Christian . . . is to work for the total abolition of war." If we fail to do so, "we tend by our very passivity and fatalism to cooperate with the destructive forces that are leading inexorably to war. . . . Peace is to be preached, nonviolence is to be explained as a practical method, and not left to be mocked as an outlet for crackpots who want to make a show of themselves."

Nor would he allow a double standard in disarmament—working to convince governments to prohibit war and eliminate the machinery of war while we fail to disarm ourselves as individuals: "Prayer and sacrifice must be used as the most effective spiritual weapons in the war against war, and like all weapons, they must be used with deliberate aim: not just with a vague aspiration for peace and security, but against violence and war. *This implies that we are also willing to sacrifice and restrain our own instinct for violence and aggressiveness in our relations with other people.*

These unambiguous statements were rare enough from anyone at the time (the last quotation comes from his first article in *The Catholic Worker*, published in October 1961). It was still more surprising to many that they were said by one of the most famous and widely read priests in the Roman Catholic Church. That such a call might later be made by the pope (John XXIII in *Pacem in Terris*) and the Second Vatican Council *(The Constitution on the Church in the Modern World)* was, at the time, beyond imagination's most fanciful reach.

Indeed, Catholics as well as others were not only surprised but troubled. Merton seemed "too political." In his autobiography, *The Seven Storey Mountain*, he had written about his flirtation with Communism, to the point of becoming a Young Communist with the secret "party name" Frank Swift. Well, some thought, maybe Thomas Merton is really Father Frank Swift.

The subsequent crisis within his monastic community regarding his peace writings is too complex to describe in this brief article. If Merton could be troubling to his monastic order, he could be troubling to his fellow pacifists as well.

He was increasingly aware in the last decade of his life of the shallowness of much that is done in the name of peace. He tried to make us think more deeply, to get rid of our own prejudices and stereotypes, to be more critical about ourselves and various "movements," and to develop a purity of life that had nothing to do with self-righteousness.

"We have to have," as he put it in one letter, "a deep, patient compassion for the fears and irrational mania of those who condemn us."

Merton's Christianity was quite Gandhian, in the sense of working for reconciliation rather than the triumph of one group over another. At the center of the peacemaking vocation, he found, was a realization that attitudes can be completely transformed, in others no less than in ourselves. There was no need to divide the world up into those who are now-and-forever right and those who are now-and-forever wrong. "The whole problem," he wrote, "is this inner change . . . an application of spiritual force and not the use of merely political pressure."

Pacifists, he noticed, have a temptation to establish halos over their heads while provoking others into fervent opposition. "We have to consider the fact that, in its provocative aspect, nonviolence may tend to harden the opposition and to confirm people in their righteous blindness." Such "nonviolence" could easily produce a kind of false martyr, whose real passion wasn't to change and deepen understanding in others but simply prove others "terribly and visibly wrong."

He argued strongly against the peace movement becoming too politicized and thus getting lost in its slogans and ideologies. Instead, it needed to root itself in the human dimension. In another letter he wrote:

> The basic problem is not political; it is a-political and human. One of the most important things to do is to keep cutting deliberately through political lines and barriers and emphasizing the fact that these are largely fabrications and that there is another dimension, a genuine reality, totally opposed to the fictions of politics: the human dimension which politics pretend to arrogate entirely to themselves.

He noticed that pacifists, no less than corporate executives, could become trapped in success addictions. It wasn't that Merton didn't care about results. Ends are implied and determined in means. But often action is needed where the only end in sight—reason's sight, at least—is utter catastrophe. Merton himself, reflecting in conversation one day on the arms race, said, "Perhaps we have already gone over the waterfall and just haven't landed yet."

There is an easy hope. It is innocent. Confronted with certain facts, certain experiences, it becomes despair. The kind of hope worth having, indeed the only genuine hope, is beyond rather than before despair. In a letter I especially value, Merton put it this way:

> Do not depend on the hope of results. When you are doing the sort of work you have taken on, essentially an apostolic work, you may have to meet the fact that your work will be apparently worthless and achieve no result at all, if not perhaps results opposite to what you expect. As you get used to this idea, you start more and more to concentrate not on the results but on the value, the rightness, the truth of the work itself. And

there too a great deal has to be gone through, as gradually you struggle less and less for an idea and more and more for specific people. The range tends to narrow down, but it gets more and more real. In the end, it is the reality of personal relationships that saves everything. . . . The big results are not in your hands or mine, but they suddenly happen, and we can share in them; but there is no point in building our lives on this personal satisfaction, which may be denied us and which after all is not that important.

Merton personally knew loss and failure quite well. His parents died when he was young. His only brother was shot down in the Second World War and disappeared into the North Sea. Becoming a Catholic while a graduate student at Columbia University, and later becoming a Trappist monk, gave him a challenging context, direction, and a deeper sense of the meaning of life—but there were sufferings of a different kind. The deeper he entered into the spiritual life, the more he encountered the suffering world. But without that encounter, the joy and peace of God weren't possible.

How to sum up in rough words the qualities of that rich, challenging life?

He was a man with an immense capacity for wonder and delight.

He could not accept murder as a virtue, no matter how official or patriotic or revolutionary the excuse.

He had no patience for the carefully contrived commercial noises—or ideological noises—of culture or counterculture; but an enormous patience for the sounds of prayer, wind, and rain.

He was a writer. A friend said Merton couldn't scratch his nose without writing about it.

He was a friend, deeply committed to friendship, yet able to retain a certain independence, space—an area for critical interaction.

He was a man confident and alive enough in his own faith to be fully open to the faiths of others. When the Fellowship arranged for Thich Nhat Hanh, the Zen Buddhist monk from Vietnam, to visit him, Merton was able to recognize him as "my brother . . . more my brother than many who are nearer to me in race and nationality, because he and I see things exactly the same way."

He was, finally, a man of marvelous and contagious compassion, whose life was an ever-widening channel for God's love to make itself felt—in his community, his church, and among his friends and readers in the world at large. Thus he helped many of us live more perceptively, more faithfully, more at peace in vocations engaged with peacelessness. He made us better able to understand God, in words he often used, as "Mercy with Mercy within Mercy."

17

CONNECTING THE ALTAR
TO THE PENTAGON

Daniel Berrigan

Daniel Berrigan, a Jesuit priest and poet, has for many years offered a prophetic witness for peace—a witness both in word and deed. In 1968 he was arrested with his brother Philip and six others for destroying draft files in Catonsville, Maryland. In 1980 they were again arrested for hammering on weapons components at a plant in King of Prussia, Pennsylvania. The following remarks were extracted from press conferences during a trip to Europe in 1979. At the time, Berrigan was vice chairperson of the Fellowship of Reconciliation (Fellowship, *November 1979*).

Why are you working in a hospital for people dying of cancer? Is this not a diversion from your efforts against the arms race?

To begin with, I find it necessary to have some physical work connected with suffering. It is a self-testing. It is an exploration of one's response to death by cancer, which now appears to be, in the world of the Bomb, the human life itself. Experiencing cancer is a rehearsal for the future as presently planned. Being with those dying of cancer is to be with those among whom the Bomb has already fallen. And this is a privilege. Those we care for, the experience of their sufferings, helps me find my way to the Pentagon and the White House and the places where our communities join in resistance to a future of death and cancer.

What is it these communities are doing at the White House and the Pentagon?

Repeating ourselves! We have been at these places time and again for seven years now, doing vigils, praying, singing, and committing civil disobedience.

This year (November 1979), during Holy Week, we attempted to celebrate the Year of the Child that the United Nations has declared. Forty children came, meeting together on their own, planning their own Holy Week action. In the end they carried out a procession. Paper cranes, the peace symbol from Japan, and balloons, these things in their hands. They sang, leafletted, waved signs they had composed themselves. They wrote a letter to Amy Carter, the youngest resident of the White House, about being a child in a bomb-ridden world. They visited the models of nuclear weapons exhibited at the Aerospace Museum and put garlands of paper cranes upon them. They met with astonished officials of the State Department.

The adults went to the Pentagon, many of them prepared for arrest.

Our purpose there was to bring home to the authorities the meaning and consequences of their decisions to build and sell weapons around the world, thus depriving the poor of life and the right use of the world. We used, as is usual in our efforts, a range of ways of communicating. Some distribute leaflets and carry on conversation with Pentagon employees. Some wear costumes and play the part of specters of death, walking through the Pentagon concourses, the acres of shops and restaurants and banks beneath the military offices, chanting "death, death, death, the bomb, the bomb, the bomb." Still others poured blood, our own blood, which earlier had been gathered clinically by a nurse in the group. The blood was poured out on pillars, walls, doorways, the floor—a terrific amount of blood dripping everywhere. And ashes were poured as well: a sign of our readiness to burn the living. A number of people fell as if dead into the blood and ashes. We carried a cross on which the names of various weapons had been written: Trident, cruise missile, neutron bomb, nuclear warhead, napalm . . . all the machinery of death.

Why such use of symbols?

At the Pentagon we are dealing with the insane, the spiritually insane. We are dealing with irrational power. So we are not only relying on rational means of communication—the leaflets, the conversations—but the a-rational, the symbolic. The symbols are an effort to make death concrete. The generals never see the other end of their decisions. There is a huge gap between decision and consequence. It is horrifying to see human blood in the immaculate corridors of the Pentagon. Nothing is more dismaying to the people responsible for that enormous Greek temple. Suddenly the truth of the situation is in the air, and under your feet, and it is terrifying.

For us, for we are mostly Christians, this is also an extension of our normal worship. Our tradition is sacramental. It is full of symbols: human blood, ashes, water, oil.

We look upon this as taking the body and blood from the table of the sacrament to the Pentagon in the same way Christ was taken from table to Calvary, all in one day. At the table Christ announced the breaking of his body and the shedding of his blood, thereby establishing this principle for his followers: you shed your own blood rather than the blood of others; your own body is broken rather than the bodies of others. This is the heart of the gospel. He said *Do this! Do this!* Which we understand to mean not only *do this* with symbols at the table, which can be very safe in the worst of times, but *do this* with our lives.

It is very interesting that the crimes that we are accused of at the Pentagon are the crimes of the altar. We have *done this* in obedience to Christ, and many of us have gone to prison for it, including my brother Philip and my sister-in-law Elizabeth.

Our conviction is that the sacraments, properly understood, are not merely a principle of worship but also a command of ethics and conduct.

Do you see what you are doing as an action of the church?

Absolutely. The role of the church is to be able to read the gospel, to be literate in the gospel, and to be able to explore it out in the world.

Is that the only reason to be a Christian?

That's the best one I have. All the other roles are secondary.

Why?

Why? Because that's our book, that's our way, that's our life, that's our leader, our Christ. And he says we are not allowed to kill other people. Which gives us a start for understanding our response to war, our response to nuclear weapons, our response to any system that results in murder.

But in fact there are very few Christians doing the kind of thing you are doing. Very few Christians seem to recognize war or the arms race as any kind of priority of religious life.

In my country one could say that if we had a hundred priests, ministers, and nuns, and as many laypeople arrested tomorrow at the White House or the Pentagon, it would make a difference. It would have some impact on the momentum of the arms race. It would render many people in government and out more thoughtful. And it would be an embarrassment to the government.

If a month or two later there were five hundred, and then a thousand, we would be getting to the point of slowing, even stopping the arms race. If we had the kind of faith that could bring us together in such resistance, such nonviolent leadership, we could move the nuclear mountain.

But will people in such numbers come forward?

That is the unknown right now.

But thirty years ago no one could imagine what lay ahead for a young man named Martin Luther King and the moral grandeur that Americans would experience in the civil rights movement. And fifteen years ago no one could imagine that millions of Americans would oppose their government in wartime, that thousands would go to the prisons in resistance, that this resistance would be so effective that the government's plan to use nuclear weapons in Vietnam would never be realized, that tens of thousands of Vietnamese lives would be saved, and that America would finally withdraw in its first military defeat. The resisters prevented the *extinction* of Vietnam. President Johnson never quite dared go ahead and use nuclear weapons. There was too much turmoil, too much resistance.

In resisting nuclear war and nuclear energy, we are only at the beginning. Ideas are beginning to change, and lives may follow.

Many people would agree with you about nonviolence being the necessary means of resistance in developed and democratic societies. But you have written—for example in your public letter to your fellow priest Ernesto Cardenal—that nonviolence must be used in completely repressive countries, impoverished countries, where there is no open press, where prisoners are tortured and murdered, where nonviolence seems completely futile.

Obviously there is a hideous difference between living under a dictator like Somoza or Pinochet and living under Carter. But I also want to say that living as a Christian in any conceivable society places upon us a certain discipline regarding other lives and opens a certain path to follow. In a sense the gospel is independent of political regimes in what it lays upon us.

Are there nonviolent means that would work in Latin America? Or South Africa? Or Korea?

I don't know. I don't live there. I know that Jesus lived—and died—in such a country. I also know that we have to recognize, after thousands of years of religious resistance to political tyranny, that there are situations in which you can do nothing. For example, occupied Israel, two thousand years ago. Nothing with guns, and nothing without guns. You can only die.

The first question of the Old Testament is not one of tactics in any event. That seems to be secondary. From a religious point of view, nonviolence is not primarily a tactic. It is a way of living and being and expressing the truth of your soul in the world. Tactics come and go. Tactics now work and now do not work. The gift of faith, as I understand it, is to be able to die well when called to. It may yet come to that for us. I recall Bonhoeffer while in prison writing that, in his situation, there was very little he could do. "One can only," he said, "tell the truth and say one's prayers." And then he went to die. That was his politics. He told the truth, he said his prayers, and he died. That was his gift to us.

So I think this concentration upon political effectiveness is very often a trap. There is in fact very little one can do in certain circumstances. One can only know effects later, or the survivors know what the gift meant. You can't immediately proclaim political effectiveness.

But you seem optimistic about the possibility of public resistance finally stopping the arms race. Where do you get your hope?

Hope is a mystery, a gift. It has nothing to do with optimism. I have never been allowed optimism. I have never seen things going well. I have seen only the continuous expansion of targets—the poor, the innocent, the unborn—continuous evidence of the blunting of our humanity. In my childhood neither abortion nor the nuclear weapon nor the Holocaust was imaginable. If I were to slog along in the political situation, as it is commonly understood, I would have gone under long ago.

The believing community has an entirely different basis that has nothing to do with cultural promises or political expectations. For us, it has to do with the promises of Christ. It has to do with looking for an act of God, God's intervention. We are looking for this act of God in our own lives.

Hope is the interplay between trust in the promises of Christ and the willingness to embody these promises in the way we live and in our resistance to the rule of death in the world.

What we do at the Pentagon is for me an experience of hope. It is a great act of hope to go back and back and back, and to sing and to offer a message that there is another way to live, and to keep trying to dissolve the boundaries.

What of your own future?
It's no different than the past. Opportunity for more growth, and more prayer, and more salvation.

Political plans?
That's the political plan.

You're sure?
Absolutely.

18

ADOLFO PEREZ ESQUIVEL

Behind the Man and the Prize

Richard Chartier

The decades of the 1960s and 1970s in Latin America easily summoned images of violence, whether the brutal repression of military governments or the guerrilla movements scattered throughout the continent. The existence of creative experiments in nonviolent action, both in the struggle for social change and in the defense of human rights, was a little-known story. In 1980 the award of the Nobel Peace Prize to Adolfo Perez Esquivel, leader of Servicio Paz y Jusiticia, shed new light on this story. For years he was among those who labored nonviolently on behalf of the Latin American people deprived of their human rights. He was interviewed in 1980 by Richard Chartier, editor of Fellowship, *who himself had worked as Methodist missionary in Argentina from 1959 to 1973* (Fellowship, *December 1980*).

"Human rights activist" and phrases like it have been used to identify Adolfo Perez Esquivel, winner of the 1980 Nobel Peace Prize, and in a sense those words do capture the nature of the work and witness of the forty-eight-year-old Argentine, coordinator of Servicio Paz y Justicia (Service for Peace and Justice) in Latin America.

Indeed, the concern for human rights had become increasingly central to the work of Servicio in the last few years. In Argentina (where the Servicio headquarters is located) and in many other countries, millions of Latin Americans had been denied any effective participation in decisions affecting their destinies because military regimes have abolished democratic institutions, procedures, guarantees, and effectively usurped all power. And among those millions generally denied any access to the democratic process are the tens of thousands who have been subjected to arbitrary imprisonment (with no pretense of due process) and tortured by government authorities, and the tens of thousands who were found dead or who disappeared (never to be seen again), presumably at the hands of self-appointed paramilitary groups with the complicity, by action or inaction, of the governing military authorities.

The courageous work of Servicio in its denunciation of human rights violations and its advocacy on behalf of the victims of those violations, of course, was not unique. The Servicio network did significant work which grew in scope and influence, but it was one expression of a growing movement of concern and protest about human rights violations in Latin America.

Similarly, Adolfo personified the countless—some known, many nameless—persons who paid the price in their own flesh, many of them the price of death at the hands of governments or paramilitary forces.

Adolfo and Servicio know full well that the recognition accorded their work must be understood and accepted in terms of all those struggling for human rights in Latin America rather than as their particular and singular achievement.

But an even more critical clarification is in order. The emphasis on human rights must be seen in larger terms than we have just employed and which have characterized so much of the media treatment of the award. We refer to an emphasis on human rights which stresses the arbitrary and ruthless violations of personal and civil liberties of those regarded as subversive or enemies of the established order.

One needs to remember that the full name of Servicio includes Paz y Justicia (Peace and Justice). The name stems from the fundamental conviction in Latin America that *peace is possible only as the fruit of justice and that the two concerns are inseparably linked.* The absence of justice has constituted the greatest violation of human rights; the struggle for justice led to repression and human rights violations in the sense of arbitrary arrests, torture, assassinations, and disappearances.

Servicio, like many of its counterparts, must be understood as an attempt to wrestle with the overriding reality of a Latin America characterized by unjust socioeconomic and political structures and the increasing determination to transform those structures in such a fashion as to make possible a more just and humane society.

In a word, the watchword or *leitmotiv* for most Latin Americans has become *liberation*—liberation from all the institutionalized injustices and structures of violence which have deprived the majority of Latin Americans of real political freedom, basic socioeconomic well-being, and human dignity. This means liberation from the internal forces ("power elites" or interests) that control the political alliances of vested and economic decision-making to their own advantage and leave the majority of Latin Americans in subhuman social conditions, "marginalized" and powerless.

It also means liberation from the relationship between the "internal elites" and the dominant forces in the "external world" (read developed, industrialized economies of the North)—a symbiotic relationship from which both elites prosper at the expense of the majority of the people.

It is in the context of the struggle for liberation that one must understand the origins of Servicio and the nature of its philosophy and program.

Suffice it to say here that Servicio was actually begun in 1971 in Costa Rica with responsibility for its then-necessarily-limited program largely in the hands of veteran missionary Earl Smith and more formally constituted in 1974 in Medellín, Colombia, at which time Adolfo Perez Esquivel was named as coordinator.

The time was ripe, indeed, for Servicio Paz y Justicia as a coordinating network with a nonviolent orientation.

The way had been prepared by figures such as Hildegard Goss-Mayr and Jean Goss. Bishops, priests, pastors, and laypeople were seeking a "way of liberation" consonant with the gospel; situations of injustice were clamoring for attention. Efforts—often limited and isolated—to bring about change nonviolently were being made; there was a need for coordination, communication, and collaboration among persons and groups concerned for nonviolent change. In a word, Servicio was needed.

It is not possible here to trace the nature and scope of the work of Servicio. In brief, it can be said that it provided inspiration, guidance, and resources (through its publications and in other ways) for the still nascent but growing Servicio network, and that it initiated or collaborated with efforts to achieve a larger measure of social justice in matters affecting urban workers and peasants in several countries.

It is ironic that Adolfo Perez Esquivel became coordinator of Servicio at a time when the forces of reaction were beginning to resist the trend toward democratization and liberation. The revolutionary thrust was suppressed by one military government after another and the patterns of repression were institutionalized. (Chilean Salvador Allende's government was ousted in 1973. At about the same time, Uruguay accelerated its institutionalization of the military's hegemony and Argentina moved toward the military coup of 1976.)

The repressive reaction was rapid, virulent, and widespread in most of Latin America. The military assumed total control and ruthlessly suppressed all democratic institutions. Civil liberties were abolished. Human rights violations abounded.

The reasons for the new wave of de facto military regimes of a near-totalitarian and repressive character are beyond the scope of this article. The immediate excuse was that the violence to which some groups had resorted (for example, in Argentina and Uruguay) justified total repression by the governments and necessarily led to some "excesses and errors."

Because of this reality of the systematic, widespread, and prolonged violation of human rights, Servicio was led to make human rights a principal program emphasis which was Latin American in scope and won worldwide interest and support. It was while active in that effort that Adolfo was arrested in April 1977 and imprisoned without charges for fourteen months, after which he spent another fourteen months in "restricted freedom."

Late last year he was granted full freedom and was able to resume his travels on behalf of Servicio and the quest for peace and justice through active nonviolence. In his absence the Servicio staff—including Adolfo's eldest son, Leonardo—had carried on under adverse circumstances.

Thus far we have tried to link the human rights work for which he was awarded the prize to the larger struggle for social justice and liberation, but it is necessary to deal with another major component: the place of nonviolence in the philosophy and program of Servicio.

It is not gratuitous or peripheral to the spirit and stance of Servicio that to its name—Service for Peace and Justice—is usually subsumed the phrase "nonviolent orientation." The commitment to nonviolence as a philosophy and method is clear-cut and unequivocal, and in the Latin American context represents a deliberate, decisive—and, indeed, daring—choice.

For years nonviolence was virtually unknown—restricted to a few familiar with its theory and practice elsewhere—or regarded as alien or irrelevant to the harsh realities of Latin America. For many, it connoted passivism, emphasis on democratic and decent deportment privately and publicly, mild reformism or the resolution of insignificant conflicts.

As the "awareness of situation" and "revolutionary ethos" gained strength in Latin America, it was hoped at first that the transformation of structures could be effected through democratic, peaceful political alternatives. Nonviolence—as a principled methodology—at best figured as an occasional legitimate and convenient technique within the broader strategy of revolutionary change, but not as a major factor or methodology in itself.

As the peaceful efforts at profound social change were increasingly resisted by the established governments and repression mounted, several things occurred:

1. The "guerrilla" movements, already convinced that violence must be the "midwife of revolutionary change," intensified their commitment to violence. (The violence of these groups/movements was often used by governments as a pretext for repressing any and all who espoused change, even by word or nonviolent deed.)

2. Most sectors of Latin American society preferred nonviolent change (though not necessarily an articulate, principled nonviolence). Nevertheless, in the face of the resistance to and the repression of peaceful efforts toward political change, increasing numbers of persons and groups became reluctantly convinced that basic transformation of unjust socioeconomic structures would have to be effected by violence in the end. Nonviolence was seen as preferable but not as viable.

3. In the face of the foregoing reality, those who were committed to nonviolence as both principle and practice (theory and praxis) found themselves increasingly obliged to demonstrate that nonviolence was consonant with and relevant to "bringing off the revolution."

This was true not in a general theoretical way but in concrete situations where peaceful change efforts of a general nature, and even some sporadic and spontaneous but deliberate attempts to use nonviolent direct action techniques, were mercilessly repressed.

Nicaragua, prior to the armed insurrection against Somoza, and El Salvador until the internecine conflict erupted there, are examples of countries where attempts were made to bring about change without violence, not so much out of a principled commitment to nonviolence per se as because the use of violence was seen as futile against the virtual monopoly of armed force by the military regimes that exercised power.

4. Even in the camp of those like the Servicio groups who were committed in principle and practice to nonviolence, the repressive nature of the situation in most countries has caused even modest nonviolent efforts (vigils and peaceful marches) to be ruthlessly squelched.

The point here is that the option for nonviolence in Latin America is a far more difficult and costly one, by and large, than North Americans may be able to understand. (Adolfo's arbitrary imprisonment is a case in point.)

Servicio has selected the nonviolent option. It seeks to "work for the dignity of the person according to the principles of the gospel and through the nonviolent methodology which also arises out of the gospel." Adolfo—a devout Catholic—personifies the reality of a church increasingly committed to liberation and a church that is discovering nonviolence as an instrument of that liberation which is at once effective and consonant with the gospel. And it has not been an academic exercise, a "coffee-house revolution."

Servicio as an organization and the persons and groups that form part of the Servicio network have *practiced* nonviolence through participation in and support of the struggles of Indians in Paraguay, landless peasants in Ecuador, exploited metal workers in Brazil. It has practiced nonviolence in its forthright and persistent denunciation of human rights violations. It has promoted nonviolence through its indoctrination in and teaching of the *liberating power* of the gospel.

The awarding of the Nobel Peace Prize to Adolfo Perez Esquivel is, indeed, a recognition of his courageous work and witness, but as he said in an early interview, "the prize is not for me but for my organization and the cause of human rights and justice in Latin America." And then he added that he accepted the award "on behalf of the poor of Latin America, the peasants and workers, and all those who strive for a more just and human society."

A paramount significance of the honor accorded Adolfo Perez Esquivel is that it can serve to call attention to the drama of Latin America, "where tomorrow struggles to be born" and where human rights and peace/justice are distinguishable but not separable terms on the Latin American agenda. North Americans who are engaged in efforts to work for that new *mañana* in Latin America are encouraged by the way in which the award has served to bring into sharper focus the issues involved in that struggle both in the sense of problems and possibilities.

The award serves to dramatize the agonizing dilemma of those who share the determination to defend human rights and effect the transformation of unjust structures, but who disagree about whether or not violence is necessary and legitimate in the liberation struggle. Many who applaud the awarding of the Nobel Peace Prize to Adolfo Perez Esquivel nonetheless are far from thinking that nonviolence is a viable and effective vehicle of liberation, given the repressive and oppressive reality of most of Latin America.

Still another value of the award is that it can encourage—one would like to say oblige—governments (particularly our own), organizations (such as FOR), and individuals to become more cognizant of and concerned about the crucial issues at stake there. It could cause us, for example, to take a more sustained and critical look at the role in Latin America of the United States, whose presence and power are so decisive in determining the outcome of the drama being enacted there. It can call all of us to ask ourselves—in our context and with our peace/justice agenda—what is required of us.

The awarding of the Nobel Peace Prize to Adolfo Perez Esquivel is an occasion for rejoicing because it recognizes and honors what has been done, but it is also the occasion for a serious appraisal of how much remains to be done.

19

REMEMBERING DOROTHY DAY

Jim Forest

Dorothy Day (1897-1980), co-founder of the Catholic Worker movement, was the preeminent Catholic peacemaker of this century. In her houses of hospitality she combined direct practice of the works of mercy—feeding the hungry, clothing the naked, sheltering the homeless—with a courageous witness against war and injustice. She was repeatedly jailed for acts of civil disobedience. Jim Forest first knew her as a member of the Catholic Worker community in New York City. He later published her biography, Love Is the Measure: A Biography of Dorothy Day *(Fellowship, April 1981).*

I first met Dorothy Day a few days before Christmas in 1960. She was spending that day at the Catholic Worker farm, sitting at the corner of a large, well-worn table reading aloud from letters newly received. Half a dozen people, mostly younger staff, were gathered around.

What a handsome woman! The face was long, with high, prominent cheekbones underlining those large, quick eyes that could be teasing one moment, laughing the next, and then reading your soul. Her hair was braided and circled the top of her head like a garland of silver flowers. The suit she wore was plain but well tailored, good quality and yet almost certainly from the Catholic Worker clothing room, a distribution point of discarded garments and the clothing of the dead.

The only letter I recall from that day's reading was one she had just received from Thomas Merton, who then as now was one of the best known and most widely read Catholic authors. I was amazed he was in correspondence with Dorothy Day. How could a monk who had withdrawn from the world be so in touch with someone both much engaged with the world and a target of controversy? In his letter Merton said he was increasingly drawn to the "derided" example of the Catholic Worker. It reminded him of the primitive monasticism of the Desert Fathers, whom he had been studying with growing interest and about whom he hoped to write (as he did later in *Wisdom of the Desert*).

Merton was only one of many people, countless in number and coming from every walk and station of life, who were deeply impressed by Dorothy Day—impressed enough to see the world differently and to live differently because of her. It would begin with admiration for the houses of hospitality she had helped found or had inspired, unpretentious places where down-and-out people were received and necessities given, all without forms, inquisitors, or unsought advice, in some of the most squalid sections of America's cities. Money was often given "to thicken the soup, not for protest," as one donor—a cardinal—explained. But an interest in the density of the soup might later enlarge to include concern with the social conditions and structures, which were destroying so many lives.

The soup could lead toward the Sermon on the Mount, which Dorothy said wasn't only for priests and nuns plus the odd layperson drawn toward some religious high road, but for everyone. This meant, she insisted, not serving soup one day and war the next. We were to live without killing, no matter what the provocation or consequence, no matter how many other Christians or Christian bishops were fighting wars or blessing them. It also meant voluntary poverty: living as poorly as possible, keeping close to those who have little or who are so destitute they would even count poverty an advance. Dorothy stood for the formation of cooperatives, voluntarism rather than coercion, decentralization, a village-oriented rather than city-centered culture, sharing of goods and talents, life in community.

It is easy enough to summarize a few facts about Dorothy Day's convictions, but it tends to become too abstract and academic. The best way to learn from Dorothy was to hear the stories she would tell, and this happened with her as easily as breathing. Letter-reading times were often funny. We might learn that the letter writer had once nearly burned down the chapel because of an excessive use of candles by a Mary statue or that he had torn out numerous pages from a volume of Shakespeare in the community library because certain scenes were offensive to piety. Or the stories could open whole new areas of understanding. We might hear how a particular writer's family sometimes took in young children who were dying of incurable illnesses and how several times the family's love had been such that the children fully recovered.

Dorothy was a storyteller. It was through stories, interspersed with her favorite quotations from the Bible and various saints, that one learned the Catholic Worker history and its vast pre-history (which leapt back century by century until you ended up with Simon and Andrew aboard their fishing boat, floating on the Sea of Galilee).

The method was informal and often irreverent. Irreverence has its place within reverence, you came to understand, and you couldn't love anyone or anything you couldn't sometimes laugh about as well.

So there was much talk and often laughter. As she says in the last line of her autobiography, *The Long Loneliness*: "It all happened while we sat there talking, and it is still going on."

Many would say we talked too much. It was, in a way, a kind of school. So much time was spent drinking tea (coffee being much too costly) that one member of the community proposed we should rename the paper *The Catholic Shirker*. There was no time for work.

But in fact there was. If not enough cleaning was done, still the most urgent cleaning occurred. If there was no hint of fine cooking on the table, the soup was filling and seldom burned. Great quantities of clothing were received, sorted, and given away. Food that had become unsellable was collected from wholesalers. Hundreds of people were received every day. Many with medical needs were helped. Prisoners and patients in various institutions were visited. The monthly paper, with nearly 100,000 copies printed, was edited, put to press, and mailed out. So were two or three annual appeals. Public meetings were arranged and held every Friday night. Very often there were demonstrations for civil rights or peace which some of the staff took part in or even helped to organize. At the farm, to move on to greater miracles, food was grown, bread baked, vegetables canned, and quite a few people given long-term hospitality.

Had God forgotten to invent Dorothy Day, or the very same person with a different name, it would not have happened. Given the very slight amount of structure she created, it is extraordinary it happened even with her presence.

I don't think Dorothy would object to my saying that she had few if any original ideas. Her convictions were as second-hand as her clothing. Ah, but what extraordinary sources! The ideas were from Jesus, mainly, and next from some of his most remarkable followers down through the centuries: Paul, a number of the great theologians of the early church, Benedict, Francis, Catherine of Siena, John of the Cross, and Teresa of Avila—these were among those she often cited. (There was also Joan of Arc. Dorothy had a small, carefully painted statue of the Maid of Orleans in shining armor on the table by her bed. She had been canonized, Dorothy said, not for her nationalism and not for her battles, but for her fidelity to conscience during the trial that led to her execution. She was therefore "a patron saint of conscientious objectors.") She loved Dostoyevsky, especially his novel *The Brothers Karamazov*; the book's Father Zossima was really one of Dorothy's guides.

I suppose one of the things most people would say was unfortunate in Dorothy was the fact she wasn't much for what might be called "democratic process." There wasn't a democratic bone in her body. You wouldn't find out the truths to live by on Election Day. There was no shortage of conversation at the Catholic Worker, but there were no committees, at least not when I was there. She was a kind of reluctant but necessary abbot. Her constant hope was that those who had particular responsibilities would manage to handle them responsibly, without infuriating everyone else. She distributed a few jobs: responsibility for money, management of the paper, running the farm, etc. Other jobs simply were absorbed one way or another. Decisions, often out of alignment with each other, seemed to occur by spontaneous combustion. This resulted at times in some nasty burns. I best remember a community crisis that occurred when the person mainly responsible for the kitchen decided that the odd pound of butter or box of eggs that were contributed should be used for "the line"—the often anonymous people who turned up for meals—rather than "the family"—the regulars who ate afterward and had various responsibilities in the household. Conflicting quotations from Dorothy's writing appeared on the bulletin board. The Great Butter Crisis ended when Dorothy returned from a trip and said the butter and eggs were to go to the family. At least two of the younger staff were outraged at Dorothy's violation of what they judged to be the Dorothy Day code and left soon afterward.

These crises, quite petty from the outside, were grueling. There must have been many of them during the forty-seven years that lay between the founding of the Catholic Worker in 1933 and Dorothy's death. It is a wonder she was able to endure. The poverty-stricken are, I fear, much less difficult than the brilliant volunteers, most of whom did not last a year.

With such endurance, it is not inappropriate to wonder if she wasn't indeed the saint she was often accused of being. This was not a favorite subject of Dorothy's, needless to say. "Don't call me a saint," she would respond. "I don't want to be dismissed so easily." Yet if the word is stripped clean of sugar and witlessness, of religious posturing, then someone as combative and stubborn and half-timbered as Dorothy may have a halo tucked under her braids.

There is no forgetting Dorothy at prayer. She was nowhere more at home than at Mass, which she sought to get to daily. She was at home in prayer anywhere. You could smell that at-homeness as surely as the smell of bread in the oven or spring in the March wind. Her absorption in prayer was contagious. She taught prayer by praying. Often the rosary was in her hands, which sometimes disturbed those who insisted the rosary was only for medieval illiterates. She was as devoted to Mary as the present pope. She was quite committed to spending time every day in prayer for those who asked her prayers. I once looked through her Mass book and found there long lists of those for whom she was praying.

One of the most disturbing aspects of Dorothy Day to many others was her complete acceptance of Catholic dogma and church structure. She was critical not of what the church taught but only its failure to live its teaching. She believed in obedience to those in religious authority. "If the cardinal asked me to stop publishing articles on pacifism tomorrow, I would do so immediately," she told me one day. "You mean," I responded with alarm, "if he says give up our stand on war, we give it up?" "Not at all. But it means then we only use quotations from the Bible, the words of Jesus, the sayings of the saints, the encyclicals of the popes, nothing of our own." Well, these were our sources anyway, but I was still appalled at the acquiescence, even if never required, which she had in reserve for such a potential abuse of authority. "I can't accept that," I said. "I'm Catholic, not Quaker," Dorothy said. "If you want to edit the Quaker Worker, you're in the wrong place."

Some might think Dorothy would have been far happier as a Quaker. Her ideas on many subjects would have been more easily received and supported.

She had at least as many complaints as a Quaker might have about the Catholic church. Despite them, she often said her main reason for being in a religious body notorious among intellectuals was that she loved it. "I love the Church of Christ made visible," she explained in *The Long Loneliness*, "not for itself because it was so often a scandal to me . . . [but because] the Church is the Cross on which Christ was crucified; one could not separate Christ from his Cross."

Let me confide three more memories of her.

I remember working with her in a tiny office she had on the ground floor of the Worker house on Chrystie Street. It was adjacent to the area in which meals were served and was the noisiest part of the building. We were trying to hear each other through the din. In the middle of a sentence, Dorothy suddenly stood up, opened the door, and then yelled loud enough for a corpse to blink, "Holy silence!" And there was, if only briefly, a midnight silence in St. Joseph's House of Hospitality.

One day another member of the staff and I were preparing a small apartment into which Dorothy was moving in order to have only one flight of steps to climb instead of five. It was a cold-water slum flat such as ought to have disappeared with Oliver Twist. The place was filled with debris, which we loaded into boxes and carried down to the street. One of the objects we found was a large piece of plywood on which some unknown hand had painted the Holy Family—Mary, Joseph, and Jesus. If there is a style called primitive, this was pre-primitive. After expressing horror with the work's aesthetic poverty, we put it out on the street with the rest of the trash. Soon afterward Dorothy walked in with it, delighted. "Look what I found outside! The Holy Family! It's a providential sign, a blessing." She put it proudly on the mantel of the apartment's extinct fireplace, and it later followed her to other rooms.

About the same time, perhaps 1962, she addressed a large meeting one night at New York University. As often happened, some of those present found her pacifism naive and infuriating. One of them demanded to know what she would do if the Russians invaded the United States. Perhaps even she would in that extremity allow that killing was in order. "I would open my heart and my arms and receive them with love, the same as anyone else," she said.

It is nearly a biblical quotation. Certainly one is hard pressed to imagine Christ with a machine gun held in his arms, or its equivalent in any age. His entire ministry occurred, after all, in a country where "the Russians" *had* landed.

The memories go on and on. But now death closes the story for us. Instead comes the time, perhaps, of better understanding the stories she has left behind. Perhaps that is the gift of death and the reason for wakes: sometimes we are more attentive to another's life in its complete absence. The utter silence can be awakening.

Dorothy Day, we can be certain, has not yet finished troubling the world and even ourselves.

20

PEACE PILGRIM

Ann and John Rush

One of the most unusual of modern witnesses for peace was a woman who called herself simply Peace Pilgrim. For almost thirty years she walked across America imparting the message of peace to all who would listen. There is no way of calculating the influence she had on literally thousands of people. This memorial was written by Ann and John Rush, members of the Society of Friends in California, who did much to promote the work and witness of Peace Pilgrim (Fellowship, *March 1982*).

"I look forward to the time when my present-day garment returns to the dust from which it came, while my spirit goes on to a freer living," the woman known as Peace Pilgrim wrote. "Free of earth, as free as air, now you travel everywhere," a friend of hers wrote after her death.

Although she had no fear of death and even looked forward to it, Peace was a completely happy person in this world, thankful constantly for the beauty of the earth. "You will never be privileged to meet a happier person," wrote one minister.

Fellowship reported last September that Peace Pilgrim was killed in a head-on collision while being driven to a speaking engagement outside Knox, Indiana. She always insisted that we should rejoice with our loved ones who make the glorious transition. During the first year of her pilgrimage (1953), she was faced with death in a blinding snowstorm and called it the most beautiful experience of her life!

But like many of her other friends across the country, we did not exactly receive the news of her death with rejoicing. Shock seemed to be the most frequently expressed feeling. Her life as a pilgrim was such a miracle, walking countless miles beyond twenty-five thousand because, she said, "I shall remain a wanderer until mankind has learned the way of peace, walking until I am given shelter, fasting until I am given food." Talking with people everywhere about the urgent need for peace, her words rang with true simplicity. As Robert Steele wrote in the Indian journal *Gandhi Marg*, "Peace Pilgrim speaks with astonishing authority and confidence; she reminds one of the spokesmen of God of biblical times." In another Indian journal the author wrote: "It's as though the voice of Gandhiji is speaking through her."

Twenty-four years ago this remarkable woman walked into our lives to begin the long friendship that was to have a profound influence on us both. We were living in the backwoods of British Columbia then, in a Quaker community; Peace was on her pilgrimage through Canada. When she spoke to Argenta Friends Meeting on the shores of Kootenay Lake, John said to her: "This is the same message the saints have given down through the ages." "I know there is nothing new in my message, except the practice of it," she replied.

Her message was always the same: "Overcome evil with good, falsehood with truth, and hatred with love." The universal truth she spoke, combined with her deep inner peace, made a profound impression on most of those who heard her. As the years went by, she became so full of a contagious zest that her audiences responded more and more frequently with spontaneous laugher. She told stories of her pilgrimage and steps she took, not knowing where they were leading. They led to inner peace. "Inner peace comes through working for the good of all," she said. "Each one has a contribution to make, and will feel within what this contribution is."

Inner peace had not come easily to this unusual woman. In her twenties she had a good job and a busy social life, but life eventually became meaningless. Out of a very deep seeking, she finally came to a complete willingness to give her life to service. That was forty-three years ago. When the decision was made, a great peace came over her. With it, she knew that her life work would be for peace. Ever afterward, she had "the great blessing of good health," she said. "I haven't had an ache or pain, a cold or headache since."

"I took daily walks, receptive and silent amid the beauties of nature, and wonderful insights would come to me which I then put into practice." Here is an example of one of those insights: "I came to feel the need for simplification of life. This was made easy for me because I felt I could no longer accept more than I need while others have less than they need." A fifteen-year preparation followed as she rid herself of "unnecessary possessions and meaningless activities" while doing volunteer work for FOR and other peace groups.

During this time, she experienced "a wonderful mountaintop experience."

For the first time, I knew what inner peace was like. I felt a oneness with all my fellow human beings, with all creation. There is a feeling of always being surrounded by all of the good things like love and peace and joy. There is a feeling of endless energy; it just never runs out. You seem to be plugged into universal energy. It was only at this time that I felt called to begin my pilgrimage for peace in the world. One day, when I was taking a short walk through New England, I saw myself in a navy blue outfit with the words Peace Pilgrim on the front, walking across America.

In her first newsletter she wrote: "In undertaking this pilgrimage, I do not think of myself as an individual but rather as an embodiment of all human hearts that are pleading for peace."

Thus, Peace left her home twenty-eight years ago, without a penny or an organization backing her, with only the clothes she wore, a folding toothbrush, a pen, a comb, and copies of her message. She also left her name and earlier identity behind forever. From that time on, she never lacked what she needed to live. "Without ever asking for anything, I have been supplied with everything I need for my journey," she said. "You see how good people really are?"

After walking twenty-five thousand miles, she stopped counting in 1964; speaking became her first priority. This is the way she accounts for her ability to walk so far, beginning at forty-four years of age: "I walk not on the energy of youth, but the energy that comes with inner peace." Through all of the years during the McCarthy era, the Korean War, the Vietnam war, and since, Peace took her message to tens of thousands of people (probably well over a million; no one kept track), on city streets and dusty roads, in ghettos, suburbs, deserts, even truck stops (once, a stream of truckers kept her talking all night).

Through all of the years when most of us were becoming increasingly afraid to go out on our streets, she walked through slums, slept in bus stations, in trucks, and in the homes of strangers. She slept on the ground, covered with leaves, in cornfields, and in a box under a bridge. Strangers became friends, inviting her into their homes and arranging speaking engagements, often a year or more in advance. In recent years she was able to sleep indoors about three-quarters of the time.

Peace Pilgrim has given us renewed hope in the future of this world, hope that many might gain enough inner peace to make world peace possible. She has strengthened our faith in the reality of the spiritual world and given us a concrete example of something we never dreamed possible: a person filled with inner peace and boundless energy that grew instead of diminished with age. She has given us hope of finding that same Universal Energy because she insists it is there for all of us.

"If I can find it, you can, too," she would say. The greatest inspiration of all is that her life and her words were one. She was her message.

21

THE EXPERIMENTS OF GANDHI

Nonviolence in the Nuclear Age

John Dear

Gandhi needs no further introduction. John Dear may. As the first Roman Catholic priest to head FOR, John brings a cornucopia of gifts that can only energize and extend FOR's mission. A Jesuit, he has lived and worked in El Salvador, Guatemala, and Northern Ireland, and has traveled widely in the Middle East, Central America, and the Philippines. He has frequently been arrested, and he served nine months in prison for civil disobedience at a U.S. Air Force base in North Carolina. He is a prolific writer whose works include Disarming the Heart, Our God Is Nonviolent, Seeds of Nonviolence, Christ Is with the Poor, Oscar Romero and the Nonviolent Struggle for Justice, *and a substantial work of theology,* The God of Peace: Toward a Theology of Nonviolence, *winner of the Pax Christi Book of the Year Award for 1997. He has also edited books on Dan Berrigan, Henri Nouwen (for which he received the Pax Christi Book Award for 1999), and Mairead Corrigan Maguire. The following article succinctly summarizes the ongoing relevance of Gandhi for our time* (Fellowship, *January/February 1988*).

January 30, 1988, marks the fortieth anniversary of the assassination of Mohandas Gandhi. He died shortly after World War II, after the atomic bombings of Hiroshima and Nagasaki, after India's independence and civil war. He was killed at a prayer service.

What has become of Gandhi's experiments in truth, his rediscovery of nonviolence as the personal and public method for positive social change? What does Gandhi's nonviolent resistance and truth-force mean for North Americans, forty years after his death?

Gandhi never achieved political office. He sought solidarity with the poorest of the poor, and in this powerlessness he found the power of love and truth. "My message is my life," he wrote, and his life was a never-ending series of experiments in truth and nonviolence. "My greatest weapon is prayer," he maintained, and through his steadfast faith and study of the Bhagavad Gita and the Sermon on the Mount, he was able to move mountains. "Truth is God," he realized, and in truth, he found a way to liberation and resistance, the way of nonviolence.

But nonviolence was never simply a tactic. For Gandhi, "nonviolence is a matter of the heart." From his inner unity, through years of discipline and renunciation, Gandhi found the ability to suffer for justice's sake, to refuse to harm others, to go to prison for peace. For his friends in the independence movement, he wrote an essay, "How to Enjoy Jail." Such an essay came as a fruit of inner freedom already realized. Gandhi's nonviolence starts from within and moves outward.

His nonviolence and truth-seeking gave him the strength to claim in all humility, "I have ceased for over forty years to hate anybody. I hold myself to be incapable of hating any being on earth." His willingness to lay down his life for suffering humanity gave birth to tremendous new life in himself and for those around him. With great care and discipline, he discovered new truths, and his discoveries were open to all. "I have not the shadow of a doubt that any man or woman can achieve what I have, if he or she would make the same effort and cultivate the same hope and faith."

Gandhi's sense of experimentation in truth continued through to the last day of his life. He was constantly growing, seeking new ways to pursue the truth of nonviolence in his own heart and therefore in his world. The world of North America has much to learn from Gandhi's experiments. As we race ahead in the mad rush of violence, his message of nonviolence waits calmly to be heard and undertaken anew. Several points may apply to our own North American context as we remember and ponder his life.

Faith was the center of life for Gandhi. Gandhi believed in God, in truth. "What I want to achieve, what I have been striving and pining to achieve these thirty years," he wrote in his autobiography, "is self-realization, to see God face to face. I live and move and have my being in pursuit of this goal. All that I do by way of speaking and writing, and all my ventures in the political field, are directed to this same end." Gandhi saw the face of God in the poorest peasant and in the struggle of nonviolent resistance and love in the public realm. He sought to uncover truth at every turn and found that justice and nonviolence spring from the journey in truth. "You may be sent to the gallows, or put to torture, but if you have truth in you, you will experience an inner joy." Truth, for Gandhi, is the essence of life.

Nonviolence is the essence of truth; one cannot seek truth, Gandhi discovered, and still continue to participate in violence and injustice within one's heart and in the world. Nonviolence is the power of the powerless, the power of God, the only power that overcomes evil, including the evil of the bomb. "Nonviolence is the greatest and most active force in the world. . . . One person who can express nonviolence in life exercises a force superior to all the forces of brutality. . . . Nonviolence cannot be preached. It has to be practiced," he insisted. "If we remain nonviolent, hatred will die as everything does, from disuse."

Gandhi's nonviolence began with prayer, solitude, and fasting. By avoiding power in all its forms of violence and control, and by renouncing his desire for immediate results, Gandhi discovered that one could be reduced to zero. From this ground zero of emptiness, the compassionate love of God—nonviolence—can grow. At this point, Gandhi wrote, the individual becomes "irresistible" and one's nonviolence becomes "all-pervasive."

Gandhi's experiments in truth revealed that the mandate of the Sermon on the Mount—to love one's enemies— is of critical importance. In all of Gandhi's public uses of nonviolence, he always manifested a desire for reconciliation, friendship, with his opponent. In South Africa he showed deep respect for General Smuts, and the two adversaries became fast friends. In India, Gandhi struggled to win over Jinnah, his Muslim opponent, through nonviolent love. His *satyagraha* campaigns began in a community of love and resistance and endeavored to extend that beloved community as far and wide as possible. When in prison, Gandhi befriended his jailers.

Gandhi always taught that "noncooperation with evil is as much a duty as cooperation with good." In order to seek God's kingdom first, Gandhi believed one must dissociate one's self from every form of evil, within and without. His noncooperation campaigns put into public practice the teachings of Jesus: "When someone strikes you on one cheek, turn and offer the other." His willingness to suffer for justice's sake (his apparent cooperation with violence) actually was a total noncooperation with violence. The violence ended there, in Gandhi's own person, as Jesus showed, and Gandhi's noncooperation with evil, his nonviolent resistance, led to the presence of new life and love.

Gandhi learned nonviolence, he confessed, from his wife, Kasturbai. "I learnt the lesson of nonviolence from my wife, when I tried to bend her to my will," Gandhi wrote. "Her determined resistance to my will, on the one hand, and her quiet submission to the suffering my stupidity involved, on the other, ultimately made me ashamed of myself and cured me of my stupidity." Kasturbai taught Mohandas that nonviolence includes feminism, the practice of the equality of the sexes. Gandhi became an advocate of women's rights and maintained that if the world was to make any progress, sexism must be banned and forgotten.

Gandhi always tried to stand with the outcasts of society and to speak up for the rights of the marginalized. In India, such solidarity primarily meant taking the radical, scandalizing public stand on behalf of the so-called untouchables. Gandhi called them *harijans*, or "children of God," and begged his fellow Indians to banish untouchability from their hearts and lives. His message needs to be proclaimed in every part of the world today, including North America. Such solidarity might mean touching the lives of the marginalized in our own society: gays and lesbians, people of color, illegal aliens, the elderly, the mentally handicapped, and AIDS victims.

Gandhi also developed a practical, constructive program to rid India and the world of poverty and injustice. He lived with the poor and taught ways to improve their lives, while always advocating voluntary poverty and simplicity of life. He tried to improve the environment and public sanitation and to encourage the personal responsibility of daily work through the spinning wheel. Gandhi's motto was: "Recall the face of the poorest and the most helpless person whom you have seen and ask yourself if the step you contemplate is going to be of any use to that person. Will he or she be able to gain anything by it?"

In our own day and age Gandhi's lessons of nonviolent resistance are more essential than ever. Perhaps the primary lesson we need to relearn from Gandhi is to choose every day for the rest of our lives, with the gift of our lives, the truth of nonviolence over the lie of nuclear violence. Gandhi's path to nonviolence—the way of the cross—is an invitation to resist the nuclear arms race at its roots, within each of us. The spiritual power of nonviolent love, when sought through prayer, fasting, and discipline, will mean the reversal of the arms race. Such nonviolent love will lead to noncooperation and loving disobedience, and possibly imprisonment and death for some.

But Gandhi believed that there is no such thing as defeat for the person seeking the truth of nonviolence. When one accepts love and nonviolence in one's empty heart, then the doors of life are opened. Everyone is seen as a sister or a brother, an image of God, a child of God. The poor are embraced and welcomed with special warmth and given everything. The truth can be told; forgiveness can be given and accepted; disarmament can begin. Suffering can be accepted willingly and transformed into a gift of love that will bear fruit in humanity. Arrest and imprisonment for nonviolent resistance become doorways to freedom. Death becomes the door to resurrection. Gandhi's nonviolent resistance is based in hope, in a vision like the dream of Martin Luther King Jr. of a new life, a new age, a new world without weapons or fear, in which all will be treated as one, as brothers and sisters, everyone a child of God.

At the beginning of the nuclear age on August 6, 1945, Gandhi wrote, "Unless now the world adopts nonviolence, it will spell certain suicide for humanity. Nonviolence is the only thing the atom bomb cannot destroy." Shortly after the bombing of Hiroshima and Nagasaki, he reflected that the bomb made clear for all the world what war is all about: the mass pursuit of death.

Ultimately, Gandhi's message of nonviolence for North Americans today is a call to resist the nuclear arms race. As the struggle for peace continues, we need to return to Gandhi's *satyagraha* campaigns, to study his discoveries, and to seek ways to apply them with the same effort in our own work to rid the land of weapons and ourselves from the arms race within. "We have to make truth and nonviolence not matters for mere individual practice but for practice by groups and communities and nations," Gandhi wrote. "That, at any rate, is my dream. I shall live and die in trying to realize it."

Nonviolence, the power of the powerless, Gandhi believed, is the power of God, the power of truth and love that goes beyond the physical world into the realm of the spiritual. This power can overcome death, as God revealed through the nonviolence of Jesus, his crucifixion, and subsequent resurrection in the resisting community. In the twentieth century Gandhi sought this power on a public level as no one else in modern times has done.

What Gandhi sought was the spiritual liberation of humanity. He wanted the kingdom of God within each person *to* be realized, and that kingdom to extend throughout humanity so that oppression, injustice, and violence would cease and love and truth would reign. "When the practice of the law (truth and love) becomes universal, God will reign on earth as God does in heaven. Earth and heaven are in us. We know the earth, and we are strangers to the heaven within us."

The life of Mohandas K. Gandhi needs to be explored today with renewed vigor if humanity is to have a future. We need to study his message, his life, and the scriptures that gave him strength. Then, we need to get together with others in our own North American ashrams, base communities of nonviolent resistance, to begin the work of nonviolent love with a deeper commitment. We need to cultivate the spirit of love and truth in our own lives through our own modern-day experiments in love and truth that may lead us to public, loving disobedience to government authority.

One of Gandhi's associates, Asha Devi, was asked by a BBC interviewer: "Don't you think that Gandhi was a bit unrealistic, that he failed to reckon with the limits of our capacities?" With joy, Asha Devi responded, "There are no limits to our capacities."

Gandhi discovered that indeed there are no limits to our capacities. May God give us the strength to undertake new lives of nonviolent love with the same conviction he had.

Part Three

SPIRIT OF PEACE

Models are not enough. There must also be disciplines. Confronting injustice can leave the soul dry and brittle. Love withers. Idealism shrivels, and the hope for meaningful change loses all its vitality. Disciplines are the spiritual calisthenics of social struggle. They are geared to keep the soul wet, elastic, growing. There are a number of such disciplines, from healthy exercise to nutritional eating, to simplified living, to recycling, to stimulating reading. But the one discipline that all our models seem to give highest priority to is prayer. They do not advocate any special form of prayer. It can be Buddhist meditation, Ignatian exercises, transcendental meditation, contemplation of nature, intercessory prayer, reflection, self-collection, study of a sacred scripture, or centering. What seems to matter is that there be pauses in the frenetic pace of struggle, work, chores, and simply getting along. Without these opened windows on eternity we simply burn out or burn up.

Some people throw themselves into social change efforts with no regard for the spiritual cost of their commitment. They fail to recognize this as a form of spiritual masochism, an act of functional atheism. They seem to believe that there is not enough time in the universe for them to stop and water their souls. They become oddly convinced of their indispensability on the battle line. Or they become so obsessed with the wrongs they seek to ameliorate that they disdain the disciplines necessary to keep them going. There is no time for walking, or contemplation, or cooking good food. No time, as Thich Nhat Hanh says in his essay, simply to "be peace." As a woman in Texas once said to me, "You cain't no more give somebody somethin' you ain't got than you can come back from somewhere you ain't been."

Here then are a few reflections on how to catch the spirit of peace. They do not touch on all the disciplines of social struggle, but they hit the most important ones, the ones that most deeply water the soul.

22

HASIDISM
AND THE LOVE OF ENEMIES

Maurice S. Friedman

Maurice S. Friedman was a conscientious objector in the Second World War and a member of FOR. In this essay he demonstrates how Jewish mystical traditions form a basis for Jewish nonviolence (Fellowship, *November 1964*).

The civil rights movement in the United States and in South Africa has made abundantly clear that our current approaches to reconciliation are often unable to meet the demands which the surging movement toward racial equality must place upon those who resist social change. It illustrates too how unsatisfactory, and sometimes tragic it is to leave "nonviolence" in the hands of those who regard "nonviolent resistance" as merely a more effective technique than violence at this moment in history. In the obscure movement of Hasidism—the popular communal mysticism of East European Jewry in the eighteenth and nineteenth centuries—there are hints of an approach to reconciliation that might be more fruitful than the doctrine of turning the other cheek, on the one hand, or that of nonviolence as a pure technique, on the other.

I came to Hasidism as a conscientious objector in the Second World War. For me Hasidism was not a negation but a fulfillment of what had led me toward pacifism and mysticism. In its founder, Israel ben Eliezer (1700-1760) popularly called the Baal-Shem-Tov or Good Master of the Name of God, I found an image of man. Although he did not blot out of my heart the images of Jesus, St. Francis, Gandhi, the Buddha, and Sri Ramakrishna, he captured my devotion in an even more powerful way than they had. The Baal-Shem knew his relationship to God as the meaning and goal of his strivings compared to which no future life was of importance. He did not emphasize mystical exercises, such as I had been concerned with, but wholehearted turning to God. He preferred a passionate opponent to a lukewarm adherent, "for the passionate opponent may come over and bring all his passion with him. But from a lukewarm adherent there is nothing more to be hoped." He turned away from asceticism and mortification of the flesh to the joyful recognition that each person is a child of the King.

After my immersion in the individualistic and world-denying forms of mysticism that I had found in Hinduism, Buddhism, and Christianity, Hasidism spoke to me in compelling accents of a wholehearted service of God that did not mean turning away from my fellowmen and from the world. All that was asked was to do everything one did with one's whole strength—not the denial of self and the extirpation of the passions but the fulfillment of self and the direction of passion in a communal mysticism of humility, love, prayer, and joy. After my concern for techniques of spiritual perfection, I now learned that fulfillment and redemption do "not take place through formulae or through any kind of prescribed and special action," but through the *kavana*, or intention, that one brings to one's every act. The humble love of the *zaddik*, the leader of the Hasidic community, was one that "knows that all is in God and greets God's messengers as trusted friends."

What is unique in the Hasidic approach to reconciliation is that it points the way to seeing justice and love as necessary complements of each other rather than as alternatives between which one must choose. Despite an emphasis on the love of enemies that is stronger than similar passages in the Old Testament, the Hasidic attitude toward justice and love is squarely based upon the Hebrew Bible. The large majority of people in our culture hold the distorted view that the God of the Old Testament is a harsh and wrathful God in contrast to the loving and merciful God of the New. Both Christians and Jews are blocked from a serious engagement with the teaching of social responsibility in the Hebrew Bible by the popular misconception that "an eye for an eye and a tooth for a tooth" represents the spirit of the Old Testament whereas "love thy neighbor as thyself" represents the spirit of the New. Actually *both statements* come from Leviticus. What is more, far from being opposites, they are the indirect and direct statement of the same principle. "An eye for an eye and a tooth for a tooth" *is not* the expression of a vengeful God but a primitive statement of basic social democracy in which no man is held of greater worth than another, because each is created in the image of God. Such equality existed nowhere outside of Israel in the ancient world. Throughout all history, indeed, the natural *inequality of* man has justified razing a whole city to revenge the murder of one privileged man. Countless others have been exterminated with impunity because they were slaves or serfs or members of an "inferior race." "An eye for an eye" is a fundamental conception of social justice. No society has ever got further than this principle in its actual administration of justice (despite all the talk about a higher "law of love"), and many, even today, are still not up to it.

What keeps "an eye for an eye" from deteriorating into an abstract principle that ignores the uniqueness of each man and each situation is "deal lovingly with thy neighbor as one equal to thyself," to use Martin Buber's translation of the familiar commandment. Justice, which regulates the indirect relations of men, and love, which channels the direct, do not oppose, but complement each other. Once the rabbi of Apt shouted "Adulteress!" at a respected woman who came to ask his advice. To this the woman replied, "The Lord of the world has patience with the wicked. . . . He does not disclose their secret to any creature, lest they be ashamed to turn to him. Nor does he hide his face from them. But the rabbi of Apt sits there in his chair and cannot resist revealing at once what the Creator has covered." Commenting on this incident, which was a turning point for the rabbi of Apt, Martin Buber writes:

> It was through error and effort that he arrived at his profound conception of true justice. . . . He learned step by step that human justice as such fails when it attempts to exceed the province of a just social order and encroaches on that of just human relationships. . . . Man should be just within the bounds of his social order, but when he ventures beyond it out on the high seas of human relationships, he is sure to be shipwrecked and then all he can do is to save himself by clinging to love.

The Hasidim, like the prophets and the Talmudists before them, saw God's justice and mercy as united, with the predominance on the side of mercy. "Just as it is man's way and compulsion to sin and sin again and again," said the rabbi of Rizhyn, "so it is God's way and his divine compulsion to forgive and pardon again and again." To be a Hasid, a loyal follower of God, means to love one's fellowmen and even one's enemies, but it would be mistaken to assume from this that Hasidism places no demand on others or that it means self-denial for the sake of others. The love of Hasidism must be distinguished from Christian love, even that so impressively present among the Quakers, by the fact that it is not a spiritualized love but a love of the whole person. By the same token, it is not like that of Dostoyevsky's Christ for the Grand Inquisitor, but one that places a real demand upon the other—the demand of the relationship itself. The "hallowing of the everyday" means making the concrete relations of one's life essential, and real relationship includes both mutuality and passion. Mutuality means that love does not simply flow forth from the loving individual to others; rather, it moves back and forth within the dialogue between them as the fullest expression of that dialogue. Passion means that one does not suppress one's humanity before bringing oneself into relation with others, but on the contrary directs one's "evil urge" into that relationship in such a way that, without losing its force, it ceases to be evil. Hasidism represents a sanctification of the profane in which every natural urge is waiting to be hallowed and the profane itself is just a name for what has not yet become open to the holy. One must serve God with the "evil urge" as well as the good, says the Talmud. The Hasidic rabbi Abraham applies this teaching to the wars of Frederick King of Prussia, who fell on his enemy from the rear rather than directly attacking him: "What is needed is not to strike straight at Evil but to withdraw to the sources of divine power, and from there to circle around Evil, bend it, and transform it into its opposite." This means that evil itself can be redeemed and transformed into the good. True reconciliation from this standpoint does not mean ignoring evil or escaping from it, but confronting it and redeeming it.

Hasidic realism recognizes that true love and true reconciliation cannot be based upon altruism and selflessness and self-denial, but only upon genuine dialogue, real mutual contact, and trust between people. "The motto of life is 'Give and take,'" said Rabbi Yitzhak Eisik. "Everyone must be both a giver and a receiver. He who is not both is as a barren tree." This means that one must demand for himself as well as others. When Rabbi Mendel of Rymanov did not eat his soup because the servant forgot to bring him a spoon, his teacher Rabbi Elimelekh said to him, "Look, one must know enough to ask for a spoon, and a plate too, if need be!" It is a false humility which denies the very ground on which one stands—that of one's created existence as a self whose freedom one can neither absolutize nor surrender. "Everyone must have two pockets, so that he can reach into the one or the other, according to his needs," said Rabbi Bunam. "In his right pocket are to be the words: 'For my sake was the world created,' and in his left: 'I am earth and ashes.'" By the same token Hasidism does not call upon people to be saintly but to be "humanly holy" unto God—in the measure and manner of humans. We approach God not by reaching beyond the human but by becoming human. Therefore, we cannot pray with Jesus, "Lead us not into temptation," except as he means a temptation that will overwhelm us, but rather, "Help us in each new moment of temptation, in each unique moment of presentness, to direct our 'evil urge' to God."

Jesus offered his disciples a counsel of perfection. Paul, in contrast, saw not only temptation but sin as inevitable. In between the teaching that man can overcome temptation altogether and become pure in heart and that which sees man as fallen and sinful is the Hasidic teaching that the daily renewal of creation also means the daily renewal of temptation and with it the strength and the grace to direct that temptation into the service of God through an essential and meaningful relation with the world.

What does Hasidism have specifically to say on the subject of peace? First, that one must begin with oneself. "When a man has made peace within himself, he will be able to make peace in the whole world," Rabbi Bunam taught. Peace in oneself does not mean "peace of mind," however, but peace in one's immediate relations with others—in thought, speech, and action, with wife, children, and servants. This means, too, that one does not set oneself, or even one's nation, as one's own goal. When Martin Buber and the other leaders of Ichud (the Israeli group for Jewish-Arab rapprochement) insist that Zion must be built *bmishpat*, with justice, they have good Hasidic precedent. When God promised to make of Abraham "a great nation," said the rabbi of Apt, the Evil Urge whispered to him: "A great nation—that means power, that means possessions!" But Abraham only laughed at him. "I understand better than you," he said. "A great nation means a people that sanctifies the name of God."

What does this attitude toward peace imply concerning reconciliation? That it is a real mutual building in a concrete situation that takes account of both sides of any conflict and never reduces the conflict to one or another of the two sides or to any "objective" or "universal" point of view from above. Human togetherness is seen by one *zaddik* in the figure of a divine vehicle whose unity must be preserved: "When you see that someone hates you and does you harm, rally your spirit and love him more than before. That is the only way you can make him turn. . . . If your neighbor grows remote from you in spirit, you must approach him more closely than before—to fill out the rift." The wife of Rabbi Yehuda Zevi of Rozdol asked him why he did not say something to the enemies who were out to hurt him but instead did them favors. He replied that the world rests not only upon the righteous man, the *zaddik*, but also "upon him who, in the hour of conflict, reduces himself to nothing, and does not say anything against those who hate him."

Rabbi David of Lelov believed that his most important mission was to keep peace among men and that he could do so even through prayer. "He taught," writes Buber, "that one should not reprimand and exhort persons whom one wishes to turn to God, but associate with them like a good friend, quiet the tumult in their hearts and through love lead them to recognize God."

We must work for reconciliation among the peoples, between the races, between labor and management, but we must also work for it in the undramatic situations of our lives—in the everyday. I once witnessed an example of such reconciliation in connection with the reading of Hasidic tales. In the summer of 1961 I conducted three Buber seminars for the Church of the Fellowship of All Peoples at its ranch in the Valley of the Moon north of San Francisco. As a part of one of these seminars, the members were asked to read Buber's *Tales of the Hasidim* and select one to bring to the group, telling what it meant to them and why they selected it. One woman read to us the tale entitled "Drudgery":

> Rabbi Levi Yitzhak discovered that the girls who knead the dough for the unleavened bread drudged from early morning until late at night. Then he cried aloud to the congregation gathered in the House of Prayer: "Those who hate Israel accuse us of baking the unleavened bread with the blood of Christians. But no, we bake them with the blood of Jews!"

When she had finished reading, she told us that her father, a simple man from a poor background, used to tell her and her sisters about his childhood in the Ukraine and about how all the children in his village were warned not to go near the Jews' quarter for fear of being captured and killed to make blood for the Jewish matzoh at Passover. Her father still believed this millennial superstition that has sprung up again and again from the fear and hatred of the alien. The story of Rabbi Levi Yitzhak struck the woman who read it to us not because she too believed this naive yet tenacious myth but because it removed the fear of the alien that lies at its base. It enabled her to experience the situation from the other side—from the side of Rabbi Levi Yitzhak, of the Jewish girls whom he befriended, and of the Jewish employers whom he called to account!

This "reconciliation in the everyday" is not unlike the dialogical approach to the peace movement that Albert Camus takes in "Neither Victims Nor Executioners":

> Some of us should . . . take on the job of keeping alive, through the apocalyptic historical vista that stretches before us, a modest thoughtfulness which, without pretending to solve everything, will constantly be prepared to give some human meaning to everyday life.

It remains to state in more theoretical form those hints that led us to put forward Hasidism as a new approach to reconciliation. In Hasidism the reality of peace and reconciliation is that of the biblical covenant. Man's task as God's partner in creation is not to work for his own salvation or for harmony with any already existing spiritual order, but it is to create justice and peace in each new situation. By the same token, creation is not seen as already redeemed but constantly in the need of redemption. For Hasidism, the demand of the historical situation prevents that familiar dualism that abandons one part of creation to "strict justice" while trying to raise the other to a purely spiritual plane of love. One may trust in creation, in the "lived concrete," not because it is all "really good," but because only in the meeting with it does one find real life and build real peace. Real peace exists neither within the individual nor in the harmony of the social order but in the meeting between persons, the encounter between group and group. In this meeting alone is it possible for creation to be completed, evil redeemed, conflict reconciled, and hostility overcome.

23

SOCIAL ACTION
AND THE NEED FOR PRAYER

Dorothy Friesen

In this essay, Dorothy Friesen stresses the complementarity that exists between prayer and social struggle. She writes for all those who have found in the nonviolent struggle itself a gateway to the inner life. Exhausted, betrayed by allies, terrified at death threats, gazing into the face of incarnate evil, some have undergone spiritual death. It was then that they opened to something greater, transcendent, by whatever name. For those who have lived through that transformation, Dorothy Friesen offers practical tips for fostering that inner life, giving it the rich nourishment it requires, and restoring us for struggle with joy in our hearts (Fellowship, *July-August 1981*).

People who are deeply involved in social justice work—even those who are religious—have often been suspicious of prayer as belonging to the realm of those pious ones who hide behind words to avoid involvement. But the split between people of prayer and people of action is a false and harmful one, especially for those of us in peace and justice work.

My husband and I were forced to our knees a few years ago when we lived and worked in the Philippines. Each day we had to deal with problems stemming from economics and our class background on a personal and emotional level. Each day we had to face our neighbors: squatters with no secure home who had been pushed off their farmland by the onslaught of multinational agribusiness. They came to the cities to find work, but most were underemployed and unable to afford both food and housing. Needing food, they had to live as squatters where they could. From begged and borrowed material they constructed makeshift houses on marginal, often swampy land, which they filled in themselves with hand-carried garbage and stones. Each day we had to face the violence of people we knew being arrested or "salvaged," a euphemistic term which means that the Philippine military killed them after they were tortured to extort any information they might have. We had to face homeless people sitting beside their bulldozed crops after business, the military, and the government joined forces to evict small rice-and-corn tenants and make way for export crops like bananas and pineapples.

How could we cope with it? How could we respond? We felt powerless in the face of this violence, fueled by the military, with economic and political support from our American government. The objective situation and our own internal longing brought us to this question:

How can we stand before God while walking with the people? We were forced to place ourselves—together with our contradictions, our guilt, and the objective wounds of Philippine society—in the presence of God. Broken, angry, and confused, we held these problems up to the light. But we had hesitations about prayer. We did not want to slip into magic or mail-order prayers, which would simply send up an order to have the goods delivered. Partly, we did not even know what to ask for. We did not know how to pray. We could only offer up our confusion. As we did that, we began to realize that it was not our definition or assessment of the problem which was determinative. When we place ourselves in the presence of God, a transformation takes place. *Who God is* becomes important. Emptying ourselves so that we may take in the person of God becomes the essential thing. It shapes our view of the situation; it shapes the nature of our involvement.

In our groping, painful search we found the writings of Catherine de Hueck Doherty, founder of Madonna House, a lay apostolate for prayer and hospitality. Her book *Poustinia* helped us to understand the need for a desert: a holy quiet place where we could hear God. *Poustinia* is the Russian word for desert, but with many more rich meanings than our English understanding. To "make a *poustinia*" is to go to a quiet, enclosed place with simple food, a Bible, pen, and notebook for at least twenty-four hours of total silence. That experience can cleanse us so that we are prepared to start anew. But it is a special discipline, perhaps better done after building up with short periods of silence daily. Silence can be terrifying.

We were helped along the way, as well, by the example of the Taize Brothers. Founded in Taize, France, during the Second World War by Brother Roger Schutz, these lay ecumenical brothers live simply among the poor, work for their living, and pray together three times a day. Some brothers lived in a little squatter house in the poorest area of the Philippine city where we were. They knew the country and the culture because of their ability to listen. At any time, they were spiritually prepared to go as deep with another person as that person was willing to go. Because they were centered within, they could act as a wedge into the world, pointing to another reality, an alternative.

In our busy, noisy lives, we can hardly imagine the time and space that would allow us the inner centeredness to stand before God. We know that in our modern, alienated society there are many internal and external obstacles to overcome before we can make contact and touch our innermost selves. Often we can't pray because we feel we aren't good enough; or we think we won't have enough discipline to continue; or we have had a fight with our husband or wife, and we know we can't pray before we are reconciled. But this concern carries in it some false understandings of the work and person of God. Doherty writes that Westerners often believe they are not worthy that God should speak to them. "Of course we are not worthy . . . but God still speaks," she writes. Pierre Yves Emery, a member of the Taize Community, offers us a new way of seeing these blockages. "The days during which we experience only a bitter powerlessness to hold ourselves in dignity before God can often be the days when prayer is most authentic, if we offer that powerlessness as an appeal and as confidence."

Another obstacle is the suspicion that prayer is an excuse to do nothing. People who are passionately concerned about what is happening to God's creatures and creation are right to be suspicious of cheap and easy answers. Jesus' prayerful life was neither cheap nor easy.

Throughout church history, saints and mystics have drawn the connection between material wealth and spiritual poverty. St. Ambrose of Milan minced no words: "It was in common and for all alike that the earth was created. Why then, O rich, do you take to yourselves the monopoly of owning land? It is not with your wealth that you give alms to the poor, but with a fraction of their own which you give back, for you are usurping for yourself something meant for the common good of all." St. John Chrysostom connects possessions with war when he writes, "It is because some try to take possession of what belongs to everyone that quarrels and wars break out. It is the poor's wealth of which you are trustees even in cases where you possess it through honest labor or inheritance. . . . And is not the earth the Lord's with all that therein is? Everything which belongs to God is for the use of all."

Economics and a healthy prayer life are deeply interrelated. Praying means readiness to let go of our certainty and to move ahead from where we are now. It demands that we take to the road again and again, leaving our houses and looking forward to a new land. Praying demands the readiness to live a life in which we have nothing to lose, so that we can always begin afresh. Whenever we willingly choose this poverty, we make ourselves vulnerable, but we also become free to see the world as it really is.

Contemplation (as part of prayer) helps us to overcome our great temptation to try to "control" God by making demands and hoping that God will do what we ask. Emery describes contemplation as "digging deep within the self to rediscover human life as it first burst forth, created by God and grafted onto Christ. God in the most inward part of ourselves, his love at the root of our being. It is there that he awaits us."

Although contemplation implies a certain withdrawal and the firm desire to quiet the inner noises, it is not an escape from life. The renunciation of control becomes the sign of God's presence. But going deep within is never disconnected from concern for peacemaking. Brother Roger writes, "One thing is certain. All contact with God leads to one's neighbor."

In our busy world, how do we prepare ourselves for this experience before God? It is important that each of us finds what is appropriate to us, without trying to squeeze ourselves into a prescribed mold. We are freed when we realize that God infinitely respects our sensibilities, our rhythms, and our inner life. After all, God created us in all our variety. Most of us will have to make changes that are essential to our becoming quiet and which are in tension with the way our society functions. We will probably have to trim our schedules in order to make room for quietness. It is possible to have brief relays of prayer in the gaps within our schedules, but sooner or later we will need a longer time to disengage ourselves and leave time for God to fill us.

Each person needs to find his or her own way, but sometimes suggestions of what other people have done can be helpful. A "baby step" is to set aside twenty minutes a day for silence or meditation. It is often helpful if one sits quietly at the same time each day and in the same place. A candle, incense, or a picture can help to focus and bring thoughts together. Sometimes beginning with a biblical passage, an event, or a question can also direct the twenty-minute reflection.

Keeping a journal can help to focus the mind over a period of time. This means not only keeping a record of events but also your reflections on events and dreams, on biblical passages, or on your twenty-minute daily meditation. While we must come to this centeredness ourselves—no one can do it for us— a partner can be helpful, either to sit with us during our meditation time or to check with periodically on the progress of our discipline.

We must always remember that centering and emptying is not done for oneself, for purity, or even to be one with God. Catherine Doherty warns that we must go beyond such motivation and "take upon ourselves the pain of humanity." The uniqueness of this kind of deep prayer for peacemaking is that it is brought into the marketplace. A *poustinia* in the marketplace, says Doherty, is carried within persons who go about their work. She makes the comparison to a pregnant woman who engages in day-to-day life like everyone else, but everyone knows she carries a special life within her. In her being, she is a witness to life.

Once we have let go, we are ready to intercede for others without getting caught in the mail-order syndrome. Overwhelming events or concern for justice action can bring us to prayer, but the movement between contemplation and action goes both ways. Justice action can rise out of the prayer meeting in the local congregation. In fact, that is a better place to root action than in the church bureaucracy or central office. If we pray together with a group, interceding on behalf of some concern, there will surely be some meaningful action that we are called to take. Real prayer is risky in that it demands commitment and responsibility when we speak our concerns out loud.

Praying is the most critical activity we are capable of. For a person who prays is never satisfied with the world of here and now. We know it is possible to enter into dialogue with God and so work at renewing the earth. Prayer can move us to take local action together, but what about larger issues, where we cannot take direct, personal action so immediately? Pierre Yves Emery offers a helpful response:

> If we dare to entrust to the love of God those problems which are vastly beyond our capacities to solve, such as peace or justice, we can do so honestly only in the knowledge that at least on our own level we must be workers for peace and justice. Our prayers must bring us back to the specific, in order to take a large view without being abstract. Our prayers must bring us back to our immediate and concrete responsibilities, as well as to that larger and more indirect relationship which is political and economic. Everything is interrelated, in a tenuous and usually hidden way. Intercessory prayer cannot get along without information on the life of the world.

But Emery adds that it is possible to pray for causes or individuals whom we cannot help personally in any way. How do we pray honestly? He says this: "Relying on the limited but serious involvement that is properly mine, my prayer can legitimately reach out to needs in areas where other men and women are seeking to bring answers." Intercession for events far away emphasizes our unity with others who also work and pray for peace and justice.

When we pray, we open ourselves to the influence of the power which has revealed itself as love. Once touched by this power, we have found a center for ourselves that gives creative distance, so that everything we see and hear and feel can be tested against this source. Prayer means breaking through the veil of existence and allowing ourselves to be led by God's vision. It is this rootedness and being in touch with the source of life that can give hope and energy to our peace-and-justice efforts. Prayer can save us from cynicism in the face of overwhelming odds.

As we receive God in our depths, we come to know that amid all the greed and selfish misuse of people and resources of the good earth, amid frantic effort and failure, there is still another stream of events that goes on. God is letting seeds grow, secretly and mysteriously, to the end that God plans. Through prayer, our inner eye is sharpened so that we can see the future sprouting, growing, and blooming from the seeds that we sow now.

24

ENVISIONING
THE PEACEABLE KINGDOM

Elise Boulding

Elise Boulding is a sociologist of international renown, but she is also a Quaker who listens closely to the "inward teacher." In this article she debunks the sentimental notion that "visualizing peace" by itself will bring in the Peaceable Kingdom. Her focus here is on the ways we can bring our love, our prayers, our creativity, and our energy together so that we are able to make our dreams come true, instead of letting our visions degrade into cynical dystopias (Fellowship, *April–May 1982*).

There has been a splendid kind of thinking going on in relation to the hundredth anniversary of the French mystic and theologian Pierre Teilhard de Chardin. There have been meetings and seminars and books to celebrate Teilhard de Chardin's extraordinary vision of the divinization of the planet. Teilhard, visioning within the Catholic tradition, saw all matter becoming spirit and the planet becoming the body of Christ.

There is a direct correspondence between our vision of the Peaceable Kingdom, and of the world becoming the Holy Mountain of Zion, where none shall hurt or destroy. This is a vision of the evolutionary process as creating one body, mind, and spirit, which becomes God's handiwork and God's garden. However, there is also an element of magical thinking that creeps into this kind of visioning, the thought that the image will simply materialize. Many people are attracted to this Teilhardian vision of the planet becoming divinized. "Isn't it great!" they say. "We can meet and celebrate it." Such people are separating out, or simply leaving to one side, the issue of *how* it will come about. The way we translate the visioning into practice is the issue that confronts us. If we limit it to blueprinting the intellectual strategy, or if we simply envision the Peaceable Kingdom in our spiritual fantasy life, we can go very far astray.

This century has been the century of Utopias. I was born in 1920, and I grew up believing that science, technology, and the development of humanitarian impulse were going to create a society in which war and poverty and disease would be abolished. I really believed that as a child. Everyone in my generation was taught this in school. That conviction is the basis on which everything that has happened in this century has happened. We haven't seriously critiqued the assumptions that led us to where we are now. We have only said, "Isn't it awful how we've misused science?" But the problem goes much deeper than that. We've never thought out how we should really link our capacity for scientific work with our capacity for prayer and our capacity for love.

Many of you are familiar with the work of Martin Buber. His greatest contribution has been his teaching about the "I-Thou" relationship and the distinction he has drawn between the I-Thou and the "I-It." The I-Thou relationship is, of course, the relationship between the human being and the creator; for Buber it is the model of all relationships. Making space is at the very heart of Buber's concept of relationship. There must be space so that you can reverence the other as a whole, remarkable, unique being. That is how we reverence our creator and each part of creation, even extending to inanimate objects. We can reverence a stone, a tree, soil, a pond.

Peace and social justice movements, the environmental movement, are all grounded in this attitude of reverencing, of making space so that the other can *be*. Martin Buber realized that you can't just go around reverencing all the time, however. Reverencing doesn't feed people. The I-It relationship, which treats the other as an object, represents an instrumental approach to reality.

You see what is there and choose how to use it. It is tempting to say that the I-Thou relationship represents all the good, and the I-It all the bad, but it's not that simple. It is in the I-It relationship that we learn the mental discipline of analysis, of identifying elements of problems, of figuring out possible recombinations of pieces of the familiar into something new. We are continually confronted with the need to "use" ourselves and to "use" others. The narrow ridge that we have to walk is where the I-It and the I-Thou meet, where our acts of relationship partake of both sets of qualities.

There is another element in the visioning process, a kind of free-flow thinking, which I call spiritual daydreaming. Spiritual daydreaming is a linking of the mind and the heart and the spirit in a looking "out there" to see what we could become. That work of looking ahead to what the whole would be like, as contrasted to what we are doing in our particular moment, in our particular project, is what gives the Teilhard de Chardin centennial such importance. In the centennial celebration the insistence has been on looking at the planet as a whole. Most of us are working in our little corner, on our little piece of the planet. We must do that kind of global daydreaming which Teilhard wrote about, but we must anchor it in what we know about the human possibility.

Visioning is one of the basic things we do, like eating, breathing, walking, working. It is a built-in part of human functioning. As far back as we have written records, we find myths and legends about a concept we may call the peaceable garden. Nomadic peoples who live in the world's deserts and arid lands all have stories of green and pleasant places where trees and flowers grow, fresh waters flow, and people live in peace. The vision of shared abundance is a vision of a loving, caring community. There is no violence, and there is peace.

Some of the basic issues we are concerned about, including peace, social justice, and environmentalism, can be traced back to the earliest legends that we can find. The peoples who created these legends were sometimes very violent in their intertribal relations. The Homeric warriors had the Elysian fields as part of their mental imagery. When they had finished with fighting, they would go off to the Elysian fields, take off their swords and shields, and hang them in the trees. They would put the war horses out to pasture and walk in the meadows talking philosophy and quoting poetry. This imagery of a sharing society is something that human beings seem to produce, whatever the cultural tradition.

What is important for us, since some of our thinking must be on a global scale, is to do more conscious affirming of the intentional experiments in creating peaceable gardens that exist today around the world. I was profoundly moved by an eyewitness account of refugee camps in which the Saharawi people from the Spanish Sahara are living under the protection of the Algerian government. The Moroccan government is literally trying to exterminate the Saharawi and take over the country. Algeria's role has been to offer the Saharawis refuge; 150,000 of them are living in camps just inside Algeria.

This is desert land. There is nothing there. It's very cold in winter; the winds blow all the time. There is no water, and little sun except in summer, when it is hot. It's the grimmest kind of environment one can imagine for human survival. In the years from 1976 to the present, the Saharawi have gone from being a people that were dying out, with children dying by the hundreds every day, to being a vigorous, healthy society. One hundred and fifty thousand people have reorganized themselves in their camp setting into a condition of health and social purpose. They are organized by provinces, corresponding to their provinces back in their home country. Drawing on all their indigenous knowledge, they have created in the windy desert the kind of society they hope to re-create when they can go back to their own country. They have done it under incredible conditions of difficulty and suffering because they have a vision of their own future society as a sharing, peaceable one. Instead of killing each other for the scanty food supplies, they have built up the physical and spiritual health of the whole people.

The re-creation of community, drawing on traditional religious ideals, is an important phenomenon in our time. In India we have the Gandhian re-creation of the image of Sarvodaya, the sharing community that seeks the welfare of all. In our own time we can see the building of mini–peaceable kingdoms in a number of places. They are springing up where a great deal of hurt has been experienced. In each case they are anchored in a deep religious tradition of that part of the world. When we are talking about a global vision of a disarmed world—a world without weapons—then we have to know what our brothers and sisters have been able to create in the way of nonviolent sharing communities under great hardships in many parts of the world. Practicality links with spirituality. The practice of community prayer, for example, always precedes a Shramadana community work project. Villagers assemble and become inwardly gathered. When they go forth to begin project activity, they go forth in a centered spirit because they have visioned the whole. Affirming the whole chain of events has to be a central aspect of our own visioning process.

So far I have pointed out that we have to bring more parts of our own being, our spiritual intuition, our capacity to love, our capacity to analyze, and our daydreaming talents together in a visioning process. Now I'd like to say something about a disciplined use of those elements on behalf of the specific goal of a world without arms. This is one thing that is truly totally lacking in our present society—in our world society. Look at any intellectual tradition. Look at the good work among the community of peace researchers, including particularly the people with whom I have been working on the federal commission to bring proposals for a National Peace Academy. One of the things we hope to do in a peace academy is to train people in alternative approaches to problems. (One of the justifications for military action is that there are no workable political solutions.) We want people to have the skills to enter into a conflictual situation and bring together the ingredients for a solution that enhances the well-being of both parties.

We have recruits undergoing training to operate in certain kinds of high-conflict settings, and to engage in certain kinds of political strategy, but we do not have any source in the modern world for a coherent image of how a society might be structured without weapons. We simply don't have it. It is rather obvious, once pointed out, that you can't work for something you can't visualize. We all know how important visualization is in our own personal planning. In that happy period of life when one is planning to marry, there is a great deal of visioning as to what married life is going to be like. Then one comes to the period where children are expected. There is visioning about what we are going to do. It is not all visioning; part of it is planning. A lot of it is daydreaming. This is a kind of positive thinking that is very important.

We generally use the term *daydreaming* to belittle the idea of people making mental images of the great things that are going to happen to them personally. This undercuts the possibility of social daydreaming, but social daydreaming is a very good thing to do. We do it for our families all the time. If we are involved in a community project, we engage in a visualizing of the possible outcomes. We *know* what we are working for. Strangely, in the peace movement we haven't got the foggiest notion of what we are working for when we talk about a world without war. What would such a world look like? No one is prepared to say. The reason no one is prepared to say is that we haven't harnessed this quadruple set of human talents—mind, spirit, heart, and fantasy— to the task of imaging interrelationships between social elements in a world without weapons.

It is extraordinarily difficult to do something that has never been done before. Once it has been done, it may become an obviously good thing to do, but the first time it's hard. We all know that. We have all been first-timers in something. The first futures invention workshop about a world without weapons was held in October 1981 in Yulan, New York. The workshop was developed by Warren Ziegler as an approach to a number of other social problems. Now we are applying it to the visualization of a world without weapons. Other types of futures invention workshops have been addressed to problems like, for example, prison abolition. If you design a community to function without prisons, then a group of people who have been involved with the existing prison system could sit down and say, "What would this part of New York State look like without prisons? There are no prisoners, and no guards. The old prison buildings are still there, used for something else. OK. What else would be useful? What are the formerly imprisoned doing? What has happened to the economic life of the community? What about the family life, civic and cultural life?"

In other words, we have to account for every aspect of life, for every sector of society, every set of roles. The device is the same, whatever specific future goal you choose. That's what we are doing now with disarmament. We're saying that there are no weapons in the year 2020. Once the fulfillment date has been set, we work from that. You may say that it can never be done by the year 2020, but it doesn't matter. In the exercise, it has happened. You have to report what's out there. You have to describe a world that you'd want to live in, that deals with its problems effectively. If it happened in 2020, then what happened in 2019? Then you begin writing history from the future back to the present. But given the magnitude of a weaponless world, you have to work it out according to your thesis. You have to draw on possibilities in a variety of countries, a variety of population sectors, paying attention to the interrelationships between the family, the economy, the school district, the voting system. Don't leave anything out. What happens in this kind of exercise is that we perceive connections we do not normally see. We develop images of strategies we never thought of.

Think of how we work in the peace movement and in all our actions and roles. We are always acting out of the present but we never get feedback about the effectiveness of what we do. Nothing happens. During the Vietnam war, university students got very excited and put a lot of time into public demonstrations. Once the University of Colorado students seized the bridge which carried the traffic from Denver to Boulder and stopped traffic cold for twelve hours. It was quite a dramatic thing and caused headlines all over the United States. Teachers like myself supported the students. Of course, they were carried off the bridge in the end, but they felt enormous satisfaction. The next day they went back to their usual activities. After a few such events, they became impatient. "Look, we've been working on the Vietnam withdrawal for three months and nothing has happened yet," they complained.

In a sense, that is the plight of all of us. We have been working for years, and nothing has happened yet! But those students on the bridge could not describe the world they hoped to bring about, and neither can we. No wonder our strategies get stale! We try the same old things with no sense of what the criteria are for nearing a goal because there is no real visualization of the goal itself.

I am not proposing a static Utopian depiction for the peace movement. I am suggesting that we return to a long-forgotten tradition of visualizing the good society and exploring what the visualizations themselves might teach us about strategies for the present. Fred Polak, the author of the macro-historical *Image of the Future*, says that twentieth-century humans have lost their capacity to visualize a future different from the present, and that only by reconstituting our visioning capacity can we make any meaningful future possible for the human race.

I believe he is right. I believe that focusing on what the social order might look like if we handled conflict without weapons is a critical part of the task of imaging any future at all. I would welcome your joining me in this work of reaching into the future and letting the inward teacher help us reconstruct the Peaceable Kingdom. Only when we can in some sense visualize that future can we find the path to it.

25

TAKING HEART

Spiritual Exercises from Social Activists

Joanna Macy

With the end of the Cold War and its sense of apocalyptic doom, most people no longer contemplate their own destruction in nuclear war. But there are other threats no less dangerous, if not as fast acting: the spread of pesticides, global warming, acid rain, nuclear spills and meltdowns, the black market for uranium and plutonium, illicit drugs, and a simply unthinkable number of deaths from malnutrition in children under five (thirty-five thousand a day). As we see species of animals and birds and sea creatures going extinct, something in us dies with them. There is a cumulative loss of beauty, of the sheer exuberance of nature's prodigality. Sensitive persons can scarcely avoid a kind of cosmic sadness that must be addressed. In this essay, Joanna Macy guides us through a series of exercises that can provide the deepening of soul that is required if one is to continue working for justice, in season and out (Fellowship, *July-August 1982*).

To heal our society, our psyches must heal as well. The military, social, and environmental dangers that threaten us do not come from sources outside the human heart; they are reflections of it, mirroring the fears, greeds, and hostilities that separate us from ourselves and each other. For our sanity and our survival, therefore, it appears necessary to engage in spiritual as well as social change, to merge the inner with the outer paths. But how, in practical terms, do we go about this?

Haunted by the desperate needs of our time and beset, as many of us are, by more commitments than we can easily carry, we can wonder where to find the time and energy for spiritual disciplines. Few of us feel free to take to the cloister or the *zafu* to seek personal transformation.

Fortunately, we do not need to withdraw from the world or spend long hours in solitary prayer or meditation to begin to wake up to the spiritual power within us. The activities and encounters of our daily lives can serve as the occasion for that kind of discovery. I would like to share some simple exercises that can permit that to happen.

I often share these mental practices in the course of my workshops. Participants who have found them healing, energizing, and easy to use in their daily activities urged me to make them more widely available. I have been reluctant to put them in writing; they are best shared orally, in personal interaction. This is especially true of these forms of what I call *social mysticism*, where the actual physical presence of fellow beings is used to help us break through to deeper levels of spiritual awareness.

The four exercises offered here—on death, compassion, mutual power, and mutual recognition—happen to be adapted from the Buddhist tradition. As part of our planetary heritage, they belong to us all. No belief system is necessary, only a readiness to attend to the immediacy of one's own experiencing. They will be most useful if read slowly with a quiet mind (a few deep breaths help), and if put directly into practice in the presence of others.

MEDITATION ON DEATH

Most spiritual paths begin with the recognition of the transiency of human life. Medieval Christians honored this in the mystery play *Everyman*. Don Juan, the Yaqui sorcerer, taught that the enlightened warrior walks with death at his shoulder. To confront and accept the inevitability of our dying releases us from attachments, frees us to live boldly, alert and appreciative.

An initial meditation on the Buddhist path involves reflection on the twofold fact that "death is certain" and "the time of death, uncertain." In our world today, the thermonuclear bomb, serving in a sense as a spiritual teacher, does that meditation for us, for we all know now that we can die together at any moment, without warning. When we deliberately let the reality of that possibility surface in our consciousness, it can be painful, of course, but it also helps us rediscover some fundamental truths about life. It jolts us awake to life's vividness, its miraculous quality as something given unearned, heightening our awareness of its beauty and the uniqueness of each object, each being.

As an occasional practice in daily life: *Look at the person you encounter (stranger or friend). Let the realization arise in you that this person may die in a nuclear war. Keep breathing. Observe that face, unique, vulnerable . . . those eyes still can see; they are not empty sockets . . . the skin is still intact . . . Become aware of your desire, as it arises, that this person be spared such suffering and horror, feel the strength of that desire . . . keep breathing . . . Let the possibility arise in your consciousness that this may be the person you happen to be with when you die . . . that face the last you see . . . that hand the last you touch . . . it might reach out to help you then, to comfort, to give water. Open to the feelings for this person that surface in you with the awareness of this possibility. Open to the levels of caring and connection it reveals in you.*

BREATHING THROUGH

Our time assails us with painful information about threats to our future and the present suffering of our fellow beings. We hear and read of famine, torture, poisonous wastes, the arms race, animals and plants dying off. Out of self-protection, we all put up some degree of resistance to this information; there is fear that might overwhelm us if we let it in, that we might shatter under its impact or be mired in despair. Many of us block our awareness of the pain of our world because our culture has conditioned us to expect instant solutions: "I don't think about nuclear war (or acid rain) because there is nothing I can do about it." With the value our society places on optimism, our contemplation of such fearful problems can cause us to feel isolated, and even a bit crazy. We tend to close them out—and thereby go numb.

Clearly, the distressing data must be dealt with if we are to respond and survive. But how to do this without falling apart? In my own struggle with despair, it seemed at first that I must either block out the terrible information or be shattered by it. I wondered if there was not a third alternative to going numb or going crazy. The practice of "breathing through" helped me find it.

Basic to most spiritual traditions, as well as to the systems view of the world, is the recognition that we are not separate, isolated entities, but integral and organic parts of the vast web of life. As such, we are like neurons in a neural net, through which flow currents of awareness of what is happening to us, as a species and as a planet. In that context the pain we feel for our world is a living testimony to our interconnectedness with it. If we deny this pain, we become like blocked and atrophied neurons, deprived of life's flow and weakening the larger body in which we take being. But if we let it move through us, we affirm our belonging; our collective awareness increases. We can open to the pain of the world in confidence that it can neither shatter nor isolate us, for we are not objects that can break. We are resilient patterns within a vaster web of knowing.

Because we have been conditioned to view ourselves as separate, competitive, and therefore fragile entities, it takes practice to relearn this kind of resilience. A good way to begin is by practicing simple openness, as in the exercise of "breathing through," adapted from an ancient Buddhist meditation for the development of compassion.

Relax. Center on your breathing . . . visualize your breath as a stream flowing up through your nose, down through windpipe, lungs. Take it down through your lungs and, picturing a hole in the bottom of your heart, visualize the breath-stream passing through your heart and out through that hole to reconnect with the larger web of life around you. Let the breath-stream, as it passes through you, appear as one loop within that vast web, connecting you with it . . . keep breathing . . .

Now open your awareness to the suffering that is present in the world. Drop for now all defenses and open to your knowledge of that suffering. Let it come as concretely as you can . . . concrete images of your fellow being in pain and need, in fear and isolation, in prisons, hospitals, tenements, hunger camps . . . no need to strain for these images, they are present to you by virtue of our interexistence. Relax and just let them surface, breathe them in . . . the vast and countless hardships of our fellow humans, and of our animal brothers and sisters as well, as they swim the seas and fly the air of this ailing planet. Breathe in that pain like a dark stream, up through your nose, down through your trachea, lungs, and heart, and out again into the world net . . . you are asked to do nothing for now, but let it pass through your heart . . . keep breathing . . . be sure that stream flows through and out again; don't hang on to the pain . . . surrender for now to the healing resources of life's vast web . . .

With Shantideva, the Buddhist saint, we can say, "Let all sorrows ripen in me." We help them ripen by passing them through our hearts . . . making good rich compost out of all that grief . . . so we can learn from it, enhancing our larger, collective knowing . . .

If you experience an ache in the chest, a pressure within the rib cage, that is all right. The heart that breaks open can contain the whole universe. Your heart is that large. Trust it. Keep breathing.

This guided meditation serves to introduce the process of breathing through, which, once experienced, becomes useful in daily life in the many situations that confront us with painful information. By breathing through the bad news, rather than bracing ourselves against it, we can let it strengthen our sense of belonging in the larger web of being. It helps us remain alert and open, whether reading the newspaper, receiving criticism, or simply being present to a person who suffers.

For activists working for peace and justice, and those dealing most directly with the griefs of our time, the practice helps prevent burnout. Reminding us of the collective nature of both our problems and our power, it offers a healing measure of humility. It can also save us from self-righteousness. For when we can take in our world's pain, accepting it as the price of our caring, we can let it inform our acts without needing to inflict it as a punishment on others who are, at the moment, less involved.

THE GREAT BALL OF MERIT

Compassion, which is grief in the grief of others, is but one side of the coin. The other side is joy in the joy of others—which in Buddhism is called *muditha*. To the extent that we allow ourselves to identify with the sufferings of other beings, we can identify with their strengths as well. This is very important for our own sense of adequacy and resilience, because we face a time of great challenge that demands of us more commitment, endurance, and courage than we can ever dredge up out of our individual supply. We can learn to draw on the other neurons in the net, and to view them, in a grateful and celebrative faction, as so much "money in the bank."

The concept here resembles the Christian notion of grace. Recognizing our own limitations, we cease to rely solely on individual strength and open up to the power that is beyond us and can flow through us. The Buddhist "Ball of Merit" is useful in helping us see that this power or grace is not dependent upon belief in God but operates as well through our fellow beings. In so doing, it lets us connect with each other more fully and appreciatively than we usually do. It is most helpful to those of us who have been socialized in a competitive society, based on a win-lose notion of power. "The more you have, the less I have." Conditioned by that patriarchal paradigm of power, we can fall prey to the stupidity of viewing the strengths or good fortune of others as a sign of our own inadequacy or deprivation. The Great Ball of Merit is a healthy corrective to envy. It brings us home, with a vast sense of ease, to our capacity for mutual enjoyment.

The practice takes two forms. The one closer to the ancient Buddhist meditation is this:

Relax and close your eyes, relax into your breathing. Open your awareness to the fellow beings who share with you this planet-time . . . in this room . . . this neighborhood . . . this town . . . open to all those in this country . . . and in other lands . . . let your awareness encompass all beings living now in your world. Opening now to all time as well, let your awareness encompass all beings who ever lived . . . of all races and creeds and walks of life, rich, poor, kings and beggars, saints and sinners . . . like successive mountain ranges, the vast vistas of these fellow beings present themselves to your mind's eye . . . Now open yourself to the knowledge that in each of these innumerable lives some act of merit was performed. No matter how stunted or deprived the life, there was a gesture of generosity, a gift of love, an act of valor or self-sacrifice . . . on the battlefield or workplace, hospital or home . . . From each of these beings in their endless multitudes arose actions of courage, kindness, of teaching and healing. Let yourself see these manifold and immeasurable acts of merit . . . as they arise in the vistas of your inner eye, sweep them together . . . sweep them into a pile in front of you . . . use your hands . . . pile them up . . . pile them into a heap . . . pat them into a ball. It is the Great Ball of Merit . . . hold and weigh it in your hands . . . rejoice in it, knowing that no act of goodness is ever lost. It remains ever and always a present resource . . . a resource for the transformation of life . . . and now, with jubilation and gratitude, you turn that great ball . . . turn it over . . . over . . . into the healing of our world.

As we can learn from modern science and picture in the holographic model of reality, our lives interpenetrate. In the fluid tapestry of space-time there is at root no distinction between self and other. The acts and intentions of others are like seeds that can germinate and bear fruit through our own lives, as we take them into awareness and dedicate, or "turn over," that awareness to our empowerment. Thoreau, Gandhi, Martin Luther King Jr., Dorothy Day, and the nameless heroes and heroines of our own day, all can be part of our Ball of Merit, on which we can draw for inspiration and endurance. Other traditions feature notions similar to this, such as the "cloud of witnesses" of which St. Paul spoke, or the Treasury of Merit in the Catholic church.

The second, more workaday, version of the Ball of Merit meditation helps us open to the power of others. It is in direct contrast to the commonly accepted, patriarchal notion of power as something personally owned and exerted over others. The exercise prepares us to bring expectant attention to our encounters with other beings, to view them with fresh openness and curiosity as to how they can enhance our Ball of Merit. We can play this inner game with someone opposite us on the bus or across the bargaining table. It is especially useful when dealing with a person with whom we may be in conflict.

What does this person add to my Great Ball of Merit? What gifts of intellect can enrich our common store? What reserves of stubborn endurance can she or he offer? What flights of fancy or powers of love lurk behind those eyes? What kindness or courage hides in those lips, what healing in those hands?

Then, as with the breathing-through exercise, we open ourselves to the presence of these strengths, inhaling our awareness of them. As our awareness grows, we experience our gratitude for them and our capacity to enhance and partake . . .

Often we let our perceptions of the powers of others make us feel inadequate. Alongside an eloquent colleague we can feel inarticulate; in the presence of an athlete we can feel weak and clumsy. In the process, we can come to resent both ourself and the other person. In the light of the Great Ball of Merit, however, the gifts and good fortunes of others appear not as judgments, putdowns, or competing challenges, but as resources we can honor and take pleasure in. We can learn to play detective, spying out treasures for the enhancement of life from even the unlikeliest material. Like air and sun and water, they form part of our common good.

In addition to releasing us from the mental cramp of envy, this spiritual practice—or game—offers two other rewards. One is pleasure in our own acuity, as our merit-detecting ability improves. The second is the response of others, who—while totally ignorant of the game we are playing—sense something in our manner that invites them to move more openly into the person they can be.

LEARNING TO SEE EACH OTHER

This exercise is derived from the Buddhist practice of the Brahmaviharas; it is also known as the Four Abodes of the Buddha, which are loving-kindness, compassion, joy in the joy of others, and equanimity. Adapted for use in a social context, it helps us to see each other more truly and experience the depths of our interconnections.

In workshops I offer this as a guided meditation, with participants sitting in pairs facing each other. At its close I encourage them to proceed to use it, or any portion they like, as they go about the business of their daily lives. It is an excellent antidote to boredom, when our eye falls on another person, say on the subway. It charges that idle movement with beauty and discovery. It also is useful when dealing with people whom we are tempted to dislike or disregard; it breaks open our accustomed ways of viewing them. When used like this, as a meditation in action, one does not, of course, gaze long and deeply into the other's eyes, as in the guided exercise. A seemingly casual glance is enough.

The guided, group form goes like this:

Sit in pairs. Face each other. Stay silent. Take a couple of deep breaths, centering yourself and exhaling into each other's eyes. If you feel discomfort or an urge to laugh or look away, just note that embarrassment with patience and gentleness toward yourself and come back, when you can, to your partner's eyes. You may never see this person again: the opportunity to behold the uniqueness of this particular human being is given to you now.

As you look into this being's eyes, let yourself become aware of the powers that are there . . . open yourself to awareness of the gifts and strengths and the potentialities in this being . . . Behind those eyes are unmeasured reserves of ingenuity and endurance, wit and wisdom. There are gifts there, of which even this person is unaware. Consider what these untapped powers can do for the healing of our planet and the relishing of our common life . . . As you consider that, let yourself become aware of your desire that this person be free from fear. Let yourself experience how much you want this being to be free from anger . . . and free from greed . . . and free from sorrow . . . and the causes of suffering. Know that what you are now experiencing is the great loving-kindness. It is good for building a world.

Now, as you look into those eyes, let yourself become aware of the pain that is there. There are sorrows accumulated in that life's journey . . . There are failures and losses, griefs and disappointments beyond the telling. Let yourself open to them, open to that pain . . . to hurts that this person may never have shared with another being. What you are now experiencing is the great compassion. It is good for the healing of our world.

As you look into those eyes, open to the thought of how good it would be to make common cause . . . consider how ready you might be to work together . . . to take risks in a joint venture . . . imagine the zest of that, the excitement and laughter of engaging together on a common project . . . acting boldly and trusting each other. As you open to that possibility, what you open to is the great wealth: the pleasure in each other's powers, the joy in each other's joy.

Lastly, let your awareness drop deep, deep within you like a stone, sinking below the level of what words or acts can express . . . breathe deeply and quietly . . . open your consciousness to the deep web of relationship that underlies and interweaves all experience, all knowing. It is the web of life in which you have taken being and in which you are supported. Out of that vast web you cannot fall . . . no stupidity or failure, no personal inadequacy, can ever sever you from that living web. For that is what you are . . . and what has brought you into being . . . feel the assurance of that knowledge. Feel the great peace . . . rest in it. Out of that great peace, we can venture everything. We can trust. We can act.

In doing this exercise we realize that we do not have to be particularly noble or saintlike in order to wake up to the power of our oneness with other beings. In our time that simple awakening is the gift the Bomb holds for us.

For all its horror and stupidity, the Bomb is also the manifestation of an awesome spiritual truth—the truth about the hell we create for ourselves when we cease to learn how to love. Saints, mystics, and prophets throughout the ages saw that law; now *all* can see it and none can escape its consequences. So we are caught now in a narrow place where we realize that Moses, Lao-Tzu, the Buddha, Jesus, and our own inner hearts were right all along; and we are as scared and frantic as cornered rats and as dangerous. But the Bomb, if we let it, can turn that narrow cul-de-sac into a birth canal, pressing and pushing us through the dark pain of it until we are delivered into . . . what? Love seems too weak a word. It is, as St. Paul said, "the glory that shall be revealed in us." It stirs in us now.

For us to regard the Bomb (or the dying seas, the poisoned air) as a monstrous injustice to us would suggest that we never took seriously the injunction to love. Perhaps we thought all along that Gautama and Jesus were kidding, or their teachings meant only for saints. But now we see, as an awful revelation, that we are *all* called to be saints—not good necessarily, or pious, or devout—but saints in the sense of just loving each other. One wonders what terrors this knowledge must hold that we fight it so, and flee from it in such pain. Can it be that the Bomb, by which we can extinguish all life, can tell us this? Can force us to face the terrors of love? Can be the occasion for our birth?

It is in that possibility that we can take heart. Even in confusion and fear, with all our fatigues and petty faults, we can let that awareness work in and through our lives. Such simple exercises as those offered here can help us do that, and to begin to see ourselves and each other with fresh eyes.

Let me close with the same suggestion that closes our workshops. It is a practice that is a corollary to the earlier death meditation, where we recognize that the person we meet may die in a nuclear war. Look at the next person you see. It may be lover, child, co-worker, postman, or your own face in the mirror. Regard him or her with the recognition that:

This person before me may be instrumental in saving us from nuclear war. In this person are gifts for the healing of our planet. In this person are powers that can redound to the joy of all beings.

26

SAYING NO TO DEATH

Henri J. M. Nouwen

Henri Nouwen (1932-96), a Dutch-born priest who spent most of his life in North America, was one of the most popular spiritual writers of his time. In dozens of books he invited his readers to enter into a more intimate relationship with God. But he always insisted on the relationship between spiritual life and compassion for a suffering world. This article is an excerpt from a manuscript on peacemaking. The full text was published posthumously in The Road to Peace: Writings on Peace and Justice, *edited by John Dear* (Fellowship, *September 1985*).

Not long ago I visited an exclusive preparatory school. Most of the boys and girls came from well-to-do families and all of them were very bright. They were friendly, good-mannered, and ambitious; it was not hard for me to imagine many of them holding important positions, driving big cars, and living in large homes within fifteen or twenty years.

One evening I joined these students in watching a movie in the school's auditorium. It was *The Blues Brothers*. I could not believe what I saw and heard. Not only was the screen filled for more than an hour with the wild destruction of supermarkets, houses, and cars, the auditorium rang with the excited cries and shouts of these well-mannered, bright young people. Watching the total devastation of all the symbols of their own prosperous lives, they yelled and screamed as if their team had won a championship. As cars were smashed, houses put to fire, and high-rises pulled down, my excited neighbor told me that this was one of the most expensive "funny" movies ever made. Millions of dollars had been spent to film a few hours of what I considered to be death. No human beings were killed, but nothing human beings made was left untouched.

What does it mean when young, ambitious Americans are being entertained with millions of dollars worth of destruction in a world where many people die from fear, lack of food, and ever-increasing violence? Are these the future leaders of a generation whose primary task is to prevent a nuclear war and stop the arms race?

I tell this seemingly innocent event to point to the fact that a large portion of contemporary entertainment is fascinated with violence and death. Huge amounts of money are spent on films and books in which death and destruction are the major themes. Long hours of our lives are spent filling our minds with images not only of disintegrating skyscrapers and cars, but also of shootings, torture, and other manifestations of human violence. Once I met a Vietnam veteran on an airplane. He told me that he had seen so many people killed on television that it had been hard for him to believe that those whom *he* killed would not stand up again to act in the next movie. Death had become unreal. Vietnam woke him up to the truth that death is real and final and very ugly.

When I am honest with myself, I have to confess that I, too, am often seduced by the titillating power of death. I look with open eyes and open mouth as stunt pilots, motorcyclists, and car racers put their lives at risk in their desire to break a record or perform a dazzling feat. In this respect I am little different from the thousands of Romans who were entertained by the life-and-death games of the gladiators, or from the crowds who in the past and even the present are attracted to places of public execution.

It is important to note that any suggestion that these real or imagined death games are healthy ways to deal with our "death instinct" or "aggressive fantasies" needs to be discarded as unfounded. Acting out death wishes, either in fact or in the imagination, can never bring us any closer to peace, whether it is peace of heart or peace in our life together.

Our preoccupation with death, however, goes far beyond real or imagined involvement in physical violence. We find ourselves involved over and over again in much less spectacular, but not less destructive, death games. During my visit to Nicaragua and my subsequent lectures and conversations in the United States about the Nicaraguan people, I become increasingly aware of how quick judgments, stereotyped remarks, and verbal rejections can make people and nations into distorted caricatures, thus offering a welcome pretense for destruction and war. By talking about Nicaragua as a land subject to the evils of Marxist-Leninist ideology, totalitarianism, and atheism, we create in our minds a monster that urgently needs to be attacked and destroyed. Whenever I spoke about the people of Nicaragua, their deep Christian faith, their struggle for some economic independence, their desire for better health care and education, and their hope that they may be left alone to determine their own future, I found myself confronted with these deadening stereotypes. People would say: "But shouldn't we be aware that Russia is trying to get a foothold there and that we are increasingly threatened by the dark powers of communism?" Such remarks made me see that long before we start a war, kill people, or destroy nations, we have already killed our enemies mentally, by making them into abstractions with which no real, intimate human relationship is possible. When men, women and children who eat, drink, sleep, play, work, and love each other as we do have been perverted into an abstract communist evil that we are called—by God—to destroy, then war has become inevitable.

Saying no to death therefore starts much earlier than saying no to physical violence, whether in war or entertainment. It requires a deep commitment to the words of Jesus: "Do not judge." It requires a no to all the violence of heart and mind. I personally find it one of the most difficult disciplines to practice. Constantly I find myself making up my mind about somebody else: "He cannot be taken seriously. She is really just asking for attention. They are rabble rousers who only want to cause trouble." These judgments are a form of moral killing. I label my fellow human beings, put them in some fixed category at a safe distance from me. By judging others, I take false burdens upon myself. By my judgments I divide my world into those who are good and those who are evil, and thus I play God.

But everyone who plays God ends up acting as the demon. Judging others implies that somehow we stand outside of the place where weak, broken, sinful human beings dwell. It is an arrogant and pretentious act that shows blindness not only toward others but also toward ourselves.

A peacemaker never judges anybody. Neither a neighbor close by, nor a neighbor far away. Neither friends nor enemies. It helps me to think about peacemakers as persons whose hearts are so anchored in God that they do not need to evaluate, criticize, or weigh the importance of others. They can see their neighbors—whether they are Americans, Russians, Nicaraguans, Cubans, or South Africans—as fellow human beings, fellow sinners, fellow saints: men and women who need to be listened to, looked at, and cared for with the love of God, and who need to be given the space to recognize that they belong to the same human family as we do.

I remember vividly encountering a man who never judged anyone. I was so used to being around people who are full of opinions about others and eager to share them that I felt somewhat lost in the beginning. What do you talk about when you have nobody to discuss or judge? But as I discovered that he also did not judge me, I gradually came to experience a new inner freedom. I realized that I had nothing to defend, nothing to hide, and that I could be myself in his presence without fear. Through this true peacemaker, a new level of conversation opened up, based not on competing or comparing but on celebrating together the love of the one who is "sent into the world not to judge the world, but so that through him the world might be saved."

This encounter continues to change my life. For a long time I had simply assumed that I needed to have my opinions about everyone and everything in order to participate in ordinary life. But he made me see that I am allowed to live without the heavy burden of judging others and can be free to listen, look, care, and fearlessly receive the gifts offered to me. And the more I become free from the inner compulsion to make up my mind quickly about who the other "really" is, the more I feel part of the whole human family stretched out over our planet from East to West and from North to South. Saying no to the violence of judgments leads me into the nonviolence of peacemaking that allows me to embrace all who share life with me as my brothers and sisters.

As peacemakers we must have the courage to see the powers of death at work even in our innermost selves. We find these powers in the way we think and feel about ourselves. Yes, our most intimate inner thoughts can be tainted by death. When I reflect on my own inner struggles I must confess that one of the hardest struggles is to accept myself, to affirm my own person as being loved, to celebrate my own being alive. Sometimes it seems that there are evil voices hidden deep in my heart trying to convince me that I am worthless, and even despicable. It might sound strange, but these dark inner voices are sometimes most powerful when the outside world—family and friends, students and teachers, supporters and sympathizers—offers compliments and covers me with praise. Precisely then, there are voices that say: "Yes, but they really do not know me. If they knew me, they would discover how impure and selfish I am and they would withdraw their praise quickly." The voice of self-loathing is probably one of the greatest enemies of the peacemaker. It seduces us to commit spiritual suicide.

To believe that we are forgiven is probably one of the most challenging spiritual battles we have to face. Somehow we cannot let go of our self-rejection, somehow we cling to our guilt, somehow we seem to find a strange kind of security in low self-esteem, as if accepting forgiveness fully would call us to a new and ominous task we are afraid to accept. Resistance is an essential element of peacemaking, and the no of the resisters must go all the way to the inner reaches of their own hearts to confront the deadly powers of self-hate. I often think that I am such a hesitant peacemaker because I still have not accepted myself as a forgiven person, a person who has nothing to fear and is truly free to speak the truth and proclaim the kingdom of peace. It sometimes seems to me that the demonic forces of evil and death want to seduce me into believing that I do not deserve the peace I am working for.

My own inner struggles are not just my own. I share them with millions of others. One of the greatest sources of human suffering in our day is the self-loathing that fills the hearts of countless people. Underneath much self-assured behavior and material success many people think little of themselves. They might not show it, as it is socially unacceptable, but they suffer from it no less. Feelings of depression, inner anxiety, a sense of spiritual lostness, and, most painfully, guilt over past failures and past successes are often the constant companions of highly respected men and women. These feelings are like small rodents, slowly eating up the foundations of our lives.

Personally, I believe that the battle against these suicidal inner powers is harder than any other spiritual battle. If those who believe in Jesus Christ were able to believe fully that they are forgiven people, loved unconditionally and called to proclaim peace in the name of the forgiving Lord, our planet would not be on the verge of self-destruction.

It might seem contrived to extend the no of the peacemakers against nuclear war to a no against violent public entertainment, destructive stereotyping, and even self-loathing. But when we are trying to develop a spirituality of peacemaking we cannot limit ourselves to one mode of resistance. All levels need to be considered. Peace activists who are willing to risk their freedom to prevent a nuclear holocaust but who at the same time feed their imagination with violent scenes, give bad names to fellow human beings, or nurture an inner disgust for themselves cannot be witnesses to life for very long. Full spiritual resistance requires a no to death wherever it operates.

Life means mobility and change. Wherever there is life there is movement and growth. Wherever life manifests itself we have to be prepared for surprises, unexpected changes, and constant renewal. Nothing alive is the same from moment to moment. To live is to face the unknown over and over again. Life requires trust. We never know exactly how we will feel, think, and behave next week, next year, or in a decade. Essential to living is trust in an unknown future that requires surrender to the mystery of the unpredictable.

In a time such as ours, in which everything has become unhinged and there is little to hold onto, the uncertainty has become so frightening that we are tempted to prefer the certainty of death to the uncertainty of life. It seems that many people are saying by their words or actions: "It is better to be sure of your unhappiness than to be unsure of your happiness." In different situations this reads: "It is better to have clear-cut enemies than to have to live with people of whose lasting friendship you cannot be sure," or, "It is better to ask people to accept your weaknesses than to be constantly challenged to overcome them." It is shocking to see how many people choose the certainty of misery in order not to have to deal with the uncertainty of joy. This is a choice for death, a choice that is increasingly attractive when the future seems no longer trustworthy.

As I reflect on my childhood experiences of fear, I remember the time when I was tempted to fail even before I had seriously tried to succeed. Somewhere I was saying to myself: "Why not run back from the diving board and cry, so that you can be sure of pity if you are not sure of praise? Why not give up this difficult game and claim the comfort of consolation, when the affirmation coming from victory is so elusive?"

These childhood memories offer me an image of the temptation that faces all of us on a worldwide scale. It is the temptation to choose the satisfaction of death when the satisfaction of life seems too precarious. When the future has become a dark, fearful unknown, isn't it then quite attractive to choose the satisfactions that are available in the present, even when they are partial, ambiguous, and tainted with death? The nuclear situation—in which the future itself has become not only dark and fearful but uncertain—has made the temptation to indulge ourselves in the short pleasures of the present greater than ever. It is quite possible that we will see an increasingly death-oriented self-indulgence going hand in hand with increasing doubt in a livable future. Fascination with death and hedonism are intimately connected.

Peacemaking requires clear resistance to death in all its manifestations. As peacemakers we have to face the intimate connection between the varied forms of our contemporary fascination with death and the deaths caused by a nuclear holocaust. By recognizing the many "innocent" death games in our daily lives, we gradually come to realize that we are part of that complex network of war-making that finds its most devastating expression in a nuclear holocaust. Real resistance requires the humble confession that we are partners in the evil that we seek to resist. This is a very hard and seemingly endless discipline. The more we say no the more we will discover the all-pervasive presence of death. The more we resist, the more we recognize how much there is to resist. The more we fight, the more we have to face battles yet to be fought. The world—and we are an intimate part of the world—is indeed Satan's territory.

The world and its kingdoms are under the destructive power of the evil spirit, the spirit of destruction and death. The nuclear threat reveals the ultimate implication of this truth. It is not that God—who created the world out of love—will destroy it, but that *we* will destroy it if we allow the satanic power of death to rule us. This is what makes saying no to death in all its manifestations such an urgent spiritual task.

27

CIVIL DISOBEDIENCE AS PRAYER

Jim Douglass

In this profound reflection Jim Douglass unmasks the violence at the core of much nonviolent action. The very desire to win through nonviolence reveals our enthrall- ment with the domination system and its view of power. The only cure for this delusion is to pass through ideology to persons (Fellowship, *March 1986).*

One way of seeing jail today is to regard it as the new monastery. In a soci- ety preparing for nuclear war and ignoring its poor, jail is an appropriate set- ting in which to give one's life to prayer. In a nation which has legalized prepa- rations for the destruction of all life on earth, going to jail for peace—through nonviolent civil disobedience—can be seen as a prayer. In reflecting today on the Lord's Prayer, I think that going to jail as a way of saying "thy kingdom come, thy will be done" may be the most basic prayer we can offer in the nuclear security state. Because we have accepted the greatest evil conceivable as a substitute for divine security, we have become a nation of atheists and blasphemers. The nuclear security state, U.S. or U.S.S.R., is blasphemous by definition. As members of such a nation, we need to pray for the freedom to do God's will by noncooperating with the ultimate evil it is preparing. Civil dis- obedience done in a loving spirit is itself that kind of prayer.

On the other hand, civil disobedience can be done in a way that, while apparently noncooperating with nuclear war, ends up cooperating with an il- lusion that underlies nuclear war. In any attitude of resistance to the state there is a kind of demonic underside, power turned upside down, which wishes to gain the upper hand. Civil disobedience which is not done as prayer is espe- cially vulnerable to its underside.

A simple truth at the root of nonviolence is that we can't change an evil or an injustice from the outside. Thomas Merton stated this truth at the conclu- sion of one of his last books, *Mystics and Zen Masters,* as a critique of "nonvio- lence" as it is understood by its proponents in the Western world. Merton questioned "the Western acceptance of a 'will to transform others' in terms of one's own prophetic insight accepted as a norm of pure justice." He asked: "Is there not an 'optical illusion' in an eschatological spirit which, however much it may appeal to *agape,* seeks only to transform persons and social structures *from the outside?*" Here we arrive at a basic principle, one might almost say an ontology of nonviolence, which requires further investigation.

Nonviolent noncooperation with the greatest evil in history is still, according to Merton's insight, a possible way into illusion, a more subtle form of the same illusion that we encounter behind the nuclear buildup. Even in nonviolent resistance, unless we accept deeply the spirit of nonviolence, we can end up waging our own form of war and contributing to the conclusion we seek to overcome. Because the evil we resist is so great, we are inclined to overlook an illusion inherent in our own position, the will to transform others from the outside.

If one understands civil disobedience as an assertion of individual conscience over against the evil or injustice of the state, the temptation to seek an "outside solution" is already present. Conscience against the state sounds like a spiritually based or "inside solution." We are, after all, stating our willingness in conscience to go to jail at the hands of the state that threatens an unparalleled evil. But our conscience set off against the nuclear state takes an external view of people acting on behalf of that state. And ultimately such a view externalizes our own conscience.

In the acts of civil disobedience I have done, I have never met "the state." In terms of my own ambition, that has been disappointing. I have met only people, such as police, judges, and jail guards, who cooperate (and sometimes noncooperate) with the evil of nuclear war in complex and often puzzling ways. I have never met a person who embodies the state of nuclear war. In their nuances of character, police, judges, and guards come from the same stew of humanity as do people who do civil disobedience.

A spiritually based nonviolence, one that truly seeks change from within, has to engage deeply the spirits of both sides of a conflict. Civil disobedience as an act of conscience against the state tends to focus exclusively on our own conscience as a source of change. Yet in the act of civil disobedience we meet particular people like ourselves, not "the state," and the most enduring thing we can achieve through such an act is, in the end, our relationship to the people we touch and who touch us. Our hope should not be for any strategic victories over such representatives of the state but rather loving, nonviolent relationships with them in the midst of our arrests, trials, and prison sentences. The danger of seeing civil disobedience as an assertion of conscience over against the evil of the state is that it may get confused into an assertion against these particular people so that we may never really see our relationship to them as primary. Making friends with our opponents—in the police, in the Pentagon, or in the Soviet Union—is our greatest hope of overcoming nuclear war.

A more fundamental question suggested by Merton is: Who is this "I," this self, that is doing the act of conscience in civil disobedience? If civil disobedience accentuates, or heightens, this sense of self—if it gives it a sense of power— is that necessarily a good thing? Civil disobedience is often referred to today as a way of empowering its participants. For socially powerless people, nonviolent civil disobedience can be a profoundly liberating way out of bondage, as one part of a larger revolution. But empowerment can also be used to cover a heightened sense of an individual self that may be a step into further bondage.

We who see ourselves as peacemakers—and don't we all?—would be deeply shocked if we could see the extent to which we act personally for war, not only in our more obvious faults, but even in our very peacemaking. Our intentions and actions for peace lead to war if they are based on a false self and its illusions. If the purpose of civil disobedience is to "empower" such a self, it is a personal act of war.

The nuclear arms race summarizes the history of a false, violent self—of many such false selves magnified in national egos—in an inconceivable evil. What the nuclear crisis says to us, as nothing else in history could, is that the empowering of a false self creates a crisis which has no solution, only transformation. We can't *solve* an arms race based on enormous national illusions, illusions which both exploit and protect an emptiness at the center of millions of lives. Those illusions can only be cracked open to the truth and fear and emptiness at the core of each national pride, then revealed as truly reconcilable with their apparent opposites in the consciousness of another people.

Civil disobedience for the sake of empowering a false self serves as the warring nation state on a smaller scale. Civil disobedience as that kind of empowerment is an attempt to solve one's problems and frustrations by externalizing them in a theater in which innocence confronts the evil of the nuclear state. But we are not innocent.

The greatest treason, as T. S. Eliot points out in *Murder in the Cathedral,* is to do the right deed for the wrong reason. Civil disobedience in response to the greatest evil in history, done to empower a self which can't face its own emptiness, is the right deed for the wrong reason. Because of its motivation, it may also twist itself into the wrong deed. An ego-empowering act of civil disobedience will in the end empower both the self and the nuclear state, which, while tactically at odds, are spiritually in agreement. Such resistance, like the state itself, asserts power in order to cover a void. Civil disobedience, like war, can be used to mask the emptiness of a false self.

Civil disobedience as prayer is not an assertion of individual conscience over the evil of the state. Protesting against something for which we ourselves are profoundly responsible is a futile exercise in hypocrisy. The evil of nuclear war is not external to us, so that it can be isolated in the state or in the Nuclear Train loaded with hydrogen bombs. The nature of the evil lies in our cooperation with it. What Merton is suggesting is that as we cease cooperating in one way with that evil, our well-hidden tendency is to begin cooperating with it more intensely and more blindly in another way, defining the evil in a way external to us, which deepens and hardens its actual presence in ourselves.

The power of the evil of nuclear war is nothing more than the power of our cooperation with it. There is no evil exclusively out there, over us. The evil is much more subtle than that. This is why it continues to exist. When we cease cooperating with evil at its source in ourselves, it ceases to exist. When we accept responsibility for nuclear war in the hidden dimensions of our own complicity, we will experience the miracle of seeing the Nuclear Train stop and the arms race end. To paraphrase Harry Truman, the Bomb stops here.

Civil disobedience as prayer is not an assertion of self over an illusion but an acceptance of God's loving will because of our responsibility for evil: Not my will but thine be done. The prayer of the gospels like the prayer of Gandhi is at its heart an acceptance of what we don't want: the acceptance of our suffering out of love. Jesus and Gandhi are precise about what is meant by God's will in a world of suffering. Gandhi in summing up Jesus' life said, "Living Christ is a living cross, without it life is a living death."

To be nonviolent means to accept our suffering out of love. The evil which causes suffering is an evil whose source is more deeply interior to ourselves than we have begun to understand. The prayer of civil disobedience which says, *"Not my will but thine be done"*—by sending us to death or to that sign of death which is jail—is a recognition that in truth we belong there, and that we will in any event ultimately find ourselves there.

Civil disobedience as prayer is not an act of defiance but an act of obedience to a deeper, interior will within us and within the world which is capable of transforming the world. "Thy kingdom come, thy will be done." To live out the kingdom of God through such an action is to live in a loving relationship to our brothers and sisters in the police, in courts, and in jails, recognizing God's presence in each of us. It is also to accept responsibility for an evil which is ours: As we are, so is the nuclear state.

The two most violent places I've ever been in my life have been the Strategic Weapons Facility Pacific (SWFPAC), where nuclear weapons are stored at the heart of the Trident base, and the Los Angeles County Jail, where people are stored. I went to SWFPAC in order to pray for peace and forgiveness standing in front of enormous concrete bunkers, the tombs of humankind, a prayer which took me in turn to the LA County Jail (on the way to a more permanent prison) where ten thousand people are kept in tombs. The deepest experiences of peace that I have had have been in these same terrible places.

I believe that a suffering God continually calls us to be in such places for the sake of peace and justice. I believe that the kingdom of God is realized there. Civil disobedience as prayer is a way into that kingdom.

28

BEING PEACE

Thich Nhat Hanh

━━━━━━━━━

Thich Nhat Hanh is a Buddhist mystic and peace activist. During the Vietnam war he staffed a mission in Paris that tried to represent a third position between the warring parties. He was instrumental in founding a network of socially engaged Buddhists that continues to the present. Thich Nhat Hanh has been especially helpful in the West in teaching social activists exhausted from the struggle for justice the art of contemplation as a means to restoring their souls (Fellowship, *July-August 1986*).

Life is full of suffering, but it is also full of wonderful things like the blue sky, the sunshine, the eyes of a baby. To suffer is not all. We also need to be in touch with the wonders of life. They are all around us, everywhere, any time. Does it require a special effort to enjoy the blue sky? Do we have to practice to be able to enjoy it? No, we just enjoy it. We don't need to travel to China in order to enjoy the sky.

You know that if a tree is a tree, that is about all it can do. If a tree is not a tree, then life is not life. The fact that a tree is a tree is very important for us. We benefit a lot from a tree's being a tree. In the same way, a person should be a person. If one person is a real person living happily, smiling, then all of us, all the world, will benefit from that person. A person doesn't have to do a lot in order to save the world. A person has to be a person. That is the basis of peace.

If a child smiles, if an adult smiles, that is very important. If in our daily life we can smile, if we can be peaceful and happy, not only we but all the members of our families will profit from it, living peacefully, joyfully, smiling. The world around us will also benefit from it. That is the most basic kind of peace work.

The other day, during a Dharma talk, children were sitting in front of me. There was a boy smiling beautifully. Tim was his name. I said, "Tim, you have a very beautiful smile." And he said, "Thank you." I said, "No, you don't have to thank me. I have to thank you. Because of your smile, you make life more beautiful. So instead of saying 'Thank you,' you should say 'You're welcome.'" When I see Tim, I am so happy. If he is aware of the fact that he is making other people happy, he can say "You're welcome."

153

Therefore, to be in touch with the wonderful things of the world, to smile, to enjoy the blue sky, the sunshine, the presence of each other: that is the first thing we must do. And that does not need a particular effort. We should just be aware of the presence of these wonderful things.

Smiling means that you are yourself, that you have sovereignty over yourself, that you are not drowned into forgetfulness. That kind of smile can be seen on the faces of the Buddhas and Bodhisattvas. So I would like to ask you all not to be observers or spectators but to be actors. Please smile and enjoy your breathing while reading. There is a *gatha*, a short verse, which I would like to share with you.

> Breathing in, I calm body and mind.
> Breathing out, I smile.
> Dwelling in the present moment,
> I know that this is the only moment.

I would like to say something about these four lines. "Breathing in, I calm body and mind." I don't just recite this, I practice it. It is like drinking a glass of ice water. You feel the cold and the freshness permeate your own body. So when I breathe in, I feel the breathing calming my body, calming my mind. I feel like a glass of orange juice just squeezed from an orange. The small particles of the orange slowly go down to the bottom and settle. So when I breathe in, I see clearly that the breathing calms my mind and my body.

When I breathe out, I smile. I actually smile. You know the effect of a smile. A smile can relax hundreds of muscles in your face, relax your nervous system, and make you master of yourself. That is why the Buddhas and Bodhisattvas are always smiling. If you smile you feel the wonder of the smile.

"Dwelling in the present moment, I know this is the only moment." While I sit here, I don't think of elsewhere in the future or the past. I sit here, and I know where I am sitting. This is very important. We tend to live in the future, not now. We say, "Wait until I finish school and get my Ph.D. degree, then I will be really alive." But after school we say, "Wait until I have a job, then I will be really alive." After the job, a house. And we are not capable of being alive in the present moment. We postpone being alive to the future, the distant future—we don't know when. Now is not the moment to be alive. And we may never be alive at all in our life.

Therefore, the technique—if we have to speak of a technique—is to be alive in the present moment, to be aware that I am here and now. The only moment for me to be alive is the present moment. So the time you are reading this article here and now—this is not just a time to read words, but to be in the present moment. Reading an article may be important, but to be here and now, enjoying the present moment, is the most important thing.

I think we can feel very happy while practicing breathing and smiling. And the conditions are available. You can do it sitting in a meditation hall or at home; you can do it walking in a park or at a riverside, anywhere. The breath is the mediator between the body and the mind. The breath unites mind and body. And it nourishes our best self.

While practicing walking meditation, you pay attention to the number of steps you make during each inhalation and each exhalation. In this way, you can make peaceful, happy steps, and you enjoy it. If you do not follow your breathing, you forget what you are doing and your steps will no longer be happy and peaceful. Following your breath is a way of reminding yourself that you are taking peaceful, happy steps.

I suggest that in each home we have a tiny room for breathing. We have one room for sleeping, one room for eating, one room for cooking; why don't we have a room for breathing? I suggest that that room be not too bright and be decorated in a very simple way—maybe just a pot of flowers to symbolize our true nature. And a table and a few cushions.

If the family has five members, then have five cushions and a few more for guests. From time to time, we may want to invite our guests to come and sit and breathe with us for five minutes or three minutes.

I know of families with such rooms. Their children go in there after breakfast, sit down and breathe for ten minutes: in-out-one, in-out-two, in-out-three, ten times, and they go to school. This is a very beautiful practice. If you don't wish to breathe ten times, three times may be more pleasant. Yes, that's a beautiful thing to do.

So a room for breathing is very important. It must be very clean and simple—only cushions and one small table with a pot of flowers. Children can arrange flowers in mindfulness, smiling. And anytime you feel a bit sad or irritated, don't say anything. Just begin to breathe and slowly open the door of that room, go in, slowly sit down, and breathe and smile for a few moments. That is a very civilized thing to do.

During a recent retreat, one friend asked this hard question, "How can I smile when I am full of sorrow? It's like forcing myself to smile. That is not natural." Maybe some of you think the same.

My answer was: "You should be able to smile at your sorrow, because you are more than your sorrow." A human being is like a television set with millions of channels to receive. If you turn the Buddha on, you are the Buddha. If you turn the sorrow on, you are the sorrow. If you turn the smile on, you are the smile. And so on. Don't let one channel dominate you all the time. You have the seed of everything in you. Therefore, you have to seize the situation in your hands, in order to recover your own Sovereignty.

When we sit down peacefully breathing and smiling, we are our true selves: we have sovereignty over ourselves.

When we sit watching a TV program, we let ourselves be invaded by it. Because we don't like ourselves, because we don't want to be with ourselves, we want to get away from ourselves, we want to have something other than ourselves enter us. Sometimes a TV program is good, but often it is just very noisy. And we let a very bad program assail us, invade us and destroy us. Even if we suffer, even if our nervous systems suffer, we don't have the courage to stand up and turn off the TV program.

We must go back to our true selves. These practices—breathing, smiling, and being aware—help you go back to your true self. Practicing them in our civilization is very difficult. All things seem to work in concert to take away your true self. You are so busy that when you have some free time, you cannot stand it. You have to pick up a book saying that you have to educate yourself. Or you pick up the telephone. You don't mind that the telephone bill will be too high. Or you turn on the TV. And there are a million other things, like video tapes and music, to help you get away from yourself. Practicing meditation to be aware, to listen attentively, to smile, to breathe—all this is on the opposite side. We want to go back to ourselves in order to see what is going on. Because to meditate means to be aware of what is going on.

What is going on is very important. I think the most important precept of all is to live in awareness, to know what is going on—not only here but there. For instance, when we eat a piece of bread, we may choose to be aware of how our farmers grow the wheat. It seems that chemical poisons are used a bit too much. And while we eat the bread, we are somehow co-responsible for the destruction of our ecology. When we eat a piece of meat, we may become aware that eating meat is not a good way to reconcile oneself with millions of children in the world. Forty thousand children die each day in the Third World for lack of food. And in order to produce meat, you have to feed the cow or the chicken with a lot of cereal. Eating a bowl of cereal is more reconciling with the suffering of the world than eating a piece of meat. An authority on economics who lives in France told me that if only the Western countries would reduce the eating of meat by 50 percent, that would be enough to change the situation of the world.

What we are, what we do every day, has much to do with world peace. If we are aware of our lifestyle, our way of consuming and looking at things, then we know how to make peace right at the present moment. If we are very aware, we will do something to change the course of things.

In the peace movement, there is a lot of anger, frustration, and misunderstanding today. The people in the movement can write very good protest letters, but they are not yet able to write love letters. We need to learn to write to the Congress and to the president of the United States letters that they will not put in the trash can. We need to write the kind of letter that they will like to receive. The way you speak, the kind of language you use, and the kind of understanding you express should not turn people off. Because the people you write to are also persons like all of us.

Can the peace movement talk in loving speech, showing the way to peace? I think that will depend on whether the people in the peace movement can *be* peace. We cannot do anything for peace without ourselves being peace. If you cannot smile, you cannot help other people smile. If you are not peaceful, then you cannot contribute to the peace movement. We know that our situation is very dangerous. A nuclear war can happen at any moment. Practicing meditation is to practice awareness of what is going on. Therefore, if we are aware, if we know what is going on, we will be peace and make peace, so that the worst may not occur.

We need people who understand, who are capable of being in touch with people. But there are few such people. To reconcile the conflicting parties, we must have the ability to understand the suffering of both sides. If we take sides, it is impossible for us to do the work of reconciliation. And humans want to take sides. That is why the situation gets worse and worse. Are there people who are still available to both sides? They need not do much. They need do only one thing: go to one side and tell all about the suffering endured by the other side, and go to the other side and tell all about the suffering endured by this side. That is our chance for peace. That alone can change the situation. But how many of us are in a position to do that?

The other morning I went with a young woman who was expecting a child. The child was due in four weeks. I told the young mother, "Please breathe and smile for the baby. You don't need to wait until the baby is born in order to take care of it. You can take care of the baby right now, or even sooner."

What if that lady tells you she cannot smile? That is very serious. What if she cannot breathe, cannot smile, cannot enjoy the blue sky? That's very serious. She cannot say, "I am too sorrowful. Smiling is just not the natural thing for me to do." Maybe crying or shouting is more natural for her to do. But her baby will get it all—whatever she is, whatever she does.

Even if you do not have a baby in your womb, the seed of a baby is already there. So those of you who are still unmarried—even men—should be aware that the baby is already there somehow. Don't wait until the doctors tell you that you are going to have a baby to begin to take care of it. It is already there. And whatever you are, whatever you do, your baby will get it. So anything you eat, anything you do, any worries that are on your mind will be for the baby. So be aware.

Can you tell me that you cannot smile? No. Think of the baby. You smile for him, for her, for the future generations. You have a baby, so you should be responsible. So smile. We have the illusion that we are only one thing, and that if we are sorrowful, we cannot be something else. This is wrong. It's like a TV set saying, "I can only be Channel 5. I cannot be something else."

I can tell you that if you are unable to smile, then the world will not have peace. It's not by going out for a demonstration against the nuclear missiles that you can get peace. It is with your capacity for smiling, breathing and being understanding that you can make peace. Practicing meditation, practicing smiling, breathing, enjoying the blue sky, we can bring a new dimension to the peace movement.

I think that if you can practice breathing, sitting with your children in your home for a few minutes every morning, that would be marvelous. Take your children out for walking meditation before going to sleep. That would make a very big difference. And a room for meditation, for breathing. These are three things I would recommend; namely, breathing and sitting with your children every morning, walking meditation with them for ten minutes before going to bed, and arranging for a room for breathing in your home. I think these things are very important. They can change our civilization.

29

GANDHI AND THE ANCIENT WISDOM OF NONVIOLENCE

Mairead Corrigan Maguire

In 1977 Mairead Corrigan Maguire received the Nobel Peace Prize, along with Betty Williams, for their efforts for peace in Northern Ireland. The Peace People, as they called themselves, served as a catalyst to bring ordinary people into the struggle to end the violence and create a culture of peace in Northern Ireland. Maguire is a member of the International FOR and honorary president of the Appeal of the Nobel Peace Prize Laureates for a Decade of Nonviolence, which the United Nations endorsed unanimously. She has traveled the world sharing the message of nonviolence. John Dear edited her writings in The Vision of Peace: Faith and Hope in Northern Ireland *(1999). These reflections were addressed to the Gandhian movement in India on the fiftieth anniversary of Gandhi's assassination* (Fellowship, *June 1988).*

Gandhi realized that the spirit of nonviolence begins within us and moves out from there. The life of active nonviolence is the fruit of an inner peace and spiritual unity already realized in us, and not the other way around. I have come to believe, with Gandhi, that through our own personal, inner conversion, our own inner peace, we are sensitized to care for God, ourselves, each other, for the poor, and for our world. Then we can become true servants of peace in the world. Herein lies the power of nonviolence. As our hearts are disarmed by God of our inner violence, they become God's instruments for the disarmament of the world. Without this inner conversion, we run the risk of becoming embittered, disillusioned, despairing, or simply burnt out, especially when our work for peace and justice appears to produce little or no result, or seems trifling in comparison with the injustice we see all around us. With this conversion we learn to let go of "all desires"—including the destructive desire to see results.

For many people, this ancient wisdom of the heart, the wisdom of nonviolence, may seem too religious and too idealistic in today's hard-headed world of politics and science. But I believe with Gandhi that we need to take an imaginative leap forward toward a fresh and generous idealism for the sake of all humanity. We need to renew this ancient wisdom of nonviolence, to strive for a disarmed world, and to create new nonviolence cultures.

As we enter the third millennium, we need to apply the wisdom of nonviolence to politics, economics, and science. For many, particularly in the West, increased materialism and unprecedented consumerism have not led to inner peace or happiness. Although technology has given us many benefits, it has not helped us distinguish between what enhances life and humanity and what destroys life and humanity. The time has come to return to the ancient wisdom.

When we examine where we are today, given the politics and technology of violence, we can only conclude that we live in an insane world.

Is it not insanity to go on producing nuclear and conventional weapons that if used can destroy millions of people, if not the whole planet?

Is it not insanity to spend billions of the people's money to produce and maintain these weapons of mass destruction, while millions of children die of disease and starvation each year? When (according to the UN) sixty thousand children die every day of starvation, even though the world's governments have the resources and capability of ending starvation and poverty immediately?

Is it not insanity to implement sanctions on some countries when their only effect is to punish the most vulnerable—as, for example, in Iraq, where because of U.S. and UN sanctions forty-five hundred Iraqi children die every month?

Is it not insanity that the developed countries—including Britain, currently the third largest exporter of arms in the world—sell huge amounts of armaments to poor and developing countries, which in turn use much of the money allocated to them for aid to pay for these arms?

Is it not insanity that India's government—currently the third or fourth most powerful military machine in the world—continues to waste so many resources on militarism, while so many of its people are in need of the basic necessities of life?

Is it not insanity to continue destroying the environment by dumping radioactive materials and poisoning the oceans, polluting the air, and destroying the ozone?

Yes, it is insanity. I believe with Gandhi that the insanity of violence can only be stopped by the sanity of nonviolence. The time has come to renew our commitment, personally, politically, economically, and internationally, to the ancient wisdom of nonviolence.

As we move into the third millennium, we are beginning to realize that the human family is multi-ethnic, multicultural, and pluralistic in nature, and that if we are going to survive and develop, we need to learn to live together nonviolently.

In Rwanda, Bosnia, and to a lesser degree in Northern Ireland, we see the consequences of ethnic, political violence. We see how injustice and militarism breed fear and hatred and release murderous passions, drowning out all reason, compassion, and mercy. Many people prefer to believe that they are themselves too "civilized" to carry out such horrors, but we need honestly to face up to Gandhi's truth that each one of us, while capable of the greatest good, is also, given the right circumstances, capable of the greatest evil.

In facing such problems we know that the "old" ways of violence, war, and militarism do not work. Fifty years after Gandhi's death, we are faced with a choice. Gandhi said, "There is no hope for the aching world except through the narrow and straight path of nonviolence." If we want to reap the harvest of peace and justice in the future, we will have to sow seeds of nonviolence. All of us need to take responsibility for the world's violence and, like Gandhi, pledge our lives to the nonviolent transformation of the world.

Gandhi taught that nonviolence does not mean passivity. It is the most daring, creative, and courageous way of living, and it is the only hope for the world. Nonviolence demands creativity. It pursues dialogue, seeks reconciliation, listens to the truth in our opponents, rejects militarism, and allows God's Spirit to transform us socially and politically.

But Gandhi's message of nonviolence is a challenge to the whole of humanity. Fifty years after his death, Gandhi challenges us to pursue a new millennium of nonviolence. This it not an impossible dream. In order to create a new culture of nonviolence, each of us can take several basic steps forward to help fulfill that dream.

First, we need to teach nonviolence to the children of the world—in India, in Northern Ireland, and everywhere. Recently, twenty-two Nobel Peace Prize laureates asked the UN to declare the first decade of the new millennium as "a decade for a culture of nonviolence for the children of the world," in the hope that every nation will begin to educate its children in the way of nonviolence, in schools and homes. I was pleased during my visit to India to launch this movement, and to see the Gandhian movement giving an example to the world in the teaching of nonviolence in schools.

Second, as individuals, we can exorcise the violence and untruth from our own lives. We can stop supporting systemic violence and militarism, and dedicate ourselves to nonviolent social change. We can take public stands for disarmament and justice, and take new risks for peace.

Third, we can urge the media to stop sensationalizing violence and instead to highlight peaceful interactions, promote nonviolence, and uphold those who strive for real peace.

Fourth, we can embrace the wisdom of nonviolence that lies underneath each of the world's religions. Every religion contains the ancient truth of nonviolence. Every religion needs to begin more and more to teach and promote nonviolence, and to worship the God of nonviolence. Gandhi said, "If religion does not teach us how to achieve the conquest of evil by overcoming it with goodness, it teaches us nothing." The world's religions need to come together in dialogue and respect, because there can be no world peace until the great religions make peace with one another. Perhaps the greatest contribution that those of us who come from a Christian tradition can make is to throw out the old just-war theory, embrace the nonviolence of Jesus, refuse to kill one another, and truly follow his commandment to "love our enemies."

Fifth, we need to pursue Gandhi's dream of unarmed, international peacemaking teams which resolve international conflict not through military solutions but nonviolent means. The world's governments need not only to reject military solutions, but to create and finance international nonviolent conflict-resolution programs.

More than anything else, Gandhi inspires me by his great love for the poor. Perhaps the greatest contribution we can pay to Gandhi is to work to eliminate poverty from the face of the earth. Gandhi said that poverty is the worst form of violence. His memorial in India contains his parting advice, which we need to keep before us every day of our lives: "Recall the face of the poorest person you have ever seen, and ask yourself if the next step you take will be of any use to that person."

As we remember his death and celebrate his life, we dedicate ourselves to the wisdom of nonviolence. Shortly before his death, Gandhi said, "We are constantly being astonished these days at the amazing discoveries in the field of violence. But I maintain that far more undreamt of and seemingly impossible discoveries will be made in the field of nonviolence."

With Gandhi we can share great hope in a future filled with peace. Like Gandhi, we can make that hope a reality by pursuing new discoveries in the field of nonviolence, building a culture of nonviolence for the new millennium, and becoming, like Gandhi, teachers and prophets of nonviolence.

As we exit the second millennium we can take great hope, too, from the many excellent achievements and discoveries made by millions of our brothers and sisters before us. They have, by their examples, enriched, inspired, and encouraged us to build lives of joy and peace for ourselves and for each other.

May the God of Mahatma Gandhi, the God of nonviolence, bless us all with peace, fill us with hope, and lead us and all humanity into a new world of nonviolence.

Part Four

INTERRACIAL JUSTICE

Curiously, the one area where nonviolent direct action achieved its greatest success in the United States is the area where the greatest disparity of income, equality, and acceptance still exists: that of racial prejudice. The civil rights movement led to the passage of the Voters' Rights Amendment, Affirmative Action, a number of programs like Head Start that disproportionately helped blacks, the rise of a black middle class, and the presence of blacks in movies, television, advertising, and many other sectors of American life.

Yet the glass ceiling also prevents African Americans from rising high in corporations or becoming fully accepted in offices, clubs, board rooms, and head coaching opportunities. Attitudes of racial prejudice still persist. Blacks represent only 13 percent of the population, but constitute 35 percent of those arrested for simple possession of drugs and a staggering 74 percent of those sentenced for possession, despite the fact that the majority of users are white. One in three young African American men is involved in the prison/parole system. Schools have resegregated. And we could go on and on.

So the civil rights struggle is not yet over. It will not be until we have achieved a color-free society, where all people are evaluated by who they are, not what envelope they arrived in. What kinds of strategies will meet our needs today? How can we adapt the tactical brilliance of a Gandhi or King or Chavez to new situations of racial injustice and economic disadvantage? Can we find in the essays that follow, guidelines and clues that can light the way forward?

30

THE WILL
TO SEGREGATION

Howard Thurman

Howard Thurman was one of the great mystics of America in a time when mysticism was dismissed as quietistic, irresponsible, and naive. Like many of Fellowship's *contributors, however, he combined mysticism with powerful leadership that sought consistently to convert church and society into something a bit more resembling the Beloved Community. This article is representative of many such reflections in* Fellowship *that sought to integrate outer struggles for justice with the disciplines of the inner life. Dean of the Chapel at Howard University when this was written, Howard Thurman clearly articulated the nonviolent alternative to race war, anticipating the civil rights movement by some dozen years* (Fellowship, *August 1943*).

Any discussion of the relationship between Negro and white people in the year 1943 must examine certain important developments that exercise wide influence in this area.

The first and most important single fact is the war. Under ordinary circumstances the Negro is at most a citizen, second class. He pays taxes on property, participates in the franchise in some sections, and holds a few offices of public trust, but for the most part normal life for him is two or three steps removed from what may be regarded as normal life for other members of the community. At a time of national peril, much of this situation is altered. Even the least citizen begins to count in terms of specific assignments that are deemed essential for survival. Thus war has caused the average Negro to become aware of counting civically in a new way: he is encouraged to buy bonds and defense stamps, he participates in the leadership program, his manpower comes under the selected judgment of the National Selective Service Act, he is involved in Civilian Defense in many of its manifestations, he is taking special training courses for carrying increasing responsibility in defense industry and the farms, he is in the armed forces.

Civic character is possible only where men are permitted to carry civic responsibility. With this new sense of civic responsibility, a new kind of civic character is beginning to appear. This new character, although occasioned by the war, makes for the development of a more careful regard for the future not only of democracy but also the particular future of the Negro in labor, professions, politics, etc. In a sense it is like the coming of age when the first full bloom of manhood possesses the mind and the body. It is unfortunate that it took a global war with its concomitant effect upon our national life to give the Negro a fresh sense of significance and power.

The second significant development stems from the fact that it is no longer possible merely to define national aspirations in terms of "making the world safe for democracy"; it is necessary now to talk concretely in terms of the four freedoms, adding footnotes to make them more definitive and less general than they would appear on the surface. The Axis nations have made clear their goals in terms of a thoroughgoing fascism, and have thus defined their political, social, and economic philosophy. The United Nations must be just as concrete and specific. Mere slogans are completely meaningless. High-ranking government spokesmen in public utterances are defining democracy in language that the simplest man can understand.

Meanwhile, the diseases in the body politic become much more acute in the minds of less privileged persons such as Negroes. As these diseases are exposed to the searching diagnosis of the meaning of democracy, the gulf between the dream as uttered and the idea as practiced is wide, abysmal, and deep. *The measure of the frustration of Negroes is in direct proportion to the degree to which the meaning of democracy is made clear and definitive.* We behold then the spectacle of the Negro with a new civic character growing out of a new sense of civic and social responsibility, yet caught in the grip of a deeper frustration and restlessness than he has ever known.

In the third place, the fact that we were attacked by Japan has aggravated greatly the tension between the races. I am not suggesting that the war between Japan and the United States is a race war, but certainly many people have thought of it in terms of a nonwhite race "daring" to attack a white race. This has given excellent justification for the expression of the prejudices against nonwhite peoples just under the surface of the American consciousness. There has been a relaxation of mutual regard and respect between the races in many walks of life where these previously existed. This has made for definite reactions on the part of Negroes, often reactions in kind with increasing bitterness, intolerance, hatred.

And in the fourth place, the attitudes described above have been met by an increasing determination and grimness on the part of white Americans. It seems perfectly clear to them that Negroes everywhere are getting out of their place. The argument runs like this: "Negroes do not know what to do with their new sense of significance. They are flippant, arrogant, bigoted, overbearing. Therefore, they must be curbed, held in check so that when the war is over they may drop quickly back into their prewar secondary citizen status." With this kind of situation facing the two groups in America, what can be done?

THE "WILL TO SEGREGATION"

The most fundamentally important thing that must be done is to relax the "will to segregation" that through the years has become the American technique for the control of the Negro minority. This "will to segregation" has taken the form of policy in business, in the church, in the state, in the school, in living zones. Let us examine this "will to segregate."

It is important to realize that segregation can exist only between peoples who are relatively weak and relatively strong, respectively. The strong may separate themselves in certain ways from the weak, but because the initiative remains in their hands they are ever at liberty to shuttle back and forth between the proscribed areas. The weak can only be segregated because, lacking the initiative, they cannot move at will between the proscribed areas. A simple case in point may be observed on any Southern train carrying day coaches. Members of the train crew, who are white, often sit in the section of the coach designated for Negroes. They may sit, by custom, in either section. The train porter, who is a Negro, may sit only in the Negro coach. White passengers move at will from one section to the other, but the passengers in the Jim Crow car sometimes experience difficulty even in passing through the other coaches en route to the diner. Waiters in the diner must always use the toilet facilities in the Jim Crow coach, while white members of the train crew may use either facilities.

The psychological effect of segregation on both groups is the critical issue. For segregation dramatizes a stigma and becomes a badge of inferiority. A group segregated systematically over many generations experiences a decisive undermining of self-respect. For the sensitive, it means a constant, persistent resentment that is apt so to disease the personality that mental health is critically attacked.

For the less sensitive there is ever the possibility of the acceptance of segregation, with its concomitant conscious admission of inferiority, of humiliation, of despair. Those who are despised, or who are treated systematically as if they were despised, are apt eventually to despise themselves. There is a sense in which society is a mirror through which individuals and groups see themselves reflected. It requires the veriest kind of vigilance and wide awareness to resist the temptation to accept the judgment of society upon one's group. Society sets the mode or the frame of reference that is apt to determine judgment. It is in an effort to overcome this that minority groups seem inclined to develop tendencies toward chauvinism, racism, and other manifestations of the "cult of segregation."

More than all of this there is at least one great fear growing out of segregation: the fear of violence. The fear of physical violence is characteristic of most human beings and other animals, but among the segregated the fear takes on a heightened significance because they are so circumscribed by society that exposure to direct violence is ever present and there are no particular types of behavior that may guarantee immunity. The basic fact is that when human beings are segregated they provide a "tethered goat" on whose innocent and unsuspecting head vengeance may be poured for deeds infinitely removed from anything for which they may have responsibility. The ghetto and the Negro section are always present, and into them may be dumped releases from frustration and from social and economic blunders, and revenge for private wrongs that originate in a world into which the victims are not even permitted to enter. *To the extent to which this is true the mere fact of being alive provides a specific liability over and above the normal fate of the average person!*

This fear of violence is not traceable merely to the fear of death. To accommodate oneself to the fact of death is one of the basic elements in a normal adjustment of life. Everyone knows that death is inevitable: "one by one the duties end; one by one the lights go out." But the fear of violence is a part of the fear that man has of dying out of his bed; dying under circumstances that degrade and debase; dying like a dog in an alley or a rat in a gutter. Death by accident, or as a result of some freakish act of nature has some of the elements of horror that are present here, but such deaths have in them something that is clean, unconscious, whole. But to be killed by others without benefit of purpose or great cause is to die ignobly and in shame. The last thread of dignity and worthfulness is stripped from personality and death under such circumstances is sordid, nasty, ghoulish.

The result of this fear makes for a definite alteration in the behavior pattern. Very early the tendency is to make the body commit to memory the ways of behavior that may reduce the exposure to immediate violence. This explains in large part why there is so little organized resistance against segregation. Each new generation of children is psychologically and socially conditioned in an effort to reduce the exposure to spasmodic, irresponsible, systematic, and calculating sadistic impulses. The injury to personality is far greater than can be adequately grasped even by the most sensitive. To be denied freedom of movement, freedom of participation in the common life, is to have the ground of personality value seriously shaken. When in moments of national crises the segregated are granted temporary citizenship, one of the first acts is to attack segregation. This is a sound instinct of self-preservation, and it provides the opening for all people of good will to give concrete expression to their commitments.

The effect of segregation on the white group is just as deadly. It gives them a false sense of superiority. What is in essence a superiority of advantage becomes rationalized into superiority based upon logical, physical, and spiritual difference. It is impossible for a white child to grow up in an atmosphere in which normal impulses of friendliness must be constantly short-circuited so as to apply only to his own kind, without there dawning upon him that the fact of this difference in attitude is not due to a difference in superior essence. The mind becomes a seedbed of all kinds of fears and superstitions with reference to Negroes, and if there is nothing in the environment at home or abroad to counteract these fears they become facts on the basis of which the life is planned and years are fulfilled. *All emphasis on brotherhood or love inherent in the Christian religion is doomed to recognize these "fear facts" as extenuating circumstances in which love and brotherhood are not supposed to be effective!*

Therefore, unless the "will to segregate" is relaxed there can be no sound basis of hope for the fulfillment of the dream of democracy in this life of ours.

THE CHURCH'S TASK

For the church this means a radical internal reorganization of policy and of structural change. I am realistic enough to know that this cannot be done overnight. My contention is that if the "will to segregate" is relaxed in the church, then the resources of mind and spirit and power that are already in the church can begin working formally and informally on the radical changes that are necessary if the church is to become Christian. This, of course, may not mean that there will be no congregations that are all Negro, or that are all white, but freedom of choice, which is basically a sense of alternatives, will be available to any persons without regard to the faithful perpetuation of the pattern of segregation upon which the Christian church in America is constructed.

How dare we undertake to teach reverence to children when we ourselves do not believe in reverence for life in general or life in particular as a valid concept in our kind of world? Shall we teach lies to children? How dare we proclaim sincerity and genuineness as essential qualities for healthy living if in our innermost selves we do not have confidence in the survival values of such ideals of living? Can we teach trust when we are bound by a vast network of impersonal social relations which create the kind of climate in which trust cannot possibly thrive? Or can we teach trust even as we confess how little of trust we have in each other, in our cause, and in our God? I wonder. What do we mean when we teach the brotherhood of man, when over and over again we give the sanction of our religion and the weight of our practice to those subtle anti-Christian practices expressed in segregated churches and even in segregated graveyards! Can we expect more of the state, of the body politic, of industry than we expect of the church? How can we teach love from behind the great high walls of separateness?

THE HUMAN TASK

But more personally, what must a person do who wishes to work effectively on this problem within the framework of Christian ethics?

In the first place I must see to it that what I condemn in society, I do not permit to grow and flower in me. The will to discriminate against others must be rooted out of the springs of my own action.

But even if my heart is pure, my motives above reproach, and my personal action unequivocal and positive, this is not enough. I must share the guilt of my age, my society, and my race. Therefore, I must exhaust all possible means that do not conflict with my ends for bringing about the kind of society in which it is possible for men to live in large groups without external limitations, to experience the good life. This means that for my second action I must put my creative mind to work in the devising of techniques, personal and group, for the achievement of these ends.

High among these techniques are those that belong in the general classification of moral suasion, attempts to make individual and social conscience articulate with reference to a specific sin. Moral suasion has only one serious limitation: the amount of moral atrophy that has taken place in the mind and character of the persons who are to be aroused. I must be patient. I must keep working and persuading and appealing on the assumption, of course, that all people are the children of God—the good and the bad. This means that the Christian will brood over the human hearts as the living instrument of the spirit of God until there is a stirring of consciousness both of sin and of kinship in their hearts.

The third type of personal action is even more difficult because a conflict of loyalties makes the decision of positive Christian action in a given situation very difficult to determine. There may be a conflict between my loyalty to the ideal fellowship viewed with reference to the weak, and my kinship with them. The strong are my kin as truly as the weak. I am apt to be caught between the recognition of fundamental kinship with the strong, and the desperation of the weak. Or the conflict may arise from a completely ethical demand of my religion that I wash my hands of the doers of iniquity and leave them to go on their recklessly destructive way, feeling that there are some types of struggle in which even God does not demand that I participate. I may say this type of action is not for me and to all the pull of the needy who are on the receiving end of the violence of the wicked I may turn a deaf ear—if I can.

But I may decide that I cannot wait for the thing to work itself out. There is too much agony, too much hunger, too much poverty and misery everywhere, too many flagrant denials of kinship all along the line. Something concrete must be done now. To wait for moral pressure to work its perfect work may be too late.

What do I do then? I may resort to the exercise of some form of shock by organizing a boycott, or widespread noncooperation, or the like. The function of these techniques is to tear people free from their alignments to the evil way, to free them so that they may be given an immediate sense of acute insecurity and out of the depths of their insecurity be forced to see their kinship with the weak and the insecure. People do not voluntarily relinquish their hold on their place. It is not until something becomes movable in the situation that they are spiritually prepared to apply Christian idealism to un-ideal and unchristian situations. Examples of these techniques are being developed by FOR groups and others in different parts of the world even now.

Action of this kind requires great discipline of mind, emotions, and body to the end that forces may not be released that will do complete violence both to one's ideals and one's purpose. All must be done with the full consciousness of the Divine Scrutiny.

31

THE COMING REVOLT
AGAINST JIM CROW

James Farmer

James Farmer graduated from college at the age of sixteen. Hired by FOR to work on the issue of racism, he helped to organize the Congress on Racial Equality (CORE), which played a prominent role in moving nonviolence toward movement status. It was Farmer's hope that returning black soldiers would be the perfect vanguard of a revolution of race relations in the United States. In this 1945 essay he sagely targeted interstate transportation and lunch-counter desegregation as the places to start, and this well before the famous demonstrations in the late 1950s (Fellowship, *May 1945*).

Nearly a million Negro youths have been inducted into the nation's armed forces. These men have been told that they are fighting against the theory of the "master race" and for freedom from the terrors of exploitation. That lofty aim they have in large measure accepted, though sensing an inconsistency in fighting abroad to protect for others the rights which they themselves have never enjoyed. Furthermore, their treatment, while in uniform, by their own countrymen and superior officers, has often been such as to lead them to question the war aims professed by their superiors and their government.

These Negro Americans upon returning to their native land, will find Jim Crow still alive and kicking. The bullets they have hurled at the master-race monster abroad, their blood that was spilt, will not have destroyed the monstrous master-race concept at home!

We do not know whether the American people realize how shameful, wicked, and tragic it is that this should be so. These young Negroes will have gone through all that other servicemen have of weariness, of danger, pain, disfigurement, horror. But in addition they will have experienced almost constant discrimination of one kind or another and frequent humiliation, and this while fighting a war allegedly fought to put an end to such things!

Even if Negroes did not object to a continuation of Jim Crow, others who profess and believe in democracy and Christianity, and especially members of such organizations as the Fellowship of Reconciliation, could not rest easy in mind and conscience. As individuals they would certainly feel that nothing could justify the continuation of Jim Crow practices, and that they must do everything in their power to persuade their fellowmen throughout the land to abandon such discrimination.

Think of the material and spiritual loss and woe, for colored and whites alike, represented by racial discrimination and segregation. Think of the certainty of racial conflict if the situation is not soon remedied. Think, on the other hand, what it would mean if, as the war draws to a close, the people of this land were to take their stand squarely on the Declaration of Independence, the Constitution of the United States, the findings of all reputable modern science, and the teachings of the Jewish and Christian scriptures, and were to launch a crusade for racial democracy and the practice of complete brotherhood in relations between the races.

But of course the Negro people are not disposed to submit to the old Jim Crow pattern. The returning Negro servicemen certainly will not be in a submissive mood. They will be resentful, bold, aggressive. After facing an inferno of the land, of the seas, of the skies, they will not be deterred by the worst that Negro-baiters can throw at them in penalty for their insistence upon equality. Even now they are saying openly that when they return they will not tolerate the same old treatment. And they won't.

Here, then, will be a veritable volcano of revolt. This is true, whether we like it or not! The experiences burning in the memories of these men, and the temper of the times will urge them on to vigorous resistance to race discrimination in postwar America. Counseling them to show no extraordinary resistance, for fear of arousing reprisals, would be like admonishing a man not to dislodge a stinging hornet from his neck lest he attract other hornets as well. His whole being cries out that the hornet must be dislodged. And even so, Negro veterans will feel irresistibly impelled to resist.

But what will be the pattern of their resistance? How will they protest? There is no question in this hour more vital. Will it be a disorganized, scattered, and aimless protest, like a man striking out blindly against his assailant? If so, it will be ineffectual. Will their training in the use of brute force on the battle front drive them to violence on the home front? When the Negro veteran is ordered to conform to Jim Crow seating in transportation or is refused service in a restaurant, will he retaliate with impetuous outbursts of resentment and vengeance? If so, his approach will be suicidal.

We have already pointed out that it would be both wrong and useless to conclude that we should counsel Negro ex-servicemen to submit to a perpetuation of practices which not only injure and humiliate them but also undermine the foundations of our democracy. On the other hand, it is certainly not for others to tell them what to do—especially others who have not shared their war experiences and might not be able to share the trials and difficulties resulting from opposition to Jim Crow. Yet it may be that these veterans have a special responsibility to remove these evils.

The returned Negro veterans may be called upon to do what the Negro people have failed to do in the past. No great and oppressive evil is ever truly wiped out until the people oppressed by that evil, together with their sympathizers, refuse to participate in and cooperate with that evil. Too often in the past we Negroes have opposed Jim Crow verbally, while in practice, however reluctantly, we have accepted it. The next step is to refuse to accept it in practice. In this the ex-servicemen can and should lead the way. The very fact that they are veterans of the "war for the freedoms" will have a dramatic and emotional appeal which can only with difficulty be ignored. Their protest will be not merely a protest of Negroes, but will be a protest of Negro youth who have risked their lives, many of whom have been wounded, crippled, and broken in a war which their nation told them was for democracy and freedom. They will be asking simply for a share of the democracy for which they fought. And with such a mild and reasonable request many will surely sympathize.

We submit for consideration and study the suggestion that one way to make the coming protest of veterans effective would be to organize an *Ex-Servicemen's Association against Discrimination*. This proposed organization should in itself bear no trace of the racism which it endeavors to destroy. To achieve maximum effectiveness, it should be open to all veterans of this war, without distinctions of race, color, or creed—it should welcome all who will completely renounce racial caste and will launch persistent planned action against Jim Crow in all its manifestations.

These men, accustomed to army discipline, should be given another discipline, equally exacting, through which they will assiduously refrain from violence, in the realization that any violence used in this program will react against the cause. This cannot be overemphasized. Entirely apart from the principle involved, violence on the part of persons opposing racial injustice in America is a boomerang—suicidal. Not only do they lack the implements for successfully carrying on violent struggle, but if they try it they alienate many friends and neutrals whose sympathy they need. In addition, the police are honestly performing their duty when they restrain persons using violence, however just the cause.

What is needed, therefore, is for the proposed *Ex-Servicemen's Association against Discrimination* to launch a systematic program of nonviolent direct action against Jim Crow in transportation, in public places, and in housing—a program coordinated with the efforts of other organizations in this direction. The more promptly and efficiently we pursue other means, such as legislation against discriminatory practices and provision of jobs for all, the less need there will be for direct action. Greater accomplishment may be anticipated also if white veterans of this war who are interested in the same cause would join with their Negro comrades in the organization and its program. We have already indicated that a grave responsibility for making democracy a reality in relations between the races rests upon the majority group and that many of them keenly feel that responsibility.

In public transportation, where Jim Crow customs and laws prevail, these Negro ex-servicemen would ignore the segregation pattern by refusing to sit in the rear sections of buses and street cars or in the Jim Crow coaches on trains. This they should do with a careful lack of belligerence, and when challenged they should show necessary credentials quietly and without antagonism, explain their action on the ground of being ex-servicemen who have fought for "democracy and freedom" in their nation's armed forces, and point out that they are simply seeking to enjoy the things here for which they fought abroad.

At the same time their white comrades should make evident their support and insist upon the justice of their position. There should be a carefully planned effort to interpret the incident to other persons present, through quiet conversations or possibly through distribution of explanatory leaflets or cards. In case violence is used against them, they should refrain from retaliating with violence, and should remain peaceful. In case the police are summoned, they should peacefully submit to arrest, and the program of interpreting what has happened should be continued by white and Negro comrades who have remained sufficiently out of the controversy to avoid arrest. This should be repeated again and again.

In places of public accommodation, a similar pattern should be followed. The ex-servicemen should enter discriminatory restaurants, for example, and seek service. If refused, they should employ nonviolent resistance against this injustice on the grounds of their status as ex-servicemen in the struggle for freedom and against the super-race theory of Hitlerism. The same program of interpreting what is happening should be carried on. If circumstances should invite, it may be well for one of the men, here as well as in transportation, preferably one of the white comrades, to make a speech on the spot, appealing to the sense of decency of the other people present.

In a campaign against racially restrictive residential agreements, Negro veterans, with the aid of white veterans, should seek to purchase homes and secure leases on apartments in restricted areas. Intimidation should be resisted nonviolently. If court cases are forthcoming, they should be carried on with the aid of the National Association for the Advancement of Colored People and the American Civil Liberties Union, and other organizations within whose jurisdiction such cases fall. Throughout the procedure, the fact that the men involved are ex-servicemen should be exploited to the utmost for its public relations value. In other areas of action, such as employment, the fact that men discriminated against are ex-servicemen should be utilized with the greatest diligence in support of the efforts of labor unions and fair employment practices committees.

It is important to emphasize that the program of *interpretation* will be quite as crucial as the program of *action*. In the past, members of veterans' organizations have used their status as ex-servicemen for reactionary ends; it would be sheer criminal neglect if they now fail to use that status for revolutionary ends.

Veterans' organizations traditionally have espoused patriotism; this one would espouse a new and dynamic, a more broadly based and genuine patriotism.

This proposal, executed with imagination, I submit, can achieve tremendous gains for racial democracy. Through it, returning Negro GIs would be genuine heroes in the home-front struggle. The indebtedness of the Negro people to them would be immeasurable. The indebtedness of all Americans and all lovers of democracy throughout the world would be as great.

32

WALK FOR FREEDOM

Martin Luther King Jr.

At Martin Luther King Jr.'s request, FOR dispatched Glenn Smiley to work with King in the Montgomery bus boycott. Thus began a long and rich relationship between the Southern Christian Leadership Conference and FOR. This brief article already strikes the themes that would remain constant in King's message, despite their never being welcome, especially in incendiary situations such as those depicted here. Love, nonviolence, forgiveness—King had found a way to take the central themes of Christianity and organize them into a movement (Fellowship, *May 1956*).

The present protest here in Montgomery on the part of the Negro citizens grows out of many experiences—experiences that have often been humiliating and have led to deep resentment. The Negro citizens of Montgomery compose about 75 percent of the bus riders. In riding buses, they have confronted conditions which have made for a great deal of embarrassment, such as having to stand over empty seats, having to pay fares at the front door and going out to the back to get on, and then the very humiliating experience of being arrested for refusing to get up and give a seat to a person of another race.

These conditions and those experiences have now reached the point that the Negro citizens are tired, and this tiredness was expressed on December 5, when more than 99 percent of the Negro bus riders decided not to ride the buses in a protest against these unjust conditions. This protest has lasted now for many, many weeks and it is still in process.

From the beginning, we have insisted on nonviolence. This is a protest—a *nonviolent* protest against injustice. We are depending on moral and spiritual forces. To put it another way, this is a movement of passive resistance and the great instrument is the instrument of love. We feel that this is our chief weapon, and that no matter how long we are involved in the protest, no matter how tragic the experiences are, no matter what sacrifices we have to make, we will not let anybody drag us so low as to hate them.

Love *must* be at the forefront of our movement if it is to be a successful movement. And when we speak of love, we speak of understanding, good will toward *all* men. We speak of a creative, a redemptive sort of love so that as we look at the problem, we see that the real tension is not between the Negro citizens and the white citizens of Montgomery, but it is a conflict between justice and injustice, between the forces of light and the forces of darkness, and if there is a victory—and there will be a victory—the victory will not be merely for the Negro citizens and a defeat for the white citizens, but it will be a victory for justice and a defeat of injustice. It will be a victory for goodness in its long struggle with the forces of evil.

This is a spiritual movement, and we intend to keep these things in the forefront. We know that violence will defeat our purpose. We know that in our struggle in America and in our specific struggle here in Montgomery, violence will not only be impractical but immoral. We are outnumbered; we do not have access to the instruments of violence. Even more than that, not only is violence impractical, but it is *immoral*; for it is my firm conviction that to seek to retaliate with violence does nothing but intensify the existence of evil and hate in the universe.

Along the way of life, someone must have *sense* enough and morality enough to cut off the chain of hate and evil. The greatest way to do that is through love. I believe firmly that love is a transforming power that can lift a whole community to new horizons of fair play, good will and justice.

Love is our great instrument and our great weapon, and that alone. On January 30 my home was bombed. My wife and baby were there; I was attending a meeting. I first heard of the bombing at the meeting, when someone came to me and mentioned it, and I tried to accept it in a very calm manner. I first inquired about my wife and daughter; then, after I found out that they were all right, I stopped in the midst of the meeting and spoke to the group, and urged them not to be panicky and not to do anything about it because that was not the way.

I immediately came home and on entering the front of the house, I noticed there were some five hundred to a thousand persons. I came in the house and looked it over and went back to see my wife and to see if the baby was all right, but as I stood in the back of the house, hundreds and hundreds of people were still gathering, and I saw there that violence was a possibility.

It was at that time that I went to the porch and tried to say to the people that we could not allow ourselves to be panicky. We could not allow ourselves to retaliate with any type of violence, but that we were stirred to confront the problem with *love*.

One statement that I made—and I believe it very firmly—was: "He who lives by the sword will perish by the sword." I urged the people to continue to manifest love, and to continue to carry on the struggle with the same dignity and with the same discipline that we had started out with. I think at that time the people did decide to go home, things did get quiet, and it ended up with a great deal of calmness and a great deal of discipline which I think our community should be proud of and which I was very proud to see because our people were determined not to retaliate with violence.

Some twenty-six of the ministers and almost one hundred of the citizens of the city were indicted in this boycott. But we realized in the beginning that we would confront experiences that make for great sacrifices, experiences that are not altogether pleasant. We decided among ourselves that we would stand up to the finish, and that is what we are determined to do. In the midst of the indictments, we still hold to this nonviolent attitude, and this primacy of love.

Even though convicted, we will not retaliate with hate but will still stand with love in our hearts, and stand resisting injustice with the same determination with which we started out. We need a great deal of encouragement in this movement. Of course, one thing that we are depending on, from not only other communities but from our own community, is prayer. We ask people everywhere to pray that God will guide us, pray that justice will be done and that righteousness will stand. And I think through these prayers we will be strengthened; it will make us feel the unity of the nation and the presence of Almighty God. For as we said all along, this is a spiritual movement.

33

FACING THE CHALLENGE
OF A NEW AGE

Martin Luther King Jr.

In this essay Martin Luther King Jr. spells out the situation that made a nonviolent movement possible, not only in the American South but all around the world, wherever oppressed people were crying out for liberation. People of color, King asserted, must take responsibility for their own freedom. They must achieve excellence in all they do, they must act out of love and not hatred, and they must bankroll the struggle and not depend on whites to do so. Even after over forty years, this essay is still an effective program for nonviolent social change. This article is adapted from Dr. King's Annual Address, delivered at the First Annual Institute on Nonviolence and Social Change under the auspices of the Montgomery Improvement Association, December 3, 1956 (Fellowship, *February 1957*).

We who live in the twentieth century are privileged to live in one of the most momentous periods of human history. It is an exciting age, filled with hope. It is an age in which a new social order is being born. We stand today between two worlds—the dying old and the emerging new.

Now I am aware of the fact that there are those who would contend that we live in the most ghastly period of human history. They would argue that the rhythmic beat of the deep rumblings of discontent from Asia, the uprisings in Africa, the nationalistic longings of Egypt, the roaring cannons from Hungary, and the racial tensions of America are all indicative of the deep and tragic midnight which encompasses our civilization. They would argue that we are retrogressing instead of progressing. But far from representing retrogression and tragic meaninglessness, the present tensions represent the necessary pains that accompany the birth of anything new. Long ago the Greek philosopher Heraclitus argued that justice emerges from the strife of opposites, and through struggle. It is both historically and biologically true that there can be no birth and growth without birth pains and growing pains. Whenever there is the emergence of the new, we confront the recalcitrance of the old. So the tensions which we witness in the world today are indicative of the fact that a new world order is being born and an old order is passing away.

We are all familiar with the old order that is passing away. We have lived with it for many years. We have seen it in its international aspect, in the form of colonialism and imperialism. There are approximately 2,400,000,000 people in this world, and the vast majority—about 1,600,000,000 of the people of the world—are colored. Fifty years ago, or even twenty-five years ago, most of the latter lived under the yoke of some foreign power. We could turn our eyes to China and see there six hundred million men and women under the pressing yoke of British, Dutch, and French rule. We could turn our eyes to Indonesia and see a hundred million men and women under the domination of the Dutch. We could turn to India and Pakistan and notice four hundred million brown men and women under the pressing yoke of the British. We could turn our eyes to Africa and notice there two hundred million black men and women under the pressing yoke of the British, the Belgians, the Portuguese, and the French. For years all of these people were dominated politically, exploited economically, segregated and humiliated.

But there comes a time when people get tired. There comes a time when people get tired of being trampled over by the iron feet of oppression. There comes a time when people get tired of being plunged across the abyss of exploitation where they experience the bleakness of nagging despair. There comes a time when people get tired of being pushed out of the glittering sunlight of life's July and left standing in the piercing chill of an Alpine November. So in the midst of their tiredness these people decided to rise up and protest against injustice. As a result of their protest, more than 1,300,000,000 of the colored peoples of the world are free today. They have their own governments, their own economic systems, and their own educational systems. To paraphrase biblical history, they have broken loose from the Egypt of colonialism and imperialism, and they are now moving through the wilderness of adjustment toward the promised land of cultural integration. As they look back they see the old order of colonialism and imperialism passing away and the new order of freedom and justice coming into being.

THE OLD ORDER IN AMERICA

We have also seen the old order in our own nation, in the form of segregation and discrimination. We know something of the long history of this old order in America. It had its beginning in the year 1619 when the first Negro slaves landed on the shores of this nation. They were brought here from the soils of Africa. And unlike the Pilgrim fathers who landed at Plymouth a year later, they were brought here against their wills. Throughout slavery the Negro was treated in a very inhuman fashion. He was a thing to be used, not a person to be respected. He was merely a depersonalized cog in a vast plantation machine. The famous Dred Scott Decision of 1857 well illustrates the status of the Negro during slavery. In this decision the Supreme Court of the United States said, in substance, that the Negro is not a citizen of the United States; he is merely property subject to the dictates of his owner. Then came 1896. It was in this year that the Supreme Court of this nation, through the Plessy v. Ferguson Decision, established the doctrine of "separate-but-equal" as the law of the land. Through this decision segregation gained legal and moral sanction. The end result of the Plessy Doctrine was that it led to a strict enforcement of the "separate," with hardly the slightest attempt to abide by the "equal." So the Plessy Doctrine ended up making for tragic inequalities and ungodly exploitation.

Living under these conditions many Negroes came to the point of losing faith in themselves. They came to feel that perhaps they were less than human. The great tragedy of physical slavery was that it led to the paralysis of mental slavery. So long as the Negro maintained this subservient attitude and accepted this "place" assigned to him, a sort of racial peace existed. But it was an uneasy peace in which the Negro was forced patiently to accept insult, injustice, and exploitation. It was a negative peace. True peace is not merely the absence of some negative force—tension, confusion, or war; it is the presence of some positive force—justice, good will, and brotherhood. And so the peace which presently existed between the races was a negative peace devoid of any positive and lasting quality.

Then something happened to the Negro. Circumstances made it necessary for him to travel more. His rural plantation background was gradually being supplanted by migration to urban and industrial communities. His economic life was gradually rising to decisive proportions. His cultural life was gradually rising through the steady decline of crippling illiteracy. All of these factors conjoined to cause the Negro to take a new look at himself. Negro masses began to reevaluate themselves. The Negro came to feel that he was somebody. His religion revealed to him that God loves all of his children, and that every man, from a bass black to a treble white, is significant on God's keyboard.

With this new self-respect, this new sense of dignity on the part of the Negro, the South's negative peace was rapidly undermined. And so the tension which we are witnessing in race relations today can be explained, in part, by the revolutionary change in the Negro's evaluation of himself, and his determination to struggle and sacrifice until the walls of segregation have finally been crushed by the battering rams of surging justice.

Along with the emergence of a "new Negro," with a new sense of dignity and destiny, came that memorable decision of May 17, 1954. In this decision the Supreme Court of this nation unanimously affirmed that the old Plessy Doctrine must go. This decision came as a legal and sociological death blow to an evil that had occupied the throne of American life for several decades. It affirmed in no uncertain terms that separate facilities are inherently unequal and that to segregate a child because of his race is to deny him equal protection of the law. With the coming of this great decision, we could gradually see the old order of segregation and discrimination passing away, and the new order of freedom and justice taking shape.

Let nobody fool you—all of the loud noises that you hear today from the legislative halls of the South about "interposition" and "nullification," and about outlawing the NAACP, are merely the death groans of a dying system. The old order is passing away, and the new order is coming into being. We are witnessing in our day the birth of a new age, with a new structure of freedom and justice.

Now as we face the fact of this new emerging world, we must face the responsibilities that come along with it. A new age brings with it new challenges. Let us consider some of the challenges of this new age.

First we are challenged to rise above the narrow confines of our individualistic concerns to the broader concerns of all humanity. The new world is a world of geographical togetherness. This means that no individual or nation can live alone. We must all learn to live together, or we will be forced to die together. This new world of geographical togetherness has been brought about, to a great extent, by man's scientific and technological genius. Man, through his scientific genius, has been able to dwarf distance and place time in chains; he has been able to carve highways through the stratosphere. Our world is geographically one. Now we are faced with the challenge of making it *spiritually* one. Through our scientific genius we have made of the world a neighborhood; now through our moral and spiritual genius we must make of it a brotherhood. We are all involved in the single process. Whatever affects one directly affects all indirectly. We are all links in the great chain of humanity.

A second challenge that the new age brings to each of us is that of achieving excellence in our various fields of endeavor. In the new age many doors will be opening to us that were not open in the past, and the great challenge which we confront is to be prepared to enter these doors as they open. In an essay written back in 1871, Ralph Waldo Emerson said: "If a man can write a better book, or preach a better sermon, or make a better mousetrap than his neighbor, even if he builds his house in the woods, the world will make a beaten path to his door." In the years to come this will be increasingly true.

In the new age we Negroes will be forced to compete with people of all races and nationalities. Therefore, we cannot aim merely to be good Negro teachers, good Negro doctors, good Negro ministers, good Negro skilled laborers. We must set out to do a good job, irrespective of race, and do it so well that nobody could do it better.

A third challenge that stands before us is that of entering the new age with understanding good will. This simply means that the Christian virtues of love, mercy, and forgiveness should stand at the center of our lives. There is the danger that those of us who have lived so long under the yoke of oppression, those of us who have been exploited and trampled over, those of us who have had to stand amid the tragic midnight of injustice and indignities will enter the new age with hate and bitterness. But if we retaliate with hate and bitterness, the new age will be nothing but a duplication of the old age. We must blot out the hate and injustice of the old age with the love and justice of the new. This is why I believe so firmly in nonviolence. Violence never solves problems. It only creates new and more complicated ones. If we succumb to the temptation of using violence in our struggle for justice, unborn generations will be the recipients of a long and desolate night of bitterness, and our chief legacy to the future will be an endless reign of meaningless chaos.

We have before us the glorious opportunity to inject a new dimension of love into the veins of our civilization. There is still a voice crying out in words that echo across the generations, saying: "Love your enemies, bless them that curse you, pray for them that despitefully use you, that you may be the children of your Father which is in Heaven." This love may well be the salvation of our civilization. This is why I am so impressed with our motto for the week, "Freedom and Justice through Love." Not through violence, through hate; no, not even through boycotts; but through *love*. It is true that as we struggle for freedom in America we will have to boycott at times. But we must remember, as we do so, that a boycott is not an end itself; it is merely a means to awaken a sense of shame within the oppressor and challenge his false sense of superiority. But the end is reconciliation; the end is redemption; the end is the creation of the beloved community. It is this type of spirit and this type of love that can transform opposers into friends. It is this type of understanding good will that will transform the deep gloom of the old age into the exuberant gladness of the new age. It is this love which will bring about miracles in the hearts of men.

Now I realize that in talking so much about "love" it is very easy to become sentimental. There is the danger that our talk about love will merely be empty words devoid of any practical and true meaning. But when I say "love those who oppose you," I am not speaking of love in a sentimental or affectionate sense. It would be nonsense to urge men to love their oppressors in an affectionate sense. When I refer to love in this context I mean understanding good will. The Greek language comes to our aid at this point. It has three words for love. First it speaks of love in terms of *eros*. Plato used this word quite frequently in his dialogues. *Eros* is a type of esthetic or romantic love. And then there is *Philia*, a sort of intimate affection between personal friends. On this level a person loves because he is loved.

DIVINE LOVE

The highest level of love is that of *agape*. *Agape* means nothing sentimental or basically affectionate. It means understanding redeeming good will for all. It is an overflowing love which seeks nothing in return. It is the love of God working in human lives. When we rise to love on the *agape* level, we love others not because we like them, not because their attitudes and ways appeal to us, but because God loves them. Here we rise to the position of loving the *person* who does the evil deed, while hating the *deed* that the person does. With this type of love—understanding good will—we will be able to stand amid the radiant glow of the new age with dignity and discipline. Yes, the new age is coming. It is coming mighty fast.

Now the fact that this new age is emerging reveals something basic about the universe. It tells us something about the core and heartbeat of the cosmos. It reminds us that the universe is on the side of justice. It says to those who struggle for justice, "You do not struggle alone, but God struggles with you." This belief that God is on the side of truth and justice comes down to us from the long tradition of our Christian faith. There is something at the very center of our faith which reminds us that the sorrow of Good Friday may be with us for a day, but ultimately it must give way to the triumph of Easter. Evil may so shape events that Caesar will occupy a palace and Christ a cross, but one day that same Christ will rise up and split history into A.D. and B.C., so that even the life of Caesar must be dated by His name. There is something in this universe that justified Carlyle in saying, "No lie can live forever." There is something in this universe which justified William Cullen Bryant in saying, "Truth crushed to earth will rise again." There is something in this universe that justified James Russell Lowell in saying:

> Truth forever on the scaffold
> Wrong forever on the throne
> Yet that scaffold sways the future
> And behind the dim unknown stands God
> Within the shadows keeping watch above his own.

And so here in Montgomery, after more than eleven long months, we can walk and never get weary, because we know there is a great camp meeting in the promised land of freedom and justice.

I have talked about the new age which is fast coming into being. I have talked about the fact that God is working in history to bring about this new age. There is the danger, therefore, that after hearing all of this you will go away with the impression that we can go home, sit down, and do nothing, waiting for the coming of the inevitable. You will somehow feel that this new age will roll in on the wheels of inevitability, so there is nothing to do but wait on it. If you get that impression you are the victims of a perilous optimism. We must speed up the coming of the inevitable.

Now it is true, if I may speak figuratively, that old man segregation is on his deathbed. But history has proven that social systems have a great last-minute breathing power, and the guardians of a status quo are always on hand with their oxygen tents to keep the old order alive. Segregation is still a fact in America. We still confront it in the South in its glaring and conspicuous forms. We still confront it in the North in its hidden and subtle forms. But if democracy is to live, segregation must die. Segregation is a glaring evil. It is utterly unchristian. It relegates the segregated to the status of a thing rather than elevating him to the status of a person. Segregation is nothing but slavery covered up with certain niceties of complexity. Segregation is a blatant denial of the unity which we all have in Christ Jesus.

CONTINUING THE STRUGGLE

So we must continue the struggle against segregation in order to speed up the coming of the inevitable. We must continue to gain the ballot. This is one of the basic keys to the solution of our problem. Until we gain political power through possession of the ballot we will be the convenient tools of unscrupulous politicians.

We must continue to struggle through legalism and legislation. There are those who contend that integration can come only through education, for no other reason than that morals cannot be legislated. I choose, however, to be dialectical at this point. It isn't either education or legislation; it is both legislation and education. I quite agree that it is impossible to change a man's internal feelings merely through law. But this really isn't the intention of the law. The law does not seek to change one's internal feelings; it seeks rather to control the external effects of those internal feelings. For instance, the law cannot make a man love me—religion and education must do that—but it can control his desire to lynch me. So in order to control the external effects of prejudiced internal feelings, we must continue to struggle through legislation.

Another thing that we must do in pressing on for integration is to invest our finances in the cause of freedom. Freedom has always been an expensive thing. History is a fit testimony to the fact that freedom is rarely gained without sacrifice and self-denial. So we must donate large sums of money to the cause of freedom. We can no longer complain that we don't have the money. Statistics reveal that the economic life of the Negro is rising to decisive proportions. The annual income of the American Negro is now more than sixteen billion dollars, almost equal to the national income of Canada. So we are gradually becoming economically independent. It would be a tragic indictment of both the self-respect and practical wisdom of the Negro if history reveals that at the height of the twentieth century the Negro spent more for frivolities than for the cause of freedom. We must never let it be said that we spend more for the evanescent and ephemeral than for the eternal values of freedom and justice.

Another thing that we must do in speeding up the coming of the new age is to develop intelligent, courageous, and dedicated leadership. This is one of the pressing needs of the hour. In this period of transition and growing social change, there is a dire need for leaders who are calm and yet positive, leaders who avoid the extremes of "hotheadedness" and "Uncle Tomism." The urgency of the hour calls for leaders of wise judgment and sound integrity—leaders not in love with money but in love with justice; leaders not in love with publicity, but in love with humanity; leaders who can subject their particular egos to the greatness of the cause.

To paraphrase Holland's words:

God give us leaders!
A time like this demands strong minds, great hearts,
True faith and ready hands;
Leaders whom the lust of office does not kill;
Leaders whom the spoils of life cannot buy;
Leaders who possess opinions and a will;
Leaders who have honor; leaders who will not lie;
Leaders who can stand before a demagogue
And damn his treacherous flatteries without winking!
Tall leaders, sun-crowned, who live above the fog
In public duty and private thinking.

Finally, if we are to speed up the coming of the new age we must have the moral courage to stand up and protest against injustice wherever we find it. Wherever we find segregation we must have the fortitude to passively resist it. I realize that this will mean suffering and sacrifice. It might even mean going to jail. If such is the case, we must be willing to fill up the jailhouses of the South. It might even mean physical death. But if physical death is the price that some must pay to free their children from a permanent life of psychological death, then nothing could be more honorable. Once more it might well turn out that the blood of the martyrs will be the seed of the tabernacle of freedom.

Someone will ask, How will we face the acts of cruelty and violence that might come as results of our standing up for justice? What will be our defense? Certainly it must not be retaliatory violence. We must find our defense in the amazing power of unity and courage that we have demonstrated in Montgomery. Our defense is to meet every act of violence toward an individual Negro with the fact that there are thousands of others who will present themselves in his place as potential victims. Every time one schoolteacher is fired for standing up courageously for justice, it must be faced with the fact that there are four thousand more to be fired. If the oppressors bomb the home of one Negro for his courage, this must be met with the fact that they must be required to bomb the homes of fifty thousand more Negroes. This dynamic unity, this amazing self-respect, this willingness to suffer, and this refusal to hit back will soon cause the oppressor to become ashamed of his own methods. He will be forced to stand before the world and his God splattered with the blood and reeking with the stench of his Negro brother.

There is nothing in all the world greater than freedom. It is worth paying for; it is worth losing a job for; it is worth going to jail for. I would rather be a free pauper than a rich slave. I would rather die in abject poverty with my convictions than live in inordinate riches with the lack of self-respect. Once more every Negro must be able to cry out with his forefathers: "Before I'll be a slave, I'll be buried in my grave and go home to my Father and be free."

If we will join together in doing all of these things we will be able to speed up the coming of the new world—a new world in which people will live together as brothers and sisters; a world in which they will beat their swords into plow-shares and their spears into pruning hooks; a world in which they will no longer take necessities from the masses to give luxuries to the classes; a world in which all will respect the dignity and worth of every human personality. Then we will be able to sing from the great tradition of our nation:

My country, 'tis of thee, sweet land of liberty, of thee I sing! Land where my fathers died, land of the Pilgrims' pride, from every mountainside, let freedom ring!

This must become literally true. Freedom must ring from every mountainside. Yes, let it ring from the snowcapped Rockies of Colorado, from the prodigious hilltops of New Hampshire, from the mighty Alleghenies of Pennsylvania, from the curvaceous slopes of California. But not only that. Let freedom ring from every mountainside—from every molehill in Mississippi, from Stone Mountain in Georgia, from Lookout Mountain in Tennessee, yes, and from every hill and mountain in Alabama. From every mountainside—let freedom ring. When this day finally comes, "the morning stars will sing to-gether and the suns of God will shout for joy."

34

BEHIND THE SIT-INS

Lillian Smith

Lillian Smith was a resident of Clayton, Georgia, who frequently spoke out for racial equality. Perhaps best known for her novel Strange Fruit, *she also was the author of* Killers of the Dream, Now Is the Time, *and* One Hour. *In this essay she predicted that once the "good" white people broke their silence, the South would change quickly. Events have proven her right. Once white Christians became convinced (through the nonviolent suffering of civil rights activists such as the ones described in this article) that racism is a sin, many of them repented. Consequently, parts of the South have made far greater strides toward ending racism than the more secular North, where whites and blacks scarcely speak to each other* (Fellowship, *July 1960*).

The South and its people have been in ordeal a long time and have had outbursts of violence and localized crises again and again: in Little Rock, Montgomery, Clinton, Nashville, Tallahassee, and in other spots in the South.

But what we are now facing is not localized and cannot be. It is something different, something that has not happened in this country before; it has a new quality of hope in it, and is, I believe, of tremendous moral and political significance. Somehow it is involving not only students but all of us, and there is a growing sense that what we say or fail to say, do or fail to do, will surely shape the events that lie ahead.

This hour of decision—and it is that for the South, certainly—was precipitated on February 1 by a Negro student, age 18, a freshman in a college in Greensboro, North Carolina. He had seen a documentary film on the life of Gandhi; he had heard about Montgomery and the nonviolent protests made there; he had probably listened to Dr. Martin Luther King—certainly he knew about him; he had his memories of childhood and its racial hurts; and he had his hopes for the future. But millions of Southerners, young and old, and of both races, have had similar experiences. What else was there in this young student that caused him to be capable of his moment of truth? Courage, of course, and imagination and intelligence—and enough love to respond to Gandhi's love of humankind, and enough truth-seeking in his mind to realize the meaning of Gandhi's teaching of nonviolence and compassion and their redemptive and transforming power. Was this all the young man had? No, there was more: an indefinable, unpredictable potential for creating something new and lasting, and doing it at the right time. Every leader and every race hero, and many artists and scientists, possess this talent for fusing their lives with the future. And yet, I doubt that the young man knew he possessed this special quality, or even now knows it.

In some strange way, however, his thoughts and memories and hopes came together and he talked about what was on his mind with three young friends. And a short time afterward, the four of them went on their historic journey to a Greensboro ten-cent store.

From this small beginning, this almost absurd beginning, so incredibly simple and unpretentious that we Americans—used to the power of big names and money and crowds and Madison Avenue and Gallup polls—can scarcely believe in it, there started the nonviolent students' protests which have caught the imagination of millions of us.

Why are we stirred so deeply? What is it we feel? What are we hoping for? I cannot answer for you. For me, it is as if the "No Exit" sign is about to come down from our age; it is as if a door is opening in a wall where there was no door. The older generations, to which I belong, have found decisions so hard to make; they have wobbled this way and that in their beliefs; they have postponed the right action until the right time for it has passed. And now suddenly, completely unexpectedly, the students' sit-in protests began, spreading from college to college, school to school. It is exciting to watch them discover a freedom and purpose within themselves that they have not experienced in the outside world; to see them acting out, actually living, their beliefs in human dignity and democracy and in the redemptive power of love and nonviolence, and going to jail for their beliefs.

I think what has impressed me most has been the way they have done this, and their attitude toward white people. They are saying, by their acts, something like this: "Look, I am Negro and you are white, but all of us are human beings; and because we are human, we have moral and intellectual potentialities; we can create our future; we don't have to be prisoners of our grandfathers' past. We who are young can free ourselves—you and me, white and Negro." By their acts, they are saying: "All of us—white and Negro—are dominated by White Supremacy; all of us are crippled by segregation; all of us have lost our freedoms." They are saying: "Freedom is like the air; we'll breathe this air, together, all of us—or we'll suffocate. You can't segregate a hunk of it for white folks and then tell the Negroes there's none left for them." They are saying: "Freedom is not an object; freedom is a relationship that each man creates with his world: freedom is a dialog between us and our God; freedom is the sacred ground on which the human spirit has its being. It can't be divided up; it is ours, together, or it is nobody's."

Thoughts like these are forming in the students' minds as they live out their new purpose. Groping, slow words, maybe; faltering sentences, perhaps, for the language of the human spirit is complex and subtle, though its grammar is structurally simple and strong.

Wait now, you say. You are giving these students quite a buildup. Do you actually think they are so extraordinary? No, I don't. I think they are probably quite ordinary young people in most ways; they are extraordinary only in their awareness that the hour we live in is an hour calling for courage and commitment, and they are making their commitment, and in doing so they are finding their courage. Actually, I suspect they were pretty shaky, those first ones who walked in the stores with their books and their Bibles to make their protest. They probably didn't have one grand noble thought in their heads; they had made their decision in all earnestness and they were going through with it; and they were probably praying that they'd find the strength just to sit there; just sit there, that's all. But afterward, they must have felt an exaltation, a sudden rush of both pride and humility.

We who have accused the young of hungering for security, of not really caring about the big important things of the spirit; we who have called the intellectual ones "beatniks" and the livelier ones "rock-n-rollers" may have been right four years ago, or even last year. But we are not right today. For what these students are doing in the South is awakening students in the North and the Midwest to action, and something is happening.

And yet, even as I say this, I know the new life that is beginning, this spiritual renascence, can be snuffed out by you and me, by our apathy and stupidity and lack of imagination. I know police measures can become so cruel and massive and overwhelming that the students may not be able to take it. I am aware that a terrific effort will be made by certain powerful groups in the South who have close economic ties with the North to smother the movement by hushing the national press and the TV networks. I know that a few men in strategic places, by saying irresponsible things, can throw pretty big obstacles in the students' path. There will be accusations of the most vicious kind, and misinterpretations, idiotic and dangerous, and there will be persistent persecution.

And it may be that these young students won't have the stamina to hold out. They may not find within themselves enough moral resources, enough psychic strength to carry them through the bitter and bleak days ahead of them. I know, too, that the white students of the South may not be able to break out of their apathy and moral paralysis in large enough numbers to help the young Negroes in this struggle for a new life, and without help the burdens may prove too heavy.

But I believe the movement *can succeed* if enough of us have the imagination to see its significance and its creative possibilities and to interpret these to others who do not see, and if we give the students the moral support and the money they are going to need. There is a tremendous power in the nonviolent protest that the sensitive Southern conscience and heart will find hard to resist, but even so, the students may have to struggle a long time. They will need friends during their ordeal. Americans in other sections can help them and should, for this not only concerns the South, it concerns the entire nation and the nation's relationships with the rest of the world. It also concerns each person's relationship with himself and his beliefs.

LET THE SILENT SOUTH SPEAK

But there are some things that only the South can do, things that only good, responsible, decent white Southerners can accomplish. Only they can create a new climate of opinion in which mob violence and the hoodlums and the police and the White Citizens Councils can be controlled, and they can do this only by breaking their silence and speaking out. To speak out for law and order is not enough, today; there is a higher law which we Southerners must take a stand on that concerns justice and mercy and compassion and freedom of the spirit and mind. Thousands of us must also speak out against segregation as a way of life, not simply racial segregation but every form of spiritual and intellectual estrangement that splits man and his world into fragments. The time has come when we must face the fact that only by speaking out our real beliefs, and then acting on them, can we avoid a bitter time of hate and violence and suffering.

But will the Southerners do it? I don't know. I hope so, but I do not know. They let Little Rock happen when they could have kept that debacle out of the history books simply by taking a stand at the right time for the right things. They are now, in Birmingham, letting even worse things happen.

Our responsible people's silence is not because they are in the minority; they outnumber the demagogues and Klansmen and hoodlums and crackpots twenty to one. In their hands are the media of communication: the pulpits, the TV and radio stations, the newspapers. They have the power and the money, the education and the techniques to create an atmosphere of vigorous health-minded concern wherein good words can be heard and the good act carried through, an atmosphere where people can plan, think clearly, and find ways to do what is right.

Why, then, are they silent? Why do they evade their responsibility at this time of crisis?

Is it fear? I don't think so. I think it is anxiety. There is a vast difference between the two.

We white people of the South think of ourselves as free, but we are chained to taboos, to superstitions, tied to a mythic past that never existed, weakened by memories and beliefs that are in passionate conflict with each other.

The tragedy of the South lies just here: segregation has made psychic and moral slaves of so many of us. We think we are a free people, but we have lost our freedom to question, to learn, to do what our conscience tells us is right, to criticize ourselves. We are torn apart inside by a conflict that never lets up, and we wall our minds off into segregated compartments. How can a man believe simultaneously in brotherhood and racial discrimination? in human freedom and forced segregation? How can he fight Communist dictatorship and surrender himself to the dictatorship of an idea like White Supremacy? How can he do and think these things and fail to see the moral inconsistency, the intellectual absurdity of his position?

But many Southerners can. And some of them are educated men who think of themselves as the community's moral and civic leaders. But the psychic result has been that a deep anxiety possesses them and they feel that any change would be only for the worse. When they are asked why they fear the crumbling of segregation, they cannot tell you that what they really fear is the crumbling of the walls inside themselves. Instead, they talk about intermarriage. It makes poor sense, but they think it explains their acute anxiety.

But there are other Southerners who have changed, who don't like discrimination, who don't believe in segregation. And I am often asked, Why don't they say so? Some are speaking out, of course, hundreds of them; others want to but are afraid they will do "more harm than good." Here, once again, we have the result of a rigid, inflexible training in early childhood, given to us during a time of panic and dread. I was born at the turn of the century when the first segregation statutes were being put on the law books of the Southern states. During the first ten years of my life there were almost a thousand lynchings in the South. It was in this atmosphere of terror and brutality, of internal and external disorder, that we were taught our lessons in segregation. No wonder so many Southerners of my age cling to it. We were told as children never to question it, never to talk about it. This silence that is today so dangerous to us and so puzzling to others is a built-in silence, its foundations go down to babyhood, to our mother's hushed whispering. There is a hypnotic quality about such learning, and only the rebellious mind, the critical intelligence, or the loving heart can defy it.

THE PRICE OF SEGREGATION

The truth is that our parents and grandparents paid a terrible price for a security which they believed segregation could give them. When they permitted the system to be set up, they did not foresee that emergency measures would be frozen permanently into state laws. They did not dream that segregation would become a ritual so sacred that it would be given priority over the teachings of Christ in our churches. They did not know a time was ahead when the politician would exert more moral force than the preacher. The history of the political and social and psychological pressures that caused our fathers to blunder in so tragic a way is too complex to go into here. Let us settle for this: the price they paid for security was exorbitant and their white children are still paying today. For they have been as surely injured in mind and spirit by segregation as have Negro children. Both have been warped, both have been kept from a free, creative life, both find it difficult to be courageous, strong individuals who can defy conformity and find their own responses to the world.

It is important for us to break the word *South* into a thousand pieces, not only geographically but economically, not only culturally, not only in terms of the sexes, not only vocationally, not only psychologically, but into generations; there are gradations of opinion in all these groups, and gradations of moral strength. What is terrifying to the older generation (those born when segregation was being set up in the South) doesn't bother the young students: the Southerner over forty is likely to suffer from taboos the eighteen year old does not feel; what paralyzes the men often releases the women; what seems easy to do for the twenty-five year old seems impossible to the fifty year old; the poor and ignorant often feel a psychic and social hunger to belong "to the white race" as if it were a club while the more sophisticated, the more secure economically and culturally, do not have this need; their sense of "belonging" has come to them in other ways. In certain areas of work, there is no racial competition; in others the competition is severe and exacerbates dominant race feelings. And too, differences go beyond the groups; the South is chockfull of individuals, each with his own ideas—this, despite our somewhat totalitarian training and our one-party political system.

These differences among our people are potentially good; this lack of conformity in feelings and beliefs keeps the door cracked. What we need to realize is that these differences exist. We need also something that will fire our imagination and stir our good feelings so that new leaders can rise up and open the way. That is why I have such hopes for the students' nonviolent protests. If white students will join with Negro students, their experiences together, their self-discipline and philosophical training will create a fine reservoir of new leadership for the South. We cannot change the South until we change our leadership and ourselves; we, as a region, can have our moment of truth only when we begin to think of ourselves as persons, when we open up our imaginations and our hearts by taking the walls down within us. Then it will come. And it will be a healing time for us and perhaps for the whole world, for we are so sensitized one to another, so closely related in the common purpose of creating a future, that whatever brings wholeness to us as persons here will bring wholeness to others across the world.

Perhaps, even now, our moment of truth is near; let us pray that it does not turn into an agonizing time of sin and error.

35

WE MUST KEEP GOING

Martin Luther King Jr.
and the Future of America

Vincent Harding

The proclamation of a national holiday celebrating the life of Martin Luther King Jr. was a cause for mixed feelings among some of his closest admirers. They wondered whether such celebration had the ironic effect of obscuring the radical challenge of his life and witness. This essay (extracted from a much longer piece) is by Vincent Harding, professor of religion and social transformation at the Iliff School of Theology in Denver, Colorado. He worked closely with Dr. King for ten years before King's death. Harding's writings on King, including the full version of this text, appear in his book, Martin Luther King: The Inconvenient Hero *(Fellowship, January-February 1987).*

It was March 25, 1968. The spring had just begun, and no one knew how late it was, how short the time, for him, for us. In the midst of a cruelly demanding schedule, Martin Luther King Jr. had flown to upstate New York to speak to a gathering of Jewish rabbis. He was introduced to the group by Dr. Abraham Joshua Heschel, one of the great teachers of that faith community.

At the heart of Heschel's introduction was a proclamation and a challenge that could not be contained by time, place, or people. For on that Monday afternoon, just ten days before the long-traveling assassin's bullet finally found Martin King, Abraham Heschel announced,

> Martin Luther King Jr. is a voice, a vision and a way. I call upon every Jew to harken to his voice, to share his vision, to follow in his way. The whole future of America will depend on the impact and influence of Dr. King.

Now, almost twenty years later, it is tempting to believe that we Americans—Jews and Gentiles alike—have a ready response to Heschel's stirring call. Now that King seems safely dead, now that he has been properly installed in the national pantheon—to the accompaniment of military bands, with the U.S. Marine Corps chorus singing "We Shall Overcome," and the cadenced marching of the armed forces color guards—we think we know the man's impact and influence. Didn't President Reagan sign a bill authorizing a national holiday honoring this teacher of nonviolence?

And didn't Coca-Cola make available one of its corporate jets to fly King's family members and friends from one celebration to another? What more impact and influence could we want?

Even those of us who feel drawn to King—and who now seek to stand as far as possible from the cruel ironies of such national hero-making—are not immune to amnesia. Perhaps the passage of time has blunted, or romanticized, our own memory. Perhaps distance has blurred our vision, the strange, bewildering times of the 1970s and 1980s confused our sense of King's voice, his vision, his way. Perhaps—and this is even more likely—each generation must forge its own understanding of King's meaning, must determine and demonstrate for itself the power of his impact and influence. Perhaps that is the way the whole future of America is being wrought.

To see King as he was in those last weeks of his life, even at the simplest levels of our perception, is to see an exhausted, hard-pressed, at times beleaguered-looking brother (didn't Malcolm look that way in his last days?), far older than the thirty-nine years of his life, often saying, "I'm tired now, I've been in this thing thirteen years and now I'm really tired." All around him we hear voices filled with accusation, fear, hostility, and disdain, calling him "traitor," "stupid," "misleading," "provocative," "communist dupe"—and "Martin Loser King." To see him as he was then is to see the disappointment in his eyes as he shared his feeling that his closest friends and assistants were failing to stand by him in his hour of greatest need.

To look carefully into King's last weeks, then, is to see darkness, both the creative and the perilous darkness of the wilderness.

Is this what Heschel meant by King's "way," this dangerous, uncharted, and often lonely path? And how did he (we?) get here? What was the road to the wilderness? Which paths led out from that bright and sunny day of August 1963—less than five years earlier? There he seemed to be celebrated by a nation, a world, surrounded by the hundreds of thousands who represented the hosts of Americans committed to his light-filled dream. There he held forth the vision of black and white children of God, holding hands, keeping faith, working for freedom. That has been our primary image of him, our primary hope for him, and for ourselves. How do you get to the wilderness from there?

Somehow we have forgotten that the movement from adulation to wilderness is not a new one for those children of the light who are consumed by a hunger and thirst for righteousness. Somehow, we have frozen the frame of the smiling, victorious hero, locked in the magnificent voice proclaiming the compelling dream; but neither the hero nor his voice, neither the vision nor the way, could be held captive, static, manageable. That was part of King's power. And what we discover through close and painful attention is that the hero, the voice, the vision, and the way continued to develop, to deepen, to expand, to burst beyond the limits that America had set for him—that he had once set for himself. Rabbi Heschel, friend, father, and follower, saw that volatile, creative transformation at work and dared beckon us toward the dangerous but necessary fellowship of hope.

By the mid-sixties, King was voicing increasingly strong opposition to the American war in Vietnam, often citing his commitment to nonviolence and his vocation as a Christian minister as his primary grounds. For instance, he said, "Violence is as wrong in Hanoi as it is in Harlem," and to those who criticized his stand against the war, he said, "I am mandated by this calling [of Christian ministry] above every other duty to seek peace among men and to do it even in the face of hysteria and scorn." He told other audiences that if he were younger and subject to the draft he would definitely take a conscientious objector position, and would not accept a military chaplaincy. Eventually, by 1966, he had pressed SCLC to move away from its caution to issue a statement condemning "the immorality and tragic absurdity" of America's role in Indochina. In this way, King and SCLC had caught up with the earlier, more stridently critical voices of Malcolm X and of the Student Non-Violent Coordinating Committee (SNCC). However, it was not a popular position in those days. Most people in the United States were still unwilling to listen to any serious criticism of their government's position. Indeed, many persons in King's own organization and in the larger civil rights community argued with him about the wisdom of taking a strong outspoken stand against the war. Some were afraid of incurring the rage of President Johnson, who seemed ever more blindly committed to a cruelly destructive, constantly expanding military solution. Others were simply unable to face the fact that Martin King had become far more than a civil rights leader and was offering leadership toward the humanizing transformation of the entire nation.

For a time, responding to the pressures, King backed off. But the powerful forces of the 1960s allowed no resting places as he continued his journey out beyond the March on Washington, as he sought to shape a new vision of struggle and hope in keeping with his commitment to the poor of America. And, as so often happens in such a dynamic, expanding social movement, King was pushed forward by unexpected, external events—like the June 1966 shooting of James Meredith in Mississippi. Meredith was the reluctant black hero of the explosive days back in 1962 when his audacity and courage had led to the official desegregation of the University of Mississippi. Now the unpredictable native son had chosen to make a solitary walk from the Tennessee border to the Gulf Coast, a "walk against fear," he called it. But he was gunned down by a white assailant (though not seriously wounded) just as he began. The immediate response of the black freedom-and-justice organizations was to try to find a way to continue Meredith's project. What emerged after much debate was a march that became the occasion for the surfacing of serious divisions within the movement, focused now on the cry of "We want black power!"

Here was another crucial element in King's transformation. The seemingly endless and sometimes rancorous debates, conversations, and arguments among Stokely Carmichael of SNCC, Floyd McKissick of the Congress of Racial Equality (CORE), and King—as well as their staffs and supporters—bore some helpful fruit in the long run. The controversy over Black Power that was fanned by the media eventually forced King to explore more deeply than ever before the power of blackness in the Afro-American communities, and the relationship of black people to social, economic, and political power in America. So, in the midst of the march, when pushed by the press, King tried to reconcile—his natural tendency—as well as to learn. Never rejecting the creative role of white allies, he said, "the term 'Black Power' does not represent racism. . . . If we are to solve our problem, we've got to transform our powerlessness into positive and creative power." Later in the summer, at the annual SCLC convention, King declared that "The majority of the people in our society are now powerless, and in no way able to participate in the decision-making. . . . Self-determination for an oppressed people requires power." By now, King could also be heard regularly saying such things as, "We must be proud of our race. We must not be ashamed of being black. We must believe with all of our hearts that black is as beautiful as any other color."

This was a blacker voice. Now King had been pressed to take up the crucial questions of how a truly multiracial and multicultural society could be built, while encouraging a sense of collective and personal self-worth within the lives of its component peoples. It was only a beginning, but he was making it, exploring the power of blackness.

This was the voice Rabbi Heschel heard. He certainly knew the voices of prophets. This was the voice he called us to hear. There was, of course, no need to deny the inspiring, moving voice we had heard on the sunlit mall, but our Jewish teacher was insisting that we allow King to become multivocal in our lives, to break out of our sound chambers, to send rushing, roaring words through our hearts, to test our faith. Indeed, Heschel's call was for us to open ourselves to all the harshness and the urgency that was King at the end. His challenge was for us to recognize, as many searchers for justice have had to, that Fyodor Dostoyevsky was right: "Love in practice is a harsh and dreadful thing compared to love in dreams."

King's way had moved beyond dreams to practice. That movement was not new in his life, for he had been a courageous practitioner when he dared accept the leadership of the Montgomery Improvement Association in 1955, surely lifetimes behind him now. What was new in the late 1960s was where the movement was going—into the midst of men, women, and children whose lives were often forced against a host of harsh and dreadful walls, with no apparent way out. Reflecting that experience, searching for an exit, his voice could not be untrue to the serrated edges of the people's lives, could not be unfaithful to his vision of the need to organize the poor for confrontation with the powers of oppression. So, by the end of 1966, King was calling SCLC to prepare itself to lead "the poor in a crusade to realize economic and social justice."

For King, it would surely have been easier to embalm his dream, to live on his memory of the Great March, the time of White House sandwiches and convivial gathering with the president, savoring the occasion for adulation by so many millions. But his basic commitment made that way impossible. Such nostalgic scenes were marvelous for his ego, but they held no promise for the poor. These sisters and brothers needed the bold, courageous practitioners. So King continued to move away from the great celebration, hoping to shape the great challenge on behalf of justice for the nation's dispossessed, beginning with all those he had met on the West Side of Chicago. (And why do we still insist on embalming the great celebration of 1963? Is it because we are not yet ready for the challenges of commitment to the struggles of the poor?)

But King found that his search for a way to challenge the government and the nation to justice was constantly blocked by the reality of Vietnam. The poor young men of America were being swept up to become victims and executioners in ever larger numbers. The poor of Vietnam were being destroyed physically and culturally. Moreover, King knew that all the cruel devastation of an unjust war was draining billions of dollars and lifetimes of energy and creativity out of the nation's potential for dealing with the needs of its own poor people. It was very clear that he would have to take on the war again, confronting it on an even broader front this time, but he wasn't certain about how or when. Then King came across the January 1967 issue of *Ramparts*, dedicated to "the Children of Vietnam," filled with the special, brutal madness that war brings to children, and heightened by all the great American technical skills of destruction. At that point, King decided. He told his staff that "after reading that article, I said to myself, 'Never again will I be silent on an issue that is destroying the soul of our nation and destroying thousands and thousands of little children in Vietnam.'" For all who would hear his voice, he was saying, "I can no longer be cautious about this matter. I feel so deep in my heart that we are so wrong in this country and time has come for a real prophecy, and I'm willing to go that road."

There he was. On the road, in the way. Now Martin King had broken even more sharply with all the narrow definitions of "civil rights," moving even more deeply into a profound commitment to the poor, and a courageous stand against his own government's ruthless blindness—all on behalf of the soul of his nation and the lives of a poor, non-white people. Heschel saw it and called us. Fittingly enough, he was there at Riverside Church in New York City on the night in April 1967 when King poured out his soul, pleading with his nation to come to its senses, accusing his government of being "the greatest purveyor of violence in the world today," calling America to stand with, not against, the revolution of the poor. (Who knew that night, April 4, that he had precisely one more year to live, that the bullet was closing in?) For King saw the larger context. He had already declared in other places that his "beloved country" was "engaged in a war that seeks to turn the clock of history back and perpetuate white colonialism." Underlying this backwardness, he said, was America's refusal to recognize that "the evils of capitalism are as real as the evils of militarism and evils of racism." Now, in all of his speeches, King's voice was heard calling for what he described as "a revolution in values" in the United States, a struggle to free ourselves from "the triple evils of racism, extreme materialism, and militarism." Without such revolutionary transformation, King said, people of good will in America would end up protesting our nation's new Vietnams all over the world, including Central America.

He would not relent. Too much was at stake. So late in the spring of 1967, at the height of the pressure, in the face of attacks on every side—including some sponsored by the FBI—with his loyalty, sanity, and humility being harshly questioned, King said to his staff, and eventually to everyone else who would listen:

> I want you to know that my mind is made up. I backed up a little when I came out in 1965. My name then wouldn't have been written in any book called Profiles of Courage. But now I have decided that I will not be intimidated. I will not be harassed. I will not be silent, and I will be heard.

By the spring of 1967, King's vision of his role in America had steadily expanded and deepened, and he was trying to make sense of its many parts. He told David Halberstam:

> For years I labored with the idea of reforming the existing institutions of the society, a little change here, a little change there. Now I feel quite differently. I think you've got to have a reconstruction of the entire society, a revolution of values.

All through that last full spring and summer, King seemed to be searching, moving, growing, on pilgrimage, often confused and uncertain, but still on his way. He was clearly pressing on, out beyond the familiar hero's place, beyond the older, easier understandings of "integration," which simply called for black people (in relatively small doses) to move gratefully, unquestioningly into the white-owned American "mainstream." By the end of the fall, King's voice, the voice that Heschel heard, was setting forth a jarring theme, declaring, "Something is wrong with capitalism as it now stands in the United States. We are not interested in being integrated into *this* value structure. Power must be relocated."

This was King's way as he moved into the last fall and winter of his life. By then, he had announced that this way of massive nonviolent civil disobedience would become the center of his movement for the next major campaign—a return to Washington, D.C. He was improvising, groping, pushing his organization to move with him. His plan was to mobilize and train thousands of the poor and their allies to come to the nation's capital and "just camp here and stay" until the country's elected leaders acted on the urgent needs of the poor. In the great black tradition, he was improvising, but he kept moving, warning that "the city will not function" until Congress created and approved "a massive program on the part of the federal government that will make jobs or income a reality for every American citizen." In the fall, King was envisioning more than Washington as target. "We've got to find a method that will disrupt our cities if necessary, create the crisis that will force the nation to look at the situation, dramatize it, and yet at the same time not destroy life or property," he said. He was challenging the nation to face the poor, to turn from its insane war and face the poor, to turn from its materialism and face the poor. He was planning to bring the poor of every color, to stand and sit with the poor where they could not be missed. He said,

> We've got to camp in—put our tents in front of the White House. . . . We've got to make it known that until our problem is solved, America may have many, many days, but they will be full of trouble. There will be no rest, there will be no tranquility in this country until the nation comes to terms with our problem.

Yes, he said, again and again, "our problem." This was the voice and the way of the man who had chosen "to identify with the underprivileged . . . to identify with the poor . . . to give my life for those who have been left out of the sun light of opportunity." He was coming back to Washington with them, but this time, he said, it would not be "to have a beautiful day." This time he was determined to create a new day, to begin a new time.

By the last months it was clear to Martin King that the vision of a new time, filled with a harsh and dreadful beauty of its own, would have to rise from a broad, ever-expanding base. For just as he had discovered that there was no way to address the needs of the black poor in America without attacking the structures of poverty-making which entrapped all the nation's poor people, so too was it impossible to isolate the American situation from its larger, international context. As a result, King continued to move beyond dreams, to declare,

> The storm is rising against the privileged minority of the earth, from which there is no shelter in isolation or armament. The storm will not abate until a just distribution of the fruits of the earth enables men everywhere to live in dignity and human decency.

Then, forever nurturing hope, forever seeing the best possibilities of the people who shared that cradle, that cauldron which had shaped him, he concluded, "The American Negro may be the vanguard of a prolonged struggle that may change the shape of the world, as billions of deprived shake and transform the earth in the quest for life, freedom and justice."

At the end, moving toward his rendezvous with destiny, King finally resisted all the powerful temptations to despair that tore at him from within and without. Speaking to himself and to others he said, "I can't lose hope . . . because when you lose hope, you die." At the end, moving toward his rendezvous with hope, he faltered, wondered if he should give up on the desperate move toward Washington, wondered if he should submit to the fears and disagreements within his staff, and the hostility and anger that were being shouted at him from all the mainstream American nation, black and white, from all who prized order more than justice, from all who feared an uprising of the poor. But he kept moving, saying, hoping, convincing himself that there was nothing else that his integrity would allow him to believe, whispering, proclaiming, "We can change this nation. We can bring it up to the point that it will live up to its creeds."

The way led to Memphis, where garbage men were marching for justice and dignity, where a bullet shaped and aimed by many hands was keeping vigil. In the midst of officially provoked violence and disturbing evidence of deep disarray within the Memphis leadership, five days before his crossing over, King considered a Gandhi-like public fast as "a way of unifying the movement and transforming a minus into a plus."

For reasons that are not fully clear (perhaps he wanted to leave the nurturing of such cleansing, empowering disciplines for us in our time), King did not enter into the fast. Nevertheless, moving on, on his last night he stood in the midst of the people, with a storm raging outside, and declared that he had seen the promised land, testified that all fear was gone, that he was ready for whatever might come, for wherever he needed to go. And he told them that they would get to the promised land. (Did they—we—remember that there is no path to the promised land for those who forget their calling: "Let my people go that they may serve me in the wilderness"?)

At the end, on the balcony, getting ready for his own movement forward, outward, as the American bullet was about to enter its chamber, King asked for a song. Faithful to the tradition that had shaped him, cradled him, prepared him, knowing what was necessary for his way, our way, he asked the bandleader, who was rehearsing for the evening's mass meeting, to be sure to play "Precious Lord, Take My Hand."

That Memphis gathering never took place. King had another mass meeting to attend. So, to the accompaniment of a black gospel song and the sound of a rifle's shout, the brother kept moving toward his rendezvous with victory.

Surely Heschel had known, had intuited it when he invited us. This was King's way, continually moving, even in stillness, grasping, being grasped by the loving hand of a justice-seeking, creator God—forever on dangerous pilgrimage toward the uncharted promised land that is always being created in the midst of the wilderness, calling others to join, to create, to overcome.

And just as surely, part of our response to the invitations must be to catch up with King. Because there are many ways in which we have not gone forward in the last fifteen years; we have tended to move, to be moved backward. For there is no stasis in nature. So we need to press on, to see as clearly as King did the challenge that American racism continues to present in all our institutions, built as they have been on white assumptions, Western values, often projecting the narrowest possible vision of America. He challenges us to catch up and move on, for now we must also deal with a temptation to racism which seeps into the black communities of the nation, especially in our responses to the new Asian-Americans and Hispanics. Now we are pressed to take up the complex but not impossible task of creating a truly multicultural and multiracial society where power, responsibilities, visions, and burdens are shared.

We catch up with King only as we face all the hard contradictions of the militarism he decried, the militarism that provides comfortable contracts and salaries for so many good, middle-class people of every race and creed, and which provides survival allotment checks for so many poor families.

We catch up and go beyond only as black and white churches and synagogues include classes on conscientious objection in the heart of their regular educational curriculum, and as pastors, rabbis, and imams teach it from their pulpits and their lives. We go ahead as we explore ways to create humane work and community-building jobs for those young people who really want to be all that they can be, and who will never reach that goal in a profession ultimately committed to the way of death. We go ahead of our brother only as we continue to call attention and to organize resistance to the militarization of our nation's budget, its children's imaginations, its foreign policy, and our lives. We catch up and go ahead by marching, picketing, sitting, undermining the ways of violence, refusing to pay taxes, giving our money to the things that make for peace, constantly searching for an answer to our brother Martin's question from long ago: Is there a nonviolent, peace-making army that can shut down the Pentagon? We go ahead by creating reservoirs of peace within us, around us, wherever we are, in whatever family and community, preparing for the coming time of great flooding, watering the small places now.

For we develop our best selves as citizens, as a nation, we catch up and follow, only when we take seriously again King's call for "a radical reconstruction" of America, relentlessly turning the nation toward the needs of our poorest, most vulnerable people. We go ahead when we refuse to believe that this politico-economic system is self-correcting for the weak and the impoverished. We go ahead when we position ourselves with King on the uncharted way toward the re-creation of America's institutions, and then confer, experiment, pray, and struggle with other fellow travelers to envision and sketch out the lineaments of a new, compassionate system. As King knew so well, the question is not a search for Utopia. Rather, it is humanity, in every age, seeking to become its best self, to manifest the image of God. Not Utopia, it is us, Americans of every kind, seeking again, in this generation, "to create a more perfect union."

Early in the 1970s one of King's closest and best known co-workers reflected on the direction his friend and leader had been taking in those last perilous years of his life. In a private conversation he said, "In a way, it was probably best for many of us who worked with Martin that he was killed when he was, because he was moving into some radical directions that very few of us had been prepared for." The man paused, then he added, "And I don't think that many of us on the staff would have been ready to take the risks to life, possessions, security, and status that such a move would have involved." Then another pause, and the final reflection: "I'm pretty sure I wouldn't have been willing." To keep moving is to become willing among and beyond ourselves, which draws us into the company of the committed, helping us to become voluntary companions, fellow travelers with our brother Martin. To keep moving is to carry, continue, and re-create the best revolutionary traditions of America.

Of course, what we also know is that the personal weaknesses of Martin King and his courageous band of co-workers are just as surely a call to us, a call to become stronger, to learn from the pitfalls as well as the mountains. So we move forward only as we discover in our own time and in our own experience a nonviolence that wells up from the deep, increasingly centered and disciplined places of our personal lives. Indeed, there can be no reflection on King's way which does not open up to us the need for a path that expresses our own searching, expanding confidence in the healing power of the universe, in the presence of a loving, leading Power, exposing us always to the harsh and the tender, to the dreadful and the compassionate, prying our lives open to the evidences of things unseen.

All these things, both in solitude and in company with fellow seekers, now become more crucial than ever before. For ultimately, it is we and our children and our forbears, we and our great cloud of witnesses to amazing grace—it is we who must keep moving, to engage at every level in the continuing struggle which seeks to turn "the whole future of America" toward the last best movements of our brother, Martin, and then to burst beyond.

For those of us who are tempted (and who is not?) to doubt that such things are possible, for ourselves, for others, for our nation, we are helped as we try to remember, to break out of our larger amnesia. For all of our best religious and spiritual traditions in the human family carry the same supportive message: We are not alone in this struggle for the re-creation of our own lives and the life of our community. It has long been written and known that those who choose to struggle for the life of the earth and its beings are part of an ageless, pulsating membrane of light that is filled with the lives, hopes, and beatific visions of all who have fought on, held on, loved well, and gone on before us. For this task is too magnificent to be carried by us alone, in our house, in our meeting, in our organization, in our generation, in our lifetime. No, King knew, Gandhi knew, Malcolm knew, Dorothy Day knew, Heschel knew, Barbara Deming knew—and said, with mystics and physicists—"we are all part of one another," and we are all part of the intention of the great creator spirit to continue being light and life. That was what Martin saw on the night before his death. That was why all the fear had drained away. That was what Heschel knew in the midst of his call.

Now the grand and urgent challenge returns to us. Now we sense the deepest meanings of the rabbi's call, the brother's way. Perhaps now we are prepared as never before to hear the authentic voice, to catch the perpetually developing vision, to join the endlessly searching way. Perhaps now we are prepared both to catch up and move beyond, to run and not get permanently weary, to walk and not faint, submitting ourselves to the magnificent, continuing struggle to redeem the soul of America, beginning with our own beautiful, needy lives.

So we must keep going. For how else shall we mount up on wings like eagles? We must keep going, for how else shall we discover and explore the harsh and dreadful beauty of that radiant darkness where the wilderness and the promised land become one, where our way and the way of our brother converge? We must keep going. The whole future of America depends on it.

36

GROWING UP BLACK

Charles Alphin

Charles Alphin, a captain in the St. Louis police department, went to the U.S.S.R. twice in 1991 with FOR delegations of nonviolence teachers and trainers. He was particularly effective in sessions with police and military personnel in Russia and in Lithuania (now independent), as he applied Kingian nonviolence to the particular concerns of law enforcement and defense. The participants wanted to know more than just Alphin's understanding and application of nonviolence. They wanted to know his story: how an African-American police officer came to believe in Dr. King's philosophy. What follows is his story as he presented it to a workshop on nonviolence in Moscow (Fellowship, *December 1991*).

I was born in 1940 and raised in an all-black neighborhood in St. Louis. At the time, we were not permitted to attend schools with whites. I remember my first experience with racism when I was nine. One hot summer day I went to a local park to swim, only to find white boys armed with bats and sticks surrounding the pool, refusing to allow any of us into the pool. They grabbed me and began beating me. And when I tried to run away, they strung a rope across the street, throwing me off my bike. Then they stole the bike. I was nine, and though I didn't understand their actions, I was very angry, an anger against whites that grew stronger with each succeeding year of my life. I never forgot that beating.

St. Louis in those years was the quintessential Southern city, with legal strictures everywhere against the mixing of races. We suffered overcrowded classrooms. Public places were barred to us. Discrimination in jobs and in housing was a regular feature of our lives. My father was a college graduate, but the only job he could get was as an elevator operator. Internally, I seethed with hatred, because, to me, by now eighteen, America was not what it was supposed to be.

When I joined the Air Force I hoped for something better, but even there—especially there—I discovered the identical racial attitudes. My friend, whose wife was white, had to leave her behind on the base because they couldn't be seen together in town.

After receiving my discharge and attending college I married, and we had two children. I had returned to St. Louis to find work. I continued to have a very strong dislike for the attitudes of some whites, so for me it was natural to continue resisting in the only way I knew how: physically, by fighting. I didn't know any other way of dealing with the frustrations of racism.

In 1965 I joined the St. Louis police department and experienced the same bars and bigotry as in civilian life. In St. Louis black cops could not ride patrol in areas inhabited by whites; we only patrolled the black housing projects. We were faced with rigid quotas. Only a handful of blacks could work for the department. There was a steady stream of racial jokes, nasty and hurtful rather than funny, during roll call, on the beat, in the station houses. We had fist fights between police officers during the district roll calls. Here was a system designed to protect citizens and uphold the law that was being aimed at us because of our skin color.

We found this injustice in the schools as well, even after the Supreme Court's desegregation ruling. Our two sons were enrolled in a school that was 80 percent white. My wife and I had made an agreement with them: academic grades were to be valued as highly as athletics. When one of my boys, a very good athlete, failed to achieve a "C" average, we docked him. No more football. He was one of the team stars, and the day we told him football was out until his grades improved, the principal and coach, both white, phoned, urging us to reconsider and allow him to play. That infuriated me. Here was a school system that cared more about winning a football game, and my son as a player than as a human being.

Here I was a police officer, sworn to obey the law, about to do some dumb thing like hit someone. I remember being consumed with fury. For twenty-five years, the system had not played fair with me or my people. Luckily, by the grace of some Supreme Spirit, the principal was absent that day. So I did a far wiser thing. I spoke with other black parents and together we called a meeting to discuss the school's lack of interest in our kids. There were about forty-five of us that night, and we vented our anger. But God, as they say, works in mysterious ways. For one of the people there was a man my age named Bernard Lafayette, whose son was in the same high school. A quiet-mannered, pipe-smoking man, I had never met him, nor did I know anything about him. (Ironically, Lafayette and the principal had been classmates at Harvard.)

We began learning more and more about how our children were being treated. Many white parents in that elitist school thought we were radicals. We held press conferences, walked picket lines, demonstrated. We decided that none of our children would be permitted on school athletic teams unless they earned a "C" grade. We gave courage to the few black teachers, offered greater chances for black kids to enroll in advanced courses, and negotiated a wide range of agreements with the school system that would deal seriously with our grievances.

In all this, Dr. Lafayette "led from the rear." We did not know then that he was a practitioner of active nonviolence in the tradition of Martin Luther King.

He did not come to us preaching nonviolence. Had he done so I would have told him that he was crazy. In time, he convinced me that by our actions, not by our words, we could find an answer to our dilemma through the power of nonviolence.

In the late 1970s Coretta King came to St. Louis to conduct a workshop on nonviolence. Dr. Lafayette was involved, and he and Mrs. King piqued my interest even more. I was like a sponge. For the next five years, I attended workshops at the King Center in Atlanta. I read every book Dr. King had written and talked to everyone I could who had worked with him, trying to glean from them what the whole thing was about and what it could mean, especially for a police officer. When King was moving America in the civil rights movement, I had been a disbeliever, feeling that nonviolence was sissi-fied and passive and could not possibly work with those who didn't like my people and insisted on hurting us. I was very comfortable using my fists and nightstick. Every day, as a patrolman and even as a police captain, I knew how hard it was to be black in white America. So what I had to know was whether nonviolence had any application in my life or in the life of my people.

Eventually—it took years—I found out that in the process of nonviolence the first person who changes is yourself. As a result, I tried very hard to under-stand my police colleagues, even those who were biased against us, trying not to hate them even as I scorned their beliefs and actions. Over time, I found that nonviolence was beginning to work in my personal life, but as a police-man I wanted to see how it worked in the black community. Earlier, Mrs. King had invited me to join the King Center faculty and teach the theory and prac-tice of nonviolence. Before long, I asked her if we could try the philosophy on some of the St. Louis gang leaders. I remember her answer: "Well, Captain, you're on our faculty, so why not bring them down to the King Center for our summer workshop on nonviolence?" I selected some of the city's toughest gang members. They were all high school students. One of them had been involved in a shooting a week before we were to depart. I was able to talk to the judge in juvenile court and got the boy released in my custody. When our bus finally departed for Atlanta, our teenage passengers included drug dealers and young men who had been in gang shoot-outs. All of them had been rejected by society long before.

The summer session was something I will never forget. The result was a remarkable turnaround in the lives of these young men. In St. Louis today, they teach nonviolence in a variety of settings. Can we say then that nonvio-lence is the panacea, the immediate answer to all our difficulties? Of course not. But nonviolence is a way of life, a lifelong journey. You have to live it, internalize it, use it every day of your life.

I am now a captain of police. When I was promoted and sent to a district in a black community, I asked, "Lord, you know I'm trying to be nonviolent. Why are you sending me to one of the most violent sections in St. Louis?" Actually, I was grappling with the problem of applying the nonviolent way of life in a district where homicide, rape, and child abuse were common. In the

United States, as we know, about 70 to 75 percent of all killings are done by blacks against other blacks. My police district had a large proportion of the 207 murders in St. Louis one year. Most of the victims were young black males. I saw death so many times that if I never see death again, it will be too soon. We used to take young people out of projects and alleys and garbage cans with four or five bullets in their heads. Something was happening to me, because the more I saw death, the more I believed in life. I had hardly made my adherence to nonviolence a secret, and many officers derided my beliefs, some even dubbing me "reverend." No matter. I soon began applying my philosophy among my officers, not by preaching but rather by example. I also began to use this philosophy in my interrogation of killers.

I recall one accused murderer who had been to jail before and was especially cold and hardened. The other police officers told me, "Captain, we can get a confession, because we know how to get confessions. Let's hang him by his handcuffs from the door and we can get a confession from him." But that sort of stuff was not in me. Instead, I began to talk quietly to the young man, telling him that I wasn't going to judge him, for there was a higher Supreme Judge who would. I told him, too, that I totally disagreed with what he had done. Before long he confessed, even adding another killing he had committed, one where he had taken a butcher knife and put it through a girl's neck. My point here is that even in the midst of violence and mayhem, one can maintain one's principles and still emerge with results. I have also used this approach to mobilize the people in my community to oppose the infestation of narcotics, to try to take charge of their own lives. Nonviolence urges you to begin taking action against injustice. As I have told people: you don't have to feel hopeless.

I have been bringing more black officers into my homicide unit, which hasn't made me very popular with my superiors. When you start rocking the boat, the system may not like you. Even so, nonviolence in my life means doing the right thing at the right time and expecting the outcome to benefit men and women, as well as glorify God. In nonviolence, you have to draw on a higher strength than yourself. For me, that strength is from God.

Part Five

NONVIOLENCE IN ACTION

In this section we move decisively from theory to practice. There were more candidates for this set of essays than any other. From the very beginning interest in nonviolence was sparked by its potential for practical action. But the mode of operating gave a whole new meaning to the word practical. *As early as 1922 John Nevin Sayre was calling for a nonviolent national defense. By then Gandhi had already mounted his nonviolent campaign to free India. Ah, some argued, of course nonviolence works with the genteel British, but it would never do so against the brutal Nazis—a sentiment contradicted by the courageous witness of André Trocmé and the citizens of Le Chambon. Well, then, at least not against the Mafia—wrong again, as Danilo Dolci proves. And on and on, actual stories of actual victories, or at least acts of bearing witness, even when the opponent is as massive as the U.S. government (the Berrigans, Ellsberg).*

How often have such nonviolent efforts been attempted? We can't say. But Gene Sharp has itemized 198 different kinds of nonviolent resistance, on a continuum from the most innocuous to the most risky. It sometimes works with muggers on city streets (Samuel), but it has also worked (not without intense suffering) in the organizing of migrant farmworkers (Chavez). It can work with only a couple of people (the Sperry Software Pair), and it has worked with whole cities (Hartsig) or whole nations (Goss-Mayr).

It doesn't always work. But we need to rehearse the times it does, because such stories arm us with hope and vision, and they enable us to continue the struggle to make and keep life human.

37

DISARMAMENT AND DEFENSE

John Nevin Sayre

In this prescient article, John Nevin Sayre outlines a new kind of national defense that can dispense with armies, not by surrender or acquiescence, but by stout refusal to cooperate with the enemy. Considered hopelessly idealistic in its time, his vision was literally enacted by the Solidarity trade union in Poland from 1980 to 1990, which did in fact demonstrate that printing presses could continue to print instructions to the people under martial law, despite all the efforts of the authorities to seize them, and that an unarmed public could bring down a hated regime. Likewise, the preposterous notion that civilians might demoralize oppressors by fraternizing with them was proven effective in Russia during the attempted coup of 1991, and in 1986 during the insurrection against the dictator Marcos in the Philippines (The World Tomorrow, *January 1922*).

Could a modern nation defend itself without arms? Suppose that it should disband its army and navy, what means of self-defense, or defense of the right, could it employ? What might it do before war comes, or when war arrives? And if a nonmilitary defense were practicable, provided the majority of a nation believed in it, could we ever hope to bring the majority to such a point of view?

BEFORE WAR COMES

It is obvious that our world is still organized on a war basis. Every nation must face the contingency of possible, if not probable, war. To devise some form of preparedness against this is vital to every people. And the time to work this out is now in the days of peace, before the sudden fires of a new catastrophe overwhelm us.

The beginnings of national defense lie in the adoption of a *national policy of friendship*. Historic examples of such a policy are the Quaker dealings with the American Indians, the hundred years of friendship between the United States and Canada, and America's return of the Boxer indemnity to China. As everyone knows, remarkable success attended these experiments, but their success is only suggestive of the much larger good which might be achieved through a national will to friendship, thoroughly applied. If for instance this should control the immigration and tariff policies of a country, and all its foreign relationships, including the selection of sincere, competent, and friendship-making men for consular and diplomatic posts, a long step on the road toward peace would be taken.

A national friendship policy could only grow out of a national friendship tradition and this ought to be taught in the schools. It would necessitate a thorough revision of almost all the history textbooks, it would call for a new order of patriotic songs and oratory, a blending of the conception of world service with the salute to the flag, and an immediate putting into practice of the theory of friendliness with regard to children of the foreign born. The thing to be aimed at would be to plant in the affections of each child the ideal of his country as a ministering servant nation. He should come to see that there is no national honor or greatness except through service, and that if a nation should lose territory or wealth in the following of this ideal, yet it would save its soul and win honor in the days to come.

A national policy of friendship would create the atmosphere in which a world league of nations could effectively function. Some league or association of nations we must undoubtedly have, not only as a safeguard against war but for the constructive organization of many world affairs. The right kind of league would greatly facilitate peace, but the wrong kind of league might easily produce war. So it is necessary not to be deceived by names but to look rather critically at any particular league the politicians may offer us.

A genuine association of nations ought if possible to include all the nations of the world. It would be disastrous should it assume the character of an alliance of one group of peoples as *against* any other group. And that the larger nations might not override the needs of the smaller ones there would have to be definite provisions for the safeguarding of minority rights. Along with this should go democratic control and open diplomacy, but with concessions of enough power to delegates and majorities for the effective performance of business. Out of the association should grow a world court and various commissions, and if they were composed of really big, broad-visioned men, they might become instruments of enormously beneficial service.

It is quite usually said that such a world court and association of nations would need an international army and navy acting as a police force to give sanction to its decrees. This is open to question. The history of the Supreme Court of the United States indicates that the force of public opinion might be enough; and then too, if the association of nations and world court were performing advantageous services for the member nations, the threat of expulsion from membership might sufficiently gain obedience to its decisions. Failing this the association could still employ nonmilitary forces like those described later in this paper. And certain it is that the more the world association accomplished its ends by persuasion and benefit, and the less by fear and force, the better would be its chance of winning the permanent allegiance of all peoples.

A further method of preparedness against war would be the internationalizing of organizations for culture. Previous to 1914 a good start in this direction had been made. There was the Socialist International comprising many from the ranks of labor, there were numerous international congresses of scientific, educational, and church groups, there were exchange professorships at some of the universities, and there were peace societies galore. But these all snapped their international bonds under the strain of the war, so that now a fresh beginning must be attempted. The reason why these associations broke down was because they could not resist the stronger organization of the state and the pull which loyalty to the state made upon their individual members; therefore, in building for the future it is necessary to develop within these organizations a *supranational conscience*, that is to say, there must develop a loyalty which will be stronger than that to the state.

The new loyalty which internationalists might seek to arouse could be occupational, humanitarian, or religious, and at its best it would be a combination of all three. On the occupational or professional side it would appeal to the worker, artist, or man of science, on the score of the good of his craft. He must work against war and refuse to take part in it because war works toward the crippling and destruction of industry, science, and art, which are universal things. On the humanitarian side the supernational loyalty would appeal for devotion to the interests of humanity as a whole—these being of greater importance than the interests of one state. And on the religious side the point would be made that war was sin and that far above all loyalty to country stood a supreme duty to God.

Now such a supernational conscience would not necessarily be anti-national, but it would be antiwar; it would be active in making preparations against war and working out better methods of international adjustment. Just as British labor struck against the proposal of war with Russia, it would be possible for technical experts, writers, and artists to withhold their skill from a government planning war; and it would be possible for the church to refuse to make any war holy. If the men and women of labor, science, art, and religion were internationally organized all over the world, and if they worked coordinately against every threat of war, they could stop preparations for war and end the ghastly business then and there.

IF WAR ARRIVES

But supposing that war actually should come and overtake a nation which had no military arms. Would that nation necessarily be defenseless or by what nonmilitary methods might it conceivably resist attack?

Mohandas Gandhi in India with, it is said seventy-five million followers, is today demonstrating some possibilities which lie in the method of noncooperation. The theory back of this method is simple. It is that no form of widespread oppression can carry on very long in any country if the people of that country *en masse* refuse to cooperate with it. If they will not trade with, nor in any way work with the oppressor or his agents, they will cut off the chance of his making financial profits. Therefore let the people lay down their tools, their books, and their pens; let them cease from buying the oppressor's wares and from accepting any titles or privileges from him; let them fold their arms and choose prison or death in preference to cooperation; let them stick solidly together and with patience wait for time's work.

The strike, the boycott, certain forms of blockade, and ability to suffer passively are the weapons of this policy. Taken separately they are not new, but the combination of them employed as a means of national defense is new, and worthy of careful study. The Chinese national boycott of Japanese goods instigated by Chinese students in order to check Japanese aggression, the five years' refusal of Sinn Fein Ireland to cooperate with the British courts and Parliament, and most of all, Gandhi's movement in India, strikingly suggest the possibility that with time for propaganda, organization, and constructive leadership, a nation might work out exceedingly effective defense tactics on these lines. They are the methods which labor has used in its struggle against oppression. Why could they not be organized about the sentiment of nationality, even more effectively than about the consciousness of class?

Now it may be said that an invaded disarmed country would not be able to keep its printing presses and airplanes going. And, of course, this might be so. But on the other hand when one considers how enormously difficult the task of suppressing a whole people's utterance would be, it is very reasonable to think that a nation of determined will, consciously depending on truth for its defense, would somehow get that truth across. Suggestive in this regard is the fact that the Germans with all their military might in Belgium were never able to suppress a little news sheet which for nearly four years during the occupation of Brussels continued to appear and denounce the German rule. *La Libre Belgique* it was called, and it bore regularly on its front page this announcement: "Bulletin of Patriotic Propaganda—Regularly Irregular—Submitting to No Censorship."

It circulated all over Belgium, and in the spirit of defiance loyal hands placed a copy of each new issue on the German governor's desk. Says Brand Whitlock, "The German police tried every device known to them, they made raids and perquisitions, they offered rewards, but they never discovered the publishers; and *La Libre Belgique* continued to appear with its announced irregular regularity on von Bissing's table. Probably nothing in all that the Belgians did irritated the Germans more."

The effectiveness of the unarmed propaganda of truth could be much further increased by combining with it a crusade of service.

During the Great War and its aftermath the Quakers gave an impressive demonstration of some things this method can do when it is earnestly and scientifically tried. *A Service of Love in War Time* is the apt title which Professor

Rufus Jones gives to his book describing this work of the Friends. In the terrible days of chaos succeeding the first battle of the Marne they established at Châlons a maternity hospital to shelter and aid the expectant mothers whose homes had been crushed by war's onslaught. Next they extended medical work widely among the civilian population in the devastated districts, most of the local French doctors having been drafted off to war duty; then they began to put back into condition the devastated fields bringing to the stricken peasants "not only a will to serve, but threshing-machines; not only good-nature, but science and trained hands." And also they brought clothes for the shivering, milk for undernourished infants, and Christmas parties—a little fun and gladness—for war-blighted children. Most needed of all, perhaps, were the houses these Quakers built, that the homeless might have somewhere to dwell.

The attacked nation, let us suppose, institutes its campaign of truth and coordinates with it the crusade of service. When the invader's army enters the land and seizes government buildings, banks, railroads, newspapers, and similarly vital properties, this army is met by no forcible resistance. If it does deeds of violence, no reprisals are made; its soldiers, therefore, learn that they need have no fear for their skins, and there is no foundation for atrocity stories with which to stir them to violence and confirm them in it. Furthermore, these soldiers find no use for their arms, for when they would compel the officers and employees of the banks, railroads, newspapers, etc., to go with them one mile, they discover that these people will voluntarily go two. Only when asked to participate in what they feel to be sin will they conscientiously refuse. And the invaded country, let us suppose opens its homes and shops and public buildings in cordial hospitality to the invading soldiers—the enemy uniform is regarded with a friendliness similar to the friendliness shown to the uniform of one's own army in time of war. If such a thing could be, what frantic orders against fraternization would begin to be issued from the enemy G.H.Q.!

Of course, I have pictured this in an extreme, almost topsy-turvy, Alice-in-Wonderland way, but in all seriousness I believe that a nation really in earnest about it could work out methods of love-to-the-enemy that would effectively disarm the enemy soldier and call into beneficent activity his humanity within.

Naturally defense by such a service crusade could not be accomplished in a day nor without cost. The people who undertook it would need to have great patience, willingness to suffer, and much faith. They would be taken advantage of, resisted by force and violence, and there might be treachery in their ranks. They would have to endure hardship, suffering, martyrdom; and they would have to develop a solidarity which could keep on sending out crusaders of service into the places where former crusaders fell. It would have to be a solidarity, moreover, which pooled financial resources and undergirded the individual's courage with a strong sense of group approval and support. But if such a course were persisted in, might not the evil will of the enemy be conquered and outmatched? And who shall say that the cost of defense by this method would be as bitter as is its cost by war?

When now the individual pacifist looks under the surface of the immediate world situation, I think he may gird up his loins and take courage. For while he is still opposed by a seemingly innumerable majority, there are good reasons to believe that this majority can be won over to the pacifist position. Of course, it will be no quick and easy task, but the eye of faith sees that the thing might be done in this generation if all those who are already pacifists would give themselves without stint to the task. And whether war is wiped out in this generation or not, one can today see many signs that "the stars in their courses" are fighting against it. The great evolutionary sweep of life on our planet is against war and for the creation of complete life by processes of wide cooperation. Religion puts this in the words, God is love and love is of God and we ought also to love one another.

38

HOW TO STOP AGGRESSORS

M. K. Gandhi

The following is Gandhi's answer to John R. Mott, who asked Gandhi what the world could do about "gangster" nations such as Nazi Germany. Mott observes that strong police measures had crushed gangsterism in the United States. Was not something comparable necessary in order to put down gangsterism on a national scale? Considering the limited but real success of UN peacekeepers in places like Cypress, some argue for a permanent international police force under the auspices of the United Nations. Gandhi, as ever, refused to accept any compromise with violence. Is not a third way possible: an international peace force trained in nonviolent methods? (Fellowship, February 1939).

DR. MOTT: *Today, I want to engage your attention on what to do with "gangster" nations, if I may use the expression frequently used? There was individual gangsterism in America. It has been put down by strong police measures both local and national. Could not we do something similar for gangsterism between nations, as instanced in Manchuria—the nefarious use of the opium poison—in Abyssinia, in Spain, in the sudden seizure of Austria, and then the case of Czechoslovakia. Can we bring something like international police into being?*

GANDHIJI: I have to deal with identical questions with reference to conditions in India. We have had to quell riots, communal and labor. The Ministries have used military force in some cases and police in most. Now whilst I agreed that the ministers could not help doing so, I also said that the Congress Ministries had proved themselves bankrupt with their stock-in-trade, I mean their avowed weapon of nonviolence. Even so, I would say in reply to the question you have asked, viz. that if the best mind of the world has not imbibed the spirit of nonviolence, the Ministries would have to meet gangsterism in the orthodox way. But that would only show that we have not got far beyond the law of the jungle, that we have not yet learnt to appreciate the heritage that God has given us, that in spite of the teaching of Christianity which is nineteen hundred years old and of Hinduism and Buddhism, which are older, and even of Islam (if I have read it aright), we have not made much headway as

216

human beings. But whilst I would understand the use of force by those who have not the spirit of nonviolence in them, I would have those who know nonviolence to throw their whole weight in demonstrating that even gangsterism has to be met by nonviolence. For ultimately, force, however justifiably used, will lead us into the same morass as the force of Hitler and Mussolini. There will be just a difference of degree. You and I who believe in nonviolence must use it at the critical moment. We may not despair of touching the heart even of gangsters, even if, for the moment, we may seem to be striking our heads against a blind wall.

Dr. Mott next asked a few personal questions. "What have been the most creative experiences in your life? As you look back on your past, what, do you think, led you to believe in God when everything seemed to point to the contrary, when life, so to say, sprang from the ground, although it all looked impossible?"

GANDHIJI: Such experiences are a multitude. But as you put the question to me, I recalled particularly one experience that changed the course of my life. That fell to my lot seven days after I had arrived in South Africa. I had gone there on a purely mundane and selfish mission. I was just a boy returned from England wanting to make some money. Suddenly the client who had taken me there asked me to go to Pretoria from Durban. It was not an easy journey. There was the railway journey as far as Charlestown and the coach to Johannesburg.

On the train I had a first-class ticket, but not a bed ticket. At Maritzburg where the beddings were issued the guard came and turned me out and asked me to go to the van compartment. I would not go, and the train steamed away leaving me shivering in the cold. Now the creative experience comes there. I was afraid for my very life. I entered the dark waiting room. There was a white man in the room. I was afraid of him. What was my duty, I asked myself. Should I go back to India, or should I go forward, with God as my helper, and face whatever was in store for me? I decided to stay and suffer. My active nonviolence began from that date. And God put me through the test during that very journey. I was severely assaulted by the coachman for my moving from the seat he had given me.

DR. MOTT: *The miseries, the slaps after slaps you received, burnt into your soul.*
GANDHIJI: Yes, that was one of the richest experiences of my life.

DR. MOTT: *What has brought deepest satisfaction to your soul in difficulties and doubts and questionings?*
GANDHIJI: Living faith in God.

DR. MOTT: *When have you had indubitable manifestation of God in your life and experiences?*
GANDHIJI: I have seen and believe that God never appears to you in person, but in action which can only account for your deliverance in your darkest hour.

39

THE STAGES OF NONVIOLENCE

André Trocmé

Writing from his experience as spiritual instigator of Huguenot resistance at Le Chambon, France, during World War II, André Trocmé, the European secretary of the International FOR, offers a penetrating analysis of the strategy of nonviolence as a technique of opposition. The events he describes took place between 1940 and 1944 and embrace both the "fighting war" and subsequent Nazi occupation. The role of Pastor Trocmé and the people of Le Chambon in rescuing Jews was described in a book by Philip Hallie, Lest Innocent Blood Be Shed *(1979) (Fellowship, October 1953).*

Totalitarian regimes, and more generally the control exercised over a nation by police and censors, render it almost impossible to organize nonviolent resistance in wartime.

If the resistance arises from individuals or from small isolated groups within a hostile mass, the resisters almost inevitably will be denounced, arrested and, at times, liquidated. One must have lived through the collective emotions created by skillful propaganda in order to understand why it is practically impossible to offer an opposition. Large towns will never be favorable ground for open nonviolent resistance.

Small towns and the countryside where everybody knows everybody else seem to be more adapted to it. Peasants in particular escape from the mastery exerted by radio and press, but they are timid conformists, incapable of initiative. Yet the initiative must be taken, and if it coincides with the deepest thoughts of the population, the latter will give reliable, tacit approval.

A religious feeling, rather than collective enthusiasm, is capable of creating that silent, individual devotion that is essential to the nonviolent campaign. Those who initiate the campaign and accept the visible risks of the undertaking cannot act without the support of hundreds of other more modest personalities. Denunciations are inevitable, but the police will generally be reluctant to act when it feels public opinion against it.

CONDITIONS IN CHAMBON

These are the conditions that existed in the Chambon district between 1939 and 1944. Since the time of the Reformation, seven or eight thousand Huguenots have been living there as if in a separate world. It is impossible to arrest seven or eight thousand persons, so the authorities have had to come to terms with them. However, before oneness of purpose was reached, several stages had to be passed through by which the public opinion of the Huguenot group was educated.

First stage. Opposition to the 1939–1944 war. The beginning of resistance is always the most difficult part. After the invasion of Czechoslovakia and of Poland, it was almost impossible to say no to the war against Hitler. Public opinion took the two pastors of Chambon, who proclaimed their conscientious objection from the pulpit, for traitors, accomplices of the Nazis, or at least dangerous fanatics.

Second stage. Search for a form of service. The war brought in its train unspeakable sufferings; refugees early became a problem. At the time of the military collapse in 1940, after the waves of despair brought from Rotterdam by the civilian fugitives who had left parts of their families along the roads as victims of air attacks, there was an influx of refugees.

SAYING YES TO SUFFERING

The two pastors saw their duty clearly as soon as the first catastrophic news arrived. It was no longer a matter of merely saying no to the war. It became necessary to say yes to human suffering and to be on the spot where it was greatest. Quakers and the International Voluntary Service for Peace have long realized that the true pacifist witness consists in fighting evil with good. The two pastors tried, therefore, to join the International Red Cross, but French military authorities refused them permission. The pastors did not know then that two weeks later human distress would come to them.

Third Stage. Sudden change of political values. June 1940 brought the armistice between Hitler and Pétain and the end of the Republic. Values were reversed overnight. That liberty for which the French had fought was presented by the new government as a cowardly lapse that had caused the defeat of France. The nationalism (German) against which they had fought was depicted as a noble discipline honoring the virtues of "work, family, and fatherland." The extraordinary thing is that few Frenchmen immediately noticed the change.

Fourth stage. First signs of collective resistance. From 1940 to 1941 three efforts were made by the government to bring into line the Old Comrades, the churches, and the youth.

With few exceptions, all the men of the district joined the Legion of War Veterans (later Pétain's party) for fear of losing their jobs. Yet, inspired by the two pastors, the chairman of the Chambon group added to the oath that imposed complete obedience to Marshal Pétain, these words: "as far as the orders I receive are in conformity with God's will." Within a year the local section of the Legion was useless for police checking of public opinion.

RESISTANT SPIRIT AROUSED

Saluting the flag had become compulsory in all schools together with the use of the Fascist salute. The College Cevenol[1] refused to obey the order. By the end of the year, the custom was abandoned in virtually all schools.

Ringing of the church bells was ordered to celebrate the anniversary of the founding of the Legion. The pastors refused. In spite of the violent conduct of some women parishioners who wanted to ring the bells themselves, a small woman caretaker refused them access to the church. These little serio-comic events contributed to the rousing of the spirit of resistance of the Huguenots.

Fifth stage. The Jewish question, 1941–1942. For some months, alarming news had been reaching Chambon about the terrible living conditions of the Jews interned in camps in the south of France. The church was very moved and decided to send one of its pastors to help the social workers there. When he arrived, American Quaker volunteers proposed that he take to Chambon any refugee children who might be got out of the camps. Soon "Guespy," the first house for children, was opened. In a few months, seven other houses were opened. A large proportion of the children, students, and adults received were Jewish, although it was already dangerous to shelter Jews. Thanks to this fraternal action, the nature of nonviolent resistance, and also its methods, became evident both to the church and to the population of Chambon.

Sixth stage. Conflict with authorities, summer 1942. Conflict eventually broke out on two counts: the setting up of youth movements and the disappearance of the Jews.

YOUTH MOVEMENTS

M. Lamiraud, the Minister of Youth, chose the summer of 1942 to pay a visit to the young Protestants of Chambon to rally them around the Marshal. (The news had just reached Vichy France of the savage operations in Paris against the Jews.) Through the decision of the local leaders of the youth movements, the visit was informal and had no official character. As people were leaving a religious service, a delegation of thirty persons from the College Cevenol went up to the minister and the prefect who was accompanying him, to protest solemnly against the anti-Semitic persecutions and to suggest that if the raids had taken place in Chambon the young people would have opposed

---

[1] A secondary school with a Christian pacifist outlook, founded by Trocmé at Le Chambon in 1933.

them in a pacifist manner. The prefect was indignant, and while admitting having received orders, repeated the official theme "There is no question of persecution, but a regrouping of the population of the Jews in Poland." Then turning toward the pastors, he added: "Beware! I have received letters from seven denouncers, and I know all your doings and gestures." That very week the youth groups were called together by the pastors to set up a hiding place for the hundred or so Jews who were in the village.

THE JEWS DISAPPEAR

The storm broke a fortnight later when Vichy police came to carry off the Jews. After two big buses had been parked in the village square (for obvious reasons!), the pastors were called upon to give the list of the Jews. On their refusal, they were urged to sign a notice calling on the Jews to give themselves up so as not to disturb public order nor to endanger the families that were sheltering them. Again the pastors refused, although they were threatened with arrest if the order was not carried out by noon the next day, Sunday. That same night they put into action the plan arranged for the "disappearance" of the Jews. The church was full that Sunday morning, for everyone expected the arrest of the pastors. The Village Council was in session under threat and signed the notorious appeal to the Jews. At noon, not a single Jew appeared.

The pastors were not arrested, and forty policemen searched every house in the village in vain. They did arrest one solitary Jew and put him in one of the big buses. The people filed by, loading him with presents! Realizing that they were by no means popular, the police were stupefied. The next day they had to release the prisoner, whose ancestry was but half Jewish. The policemen remained in the village for three weeks, at first zealous and convinced of the rightness of their action, but soon losing all enthusiasm. Subsequent raids proved equally futile.

ARRESTS AND VIOLENCE

Seventh stage. Development and perseverance in the test. The success of the methods employed at Le Chambon attracted an increasing flood of Jewish refugees. Soon there were several hundreds of them. (The Jewish Relief Agency states that more than two thousand of them stayed temporarily in the region, hidden on the farms.) This was when Cimade (a Protestant student group) came into the picture. It provided the Jews with false identity papers, absolutely necessary to get rations and safe conduct to the Swiss frontier. The resisters did not hide their activities from the authorities; they merely prevented identities being known, and in the end the police shut their eyes. But the Vichy government was not satisfied, and in the spring of 1943 had the two pastors and the headmaster of the school arrested. After six weeks, however, the pastors were liberated.

Eighth stage. Beginnings of violence, 1943. It was at this time that the pastors were first approached by representatives of the Secret Army (Maquis). While expressing their sympathy, they made quite clear the difference in aims (national liberation for the Maquis, the defense of man for the others) and in methods (armed resistance for the Maquis, non-collaboration for the others). The two patterns of action existed side by side, often intermingled right to the Liberation. It is difficult to say whether the Maquis protected the nonviolent groups, or if the latter saved the Maquis in this district from the tragic fate of the Maquis elsewhere (Vercors, for instance). In any case, the nonviolent ones raised no question of keeping their hands clean or of dissociating themselves from those who, like themselves, were bravely risking their lives. Neither did the Maquisards accuse the nonviolent ones of cowardice.

In the beginning of the summer of 1943, one of the refugee homes housing twenty-three students was raided. The director and all but three of the students died in extermination camps.

Violence broke out on the day a Vichy policeman, a spy against the Resistance, was assassinated by four Maquisards. The pastors publicly expressed disapproval of this act but were held responsible, nevertheless, by the Gestapo and condemned to death. An indiscretion on the part of a "supposed spy" (some of the spies serving the Gestapo were actually spying *on* the Gestapo for the Resistance) gave adequate warning for a successful escape. For the ten months that the pastors were in hiding, the church passed through a wonderful period, for the nonviolent movement had spread throughout the district.

Ninth stage. Resistance to the Resistance, 1944. From the time of the Normandy landing, the situation was extremely complex. The whole region had come under the authority of the 4th Republic (Gaullism). Raids by German troops, the shooting of the inhabitants of certain villages and farms, the burning of houses—all these caused great emotion among an overexcited people.

Allied planes parachuted arms during the night and many of the youth of the church and the village joined the Maquis. A few preferred to remain nonviolent and served in other ways.

PREACHING REPENTANCE

Six weeks before the Liberation, almost without firing a shot, the Maquis made prisoners of 120 Germans trying to flee to Lyons and imprisoned them in a country house in Chambon. This was the time when the story of the Oradour massacre was being circulated, when every German was held responsible for the crime. The pastor made himself unpopular with the Maquisards by visiting the prisoners. On Sunday mornings in a full church the pastor preached several sermons to those Maquisards present; in the afternoon the same sermon, translated word for word, was repeated to the Germans. On both sides, consciences were aroused, and rarely has the evidence of the gospel of peace been so striking.

Tenth stage. Martyrdom, 1944. This last stage was passed through by two men alone.

Daniel Trocmé, professor, headmaster of two homes for refugee children and students, was arrested in 1943, at the same time as his Jewish students. Held a prisoner, he continued to defend the Jews and was identified with them by the Gestapo. He died in the concentration camp at Mazdanek, Poland, probably gassed, in the spring of 1944.

Roger Le Forestier, a doctor at Chambon, arrested after an imprudent step taken at the Prefecture, gave so powerful a witness for nonviolent Christianity that he was let off but required to go to Germany as a "volunteer." While being transferred to Germany, he again fell into the hands of the Gestapo and was massacred with 120 other innocent victims.

One cannot draw from the success of the nonviolent resistance in the Chambon district any lesson of a line of conduct that would ensure success at another time and place. As a matter of fact, the attempt at resistance in Chambon was very imperfect. Rarely during the course of it did those taking part have a feeling of dazzling success. Only when it was all over, trying to evaluate what had happened to them, did they feel obliged to thank God for the daily proof he had given of his existence, and of his intervention in human affairs as soon as a few men place complete confidence in him.

MORALITY FOR LIVING

At one point, the experience was dissatisfying. It was not possible for non-violent resisters to avoid using false identity papers. To show a true identity paper was the equivalent of a denunciation. It seemed to us preferable to violate a formal moral rule (absolute truth) in order to apply a living moral rule (the absolute value of the human person). Jesus preferred to violate the Sabbath in order to help the men of his day.

On another point, the experience was positive. We learned that to resist war is but half our duty; saying no to evil is not enough. War resistance must include something else, and that something else is the salvation of the physical and moral life of humankind. That salvation is better assured by nonviolent resistance than by violent resistance, although nonviolent resistance also has its failures and its martyrs. We have never been able to console ourselves for having been unable to save from death the twenty students of the Maison des Roches.

And yet we ask ourselves, how much ruin and mourning would have been caused if the two pastors and the Christians at Chambon had felt obliged to lay ambushes and throw plastic (a special sort of explosive used by the Maquis) on the German police as they passed?

Let us leave aside the problem of national liberation. Gandhi alone could deal with it. But can we imagine a Europe that is entirely nonviolent, offering total resistance to Hitler, a Europe that the dictator and his police would have been unable to conquer? We can.

40

ON NONVIOLENT REVOLUTION

Danilo Dolci

Danilo Dolci was a reformer-revolutionary of the Gandhi-King mold, who talked like a college professor, looked like a well-fed member of the petty bourgeoisie, and lived in a Sicilian slum with his wife and five children. Known as the Gandhi of Sicily, he took on the corrupt "illegal invisible government," the Mafia, which did not assassinate him, perhaps because of his immense popularity. He effectively used fasting and the "reverse strike," where people voluntarily work harder or longer than usual in order to draw attention to a situation needing change. He raised the consciousness of millions of people and helped many to overcome situations of grinding poverty. A longtime friend of FOR, he died in 1997. His remarks are from a pamphlet, "What Is Peace?," selected and translated by Nicholas Parsons and Antonio Cowan (Fellowship, May 1970).

It is not true that everyone wants peace. We must have the courage to point to those who prepare for war in order to exploit. We must clearly distinguish between the parasites and the victims they bleed, between the violence of those who are defending their parasitism and the courageous energy of those who are defending their lives. And we must be clear about which side of this line we ourselves are on.

Real commitment to achieving peace is not to be confused with the attempt to remain equally aloof from all sides when conflicts arise.

Because the world is not at peace, any conduct—individual, group, or mass—that essentially maintains the status quo, or admits only slow change, is not real commitment to peace. *To achieve peace, we must be revolutionaries, nonviolent revolutionaries.*

The problem of the new revolution that we must have is to find how best to eliminate exploitation, murder, and the investment of energy in weapons of destruction—how to provoke chain reactions not of hate and death but of new constructiveness, of a new quality of life.

It is easy to doubt the efficacy of nonviolent revolution while it has yet to be proved, historically and systematically, that it can change *structures*. But in a

224

world tired of murder, betrayal, and pointless death, there can be a more direct appeal to people's consciences when a movement for change is both robust *and* nonviolent.

In Partinico in the winter of '55 there was really desperate hunger among most of the population, outlawed in every sense from the life of the nation. When we held the first peasant meetings, quite a few proposed flinging stones through the carabinieri's windows or setting fire to the Town Hall. But the majority objected that this way would be less effective, since people would be unwilling to participate if it meant putting themselves in the wrong. After fuller discussion we decided on a day's fast by one thousand people, to be followed by a "strike in reverse"—working on a dilapidated country road. The people joined in with scarcely any fear at all, despite massive intervention by the police—because they knew they weren't doing anybody any harm. Within a few days they had succeeded as never before in penetrating the public conscience with their protest and their own positive proposals.

With this profound capacity for awakening consciences, nonviolent action is also revolutionary in that it activates other forces that are revolutionary in different ways. And everyone who wants change makes the sort of revolution he can.

Often the situation in Partinico was so grave, the terror of the Mafia so widespread, that it was like working on the edge of a landslide. When some of us felt the situation demanded action, we decided to fast (as one has to in prison when it is the only action possible), in order to try to bring the peasants out of their isolation by joining with them in exposing the intolerable reality and making specific suggestions. At first many people disagreed with this method, but gradually as the days passed almost everyone's conscience was galvanized; discussions became animated; enterprises proliferated—among the embryonic trade unions, the local Councils, parties, individuals, and groups, often even in rivalry with one another. And many people now, as they look at the new lake with its ducks, inevitably reflect on the method which, from the first few stones to the final great mass, brought about the construction of this magnificent dam.

Sometimes we may admire violent revolutionary forces not because they are the only possible ones, or the most suitable to the circumstances, but because where they are active they are often the only ones brave enough to exist at all. But anyone who thinks war the *highest form* of struggle, or the *means* of resolving conflicts, still has a very limited vision of humanity. Anyone with effective revolutionary experience knows—and has to admit—that to succeed in changing a situation he must have not only a material appeal but a higher *moral* appeal; he knows that the appeal to truer principles, to a superior ethic, itself becomes an element of strength: and thus his action is revolutionary also insofar as it helps create new feelings, new abilities, new culture, new instincts— a new human nature.

Personally, I am absolutely convinced that peace means action—when necessary revolutionary, but *nonviolent*. I recognize that a diseased situation can be brought nearer to health, and therefore nearer to peace, by other means too; but I know that violence, even when directed to good ends, still contains the seed of death.

Which are more numerous—those who would gain by changes, or those who think they benefit from maintaining the status quo?

There are thousands of millions of people in the world at present excluded from progress and social justice. By interpreting and expressing the profound needs of *these* people, by helping them to take stock of their problems, by helping them to initiate enterprises of every kind, at every level, and to press effectively for changes, we can activate a positively revolutionary force.

Though planning from a position of power is more likely to be effective, we must not underestimate the possibilities of opposition planning.

Many revolutionary movements, though good at rousing consciences and effective in protest and pressure, suffer from weakness on their *constructive* front. But the demolition of old systems and the building of new organic groups should be simultaneous coordinated activities which potentiate each other; the growth of convincing alternatives encourages attack on the old groups, while the loss of authority of the old structures facilitates development of the new.

41

"PEOPLE ARE WILLING
TO SACRIFICE THEMSELVES . . . "

An Interview with Cesar Chavez

In organizing farmworkers in California, Cesar Chavez (1927-93) did something few have ever been able to do: apply nonviolence to the economic sphere. Throughout the 1960s and 1970s the United Farmworkers Union employed a range of nonviolent tactics, including strikes, consumer boycotts, marches, and public fasts. For Chavez himself the struggle reflected a personal commitment to nonviolence with deep spiritual roots. This interview was conducted by Jim Forest, editor of Fellowship, *in 1973* (Fellowship, *September 1973).*

CHAVEZ: Nonviolence is very difficult. In our case our job is never done because we're always dealing with new people in these situations. We're always at the beginning point. Where you happen to deal with people you've dealt with before, it's no problem, but that's not afforded us very often. And so we now have ten thousand people on strike in seven different places and in almost every single case—with 98 percent of the people—they've never had the experience. That's difficult.

You have to deal with them in such a way that you don't *impose* the idea of nonviolence on them but that they *accept* it. Because if you try to impose it in a situation as difficult as this one, a situation that's so charged up, they'll reject everything. You have to have a very skilled method of convincing people.

I think the first prerequisite of nonviolence is for the nonviolent person to assume that there are other feelings and not to impose. Trying to impose is a mistake a lot of *non-activist* nonviolent people fall into, just as they fall into the trap of thinking nonviolence is a land of milk and honey. Nonviolence is really *tough*. You don't practice nonviolence by attending conferences—you practice it on the picket lines. And if you've been here two or three days, you know how difficult that is.

But once the workers make that first step toward nonviolence and they accept the idea, then you begin to work at carrying it out. It goes by steps.

We're fortunate. We've been able to hang on to nonviolence in these really large confrontations we've been having. Some people still throw rocks—but they're not carrying guns or knives or baseball bats, and the rock throwing is only occasional, so we think we're 99 and 9/10ths percent successful.

FOREST: *How do the people do it? How do they remain nonviolent in that heat, under those conditions, with those pressures?*

CHAVEZ: A lot has to do with leadership and the people running the strike. I'm *not* running the strike, as you know.

In some places they've been striking a long time. They're disciplined. In some cases, they're not disciplined, but they've got the idea—initiating, creative picketing, never permitting the people to feel they're up against a stone wall, that they've come to the last. And that's more important than *talking* about nonviolence.

The thing we have going for us is that people are willing to sacrifice themselves. When you have that spirit, then nonviolence is not very difficult to accomplish. It becomes mechanical then—just a matter of working on mechanics.

But I think that we're just blessed with the idea that the workers accept and understand—as part of their tradition—the meaning of sacrifice. Because they're willing to do that, you're well on your way to putting the whole idea of nonviolence before them. And with some creative picketing, as I said, this does the trick.

FOREST: *Cesar, it has been eleven years since you began organizing the farmworkers. Have there been times when your convictions about nonviolence were shaken?*

CHAVEZ: No. Because I'm an extremely practical man. I don't think any one event, or any one day, or any one action, or any one confrontation wins or loses a battle. You keep that in mind and be practical about it.

It's foolish then to try to gamble everything on one roll of dice—which is what violence really gets down to.

I think the practical person has a better chance of dealing with nonviolence than people who tend to be dreamers or who are impractical. We're not nonviolent because we want to save our souls. We're nonviolent because we want to get some social justice for the workers.

If all you're interested in is going around being nonviolent and so concerned about saving yourself, at some point the whole thing breaks down—you say to yourself, "Well, let *them* be violent, as long as *I'm* nonviolent." Or you begin to think it's okay to lose the battle as long as you remain nonviolent. The idea is that you have to *win* and be nonviolent. That's extremely important! You've got to be nonviolent—and you've got to *win* with nonviolence!

And there's no cop-out. If I lose, I can't blame nonviolence. I lost for other reasons. Right at the beginning I have to accept the fact that, if I lose, it's my fault more than anyone else's.

FOREST: *You mentioned that the workers are sustained by a tradition of sacrifice. What sustains you?*

CHAVEZ: People. I have to touch people, and I have to get so close to them that my skin rubs with them. That's where I get my strength. I'm at least experienced enough to know that all power comes from the people. So I stay close to them. That's where I get my strength. *They* give it to me.

And sometimes it works the other way. When we meet, especially under these very difficult situations, people often say, "Oh, it's so good to see you here. We feel strong when you come." And I say, "How funny! I feel the same way!" *(Laughter.)* "I feel strong when I see you."

But the business of nonviolence in struggle is not angelic. It's the business of working with people—at best it's a very tough proposition.

FOREST: *I noticed in your office many of Gandhi's books as well as drawings of him. There was a photo of Martin Luther King. There were various editions of the Bible. To what extent do you find yourself turning to these sources?*

CHAVEZ: Well, number one, in our movement most of us are the action type and not the philosopher type. This is probably the most I'll ever do on nonviolence—talking when someone comes around and asks questions about it. I won't write about it. I don't want to write about it. I haven't got time.

The philosophy is great, but you take Gandhi and King and learn from them because they were activists and strategists. What people have to understand is that Gandhi—besides being a saint (not an angel but a saint!)—Gandhi was a masterful strategist. When I read him, I read him for that.

I think I've read almost everything Gandhi wrote on nonviolence. I have the concept. I may not understand everything, but I understand enough to carry me through.

But then I go behind the scenes to find out the *strategy* that he used—which in many cases makes nonviolence workable.

FOREST: *You make me think of a phrase I heard in Berkeley the other day— "cheap pacifism." The phrase was meant to describe the stance of people who use the highly moral rhetoric of nonviolence while in reality excusing themselves from any real response to human suffering . . .*

CHAVEZ: That's not nonviolence! There's no reason to be nonviolent—there's no challenge—unless you are living for people. These two men—Gandhi and King—did it for the masses, for the people. That's how it has to be done—for a purpose.

It's amazing how people lose track of basics. Gandhi was one of the best fund-raisers the world has ever seen! *(Laughter.)* But people don't look at it that way! They don't!

One millionaire Indian said, "It costs me millions to keep Gandhi poor." *(Continued laughter.)*

When you put that together with Gandhi's political acumen—well, you find he's a living, operating guy working with people.

What I'm trying to say is that you can't go around pretending to be an angel when you're not an angel for the sake of making people believe you're nonviolent. That's cheap. It doesn't work that way.

I get continually irritated by people who walk around as if they were on eggshells. I don't buy that. I resent it. I can't stand it. Nonviolent people aren't part angel. "Let the world go to hell over there"—that's what that says to me.

FOREST: *You draw a distinction between saint and angel. For you the saint isn't an eggshell walker?*

CHAVEZ: Right! You think about St. Paul—there was a man! And you think about Gandhi.

You know, Gandhi's secretary was once asked by some Westerners who came idolizing Gandhi, "Oh, how is it to live with Gandhi?"

And his secretary says, "To live with Gandhi is like living in the mouth of a lion." *(Burst of laughter.)*

You see, he was difficult to work with. I suppose living with Martin Luther King was also difficult. It was push and push and push. So you learn that from them.

And you go to the source and read the story of Christ's life here on earth and you get the message. He went over, you know, and upset some tables and said some very tough things to the rich.

FOREST: *The same people who spoke of "cheap pacifism" said it is extremely important to distinguish between nonviolent conflict resolution and the building up of justice. They said the main problem now is getting people to stop using violence as a method. We should worry more about that, they said, and less about justice. Your own approach seems very different—struggling first with the problem of injustice . . .*

CHAVEZ: With the struggle here, we'll sit back and we'll talk about non-violence and we'll have made more converts than you'll ever make by going to ten million seminars. But also you'll have accomplished just what they want to accomplish. What do the poor care about strange philosophies of nonviolence if it doesn't mean bread for them?

FOREST: *I recall Gandhi saying that there are so many hungry people in the world that the only way God can appear is as a piece of bread.*

CHAVEZ: Right. You know, if people are not pacifists, it's not their fault. It's because society puts them in that spot. You've got to change it. You don't just change a man—you've got to change his environment as you do it.

42

DISREGARDED HISTORY

The Power of Nonviolent Action

Gene Sharp

Dr. Gene Sharp is one of the most influential scholars in the field of nonviolent conflict resolution. He is the author of The Politics of Nonviolent Action, *a massive study of the nature of nonviolent struggle as a social and political technique. In 1954, after serving nine months in prison for refusing military service, he worked as secretary to A. J. Muste. From 1955 to 1958 he was assistant editor of the British periodical* Peace News. *Since receiving his doctorate in philosophy from Oxford University, he has taught at many universities. The remarks that follow are extracted from a much longer piece. In the earlier sections Dr. Sharp had reviewed a largely unknown history of successful nonviolent actions in such widely differing contexts as Germany and Norway under the Nazis, Guatemala in 1944, and the American colonies during the struggle for independence* (Fellowship, *March 1976).*

Now what is the condition of the peace movement, and how is all this relevant? Let us try to look at the "peace movement" not simply in the perspective of the period of Vietnam but in the perspective of peace movements since they began to exist as organized entities, which certainly goes back at least to the nineteenth century.

The objective of peace organizations, originally at least, was to abolish war. It is doubtful that you will find that objective very clearly stated in the current programs as an achievable objective, within the foreseeable future, of any present American or foreign peace organization.

This is very instructive. Peace groups have been willing to settle for things far short of abolishing war: witnessing to one's piety and purity—and the stupidity of everybody else; witnessing to being a "holy remnant" or the only sane people around; struggling for the rights of conscientious objectors to war. There is nothing intrinsically wrong with any of these things. The point is not that.

But they serve as substitutes for serious efforts to abolish war as such. Peace groups oppose a particular war and try to speed up its end with no confidence whatsoever that, even if successful, the military systems will thereby be weaker. Peace groups oppose the development of a particular weapon or a particular piece of technology—without that necessarily being a vehicle for reversing the whole dependence upon military hardware and military weapons. Or advocates of peace support giving all of the world's weapons to one government—a world government—or support the army of the other side—and call that antiwar activity! Or peace workers support universal negotiated disarmament when there is no historical evidence that that has ever worked or ever will. Or peace workers settle for some measures of arms control and arms regulation, which—although they may help and may prevent a particular outbreak, or destruction, or attack under certain circumstances—can easily be broken and leave the military system more or less as it is.

Where is there a peace organization that really expects that, in something less than a few hundred or a few thousand years, war is going to be removed from human society? There is no chance of a major popular uprising against war—as even I (with all of my cynicism) thought might be thinkable in the 1950s. At that point there were still people for whom nuclear weapons and intercontinental rocketry were new and therefore shocking. There was still moral indignation about it. But now whole generations have grown up in which nuclear weaponry is just part of the world, like mountains and rivers, cities and poverty. There is no fresh thinking among peace groups. There is no effective challenging of the political assumptions which underline the war system itself. One hears that the war system is all wicked. Peace groups imply that to get rid of war, one has to change whole generations and the way people are brought up. These may be wonderful things to do, but it implies that it is not possible to get rid of war until then. Others argue we must first have social revolution—ignoring the fact that wars existed for centuries before capitalism, and ignoring the fact that so-called socialist countries attack and invade each other, and that following most "revolutions," the military system is often more powerful than under the old regime.

Yet human nature may provide other clues. You all have done various things in your lives you don't tell everybody about. When you were a little screaming brat, you got mad at mommy and daddy. "I'm not going to eat!" You engaged in a "hunger strike." Or, if mommy and daddy were going to wallop you on the bottom and they hadn't touched you yet and whoever was your defender in the family was in the other room, you started screaming like mad, lying on the floor as if you had been slaughtered. And they hadn't even touched you. You were appealing to "martyrdom" and sympathy against the persecution of a poor, nonviolent, helpless person! Or you wouldn't take out the garbage, at least not on time. This was a refuse worker's strike. Or you wouldn't clean up your room until someone was standing there: "Now take that and put that in that drawer. . . . " That is "non-obedience without direct supervision" or "slow and reluctant compliance." Or you wouldn't study when you went to school. You'd look out the window, daydream, or even sleep in class.

Many animals and pets do all these things. Haven't you had dogs or cats act this way? They want to go with you in the car somewhere—when they know they are not supposed to—they go and jump right in. It's a "sit-in." Or, they know very well what you're saying to them and pretend they don't, just like you've done yourself. Or you say "move," and they lie down, whimpering, and look up at you with the saddest possible look—like some demonstrators do to police. Sometimes they're being ignored, particularly if there's company coming and there's a big fuss in the house and nobody's paying attention to them when they're trying to say, "Come and play with me." The dog then goes into the middle of the living room rug and does a "nonviolent intervention"—not biting anybody, not growling at anybody—but getting attention! So we don't have to change human nature—or even animal nature—in order to be nonviolent. We can be the same stubborn, obnoxious people we've always been, under the guise of our halos and piety, while accomplishing things collectively that have a political objective. We can draw upon the experiences of other people in other situations. We don't have to convert people to a new religious revelation, or worry about the sensitivity of our souls. That's all nonsense on the political and social level.

The focus here is on a very simple question. It isn't even: how do we change all of society? It isn't: how do we create the perfect nonviolent society of the future? It is simply: *how do we get rid of major political violence, including war?*

Nobody who has tried to get rid of war has succeeded. What we do is go on repeating the same things year after year, decade after decade. You read this and that report, change a few words, and it's the same story and the same methods that were used way back—with no evidence that they had the kind of effects that are sought this time. People try to choose between one of the bankrupt political ideologies and another one. It's ludicrous. If we've not been able to solve a problem, maybe the humility that we talk about so often and so smugly should be rooted in the awareness of our ignorance and our failure.

Most people have been totally unaware of the history of struggle without violence. Thus, every time they have engaged in nonviolent struggle, people have had to improvise anew. *Suppose that had been the case with war?* Suppose no armies had been organized. Nobody had studied military strategy and tactics. Nobody had tried to invent new weapons or even develop training in the use of existing weapons. There were no West Points. Then the Martians and the Eskimos formed an alliance to conquer all the terrible Southerners who had destroyed their way of life. President Ford would go on television and declare: *"We're going to be invaded from the North. Now you all remember we have experience in fighting with violence. You remember all those times in the kitchen when you threw things at each other, all those barroom brawls that you've had, and all the feuds you've heard about beginning with the Hatfields and the McCoys. Now, with true spontaneity and creativity and with that freshness without regimentation that makes it effective, get out there and fight the invasion from the North."*

Ludicrous!

That's the situation nonviolent struggle has always been in—even against the Nazis. It's amazing it hasn't been wiped off the earth. The explanation must be that there is something very powerful in this technique, so that even when improvised, even when facing an organized terroristic Nazi system, even when confronting one powerful government or another, it has somehow, in many situations, prevailed. But peace workers have often talked nonsense: "Nonviolent means should be used, even if they don't succeed, because it's right to be nonviolent." But if nonviolent struggle has been able to prevail despite highly unfavorable circumstances, it's possible that nonviolent struggle has a power potential many times greater than violence and war. This is possible because it is based—among other things—upon a more accurate perception of the nature of power as deriving from people and ultimately dependent on people.

If we take all this past human experience in nonviolent forms of struggle that have been improvised, and we study and research them and try to learn how to refine and develop them to make them more effective than they have ever been, we won't have to argue *against* violence and war. If *nonviolent* struggle can be shown to be so much more *effective*, then people will *want* to use it. After all, war isn't that effective. In every case, at least one side loses, which is only 50 percent effective, if you're lucky. The winner pays a very large price, as well. Nonviolent struggle has the potential for building a solution to the problem. We have primitive prototypes of nonviolent defense policy, or civilian-based defense policy, as it is preferably called. We have the experience in the use of this technique in revolution against dictatorships. Civilian struggle has been used in struggles for reform and in land redistribution, instead of guerrilla warfare.

Throughout history we have overlooked or deprecated the crucial role of nonviolent struggle. It is hardly ever presented in terms to evoke a response in people who read about it. But there is a vast, long history of this underdeveloped, crude political technique that has used a myriad of nonviolent weapons: economic boycotts, sit-ins, civil disobedience, protest marches, mutiny, parallel government—about two hundred different methods, capable not only of converting opponents, but, more importantly, of destroying the power of a dictator.

The question isn't—as some pacifists have asked—whether one is able to love a Hitler. The question is, are we capable of *destroying* a Nazi system by nonviolent struggle. If one argues that we have to wait until every last human being is capable of loving a Hitler before we can get rid of war, it's either spiritual arrogance or political bankruptcy. The problem is how on earth do you fight tyranny? How do you prevent and defeat genocide, whoever attempts to commit it? Unless we answer that question, in the worst racist situations, people are not going to give up war.

With this view of the nature of the problem of war, and the existence of nonviolent alternatives, we need a variety of things. First and foremost is research, so we know what we are talking about, and so other people will respect what we have to say, and respect the product of that research. That involves people participating in the research who hold widely diverse beliefs and are skeptical of nonviolent alternatives.

We should look forward to the time when we can establish a new national priority: a ten-year crash program of research and evaluation of whether we can develop an effective nonviolent substitute for war that would provide real defense. This could be undertaken for a mere 1 percent of the Pentagon budget for a year, every dollar of which could be very usefully spent. Either the nonviolent stuff that peace advocates have believed in is utter nonsense (which most pacifists will go on believing anyhow, irrespective of all the evidence against it, so the research won't harm it), or, as I suspect, the research will substantiate many of the claims about the potential of nonviolent means. Even the most informed advocates of nonviolent alternatives may repeatedly have their minds blown at the continuing revelations of the potential that nonviolent struggle has already demonstrated—and the discovery of what it is capable of becoming. The abolition of war does not require antiwar, anti-military lobbies or demonstrations and protest *but the development of effective nonviolent alternatives to military struggle.*

The view that there is only limited constituency from the peace movement that would take nonviolent alternatives seriously is idiocy. That view is a reflection of the incapacity of the peace organizations' perceptions, dreams, and programs. Why can't we, in an age in which military people know how little military means can really accomplish, convince them of alternatives?

The point is, this nonviolent struggle is harmonious with what we crudely call "human nature." Civilian struggles have occurred throughout history. We don't have to carry out vast sweeping changes that take decades or generations before we can eliminate major political violence. In dozens and hundreds of significant conflicts, including international ones, in ignorance and with improvisation, nonviolent struggle has already taken the place of military violence. The only question is, can we improve it and make it more effective? Can we provide the necessary vehicles and stimuli and resources to speed up the changeover? *Can civilian struggle be made a realistic choice for ordinary people (who don't really like war, anyhow) and for professional soldiers (many of whom hate war because they have seen it firsthand) and for politicians (who often want these kinds of things too)?* Pacifists and other peace workers are so used to being a minority that they have no idea how many people are ready to join in a search for a substitute form of defense and struggle. But when we see that the basis of an alternative and the readiness of people to explore it are there, then the potential of what is possible to accomplish has been changed. It becomes possible once again to dream the dream of the abolition of war—but this time on the basis of realism and substance.

43

AWAKENING FROM A DREAM OF KINGS AND WIZARDS

Daniel Ellsberg

Daniel Ellsberg served in the 1960s as a high-level analyst in the Defense Department. This work, along with his experience of two years in Vietnam, turned him into an outspoken critic of the war. In 1971 he copied and released a top-secret history of the war, which came to be known as the Pentagon Papers. As a result he was arrested and tried, though ultimately the charges were dismissed because of gross governmental misconduct. He has continued since then to work for peace, particularly in the struggle against nuclear weapons. The following remarks were delivered on the occasion of his receiving the 1976 Gandhi Peace Award from Promoting Enduring Peace in New York City (Fellowship, *November 1976*).

Do you remember, in the movie of *The Wizard of Oz*, how the Wizard is first introduced? He appears as an enormous, ominous, glowing, green face, whose voice resounds, *"I am Oz, the Great and Terrible! Who are you? And what do you seek?"* After Dorothy and her friends are sufficiently terrified, he agrees to fulfill their petitions, but only if they can bring back the witch's broom. They finally bring it back, after dissolving the witch in a splash of water, but then the great Wizard renounces his promises. While Dorothy and her companions are shuddering amid bursts of lightning and sheets of thunder, however, Dorothy's little dog Toto has gone to the corner of the great throne room and pulled back a small curtain—and there, within, is a little man pulling levers and shouting into a microphone. The voice then comes from the huge green face, *"I am Oz, the Magnificent, pay no attention to that man behind the curtain . . . "*

Such sounds were made more recently by the White House as the Pentagon Papers began to appear, bit by bit. The curtain came down, along with various trousers. The aura that had been blinding us began to dim and people began to rub their eyes and awake from a dream of kings and wizards—and to rediscover what difference it is supposed to make to be an American and to be descended from those one-time "traitors" of 1776 who, in constitutional invention, helped to give us unprecedented liberties in which loyalties to human values took priority over loyalty to a single executive.

Most of us have long been aware of the limitations of those liberties, unassociated as they are with economic and political equality. We have noticed that, despite having the freest press in the world, one of the highest literacy rates, widespread higher education, freedom to speak as great as any nation—despite all that, eight million tons of U.S. bombs fell on the Indochinese people, and eight million more tons would have fallen had people not acted.

On the other hand, when the bombs stopped falling on Indochina *despite* the wishes of the executive branch, we learned the worth of those written freedoms that were given us and discovered again the living substance of those rights that, despite all erosion, remain.

I am often asked whether I still believe in the American system. Usually, the questioner identifies the system almost exclusively with the executive branch—one of those Wizard of Oz myths foisted on us during the last thirty years. I find myself reminding others that we have a three-branched government, plus the press, and that sovereignty is vested in the public. For the first time in my lifetime, all those non-executive branches have functioned, as they were meant to function, to limit and control executive tyranny. The system has never worked so well as it has in the last few years—but this only because of the efforts of very many Americans.

I received two Gandhian awards this week, one from private, the other from public authority. One included a medal, the other a citation—a notice filed in U.S. District Court ordering me to appear for arraignment, with fifty-three others associated with the Continental Walk, arrested on the steps of the Pentagon. The citation accuses me of "failure to comply with official directions."

One might ask, and some have already, why is it important, in a time of peace, still to be marching for disarmament? Why is it still important to be arrested?

The reason that we are enjoying a degree of peace at the moment is precisely because many of those now marching for disarmament had earlier marched against the war in Indochina and, before that, for an end to the testing of nuclear weapons—weapons that would be exploding in the atmosphere today if we had kept silent. The attitudes and methods espoused by Gandhi years ago have given us a measure of hope about what could be achieved.

I'm more impressed with those methods now than I was a few years ago because they have helped us to achieve so much. We've learned not only that what we did was worth doing. We now know that our efforts saved hundreds of thousands of lives in Indochina. The secrets of that war are still not all public, but that war would be going on today if it weren't for its opponents in this country. We had a sharp effect on the president and his men. The hemorrhage of truth which was occasioned by the publication of the Pentagon Papers, and other revelations of executive deception, led them to take drastic actions to maintain secrecy that were criminal and illegal and led to their downfall. The Wizard of Oz was exposed.

How had I gotten to this disobedient course, after years of commitment to obedience?

What moved me were the writings of Gandhi and Martin Luther King—and above all meeting people whose lives reflected the values of those teachers. My tendency to identify patriotism with loyalty to executive authority gave way to an agreement with the teaching of Gandhi,

> I have found it our first duty to render voluntary obedience to law, but while doing that duty I have also seen that, when law fosters untruth, it becomes a duty to disobey it. How may this be done? We can do so by never swerving from truth and suffering the consequences of our disobedience. This is civil disobedience.

For Gandhi, nonviolence was inseparable from the search for truth, and thus honesty and openness. His key word, *satyagraha*, literally means "truth-force."

A certain point came in my life when I realized that I had materials to free at least some truth from the safe and that, in principle at least, I had an obligation to do so. But the catalyst was an experience similar to an event in Dr. King's life.

Martin Luther King had read Gandhi, but as a young Alabama pastor, he wasn't eager to make waves. It took Rosa Parks and her refusal to give her seat up to a white man on a Montgomery bus. Dr. King searched for reasons not to respond, until he realized that Rosa Parks had not only acted in her own life but was challenging others to act out the precepts they had intellectually accepted—in his case, from Gandhi. He remembered Gandhi's principle: "To fail to resist evil is to be an accomplice to it."

For me, the decision to release the papers didn't come simply from reading Gandhi but rather from meeting young draft resisters at a meeting of War Resisters International. They calmly, casually, informed an audience that they were going to prison shortly rather than join in a wrongful war. The immediate effect was to make me cry. It was a very painful time, as an American, to see what our country was forcing on some of the best of our young. I discover my patriotism these days in moments of shame—but also in pride at those acts of Americans who discover how to resist the shameful policies of their government.

Had I not met such people, had I only read a book, I might not have been forced to ask myself so suddenly, "What could I do if I were ready to go to jail???" As soon as I said that, the question could no longer be escaped. And the answer came easily. I had a lot of truth to lay on the public.

My actions were an experiment, as Gandhi put it, in the power of truth—and an experiment that verified that power.

When I agreed to speak at the Pentagon last Monday, I did so because it was my old office and I couldn't pass up the opportunity to speak to my former colleagues and perhaps suggest a few thoughts that might draw them away from their sense of being powerless ciphers significant only because of their obedience to great engines of power, the mighty wizards that they serve. It is only, I wanted to explain, when you first ask the question—"What if I were willing to risk my job?"—that your realization of alternatives suddenly expands. You discover that there are all sorts of powerful actions that you can undertake.

Thousands of people in the military have documents, for example, on the Nixon plans for the bombing of Laos and Cambodia. They could have been put out before the event, after the event—and it is still not too late to show the pattern of policy and have an enormous impact.

So I decided to speak at the Pentagon. "Here I am—life does exist outside the Executive Branch. And you needn't think there is nothing you can do—you can tell the truth. For some of you there are important truths no further away than your nearest file drawer."

Speaking at the Pentagon was something of a nostalgic occasion for me. I had last marched to the Pentagon in 1967. At that time, with my Defense Department pass, I went inside. Going from the room where we were studying the Pentagon Papers, I stood one window away from Secretary McNamara. I wanted to be able to see his face when the Yippies succeeded in levitating the building. But they didn't succeed. It only occurred to me later that levitation is best done from the inside—and that what had weighed the building down so much wasn't the cement and not even the safes but the moral weight of the lies and crimes recorded in those safes.

When I finally lightened the load by seven thousand pages, damned if the building didn't wobble a little bit.

I suggested to those in the Pentagon's windows Monday that they empty the truth from the safes behind them and ship it across the river to Congress, to the press, and to the people, and that, if they did that, the building would rise six feet in the air—and off the backs of the poor people all over the world.

A little later I was arrested. When some of the walkers tried to read a statement based on the Declaration of Independence from the Pentagon, they were informed that they had crossed a line. They were getting so close to the windows that the Secretary of Defense might actually hear the call for new priorities, to shift money being drained away by the Pentagon to meet more human needs. These were people, mind you, who had walked seven thousand miles to deliver this petition. They hadn't come that distance to be told there was free speech on one side of a line but not the other. So they stepped across the line, tried to read the petition aloud, and were arrested. Now when Americans are arrested for peaceable assembly and the presentation of petitions for the redress of grievances, then it is a good day to be arrested and to be in trouble with one's government. So a number of us crossed the same line.

At the Pentagon, a newsman—was he from the *Oz Post?*—asked me in a deprecating way. "What is this? The last rally of the Vietnam War?" "No, that was last year," I said. "This is the first rally of the rest of our lives."

44

THE VIOLENCE IN OURSELVES

Dorothy T. Samuel

Dorothy Samuel is a writer and television commentator. A longtime member of FOR, she is the author of Safe Passage on City Streets (Fellowship, *November 1976*).

Consider the Richard Nixons, the My-Lai participants, the rapists brutally assaulting our freedom of movement, the stubborn and unethical bosses—even the husbands and wives and children who continually grate on our nerves. Pacifists though we may be, we are constantly reminded that there are surges of hatred, impulses to violence, within our own natures. And just because we are pacifists, people dedicated to love and compassion and tenderness, we are often paralyzed by these emotions in ourselves. Often we know no other response but to straitjacket them, even to deny them. We are ashamed of feeling fury, of experiencing violent anger, of the occasional mounting within us of a desire to see someone actually hurt.

It is my belief, based on years of experience with my own anger supplemented by recent exploration into the angers of other nonviolence adherents, that much of the ineffectiveness of peace people stems from this sense of shame. We are often incapacitated by our own angers, even by the remembrance that we have felt anger—real, nasty, pervasive anger. This shame can make us too tolerant of others—the criminal on the streets or the bully-child on the playground. Frequently, we hesitate to confront these people with the firmness they need—the very firmness their actions may be begging for. We are paralyzed by our own sense of guilt.

When this occurs, we actually become pliant victims of the vicious and the violent lest we loose our own anger, lest we become as coercive as they. We acquiesce in the less overt domineering and manipulation practiced by bosses or club associates or even self-selected pacifist leaders in the fear that confrontation might lead *us* to violence, if only psychic violence. We at times pamper and encourage the ruthless and insensitive behaviors of our own family members by giving positive, accepting feedback to negative and unacceptable affronts.

240

We feel that love means inoffensiveness at all costs. And we worship love, we pacifists, sometimes identifying love with a kind of patience and long-suffering quite unlike the personal example of that St. Peter whose thirteenth chapter of First Corinthians we quote. We may forget, in judging our own angers, that the love demonstrated by St. Paul and Jesus and Gandhi and Martin Luther King was a tough, firm, outspoken honesty that demanded the best from people, a love more accurately described by the Quaker injunction "speak truth to power" than by the passive acquiescence of "never make anyone unhappy."

I believe these great people accepted their anger, learned to use their anger. To "use" anger releases one from the destructive effects of anger—upon oneself and upon others. It is only diffuse, blood-heating, unfocused, and unexpressed anger which short-circuits our rational powers, constricts our physical muscles, and makes us prisoners of fear—if only the fear of our own incapacity to act in a manner we consider worthy.

In my own experience, though I have not since I was a child touched anyone with physical violence, I have most certainly offered verbal and psychic violence to others at a level which appalls me. And I have found, on looking back, that this occurred only when I bottled up the anger in me with all the strength of my being. At such times, if the provocation continued too long for my powers, I finally exploded in nasty, vicious, and totally unredemptive abuse of the people involved. Unwilling to admit my anger, I was unable to use that anger, and the anger took control of me.

I am no longer ashamed of my anger and I no longer deny the existence of anger. I have, in fact, learned from less guilt-ridden areas just how effectively anger can be used.

I am not a large woman, nor an unusually strong one. Yet throughout my life, I have deliberately used anger to enable me to accomplish physical tasks otherwise beyond my strength—moving a piano, stretching a broken clothesline, lifting an injured child. In all these cases, I focused my anger on the situation—not on myself or my weakness, not on the person who "caused" the need, or the person who "should have been there when I needed him." I focused my anger on the demands of the situation; I enjoyed the rush of adrenaline and the surge of strength; and I exulted when I had accomplished an "impossible" task. My anger was transformed into a tool under my conscious control, and its use as a tool left me with a kind of glory.

At first, of course, I did this without conscious understanding. But having experienced my own physical strength when angry, I began deliberately to call anger up when such strength was needed. Only much later did I recognize the same pattern in cases where I had used my anger constructively to meet violence or threat from the world around me. And I began to see the same use of anger in the great pacifists—and in the great acts of pacifists around me.

They used their anger; they were not engulfed by it. Neither were they incapacitated by a sense of guilt over feeling anger. They did not retreat in shame before their anger at persecution of German Jews, or the lynching of black people, or the carpet bombing of Vietnamese. They used that anger to confront an otherwise overwhelming situation. And in one-to-one situations they did not deny their own anger at bullying of peaceful demonstrators or senseless attacks offered them on the street. They did not draw back in fear that their own anger might hurt the feelings of those caught up in violence.

Instead, they spoke truth to violence—in the home and on the job as well as in Washington. They stood up to attack—in the meeting houses and FOR conferences as well as on the protest lines. Their anger at the situations became a source of strength, an energizing power for creative response, for initiative action.

Anger is not the only source of strength, fortunately, nor is it the only motivating force for creative response to attack. But when anger springs up as a natural response to an intolerable situation, it can be used with the same deliberate control as one uses any attribute or talent. Anger directed at the situation—not at individuals—releases one from *passivism* to creative *pacifism*—aggressive good will by which situations are transformed, and sometimes people too. It was anger-at-the-situation which moved the retired school teacher in New York to draw herself up and tell the young hood, "You put that gun away!" Anger-at-the-situation wiped out fear in a younger teacher in a large suburban high school when a boy she had just corrected slipped up behind her and held a gun at the back of her head. Turning at his call, she told him smartly, "School is no place for guns. Give that to me!" Both attackers obeyed. Confronted by a positive response empowered by fully controlled and focused anger—anger at the situation, not anger threatening them personally—their shoddy, diffused violence evaporated.

Gandhi, we all know, used his anger at the treatment of Indians in South Africa to launch a campaign which not only freed hundreds of thousands eventually from oppressive laws, but which immediately freed those who accompanied him from the corrosive inner decay and self-doubt of frustrated, repressed anger. Martin Luther King did the same for American blacks, and in the process both leaders actually did more for the oppressors' ultimate well-being than had generations of subservient encouragement to be their worst selves.

But I am not only thinking of the leaders of vast movements. I recall one instance when anger turned a thief's purposes inside out. A mother was cooped up in a hot car with three small, protesting children when a man came up to the open window, hand in pocket, and demanded her pocketbook. Out of her frustration and pain and absorption in her own lifestyle, she burst out, "Pocketbook! Do you know what's in my pocketbook? I haven't even enough money to buy the baby's milk, and the rent is due, and my husband just got laid off. My God! The price of eggs has gone up again, and . . . " On and on it flowed as she poured out her troubles as she might have to a friend or neighbor. The thief entered her scenario so fully that he dropped a ten-dollar bill into the car before he left.

Violence is never redemptive, never healthful. We are right to deny it a part in our lives. But we must not confuse violence with anger. Anger is normal, human response to outrage, a biochemical marshalling of our forces and our strength. It is a response pattern to be admitted, controlled, and used like any other human quality—even, in time, to be enjoyed as one enjoys second wind. It is in the frustration of anger, the repression and denial of anger as something shameful, that it turns into an explosive force of destruction and violence.

45

JUSTICE
AND MILITARY MADNESS

The Case of the Sperry Software Pair

In August of 1984, Barb Katt and John La Forge of Pelican Rapids, Minnesota, entered the Sperry Corporation's Eagan, Minnesota, plant, where weapons guidance systems are made. They proceeded to spill blood on a prototype computer before smashing it with hammers. Their eloquent statements to the court at their trial express the sentiments of antiwar activists in similar cases, while the judge's equally eloquent response was nothing less than extraordinary (Fellowship, *March 1986).*

STATEMENT OF BARB KATT: Most of us build prisons for ourselves and after we occupy them for a period of time we become their walls and accept the false premise that we are incarcerated for life. As soon as that belief takes hold of us, we abandon hope of ever doing more with our lives and of ever giving our dreams a chance to be fulfilled. We begin to suffer living deaths; one of a herd heading for destruction in a gray mass of mediocrity.

In our act of disarmament, in all its preparations and what has come since, I have found a lifeline to hope, the resurrection of hope from a living death. I resist not only the nuclear arms race, but the spiritual darkness of futility and self-pity as well. Hope is alive in the courtroom today.

STATEMENT OF JOHN LA FORGE: Sperry wouldn't admit to building modern crematoria. So it is our word against Sperry's, and you know as well as anyone that Sperry's word is not to be trusted. The company is corrupt and has lied to the government before. It has conspired to rob the taxpayers, and when its weapons are used, it gets away with murder.

We all know that hydrogen bombs cannot be used with either military practicality or ethical justification. We've banned not only the wanton burning of innocent people, but the planning of such an act. In human terms, then, nuclear weapons are useless and blasphemous and absurd. Building more, like the misuse of drugs or alcohol, is a form of chronic suicide.

We were nearly unable to overcome our fear of failure in our disarmament action. Indeed, I may never have truly believed it was possible to succeed, only that it was right to try; that the attempt was, and still is, universally correct.

And so the rightness, the correctness, and the justification swept us into Sperry's Dachau. And there, after letting go of the hammers and baby bottles, we were allowed an experience rare in one's lifetime. We were filled with the "feeling of inner peace" that Aristotle referred to simply as justice.

No matter what happens now, the action will always be invaluable to me for at least these reasons. It convinced me that the arms race can be halted nonviolently. It is possible to arrest the forward momentum, because the two of us, with the help of our friends, delayed for months the delivery of prototypes. And finally, it embodied and affirmed for me Henry David Thoreau's assessment of his risk, his civil disobedience, and his life in the woods. Thoreau wrote: "If one advances confidently in the direction of one's dreams, and endeavors to live the life which one has imagined, one will meet such a success unexpected in common hours."

STATEMENT OF JUDGE MILES LORD: It is the allegation of these young people that they committed the acts here complained of as a desperate plea to the American people and its government to stop the military madness which they sincerely believe will destroy us all, friend and enemy alike.

As I ponder over the punishment to be meted out to these two people who were attempting to unbuild weapons of mass destruction, I think we must ask ourselves: Can it be that those of us who build weapons to kill are engaged in a more sanctified endeavor than those who would by their acts attempt to counsel moderation and mediation as an alternative method of settling international disputes? Why are we so fascinated by a power so great that we cannot comprehend its magnitude? What is so sacred about a bomb, so romantic about a missile? Why do we condemn and hang individual killers while extolling the virtues of warmongers? What is that fatal fascination which attracts us to the thought of mass destruction of our brethren in another country? How can we even entertain the thought that all people on one side of an imaginary line must die and, if we be so ungodly cynical as to countenance that thought, have we given thought to the fact that in executing that decree we will also die? Who draws these lines and who has so decreed?

How many of the people in this democracy have seriously contemplated the futility of committing national suicide in order to punish our adversaries? Have we so little faith in our system of free enterprise, our capitalism, and the fundamental concepts that are taught us in our constitutions and in our several bibles that we must, in order to protect ourselves from the spread of foreign ideologies, be prepared to die at our own hands? Such thinking indicates a great lack of faith in our democracy, our body politic, our people, and our institutions.

There are those in high places who believe Armageddon is soon to be upon us, that Christ will soon come to earth and take us all back with him to heaven.

It would appear that much of our national effort is being devoted to helping with the process. It may even be a celebration of sorts. When the bombs go off, Christ won't have to come to earth—we will all, believers and nonbelievers alike, meet him halfway.

The anomaly of this situation is that I am here called upon to punish two individuals who were charged with having caused damage to the property of a corporation in the amount of $33,000. It is this self-same corporation which only a few months ago was before me accused of having wrongfully embezzled from the U.S. Government the sum of $3.6 million. The employees of this company succeeded in boosting the corporate profits by wrongfully and feloniously juggling the books. Since these individuals were all employees of a corporation, it appears that it did not occur to anyone in the office of the Attorney General of the United States that the actions of these men constituted a criminal conspiracy for which they might be punished. The government demanded only that Sperry pay back a mere 10 percent of the amount by which the corporation had been unlawfully enriched. Could it be that these corporate men who were working to build weapons of mass destruction received special treatment because of the nature of their work?

I am now called upon to determine the amount of restitution that is to be required of the two individuals who have done damage to the property of Sperry. The financial information obtained by the probation officers indicates that neither of the defendants owes any money to anyone. While Ms. Katt has no assets, Mr. LaForge is comparatively well endowed. He owns a 1968 Volkswagen, a guitar, a sleeping bag, and $200 in cash.

The inexorable pressure which generates from those who are engaged in making a living and a profit from building military equipment and the pork barreling that goes on in the halls of Congress to obtain more such contracts for the individual state will, in the ultimate, consume itself in an atomic holocaust. These same factors exert a powerful pressure upon a judge in my position to go along with the theory that there is something sacred about a bomb and that those who raise their voices or their hands against it should be struck down as enemies of the people, no matter that in their hearts they feel and know that they are friends of the people.

Now conduct of this sort cannot be condoned under the guise of free speech. Neither should it be totally condemned as being subversive, traitorous, or treasonous, in the category of espionage or some other bad things. I would here in this instance take the sting out of the bomb, attempt in some way to force the government to remove the halo with which it seems to embrace any device which can kill and to place instead thereon a shroud, the shroud of death, destruction, mutilation, disease, and debilitation.

If there be an adverse reaction to this sentence, I will anxiously await the protestations of those who complain of my attempts to correct the imbalance that now exists in a system that operates in such a manner as to provide one type of justice for the rich and a lesser type for the poor. One standard for the mighty and another for the meek. And a system which finds its humanness and objectivity is sublimated to military madness and the worship of the bomb.

A judge sitting here as I do is not called upon to do that which is politically expedient or popular but is called upon to exercise his calm and deliberate judgment in a manner best suited to accomplish and accommodate and vindicate the rights of the people acting through its government and the rights of those people who are the subject matter of such actions. The most popular thing to do at this particular time would be to sentence them to a ten-year period of imprisonment, and some judges might be disposed to do just that.

(At this point, six-month suspended sentences were imposed and the judge addressed the defendants, as follows:)

I am aware of the thrust of the argument which would say this would encourage others to do likewise. If others do likewise, they must be dealt with at that time.

I am also impressed with the argument that this might in some way constitute a disparity of sentence, that you individuals have not been properly punished for your offense because some others might not be deterred from doing that. I really wonder about the constitutionality of sentencing one person for a crime that may be committed by another person at another time and place.

It is also difficult for me to equate the sentence I here give you—for destroying $33,000 worth of property, because you have been charged—with those who stole $3,600,000 worth of property and were not charged, demoted, or in any way punished.

My conscience is clear.

46

WHEN PRAYER AND REVOLUTION BECOME PEOPLE POWER

Hildegard Goss-Mayr

When a four-day massive outpouring of "People Power" drove the Philippine dictator Marcos into exile, the press treated this successful demonstration of the effectiveness of nonviolence as a freak of nature. The media missed the real story, however. For a year and a half before that revolution the leaders of the Roman Catholic Church had themselves received training in nonviolence and had encouraged such training for masses of Filipino people. Hildegard and Jean Goss-Mayr from the International FOR and Richard Deats from the U.S. FOR trained nonviolence trainers. These in turn trained half a million people *in nonviolent defense of the ballot boxes, in anticipation of voting fraud. When the election took place, and it became clear that Marcos and his accomplices were stealing it, people turned out into the streets by the hundreds of thousands. The nuns that the media photographed stopping tanks by standing in their path were not acting "spontaneously." They had been trained in such responses and were receiving information on troop movements and encouragement in nonviolence from the Catholic radio station through transistor radios. This revolution was not a lucky "happening" but the result of careful planning and preparation that became a model for other people striving for liberation as well* (Fellowship, *March 1987*).

We know that not one step, not one seed, not one action that is carried out in the spirit of nonviolence is ever lost. It bears fruit in the history of nations and of the world. But even though we know this, it is encouraging and helpful to be able to see the practical results of nonviolent action from time to time. That is why I would like to share with you some of the things that happened in the Philippines during the recent liberation struggle, although—I should like to add immediately—it is only a first step in the struggle for a life of dignity for all Filipinos.

The international press has covered it quite well, but there are aspects of what the people of the Philippines lived through that very few journalists have been able to grasp. The press could not relate the events that occurred to the traditions and attitudes of the people that made them possible.

Nonviolence—this power of truth and love—always develops out of a given historical and cultural background. The Filipino people were under Spanish domination for three centuries, and a U.S. colony for half a century. Later on, during the Second World War, they were occupied by the Japanese and liberated by the Americans. While the United States did not set up another colonial regime, it established a strong military presence in the Philippines and made that country economically dependent upon the multinational firms.

Three centuries of Spanish rule brought Christianity to the Philippines, leaving behind, as in Latin America, a mostly Catholic country in the Spanish tradition. It is important to understand that the majority of the Filipino people are a believing people, with a faith like that of children, but not in a negative sense, at all. Our children often have a very close relationship to God. There is no theology in between. Many Filipino people are like those in Latin America who have said to me, "God has spoken into my ear, He said this and this." Sometimes the gospel comes directly into the hearts and minds of the people, in a way that is not rationalized, as it is in other countries.

More recently, there was almost twenty years of the Marcos regime, which began well but deteriorated badly in later years. As the Marcos regime went on, the suffering of the people increased: the unemployment, the hunger, the misery. Whenever groups in some of the dioceses began to form in the struggle for justice, repression set in immediately. Very great atrocities were committed. This repression came down upon the peasants, students, labor unions, and committed Christians. Only a small part of the church opted to stand on the side of the people and work for social justice. There were perhaps some thirty dioceses where Christian base communities were formed.

Bishop Claver in Mindanao was one of the first to develop nonviolent liberating action in his diocese. There were sisters and priests and laypeople who were persecuted because of that stand. But the majority of the church leadership and most of the middle class were linked to the regime. As in Latin America, the church as an official institution was linked to those in power much too long. It is easy to understand why idealistic young people—seminarians and laypeople alike—saw no other way out but to join the guerrillas. Known as the New People's Army, they were established as the armed branch of the Communist Party, more or less on a Maoist basis. These young people saw no other way to struggle for justice against an unjust regime. I think the church must bear a large part of the responsibility for this development, due to the cowardice of large sections of the official church.

People cannot remain passive under certain circumstances. Unless there is the offer of a nonviolent alternative, they will have to take to counterviolence. Gandhi has said that the lowest possible attitude is to remain passive; if you don't know another way, you have to choose counterviolence. This is not to defend counterviolence, but I think it is a reality of which we must be aware. Wherever the moral authorities— whether it be Christian churches or other moral authorities—do not take the lead in nonviolent resistance there will be counterviolence and, sooner or later, civil war. I think we should understand this, and never condemn those who join the guerrillas because they see no other way. But we must try to live the alternative.

Another important event in the Philippine story was the assassination of Ninoy Aquino. This opposition leader had been imprisoned for seven years when he became very ill and had to be operated on in the United States. It may not be well known that while he was in prison Ninoy Aquino underwent a radical change, a kind of conversion. He was certainly an honest person, but like all politicians he had been trying to get power. While in prison, he read the Gospel and Gandhi and began to understand that a politician must serve the people. He decided then that if he ever had the chance to assume responsibility for his country, he would try to be a politician who worked with nonviolence and served the people rather than himself. It is important to understand that this man, who sought leadership in a country where corruption among the political and economic leaders was a way of life, underwent a deep conversion.

When Ninoy Aquino returned to the Philippines in 1983, he knew he had been condemned to death, so that when he stepped off the plane and was shot to death, his act of courage in returning held great meaning for the Filipinos. They saw in him, as we say in the Old Testament, a "just one," who gives his life for the people rather than take the life of the enemy. And we also know from the early church that the blood of the martyr is fruitful; it has the strength to renew a people, to bring a challenge and change to those who are passive, or those who collaborate with the dictatorship. Ninoy's giving the gift of his life was really the beginning of a strong popular effort in the Philippines to try to overcome the dictatorship through nonviolence. Following the assassination, demonstrations began to take place all over the Philippines. The fact that one person had the courage to give his life encouraged thousands and thousands of others to overcome the fear that had kept them passive. They poured into the streets to witness to truth and justice, and to demand that martial law be discontinued and human rights respected.

The demonstrations lasted for months, but there was no ongoing nonviolent action; people were not yet prepared for that. Polarization increased; repression became fierce; and the economic situation continued to deteriorate. NPA actions were on the increase in two-thirds of the provinces of the Philippines.

It was then that a few religious communities wrote to Jean and me, asking if we would like to come just to study the situation and see whether there might be the possibility of developing a well-organized, coherent, nonviolent resistance to the existing injustice. We thought perhaps our Latin American experience might help us to understand the Philippine situation, so we accepted. We went to the Philippines for the first time in February 1984. With the help of religious sisters and priests, we traveled throughout the islands and met many people: people close to the regime, people in opposition, peasants, laypeople, union leaders, priests, bishops, and politicians.

Jean and I felt that we were coming into the situation with nonviolence at a very late hour. I think we must say to our shame that we all close our eyes for a long time in the face of injustice. Very often those who see no other way than counterviolence are the first ones to take action against injustice. It is very difficult to come in later and say no, we should take another path. We Christians should be the first ones to open our eyes to injustices, and to speak out and bring the power of nonviolence into the revolution. We felt it was late, but we felt that there were people really searching for the nonviolent alternative.

One thing that made us decide to accept the challenge was when, on the last day of our first visit, the brother of Ninoy Aquino—he's called Agapito "Butz" Aquino—came to see us. He said to Jean and me: "A few days ago, we were approached by arms merchants, who said, 'Do you think you will be able to overthrow this regime with demonstrations? Don't you think you need better weapons than that? We're offering them to you. Make up your mind.'" And then he said to us: "It is providential that you have come at this time, because ever since their visit I have been unable to sleep. Do I have the right to throw my country into a major civil war? What is my responsibility as a Christian politician in this situation? Is there really such a thing as nonviolent combat against a system as unjust as this one?" Jean and I told him that at least he could try. "You don't lose anything if you try with nonviolence," we said. "But you must make up your own mind, and if you decide to try it, you must prepare yourself for nonviolent resistance. Nonviolence is not something that you do spontaneously and without preparation. You have to prepare yourself inwardly, because nonviolent methods are the fruit of the vision of man that we have. If you want to have seminars in preparation, let us know, and we will come back."

A few weeks later, we were invited back to carry out a series of seminars on nonviolent liberation. One of these seminars was with the group of bishops that had already committed itself to working for social justice. Bishop Claver had organized a seminar for them. The others were mainly for leaders from the political opposition, for labor unions, peasants, students, and church people—priests, sisters, and laypeople.

In each of these seminars we would first analyze the situation of violence together and how we were part of it. The seed of the violence was in the structures, of course, and in the dictator. But wasn't it also in ourselves? It's very easy to say that Marcos is the evil. But unless we each tear the dictator out of our own heart, nothing will change. Another group will come into power and will act similarly to those whom they replaced. So we discovered the Marcos within ourselves.

In some of these seminars, there were political leaders of the opposition, and there were peasant leaders. In one seminar the peasants would not speak to the politicians. "We have no faith in the politicians," they said. "Even if they are from the opposition. They have betrayed us too often." So one evening when we celebrated the Eucharist together, Father Jose Blanco, a Jesuit priest, distributed the host immediately after the consecration. "Let us now break this bread," he said, "and bring one part of the host to those with whom we have not yet spoken." We saw the peasants bring the host to the politicians, and the politicians bring theirs to the peasants. And we saw labor leaders breaking down in tears because, they said, "So far we have only been educating the workers in polarization, and not in really overcoming the injustice in the hearts and minds of those who carry responsibility." These seminars were more than just training people in methodology. The goal was for each one of us to undergo a deep change, a conversion.

The nonviolent movement of the Philippines, called AKKAPKA, developed out of these seminars, under the leadership of Father Blanco. AKKAPKA is Tagalog for "I embrace you," as well as an acronym for Movement for Peace and Justice. Those who took part in a seminar were asked to pass on what they had learned, what they had experienced. And during the first year AKKAPKA was in existence, those few people held forty seminars in thirty provinces of the Philippines. They saw an urgent need to share what they had learned, so that the people might be prepared, at least to some extent, for nonviolent change in the country.

When the so-called snap elections were announced at the end of 1985, AKKAPKA discontinued the training to work at preparing for the electoral process. Its members encouraged people to have the courage to vote for the person whom they really believed should be the leader in the country, and to refuse to accept the money that was offered by the government for Marcos votes. They prepared people to defend the ballot boxes nonviolently against the attacks of organized, armed agents who were sent to steal them. Half a million people were prepared to defend the ballot-boxes. Young and old, men and women, priests and laypeople stood unarmed around the urns that held the ballots in the face of armed agents who came to steal them.

AKKAPKA also decided that from the middle of January to the end of the struggle, they would have "prayer tents."

One tent was set up right in the banking center in Manila, where the financial power of the regime was concentrated. This big prayer tent was set up there in a little park. And around it, people who promised to fast and pray had a presence day and night. We cannot emphasize enough the deep spirituality that gave the people the strength to stand against the tanks later on. People prayed every day, for all those who suffered in the process of changing regimes, even for the military, and for Marcos, that he would find the strength not to use his huge arsenal against the people—that the little love for his people that was perhaps left in his heart might prevent him from giving the order to shoot into the millions of people who were demonstrating.

It makes a great difference, in a revolutionary process where people are highly emotional, whether you promote hatred and revenge or help the people stand firmly for justice without becoming like the oppressor. You want to love your enemy, to liberate rather than destroy him.

Radio Veritas, the Catholic station, helped tremendously in this task. It coordinated the whole resistance, around the clock, with news of events as they happened. Day and night, it broadcast passages from Martin Luther King, the Sermon on the Mount, Gandhi, and so forth—asking the people to follow those examples. Radio Veritas also encouraged the soldiers to remember their vow of loyalty to the nation, and not to one person. They kept urging the troops, "Refuse to shoot at the people, on whose side you should stand. Refuse unjust orders."

To do all this in a situation where the dictatorship was still powerful took more than human courage. It was marvelous to see the atmosphere in which it all took place, where prayer and revolution had become one. The revolutionary effort was really a revolution of the strength of truth and love. This is why, in the midst of it all, people were able to sing and dance. They knew they had a strength within them that was stronger than their own little human strength, that the power of love and truth was carrying them along. Therefore, while they were afraid, they knew at the same time that victory was possible. Because truth is stronger than lying, and love is stronger than the hatred and the repression of the regime, it will win in the end.

Now I should like to say a word about Cory Aquino, because it still seems like a miracle that this nation was able to unite in so short a time. One factor was certainly the deep suffering the people shared. Their suffering and their faith united them. But I think the pole around whom everything revolved was Cory Aquino. In the eyes of the people, she represented the opposite of all the corruption, oppression, and violence of Marcos. When the Filipino people united around Cory Aquino, I think it was because they felt the authenticity of this woman.

In the end, there were only two pillars of the regime left. One was the United States, which gave its support to the new government at the very last moment. And one was the army. While we were there last year, with Cory Aquino, Cardinal Sin, and the others, a number of scenarios of possible conflicts that might evolve in the struggle were developed. The scenario everybody feared the most was that the army would split. We knew that if the army split, a great deal of blood would be shed. We had to ask ourselves what could be done if this should happen. That was, in fact, the scenario that evolved. When the reform movement of the army separated from Marcos, he gave the order to his armed forces to crush the dissidents. As planned, Radio Veritas immediately called upon the people to fill up the street, to stand in front of the tanks, to speak to the soldiers. Eventually there were several hundred thousand people who spent a whole weekend in the road, blocking the tanks so that they could not move against the dissident groups. They spoke to the soldiers, gave them flowers, hugged them, and said, "You belong to the people; come back to those to whom you really belong."

While it was very important for the people to experience the strength of the poor and the power of love and truth to overcome evil, we all know it is only the first step. What is before the Filipino people now is at least as difficult, if not more difficult, than what has gone before. It will require perseverance. And it will need the continued conversion of those who still adhere to the old regime, who have important places in the provinces: to dismantle the private armies of the landlords; to carry out land reform so that the mass of the people can live in dignity; to negotiate with the Muslim minority; to negotiate with the NPA, so that perhaps they will be willing to put down their arms and become one of the democratic parties in the country; to rebuild the economy.

It is important that we do not forget Cory Aquino and those who support her, and that our prayers accompany her. We must also encourage our own governments to give economic and moral support to this new government. Not the kind of economic support that makes the Philippines dependent upon others, but economic support that will enable the Philippines to realize its own model of economy and its own model of social reforms.

The nonviolent revolution in the Philippines comes to us as a great gift. It has given hope to countries like Chile, South Korea, and others where there are still dictatorships. Perhaps the peace movement can help these countries toward a similar change. We have lived a moment where we have experienced a little bit of what the strength of God in the poor can mean, if we really believe in it and if we act accordingly.

47

SHINE ON IN MONTANA

Jo Clare Hartsig

The following piece is from "Nonviolence in the Arena," a regular column by Jo Clare Hartsig and Walter Wink. It was begun in the early 1990s in an attempt to preserve stories of nonviolent actions that would otherwise be irretrievably lost. Textbooks tell the "Great History" of societies: their wars, rulers, momentous events. But there is another history that often is ignored and finally lost: the "Little History" made by the common people. This column seeks to save such stories before they are forgotten (Fellowship, *January-February 1995*).

Montana, long known as "Big Sky" territory, is vast and beautiful, like all its Northwestern neighbors. One might assume there is room enough for everyone. Yet over the last decade the five-state area of Washington, Oregon, Wyoming, Idaho, and Montana has been designated a "white homeland" for the Aryan Nation and growing numbers of attendant skinheads, Klan members, and other white supremacists. These groups have targeted non-whites, Jews, gays and lesbians for harassment, vandalism, and injury, which in some cases has led to murder.

In Billings, Montana (pop. 81,000), there have been a number of hate crimes including the desecration of a Jewish cemetery, threatening phone calls to Jewish citizens, and swastikas painted on the home of an interracial couple. But it was something else that activated the people of faith and good will throughout the entire community.

On December 2, 1993, a brick was thrown through the window of five-year-old Isaac Schnitzer's bedroom window. The brick and shards of glass were strewn all over the child's bed. The reason? A menorah and other symbols of Jewish faith were stenciled on the glass as part of the family's Hanukkah celebration. The account of the incident in *The Billings Gazette* the next day described Isaac's mother, Tammie Schnitzer, as being troubled by the advice she got from the investigating officer. He suggested she remove the symbols. How would she explain this to her son?

Another mother in Billings was deeply touched by that question. She tried to imagine explaining to her children that they couldn't have a Christmas tree in the window or a wreath on the door because it wasn't safe. She remembered what happened when Hitler ordered the king of Denmark to force all Danish Jews to wear Stars of David. The order was never carried out because the King himself and many other Danes chose to wear the yellow stars. The Nazis lost the ability to find their "enemies."

There are several dozen Jewish families in Billings. This kind of tactic could effectively deter violence if enough people got involved. So Margaret McDonald phoned her pastor, Rev. Keith Torney at First Congregational United Church of Christ, and asked what he thought of having Sunday School children make paper cut-out menorahs for their own windows. He got on the phone with his clergy colleagues around town, and the following week hundreds of menorahs appeared in the windows of Christian homes. When asked about the danger of this action, Police Chief Wayne Inman told callers, "There's greater risk in not doing it."

Five days after the brick was thrown at the Schnitzer home, the *Gazette* published a full-page drawing of a menorah, along with a general invitation for people to put it up. By the end of the week at least six thousand homes (some accounts estimated up to ten thousand) were decorated with menorahs.

A sporting-goods store got involved by displaying "Not in Our Town! No hate. No violence. Peace on Earth," on its large billboard. Someone shot at it. Townspeople organized a vigil outside the synagogue during Sabbath services. That same night bricks and bullets shattered windows at Central Catholic High School, where an electric marquee read "Happy Hanukkah to our Jewish Friends." The cat of a family with a menorah was killed with an arrow. A United Methodist Church had windows broken because of its menorah display. Six non-Jewish families had their car and house windows shattered. One car had a note that said "Jew lover."

Eventually these incidents waned, but people continued in their efforts to support one another against hate crimes. After being visited at home and threatened by one of the local skinhead leaders, Tammie Schnitzer is now always accompanied by friends when she goes on her morning run. During the Passover holiday last spring, 250 Christians joined their Jewish brothers and sisters in a traditional Seder meal. New friendships have formed, new traditions have started, and greater mutual understanding and respect have been achieved.

This winter families all over Billings took out their menorahs to reaffirm their commitment to peace and religious tolerance. The light they shared in their community must be continuously rekindled until hatred has been overcome.

Part Six

THE PATH OF RECONCILIATION

One indispensable element of peace is reconciliation. Where possible, reconciliation should be sought throughout a struggle. It should not be left to the end of a conflict, otherwise those who will be required to coexist with each other may be so alienated and hostile as to make reconciliation virtually impossible. This point was constantly reiterated by Gandhi and King. Gandhi insisted that he wanted the British to leave India, but to leave on good terms, so they could work together in the future. And that is exactly what happened. Had the ten-year-long nonviolent struggle in Kosovo been supported by the nations of the world, rather than their belatedly stepping in and backing the armed revolutionaries, reconciliation might have eventually been possible somewhere down the line. But the attempt through violence to force the Serbian government to honor the autonomy of Kosovo created hundreds of thousands of refugees who then, on their return, dealt out the same ethnic hatred and violence that they had been dealt. Now it is questionable whether any future reconciliation is possible, and Kosovo may end up either "ethnically cleansed" in reverse, or partitioned along ethnic lines.

Reconciliation may not always be possible. As long as the oppressor has power over us, it may be necessary simply to establish whatever distance is possible in order to prevent further pain. But removal may be only a temporary expedient with an eye to eventual reconciliation, if such be possible.

I was simply amazed in South Africa to see how many black people who had been incarcerated and tortured had forgiven their torturers. This forgiveness took place, not after the fall of the apartheid system, but during the most brutal reign of terror. These people forgave, not for their own sakes, but out of a deep religious conviction that they had to do so, that it was an imperative of their faith. For the writers of these essays, reconciliation was nothing less than daring to be human, as one remarked, because, as another put it, we are all part of one another.

48

DARING TO BE HUMAN

Magda Yoors-Peeters

*This story was told by Magda Yoors-Peeters, a young Belgian woman, at the confer-
ence of the International Fellowship of Reconciliation at Nyborg Strand, Denmark, in
1923. It was an experience of hers during World War I that she shared with the
German delegates at the conference* (The World Tomorrow, *October 1923*).

I am a Belgian woman. During the Great War I hated the Germans with
the bitterest hatred. I wanted the French and the Belgians to fight more and to
crush Germany. So I preached hate. I not only talked it, but I wrote it. I wrote
articles for the magazines and the papers to create more hatred of the Germans. And I succeeded. People listened and read what I wrote. Then they too
would hate more deeply and more bitterly than before.

It was one winter in the war time that I was in Holland with my husband.
We were doing relief work there among the Belgian refugees. We rented a
room from a Dutch family, and the man and woman felt as we did about the
Germans. They also hated, as we hated. We had many Belgian refugees to care
for, and we were very busy.

One day my husband and I were walking along a road near the town, not
many miles from the border of Germany. We saw ahead of us something lying
in the mud, and when we came nearer we saw it was a man. We stooped over
him and saw he was in the uniform of a German soldier. He was a German.
His shoes were broken, so his feet showed through, and his feet were all muddy
and bleeding.

We looked at him. We could not leave him lying there in the cold. What
could we do? We could not take him to the house of the Dutch people, because they hated the Germans just as we did. But he needed help; he was faint
with hunger and cold. He did not even know he was in Holland and not in
Germany. We stood looking down at him.

Then suddenly we decided to take him to the house and try to get him in
without the knowledge of the landlady. We helped him, between us, back to

the town and into the house. The landlady fortunately was not around. We put him on the bed in our room.

What could we do? His feet were bloody and dirty. I had to wash them! So I got some water and a cloth and knelt down to wash his feet. While I was washing his feet something happened inside me. Something fell down from my eyes, and I saw that he was a brother. A German was my brother. The Germans were our brothers.

Then we had to get him something to eat, he was so hungry. It was war time, of course, and we had only one egg apiece every two weeks. But I went downstairs and asked the landlady for two eggs!

"Two eggs," she exclaimed, "and what would you be doing with two eggs at once in war time?" I had to tell her the truth. There was a German soldier upstairs; his feet were bleeding; he was hungry and faint and cold. Yes, he was a German, but—

The landlady looked at me a moment. Her eyes filled with tears, and then she said, "Take the two eggs. And here's some jam I made; take that up to him. But don't you tell my husband!"

When he had eaten and was warm, my husband and I put on him some of the clothes we had ready for the Belgian refugees—a new pair of shoes and a suit of clothes.

It was late in the afternoon and almost dark. He started out from the house to find his way back to the German border. We stood at the window and watched him go. The snowflakes began to come down, slowly and steadily, then faster and faster. He would be wet through in the storm. Would he get back to the border? Would he be safe? We never knew. We never heard of him again.

49

TALE FROM VIENNA

Muriel Lester

Muriel Lester (1883-1958) was a traveling secretary for the International Fellow-ship of Reconciliation from 1933 to 1958. A passionate and convincing speaker, she lectured and preached in churches, universities, and national and international con-ferences all over the world. Typically she spoke on both the outer and inner journeys of faith (Fellowship, *January 1950*).

When victorious Russian troops marched into Vienna near the end of the war, living there was a FOR family—Roman Catholic, as many European FOR members are. A son from the family had been killed on the Russian front. At home lived the parents, their second son, and their beautiful teenage daughter.

The troops' entry was orderly, but the family knew that after the occupa-tion was completed there would be a few days during which soldiers would be allowed to do whatever they pleased. It is generally so with invading armies— not just Russian but British and American as well. What, then, was the family to do with its treasures and valuables? Strip its home quite bare and hide or bury things that the soldiers might carry away? And what was to be done with the daughter? How could she be safely concealed? Should she, as some neigh-bors were suggesting for their daughters, take poison rather than suffer Rus-sian outrages?

Fully realizing the seriousness of their plight, the family prayerfully consid-ered what to do. The point became clear to them that the invading troops were boys who were hundreds of miles from home, who had been conscripted into the Russian army, and who ought during their stay in Vienna to be offered some home life. The decision therefore was to hide or bury nothing, for the daughter to remain at home as if friends were coming, and for the family to ready the house and the cupboard for the expected guests.

In a few days the expected lawlessness began. The clack of military boots, the thunder of doors being crashed with rifle butts, human shouts and screams were often heard. Inevitably footsteps sounded up the front steps of the house of the expectant family.

When the Russians reached the front door, expecting it to be locked and therefore a barrier to be beaten in, they found it open. This utterly surprised them and took the first prop from under their previous designs.

Looking in the door they saw a man descending the stairway. Not in flight or fear but with calm and ease. Out came another prop.

He came straight to the door, welcoming them. "Won't you come in? We have been expecting guests and are delighted to have you with us!" They stepped inside.

The next thing they noticed was a crucifix on a shelf across the hall from them. Several of them crossed themselves. After all, one-third of the Russians are Christians.

"Won't you remove your coats and caps and stay awhile? The rest of the family is waiting to meet you. And I believe there is some coffee that will soon be ready in the kitchen." The coats and caps came off and in the process, of course, guns came to rest on the floor.

In came the visitors, minus guns, to meet the rest of the family, including the daughter. Coffee was soon served. Questions about the families of the Russians soon elicited questions about the young man whose picture stood on the piano. "He was killed during the war." To the question, "Where?" came the hesitant, but nevertheless candid, reply, "In Russia."

The mother sat down at the piano and commenced playing folk songs. Although she began with Austrian ones, the similarity of folk songs in various parts of Europe elicited an enthusiastic response from the Russians. Soon the whole party was singing and the mission of the Russians forgotten.

Thus time flew until finally the soldiers remembered that they must be back in barracks in a short while. Hurriedly they put on their hats and coats and picked up their guns. Thanking the family for a wonderful time, they asked if they could return. To which the answer was, "Please do. And bring your friends!"

50

THE PRÉFET'S DIRTY JOB

Magda Trocmé

Magda Trocmé describes some of the moral questions and tensions that confront people under tyranny. Magda Trocmé's husband, André, was the Protestant pastor of the French village of Le Chambon, which, during World War II, offered a haven to thousands of Jews. The remarkable story of that community has been told at greater length in Philip P. Hallie's Lest Innocent Blood Be Shed *(Fellowship, May 1953).*

Even now, years later, we keep hearing reminders of the terrible moral dilemmas with which the war confronted government officials.

Not long ago my younger son came back from a trip to Italy, and a gendarme examining his passport at the border, said: "Trocmé? Are you the son of Pastor Trocmé?"

"Yes," said Daniel, surprised.

"During the war, when I was near Le Chambon, I was told to arrest your father, but I managed not to do it, because it was a dirty job!"

Yes, it was a dirty job, and that man managed not to do it, but how many others had to do dirty jobs because they were officials! Some of them believed that the Government was right; others felt they must obey even if the Government was not right, as a soldier who obeys even though he feels that war is wrong.

We had two interesting experiences of this kind with the Préfet of the Haute Loire and the captain of the gendarmerie in Le Puy. Both of them helped to execute unjust laws and both of them had to ask for help for themselves later on, when things had changed and those whom they had arrested were powerful and free.

It was February 13, 1943, around 7 o'clock in the evening, when two gendarmes knocked at the door of the old presbytère in Le Chambon sur Lignon and asked to see Pastor Trocmé. I replied that he had gone to a meeting and would return later, but that I could answer all their questions, since I knew all about my husband's work. They explained that it was something very personal and that they would wait. I took them to my husband's office and forgot all about them. We had so much work, and so little time to waste!

When my husband came back, he rushed to his office, found himself face to face with the gendarmes, and was told that he was under arrest. Why? In those days no one dared to ask why such things happened.

André went to the attic where a German Jew lay hidden and told him not to worry because the gendarmes were not for him, and I went to the cellar to warn the old German Jewish woman there not to keep putting her head into the kitchen, because it was dangerous for her and for us.

I asked the gendarmes if I might prepare André's clothes and they said I could have all the time I needed but that I should not notify any friends or neighbors of what was happening. A few days earlier, needing clothes, I had undone the "prison suitcase" I had prepared months before. So many times André had been menaced by prison that I had a special suitcase for this purpose, but clothes had become scarce!

While Mlle. Roynier and I prepared things, André and the children had supper with the gendarmes. The latter were so bewildered by the invitation that they could not eat and the conversation was rather dull!

It happened that André and I had been invited for supper that evening by a church counselor, M. Gibert. As so often happened in the rush of work we forgot the invitation, and M. Gibert sent his daughter to remind us of her father's birthday. She came, saw the police, ran away, and told everyone what was happening in the parsonage. A few minutes later, the people of the village started a sort of procession, coming to say goodbye and to bring presents. Queer presents, things not seen for years, put aside as precious items for very special days—things like sardines, soap, sausage, toilet paper, eau de cologne, and candles. But at the end we discovered that the matches were missing and the gendarme (the captain) gave his own, saying he would make a report of the way events had proceeded that evening, how everybody had been calm, and the population friendly and full of love. Later we discovered that the police had been frightened, suspecting some kind of revolt. Many police cars arrived, and the telephone and telegraph had been stopped. At the same time, M. Theis, the headmaster of the College Cevenol, and M. Darcissac, the headmaster of the elementary school, were arrested, too.

André had the honor of being arrested by the *capitaine de gendarmerie* himself! In Le Puy the prisoners were put to sleep with sheets, but with the door locked, and next morning they had no more private cars, but only the *panier à salade*—the special car for prisoners. At the station they had to walk between two gendarmes and they were taken to the concentration camp of St. Paul d'Eyjeaux, without any more consideration at all.

Next morning—and here comes the conflict of conscience—two gendarmes of Tence, the next small town, came to see me and tell me that they wanted to apologize for what had happened the evening before! They knew perfectly well that my husband was a fine man, but they had had to execute the orders from above. The *capitaine de gendarmerie*, the evening before, watching us all singing Luther's hymn as my husband left the house, told me that never in his life had he been obliged to perform such a job and that it was against his will because he admired and respected the man he was to arrest.

Years went by and the liberation came. Everything was changed. M. Laval was executed, and M. Pétain arrested. The crowds who had acclaimed Pétain turned against him and completely forgot that once they had admired him. Once more André preached against the public opinion, saying that the Pétain actions had been the actions of almost all the French nation.

M. Bach, the préfet who had sent the order to arrest André, was in prison and the captain was in difficulties. Mme. Bach wrote asking André to be a witness for her husband at the trial, and the captain asked for a letter stating how kind he had been the day of André's arrest.

Yes, we could do it, because both of them had obeyed their government, being only human, and with right and wrong judged by men so difficult to establish. If Hitler had won the war, Pétain would have been a great man, and M. Bach and the captain would surely have had promotions and honors instead of prison, trials, and difficulties.

When the time of M. Bach's trial came, André was in Sweden and I went to the Court and spoke of Le Chambon, of the mysterious telephone calls telling us that the police would come, or simply advising us to be cautious. I told them that M. Bach had offered to help me when André was in concentration camp, and if M. Bach had really wanted to obey the Government's orders, the work of Le Chambon would have been stopped immediately.

Mme. Bach sat next to me during the trial and cried most of the time. I told her I was sure that her husband would be free, that the trial was turning out well, but she still was in despair, fearing that he would lose his grade in the army, his decorations, and perhaps his French nationality!

I was amazed—yes, it was a French soldier being judged, and that French soldier had obeyed Marshal Pétain, the hero of Verdun. He had intended to do his duty and freedom would not mean anything to him if his loyalty to France was not recognized.

My husband, too, had acted as he thought a French citizen should have acted, and both these men had been arrested for their convictions, history condemning one of these men in a certain time, and condemning the other at another. Right and wrong are not always clear and easy to understand, and this is the great problem of humankind, the great problem of human conscience.

51

WE ARE ALL PART
OF ONE ANOTHER

Barbara Deming

Barbara Deming (1917-84) was active in the nonviolent movement for peace and justice from the early 1960s until her death. She was the author of six books and many articles and was an accomplished and recognized poet, essayist, and short-story writer. She was arrested numerous times for civil disobedience, and was jailed in Alabama, Georgia, New York, and Washington, D.C. When she went to South Vietnam, she was expelled for protesting the war. She also visited North Vietnam while U.S. planes were bombing it. She committed the later part of her life to the feminist community and its efforts to end patriarchal domination of society. Among her books are Prison Notes, Revolution and Equilibrium, _and_ We Cannot Live without Our Lives. _These remarks were delivered on the occasion of her receiving the Annual Peace Award of the War Resisters League in 1984_ (Fellowship, _October-November 1984)._

In other years, when other individuals were singled out to receive this award, it never seemed strange to me. But this year, when I learned that I was being singled out, it suddenly did seem very strange to me. I asked myself why. It's not that I have any less ego than the next person. But knowing myself a little, I am very conscious that the actions I have taken for which, I assume, I am given this award, were all taken not only with other people but because of them. It seems strange to be standing here without them.

I think, for example, of the trip I took to Saigon last April—along with A. J. Muste, Brad Lyttle, Bill Davidon, Karl Meyer, and Sherry Thurber. I remember very clearly the day on which the call to volunteer for that project arrived in the mail. I had heard about the project for some months, and it had always seemed to me a particularly right and necessary project—to protest the war on the very spot where it was being waged. But it had never occurred to me for a moment to volunteer to be one of those to go. I remember the day the call arrived. I read it and thought: "Wonderful! It's really going to happen, then!" (because there were a lot of people who had volunteered already). But I still didn't even pose the question to myself: Would I volunteer? The answer was so plain to me: I was much too scared to. But I wanted to be present at the meetings at which the project was discussed. I turned up at the first meeting, and there was Mary Christiansen, who was one of the first to volunteer, and I went up to her and told her that I thought it was wonderful that she had. And I asked her, "You're not frightened?" She said, "I hadn't really thought about that yet." I thought, That is really the correct order of priorities to give things—to think first about an action that is right to take and to think later about coping with one's fears. And the moment she said what she did, by a familiar but mysterious process, everything was a little different for me, and for the first moment it occurred to me that I might be able to cope with my own fears.

Then we sat down to the meeting. I particularly remember A. J. Muste at the meeting—with that extraordinary concentration he had on a particular situation and a particular action proposed to speak to the situation. Sitting next to him, I felt my own concentration on such an action sharpen, and my fears did begin to fall into second place. By the end of the meeting I said tentatively, not to put me down as a volunteer, but to put me down as a possible volunteer.

I could tell very much the same kind of story about any of the other actions I have taken. I make a point of this not to be humble but because I think it touches us all. I know there are those among us who are more capable than others of acting on their own; but surely none of us acts quite alone—of and by himself. Surely all of us are nerved by one another, catch courage from one another. As I. F. Stone quoted at the memorial for A. J., "We are all part of one another."

So I would like to talk a little more about some of the fears I experienced on that trip to Saigon. Because my fears didn't end, of course, when I found myself able to volunteer. And in each case these fears taught me again to recognize our interdependence.

Perhaps the most oppressive fears I felt were in the several days before we left this country. I remember being so hypnotized by the fear of being killed over there that, sitting talking with friends and family, I would realize again and again with a shock that I was hearing the sound of their voices but not hearing the words they were speaking. Then the evening we were to set off arrived and I met the rest of the group at the airline terminal—and the moment I walked up to them I suddenly didn't feel any more fear; I felt a very peculiar kind of joy. And we all seemed to be feeling it. We were all smiling at each other almost foolishly. Of course we could all be happy that we were finally acting, not brooding about it. And of course we all believed in what we were doing—which is a happy feeling. But there was something about setting out together—at least for me—that made it very much easier to feel the joy and not the fear of acting. One smiled at the next person with a kind of tentative happiness in acting, and when that person smiled back the happiness was no longer tentative. This giving and taking of spirit—one *from* another and *to* another—involves a wonderful kind of mathematics. There are situations in which, as e. e. cummings noted, 2 and 2 "is 5"—at least. Given this exchange, we are all of us more than ourselves.

Now I would like to talk about one other experience of fear. It is the experience I think, through which I learned the most on that trip—with the exception of conversations with some of the Vietnamese we were fortunate enough to meet.

When we first arrived in Saigon I was uneasy in a way that was unfamiliar to me on such projects. Every project in which I had taken part before had been completely open—that is, our purposes had been frankly announced. In this project there was of necessity an element of secrecy: unless we postponed an announcement of our presence and our purpose until the end of our week there, we would have little chance of taking the action we wanted to take, and little chance of making first the many contacts with Vietnamese which might allow us to speak for them as well as for ourselves. But this meant that we would have to be guarded in encounters with strangers; and it was this that made me uncertain of myself. Because I had learned to rely above all in situations of danger on creating an atmosphere of friendliness about us. One could hardly count on this to prevent violence as if by magic, but it was the best deterrence we had, and sometimes a remarkable one. It is difficult to create an atmosphere of friendliness when one has to be secretive. So having learned to trust in myself by learning to open myself to the most direct human contact with others that was possible, I found it difficult now to summon up the right spirit on which to rely.

Some of the others on the project clearly had a similar problem. And everyone met the problem in a different way. There were those who still put the greatest emphasis on being friendly to everybody, and who were in the process somewhat indiscreet—for example, about revealing to strangers our attitude toward the war. There were others who put the emphasis on discretion and were in the process stiff with curious strangers—even to the point of making them angry. And what began to happen was that one team member would become alarmed at the first kind of action and another would become alarmed at the second. It was too easy for all of us in that situation to imagine encounters that would suddenly endanger us all. In short, we began in those first days to scare *each other*. What followed, of course, was that some began to wish that this person or that person had never come on the project. I could see this happening in other people and I could feel it in myself. As one pictured in imagination some encounter in which he or she would do just the thing that would be fatal, and one began to tremble, the simplest resolution was always to imagine the person who—supposedly—would do the wrong thing, just magically not there.

I remember at a certain point recognizing with a shock that *nothing* put us in such danger as precisely this relation to each other which I have been describing. If any of these imagined situations were to occur, to be concentrated on the futile wish that one or the other of my companions were not there would hardly enable me to cope with it imaginatively. And if any of my companions sensed my fear of them, it would hardly help *them*. Instead of finding new spirit now, when we looked at each other, we would lose it, we would paralyze each other. I had learned on earlier projects to beware, when confronted by an *antagonist*, of letting myself panic. And I think one can define the state of panic precisely as that in which one tries to wish that other not there—instead of trying, persisting in trying to establish some kind of human contact with him, which could possibly, in the case of an antagonist, disarm him—and in the case of a companion, it occurred to me slowly now, help him to recover himself if he has made an error. It slowly occurred to me that while we were here, all of us were sure to make mistakes of one kind or another (and this would certainly include me) and the way to ensure that these mistakes would be fatal was to freeze toward one another.

Why have I talked at such length about this particular experience? I might add, before I answer my own question, that by the time we did announce our presence in Saigon and attempt to stage our protest, we were all again at relative ease with one another and again able, in the various moments of strain which followed, to borrow the extra courage from one another that we sometimes needed. But why have I talked so much about this particular experience of fear? It is because I feel very strongly that in the days ahead of us, unless a very great many of us move from words to acts—from words of dissent to acts of disobedience—we are going to have no effect at all upon our government's policy, no effect in halting the terrible momentum of this war. If we do become more bold, and therefore more effective, I think it is fair to predict that our government will, in turn, move more boldly to discourage us. And then if we do not all stand together, helping always *whomever* is singled out for punishment, our effectiveness will end.

To stand together is going to be hard. Our movement is composed of all kinds of groups and all kinds of individuals. It is certain that many of us will make all kinds of mistakes. It will become very tempting to wish that this group or that group, this individual or that individual, were simply not among us. My particular plea is that we not surrender to this temptation. We must certainly be frank with each other when we disagree, but my plea is that we not begin to be afraid of any of us and, in a panic, try to wish any of us out of the picture. We will need every one of us. We are all part of one another.

52

THE ROAD TO TRANSFORMATION

A Conversation with Brian Willson

Longtime peace activist Brian Willson became an international symbol of resistance when he was run over by a train carrying weapons to Central America at the Concord Naval Weapons Station on September 1, 1987. He lost his legs and received a severe head injury. A subsequent investigation revealed that the government train was speeding, could see him for 650 feet, and never even applied the brakes as it ran over Willson as he sat on the tracks to protest U.S. military intervention in Central America. He was interviewed in his home in San Francisco, California, by John Dear, S.J. (Fellowship, March 1990).

DEAR: *When did you go to Nicaragua and what did you learn there?*

WILLSON: I went to Nicaragua for two months in January and February 1986. I was in school in Esteli for one month, and then traveled around Nicaragua for a month to see as much as I could.

In the first two weeks in Esteli, there were a series of Contra attacks. Eleven people were killed by the Contras and that really provoked me. It brought Vietnam right to the front of my forehead, very vividly. All the years since Vietnam, I was in conflict between what I had learned viscerally in Vietnam and the desire to be middle class and respectable. Nicaragua clarified the conflict real fast. So, when I came back, I started organizing the Veterans Peace Coalition with Charlie Liteky and others to oppose Contra aid.

I came from a working-class, right-wing reactionary home. I was in the Boy Scouts. I didn't come from money or an educated family. During that first trip to Nicaragua in 1986, I think what happened was that I dared myself to be the real Brian Willson. That's what I'm trying to do now. I'm just clumsily walking along on that journey.

DEAR: *Why did you go on a long fast in the fall of 1986 on the U.S. Capitol steps?*

WILLSON: To express my heart and conscience to the North American people in a way that I couldn't do rhetorically, verbally, specifically about the

U.S. war in Central America with a focus on Nicaragua. It was an effort to speak to the hearts and minds and souls of North Americans about U.S. murder.

DEAR: *What are your reflections on the experience of the fast as you look back on that time now?*

WILLSON: I don't know if I can fully comprehend it. It was liberating, because I was putting my life on the line and working on being free every moment, literally, of my life, to be exactly who I am. There were no career factors, no money factors, no concern about credibility, about what I was going to do next. It meant being all that I am every moment. And I had never experienced that before.

DEAR: *What happened after the fast that led you to the Concord Naval Weapons Base in California?*

WILLSON: After the fast, I helped organize the Veterans Peace Action teams. We gathered together a group of vets that wanted to go into the war zones of Nicaragua to make a statement as former warriors, to begin an atonement process. We wanted to speak with our lives and our bodies, as well as our minds and our souls. We felt that we should go into Nicaragua's war zones to show our solidarity with the Nicaraguan people and to express our revulsion at the U.S. policy of murder.

The first team went down in early 1987. I was there for several weeks, and we were in war zones much of the time. It was incredible. We saw so much blood and death and maiming. We often were either just ahead of or just behind the Contras. Some days we would go back where we were the previous day and find the people had just been attacked. I visited several hundred amputees in six hospitals. The experience was very visceral and profound.

Some of us decided to have an action back in the United States that would interdict the supplies of arms to Central America. Concord was the largest Defense Department munitions base in the West. It has been the largest munitions depot for Vietnam. It's where most of the napalm came from for Vietnam. It had a public right of way dividing the base in two, which the munitions had to pass through. It was a logistically convenient spot to block the flow of the munitions.

We began to block munitions trucks in June of 1987. Later, we decided to escalate our presence by blocking munitions trains.

DEAR: *What are your reflections now about what happened on September 1, 1987?*

WILLSON: I became one of thousands in the Americas made legless by U.S. militarism.

DEAR: *How do you continue your nonviolent spirit toward the people at the Concord base?*

WILLSON: I had really hated my father, and had to work through that in the earlier part of this decade. It so affected my life, my work. I learned how to love my father unconditionally. If I could love my father unconditionally, who was mean and cruel much of my life, I could love anybody unconditionally. I didn't have to like people to love them. People can be mean, but I can understand a sense of connection with them, though not without great difficulty. I increasingly understand about this profound connection in life. There's something about the sacredness of life that calls me to stand in the way of people who might be participating in evil without hating them as people.

I was on the tracks because I felt this was a right thing to do; it was a conscientious thing to do. It was an act of conscience. I felt called to do that. Whatever the train crew and the Navy wanted to do in response to that was their business and their problem.

Lying in the hospital without my legs and with this big hole in my head, I was happy to be alive. I was very appreciative that I had survived, and I knew that my work was going to continue; that the real Brian Willson was still intact; that I was going to continue my life and my work, hopefully in some cooperative manner with the will of the Great Spirit. The train crew was caught between following their conscience and following orders. They weren't doing, it seemed to me, what they really wanted to do. I don't think people really want to be running over other people. I saw them as victims, as well as participants in the crime of the U.S. government. They're front line people like we vets were in Vietnam. In some way, I felt sympathy for them, without in any way condoning what they did. But I have a deeper sense of commitment and connection to the life force and the people of Central America who continue to be maimed and devastated by the policies of my government. I was trying to take responsibility as one person for that war being waged in my name.

DEAR: *What is your understanding of nonviolence?*

WILLSON: I think nonviolence is not so much a tactic as a way of experiencing the world within yourself, of understanding the sacred connection with all of life.

It's an understanding of how everything is interconnected and how everything is in a continuing state of interrelationship. We are going against our own nature when we start disrespecting all the other parts of life: people, plants, animals, water, sunlight, clouds. I think nonviolence is an attitude and way of life with a spiritual ecological dimension that is aware of how everything is interconnected and responds honestly to that.

DEAR: *Some of us in the peace movement have been talking lately about moving beyond this concept of resistance to transformation. Could you share your own understanding of the transformation which we all need to undergo?*

WILLSON: Resistance is part of affirmation. I don't believe in responding solely by resisting. It may be necessary to resist trucks and trains carrying weapons, but that occurs, I think, while you're advocating a vision.

Although there were many seeds planted in my early life, transformation started in Vietnam. When I saw dead bodies of Vietnamese I realized they were my sisters and brothers. I had been taught they were the enemy. At some deeper place, the real Brian Willson was trying to come out. I remember looking at the face of a Vietnamese mother as she lay on the ground dead and wondering, "What makes her a communist?" In a half second, all that upbringing about "communism" completely evaporated. That transformation in me and in us all is a constant process. It took me until Nicaragua to decide that I needed to live my life as holistically as I could, with my mind, body, and soul in sync, like a synthesis, an integration.

Transformation begins when we realize that everyone and everything is connected. Truth is tied to justice. Justice concerns replace our focus on material things, careers, money. Transformation means a change from "getting what you can" to an understanding of justice and the insight that injustice anywhere is a threat to justice everywhere. That transformation means for me that every day is a new commitment to be part of the life force of the world, which I call the Great Spirit. The Great Spirit is in me, not just out there. It's in here and out there, and everything, everyone, is inextricably connected.

A theology of transformation would include the resistance of evil and standing in the way of evil, but I believe its effectiveness increases as we proclaim with our lives a total affirmation of life. Transformation is a daily process, for the rest of my life, developing new consciousness. My challenge is to be open to that process constantly wherever I am, in whatever I'm doing. A theology of transformation has to do with forgiveness, atonement, and reconciliation, and that means dramatic changes in the way I live, the way I express myself, the way I relate to everyone.

That's the message I want to convey to our culture. Our lifestyle is so violent; it violates every principle of life on this planet. It causes tremendous destruction and death to the sacredness of life everywhere. We need to understand that and we need to change our conscientiousness, and the way we live our lives and make our living. A new consciousness understands how everything is connected. I happen to believe that that consciousness is already in process. The prevailing value system is going to fight like hell to survive, but it's a totally unsustainable mode. It has to keep lying, staying in denial, putting out more propaganda, building more weapons. That process is in painful conflict with an irreversible development of consciousness all over the planet. I find that very powerful.

53

BAGHDAD AFTER THE WAR

Don Mosley

Don Mosley, former chair of the FOR national council, is a founder of Jubilee Part-ners, a Christian service community in northeastern Georgia. As a member of Wit-ness for Peace, he was a frequent visitor to Nicaragua during the Contra insurgency. He helped organize the Pledge of Resistance, whose signers promised that, in the event of a U.S. invasion of Nicaragua, the signers would participate in and encourage mas-sive public resistance. Actions would include occupation of local or congressional offices and large demonstrations in Washington, D.C. Just the threat of such action may have helped avert that invasion. He has worked closely with Habitat for Humanity and a flood of refugees. His book With Our Own Eyes *is an inspiring account of how much good a few dedicated people can do* (Fellowship, *June 1991*).

Parked in my car in downtown Washington, D.C., I had just turned on the radio for a minute to catch the five o'clock headlines when I heard "My wife! Oh, my wife! She was such a good woman who hurt no one . . . " The anguish in the man's voice cut through me, and I stayed to find out what had hap-pened.

It was February 13, Ash Wednesday. A couple of hours earlier twenty-two of us had held a service on the lawn of the Capitol to launch a fast for peace in the Middle East. I had come back to add coins to the parking meter.

The reporters began to give the terrible details of the destruction of the Ameriya shelter in Baghdad. "Struck during the early morning hours by one or more missiles . . . probably hundreds killed . . . claims by the Iraqis that it was filled with women and children . . . too hot to begin rescue attempts." And then a repeat of the interview with the weeping man whose family was still inside. For the first time since the bombing had started I also wept, grieving with this man who had lost the wife and children he loved.

My own sadness became mixed with shame and anger as I heard the imme-diate response from the White House, an insistence that if there really were women and children in the shelter they had been put there to disguise an Iraqi military command post. Then came the totally inappropriate statement by

Marlin Fitzwater that Saddam Hussein "does not share our belief in the sanctity of human life." No trace of remorse, only boasting about our own high principles.

A week later I was packing my bags to go to Baghdad as the representative of the Fellowship of Reconciliation. I felt a strong need to meet face to face with the victims of our bombs. I wanted to reaffirm their humanity while apologizing for the violence being done to them by our weapons. Our trip was delayed for three weeks by the closing of the Iraqi border, and by the time we left I was carrying letters of apology from nearly eight thousand other people as well.

We were also to have taken five thousand pounds of medicine with us, but the U.S. Customs officials refused to release it in time for our trip. After FOR held a news conference, it was finally released and shipped a week late.

We flew to Amman, Jordan, and then traveled overland to Baghdad as guests of the Jordan National Red Crescent Society. No commercial flights to Baghdad are allowed; the sky belongs to the victorious allies. For hundreds of miles along the desert highway we saw bomb craters, shells of destroyed power stations, ruined relay towers and power lines, and the blackened remains of busses and trucks. Our minibus scraped down and back up again across a sagging section of the bombed bridge over the Euphrates River. Its shattered concrete hung by a few reinforcing rods like a hammock high above the water.

Two hours west of Baghdad we began to see crowds of children ahead, running out onto the highway in front of us with their arms waving. "Do they want a ride?" I asked the stupid question before thinking. "No," one of the drivers answered, "they are hungry. They are begging us to give them food."

Baghdad is a modern city with well over a million inhabitants. Middle-class neighborhoods are interspersed with commercial districts and parks. Graceful minarets rise above elaborately tiled mosques. Modern sculptures stand beside the intersection of wide boulevards. The city reflects the wealth brought in by Iraq's prolific oil fields, and at first, it looks surprisingly familiar to a visitor from Europe or the United States. But as the visitor drives through the city the differences begin to emerge. Many of the tallest buildings are ruins, their steel frames supporting tons of debris left from multiple strikes by laser bombs and Tomahawks. One of the modern bridges across the Tigris River is broken in half like a toy. Here and there are private neighborhoods and less conspicuous buildings that have been leveled by bombs.

In the evening, the most general problem of the city becomes more obvious: the municipal power system has been destroyed. Lights are on only where there are generators. Water is available only here and there, and at best the pressure is quite low. The lack of electricity forces the city to dump huge amounts of sewage into the river untreated, raising the threat of a cholera epidemic as the weather gets warmer.

We visited the Saddam Central Teaching Hospital for Children. The director, Dr. Q. M. Ismail, told us that some of the very first victims of the war were babies in his hospital. He described the panic that swept the hospital when the first bombs hit Baghdad. Mothers took premature babies out of incubators or disconnected their children from transfusion equipment and rushed them to the shelter in the basement. No bombs ever hit the hospital, but the babies that died were war victims nevertheless,

Dr. Ismail believes it will be the children who will continue to suffer most from the war, long after the last bombings. He confirmed that the hungry children we had seen west of Baghdad are a regular feature of rural Iraq, even though the food shortages are less severe in Baghdad itself. He said that for the first time in his medical career he is beginning to see kwashiorkor, severe malnutrition, among children. At the same time, the rate of diarrhea cases is rising rapidly, heralding the possible outbreak of cholera as well.

Both Dr. Ismail and Dr. Paul Boghossian, director of the Yarmuck Hospital, spoke of their fears of diseases spreading out of control in the weeks ahead, including typhoid, malaria, meningitis, and polio. Always it is the children and the elderly, especially those weakened by hunger, who are most at risk.

Meanwhile, there is a steady, pitiful flow of severely burned children through the hospitals. Without electricity, most households have to depend on makeshift kerosene lamps and heaters, and the inevitable result is that children are scalded and burned in accidents.

Dr. Boghossian estimated that his hospital treated about one thousand wounded patients during the bombing. Of those, he guessed that between one hundred and two hundred died in the hospital, with others likely to have died after they were discharged.

"Of course, that is not counting the many who were brought here from the Ameriya shelter, all dead when they arrived," he added. He proceeded to tell us of that terrible night. "I was sleeping here in my office, as I usually did during the war. When the first word of the attack came, I began to prepare the beds for the wounded." He then told of the arrival of the truck that should have been bringing the first patients. The driver came toward him slowly, simply waving his hand sadly when Dr. Boghossian asked him where the casualties were. He was so overcome with emotion that he couldn't speak. All he had brought were burned bodies.

As the bodies continued to arrive at the Yarmuck Hospital Dr. Boghossian remembered the Western reporters assembled at the El Rashid Hotel. "I sent a truck for them. When they arrived with their cameras, one of them hesitated to film the charred remains of a child, saying that it would be 'inhumane' to show such pictures on television. I shouted at him, 'Why? Is it humane to do the deed but inhumane to show it afterward?'"

"Come," he said to us suddenly. "Would you like to see the Ameriya shelter for yourself? I will take you there." A few minutes later, we were picking our way through the charred interior of the shelter. The room was eerily lighted by the sun's rays filtering down through the hole blasted through the six feet of reinforced concrete in the roof. Built to withstand the shock of a possible nuclear attack by Israel, the roof had been penetrated by the first of the two missiles that hit it. Many of the survivors of the initial blast had made their way in the pandemonium through one set of steel doors, only to find that the outer doors were still locked. About four minutes after the first explosion, a second missile had plunged precisely through the opening made by the first one, killing everyone except some who were trapped between the two sets of doors. Many of those died of the heat before rescuers finally managed to open the outer doors. After the attack, fire trucks had sprayed water into the shelter for days to cool it. While we were stumbling through the horrible wreckage of the upper chamber of the shelter, workers were still pumping the water out of the lower levels. No one knew how many more bodies were going to be found there to add to the hundreds already recovered.

Dr. Boghossian explained that the shelter had been reserved initially for people like himself: doctors, administrators, professors, and government officials. However, he said, after the first few days of the war they had decided they did not like hiding in the shelter while other people, such as the patients at the hospital, had no such place to go. As the VIPs stopped making use of the shelter, the families of the Ameriya neighborhood requested and were granted permission to use it By the time the bombs hit, the occupants were largely, if not totally (as Dr. Boghossian insists), women and children.

While the wailing call to prayer came from a nearby minaret we emerged from the shelter and crossed the street, a street where there are few women or children left. I talked to three men about the family they had lost. "How can human beings do such things?" one of them kept shouting. The oldest man stood silently, tears running down to his chin. A crowd gathered as we talked to a second man whose family had been in the shelter. "What has happened to the higher values of America," he asked, "the values of people like Lincoln?" Not only were the atrocities of the United States brutal, he complained, but President Bush and his generals insist on adding insults with brutal language, as well.

Of all the victims we met, the man whose life reflects the suffering of the Middle East most clearly was M. Mohammad Ahmed Khader. Born a Palestinian, Mohammad was forced to become a refugee early in life. He went to Libya, where he got a master's degree and married Adiba. Later they moved to Iraq, where they bought a home in the Ameriya neighborhood. Mohammad became a professor at the University of Baghdad. When the bombing became more than they could bear, Mohammad sent his wife and four daughters to the Ameriya shelter. They tried once unsuccessfully to go to Jordan to live with relatives in Amman. Returning to Baghdad, they made preparations to try again on February 14, but for Adiba and her daughters that was one day too late. For a while, Mohammad joined the grieving, helpless men in front of the burning shelter. Then he returned to his empty house and tried to burn himself to death. An alert neighbor intervened and saved him.

As I took a picture of Mohammad seated beside the portraits of his wife and daughters, he said quietly, "They were all so beautiful and so intelligent. But now . . . " Only Mohammad and his eighteen-year-old son are left.

After the interview with Mohammad, I went outside into the night and walked the dark streets of Baghdad for a while, trying to sort out my own feelings. Gradually I became more aware of the full moon shining down through the date palms and the eucalyptus trees. The sweet smell of jasmine was everywhere. Just as I was beginning to settle down, a U.S. jet suddenly roared overhead at low altitude, the nightly reminder that Iraq has been defeated and that the U.S. Air Force controls the skies. For a few minutes I struggled with my rage on behalf of thousands of children who inevitably connect such nightly fly-overs with the terror of bombs and missiles, with the impotent fury of their parents. I found myself wanting to scream curses up at the plane. Three days later I read an interview in the *Jordan Times* with a U.S. pilot as he returned to Saudi Arabia from a nightly flight over Baghdad, quite possibly the same one who had passed just a few hundred feet above me. "Routine, boring," he reported, "not like the excitement of the bombing raids."

But as I gradually calmed down again, I realized that I must learn from the example of the many people I had met these past few days, people who—despite their grief and frustration and anger—had concluded our interviews with a handshake, a smile, or even an invitation to dinner. Despite all the calculated humiliation they had suffered, there was still the urge to forgive and to build friendships. Earlier in the afternoon, I had delivered my heavy suitcases of letters to Mrs. Haddan, the head of the National Women's Federation. I showed her some of the many pictures drawn by children all over the United States and the many awkward requests that we be forgiven for our part in what the Iraqi people have suffered. She received them graciously and promised to distribute them through schools and other channels to the people of Iraq. "But," she said sadly, "it seems that such feelings have come too late to prevent the war." I agreed with her, but as we talked further we also agreed that we must begin working now to prevent the next war.

The immensity of the task facing peacemakers right now is obvious. From a rational perspective it seems clearly beyond our capability. This is the very time when it becomes most important to be part of that "company of people of faith." Not passive faith, but the kind of faith that seeks "reconciliation through compassionate action." Clearly, we have a lot to do.

54

GOD MAKES
THE CROOKED PLACES STRAIGHT

Joseph E. Lowery

The Rev. Joseph E. Lowery is president of the Southern Christian Leadership Conference in Atlanta, Georgia (Fellowship, *July-August 1995*).

In 1965, following the historic Selma-to-Montgomery voting-rights march, Martin appointed me to chair a committee of march participants to present our demands to Governor George Wallace. We checked with the general who was in charge of the National Guard. He advised us to proceed. However, when we started up the steps to the capitol, a sea of blue-uniformed state troopers formed a human barricade. I looked back at the general, who was surprised. He barked orders to members of the National Guard, who faced off with the troopers (with their hands on their bayonets). I had the feeling Moses must have experienced when the Red Sea opened and let him and the Israelites pass. We saw the "Blue Sea" part, and the children of the march walked through.

In March of this year we retraced those historic steps from Selma to Montgomery. It is a sacred trail, stained with the blood of martyrs, yet hallowed with the hopes, dreams, and footprints of the faithful. We marched again to remind the nation of the bitter price we paid for the right to vote thirty years ago, as well as the painful cost of failing to exercise that right today. We wanted to encourage a heightened level of voter activism and revive a political energy drained by disillusionment and disgust.

At the end of this reenactment, we found reason to sustain a hope for redeeming the soul of America. George Wallace, now weak, ill, and crippled from an assassination attempt in 1972, asked to greet us upon our arrival in Montgomery. The man who demonized the Federal government and deified states' rights, the man who stood defiantly in the schoolhouse door, the man whose lips dripped with interposition and nullification, wanted to welcome us to Montgomery!

When we met with Wallace in 1965 (only after the Methodist bishop in Alabama urged him to meet with us following the march), I advised him, as a Methodist preacher to a Methodist layman, that God would hold him accountable for his hateful words which others transformed into hateful deeds. Viola Liuzzo, Jimmie Lee Jackson, and others were victims of those hateful deeds.

While there were those among our marchers who didn't think I ought to grant Mr. Wallace's request, I did not dare "stand in the door" against what appeared to be an act of repentance. Since Wallace had nothing to gain politically, I welcomed his offer of reconciliation. That he wanted to come and welcome us and affirm our purpose was like a flash of lightning that blinds, and yet shines across a way filled with shadows cast by those who interpret the November election as a mandate for malice.

By car, it is less than three hours from the university in Tuscaloosa to St. Jude High School. But it is more than thirty years by way of the heart—the tortured distance Governor Wallace has traveled between the time he stood in the schoolhouse door and the time he welcomed many of the same marchers his troops had brutalized thirty years earlier. Perhaps George Wallace sends a message to today's demagogues who, with their efforts to invalidate Congressional district lines and their assaults on all forms of affirmative action, their use of hateful words and terrorist acts, now embrace a new brand of nullification and interposition.

The arc of the universe bends toward justice. I thanked George Wallace for his act of courtesy. Marchers applauded his welcome. We could not, would not, deny him an act of repentance. We serve a God who makes the crooked places straight. God makes the desert bloom and the lion lie down with the lamb. There was an air of regeneration and reconciliation in those moments! Isn't that what the world needs now? I think so!

CONCLUSION

Where is nonviolence now taking us? In summary form, we can say that it is moving us from solitary, individual expressions of nonviolence to collective nonviolent actions that involve groups ranging from a few to millions. It is moving us from passivity to proactive direct action. It is moving us from nonresistance to nonviolent resistance. It is moving us from cowardice to coercive nonviolent strategies. It is moving us beyond both just-war theory and pacifism to a third way that gathers the contributions of both into a new synthesis.

Nonviolence has been around a very long time, but it has only begun to come into its own. The Jews taught us civil disobedience, practiced for the first time in recorded history by the Hebrew midwives Shiphrah and Puah (Ex 1:15-22). The book of Daniel is full of nonviolent resistance that the authorities punished with the maximum penalties. Only a few years before Jesus' ministry began the Jews had mounted a massive nonviolent protest in Palestine. Jesus was merely developing his own tradition when he taught about turning the other cheek and walking the second mile (which must be understood as active nonviolent resistance rather than as passive nonresistance). People in many other traditions have reclaimed their own nonviolent roots as well: the Hindu Gandhi, the Muslim Basdah Khan, and socially conscious Buddhists like Thich Nhat Hanh and Aung San Suu Kyi. We are now embarking on a worldwide cooperative struggle for justice and peace through active nonviolence.

Since Gandhi and King, pacifists have been moving away from passive nonresistance to nonviolent direct action. Whereas some pacifists once argued that all force was wrong, even such forms of protest as civil disobedience, today they are more likely to support nonviolent forms of coercion and even legitimate nonviolent force. Many peace activists are beginning to see local police and an international police force under the auspices of the United Nations as necessary and even legitimate, as long as they use nonviolent methods.

Active nonviolence is an idea whose time has come. It has had spectacular successes in the last decades of the twentieth century. It has shown itself effective in overcoming political tyranny. We have only begun to use it to bring about economic justice. As I write, FOR is planning, in collaboration with other peace-and-justice groups, massive and continuous demonstrations beginning July 1, 2000, and quite possibly continuing over several summers.

But nonviolence proved almost useless in Bosnia, Rwanda, Burundi, and to a lesser extent, Kosovo. The fact is that nonviolence is still in its adolescence. We simply do not know how to use it effectively in many situations. But its unparalleled successes in the last decades give us every reason to believe that its effectiveness can be extended and enhanced, as the leaders of tomorrow apply their own creative energies to making it work.

All that is the work of the world tomorrow. The farseeing writers in this collection of pieces from The New World, The World Tomorrow, *and* Fellowship *discerned a brilliant new method for resolving the conflicts that so afflicted the twentieth century. Standing on their shoulders, we are now asked to see farther, to go farther, to dream farther, to risk and improvise and sacrifice, that the world might have a tomorrow. Thank God for these seers and prophets who led the way.*

55

THE GLOBAL SPREAD
OF ACTIVE NONVIOLENCE

Richard Deats

Richard Deats has served on the staff of FOR in a variety of positions since 1972. He is currently the editor of Fellowship *magazine. Having traveled all over the world teaching nonviolence and linking peace people together he is especially well-equipped to make this survey of the exponential increase in nonviolent actions around the world* (Fellowship, *July-August 1996 [updated for this volume]*).

In the last century Victor Hugo wrote, "An invasion of armies can be resisted, but not an idea whose time has come." Looking back over the twentieth century, especially since the movements Gandhi and King led, we see the growing influence and impact of nonviolence all over the world.

Mohandas Gandhi pioneered in developing the philosophy and practice of nonviolence. On the vast subcontinent of India, he led a colonial people to freedom through *satyagraha* or soul-force, defeating what was at the time the greatest empire on earth, the British Raj. Not long after Gandhi's death, Martin Luther King Jr. found in the Mahatma's philosophy the key he was searching for to move individualistic religion to a socially dynamic religious philosophy that propelled the civil rights movement into a nonviolent revolution that changed the course of U.S. history.

The Gandhian and Kingian movements have provided a seedbed for social ferment and revolutionary change across the planet, providing a mighty impetus for human and ecological transformation. Many, perhaps most, still do not recognize the significance of this development and persist in thinking that in the final analysis it is lethal force, or the threat of it, that is the decisive arbiter of human affairs. Why else would the United States continue to pour hundreds of billions into weapons even as non-military foreign aid is cut, United Nations dues are not paid for years, and U.S. armed forces are sent abroad on peacekeeping missions without being given the kind of training that would creatively prepare them for the work of peace?

Public awareness of the nonviolent breakthroughs that have been occurring is still quite minimal. This alternative paradigm to the ancient belief in marching armies and bloody warfare has made great headway "on the ground," but it is still little understood and scarcely found in our history books or in the media.

While "nonviolence is as old as the hills," as Gandhi said, it is in our century that the philosophy and practice of nonviolence have grasped the human imagination. In an amazing and unexpected manner, individuals, groups, and movements have developed creative, life-affirming ways to resolve conflict, overcome oppression, establish justice, protect the earth, and build democracy.

More and more, active nonviolence is taking the center stage in the struggle for liberation among oppressed peoples across the world. This is an alternative history, one that most people are scarcely aware of. What follows, in necessarily broad strokes, are some of the highlights of this alternative history.

THE PHILIPPINES

In 1986 millions of unarmed Filipinos surprised the world by nonviolently overthrowing the brutal dictatorship of Ferdinand Marcos, who was known at the time as the Hitler of Southeast Asia. The movement they called "people power" demonstrated in an astounding way the power of active nonviolence.

Beginning with the assassination in 1983 of the popular opposition leader, Senator Benigno Aquino, the movement against Marcos grew rapidly. Inspired by Aquino's strong advocacy of nonviolence, the people were opened to the realization that armed rebellion was not the only way to overthrow a dictator. Numerous workshops in active nonviolence, especially in the churches, helped build a solid core of activists—including many key leaders—ready for a showdown with the dictatorship.

In late 1985, when Marcos called a snap election, the divided opposition united behind Corazon Aquino, the widow of the slain senator. Despite fraud, intimidation, and violence employed by Marcos, the Aquino forces brilliantly used a nonviolent strategy with marches, petitions, trained poll watchers, and an independent polling commission. When Marcos tried to steal the election and thwart the people's will, the country came to the brink of civil war. Cardinal Sin, head of the Catholic church in the islands, went on the radio and called the country to prayer and nonviolent resistance; he instructed the contemplative orders of nuns to pray and fast for the country's deliverance from tyranny. Thirty computer operators tabulating the election results, at risk to their very lives, walked out when they saw Marcos being falsely reported as winning. After first going into hiding, they called on the international press and publicly denounced the official counting, exposing the fraud to the world. Corazon ("Cory") Aquino called for nonviolent rallies, vigils, and civil disobedience to undermine the fraudulent claim of Marcos that he had won the election.

Church leaders fully backed her call; in fact, the Catholic bishops made a historic decision to call upon the people to nonviolently oppose the Marcos government. Crucial defections from the government by two key leaders and a few hundred troops became the occasion for hundreds of thousands of unarmed Filipinos to pour into the streets of Manila to protect the defectors and demand the resignation of the discredited government. They gathered along the circumferential highway around Manila, which ran alongside the camps where the rebel troops had gathered. The highway, Epifanio de los Santos—the Epiphany of the Saints!—was popularly referred to as EDSA. Troops sent to attack the rebels were met by citizens massed in the streets, singing and praying, calling on the soldiers to join them in what has since been called the EDSA Revolution. Clandestine radio broadcasts gave instructions in nonviolent resistance. When fighter planes were sent to bomb the rebel camp, the pilots saw it surrounded by the people and defected. A military man said, "This is something new. Soldiers are supposed to protect the civilians. In this particular case, you have civilians protecting the soldiers." Facing the collapse of his support, Marcos and his family fled the country. The dictatorship fell in four days.

Ending the dictatorship was only the first step in the long struggle for freedom. Widespread poverty, unjust distribution of the land, and an unreformed military remained, undercutting the completion of the revolution. Challenges to the further development of an effective people power movement have continued with a determined grassroots movement working to transform Philippine society.

LATIN AMERICA

The dictatorships that characterized Latin America in the 1980s were ended for the most part by the unarmed power of the people. Consider Chile, for example. The Chileans, who like the Filipinos suffered under a brutal dictatorship, gained inspiration from the people power movement of the Philippines as they built their own movement of nonviolent resistance to General Pinochet. To describe their efforts, they used the powerful image of drops of water wearing away the stone of oppression.

In 1986 leftist guerillas killed five bodyguards of Pinochet in an assassination attempt on the general. In retaliation the military decided to arrest five critics of the regime. A human rights lawyer alerted his neighbors to the danger of his being abducted, and they made plans to protect him. That night cars arrived in the early morning hours carrying hooded men who tried to enter the house. Unable to break down reinforced doors and locks, they tried the barred windows. The lawyer's family turned on all the lights and banged pots and blew whistles, awakening the neighbors who then did the same. The attackers, unexpectedly flustered by the prepared and determined neighbors, fled the scene.

Other groups carefully studied where the government tortured people and then, after prayer and reflection, found ways to expose the evil. For example, they would padlock themselves to iron railings near the targeted building; others would proceed to such a site during rush hour, then unfurl a banner saying, "Here they torture people." Sometimes they would disappear into the crowd; on other occasions they would wait until they were arrested.

In October of 1988 the government called on the people to vote "si" or "no" on continued military rule. Despite widespread intimidation against Pinochet's critics, the people were determined. Workshops were held to help them overcome their fear and to work to influence the election. Inspired and instructed by Filipino opposition to Marcos, voter registration drives and the training of poll watchers proceeded all over the country. The results exceeded their fondest expectations: 91 percent of all eligible voters registered and the opposition won 54.7 percent of all votes cast. Afterward over a million people gathered in a Santiago park to celebrate their victory.

In the late 1980s throughout Latin America dictatorships fell like dominos, not through armed uprisings but through the determination of unarmed people—students, mothers, workers, religious groups—persisting in their witness against oppression and injustice, even in the face of torture and death. In Brazil such nonviolent efforts for justice were called *firmeza permamente*—relentless persistence. Base communities in the Brazilian countryside, for example, became organizing centers of the landless struggling to regain their land. In Argentina Mothers of the Disappeared were unceasing in their vigils and agitation for an accounting of the *desaparacidos*—the disappeared—of the military regime. In Montevideo a fast in the tiny office of SERPAJ (Service for Justice and Peace) brought to the fore the first public opposition to Uruguay's rapacious junta and elicited widespread sympathy that turned the tide toward democracy.

HAITI

Nowhere has the struggle for democracy been more difficult than in Haiti, yet even there the people developed courageous and determined nonviolent resistance against all odds. The people's movement is called *lavalas*, the flood washing away oppression. Defying governmental prohibitions and military abuse, the people demonstrated and marched and prayed. In 1986 Fr. Jean-Bertrand Aristide was silenced by his religious order and directed by the hierarchy to leave his parish and go to a church in a dangerous area dominated by the military. However, students from his church in the slums occupied the front rows of the national cathedral in Port-au-Prince. Seven students fasted at the altar, persisting for six days until the bishops backed down and allowed

Aristide to continue working in his parish. Then, in December 1990, Aristide was elected to the presidency. Driven from office and exiled abroad, he returned only after U.S. troops went into Haiti.

The long-term building of a democratic society there faces enormous odds. Even though the Haitian army has been abolished, a culture of violence remains. It will require time and persistence and the strengthening of the grassroots movement from which a civil society will emerge, as happened in Costa Rica where the abolition of the army was part of a larger effort to improve education, health care, work and living conditions. Costa Rica, without a military, remained at peace during the 1980s while much of Central America was in turmoil.

CHINA

Stunning developments took place in China in the spring of 1989. What began as a memorial march for a deceased leader quickly led into a mass expression of the pent-up longings of the Chinese people. With slogans such as "people power" and "we shall overcome," students—later joined by workers—called for democracy, an end to corruption, a free press, and other democratic reforms. Hundreds of thousands of Chinese joined the protesters in Tiananmen Square. Day after day, week after week, they peacefully called on their government to accede to their demands. First a few, then hundreds, joined in a fast. Growing numbers of citizens, including police, soldiers, even many generals, expressed sympathy for the movement. The first soldiers sent to stop the demonstrators were disarmed with gifts and good will, just as the Filipinos had done in Manila. The top leaders of the government, in an important concession, met in a televised session with the students. The movement spread, beyond control it seemed, to other cities. Finally, however, a confused and divided government replaced the troops in the capital with soldiers from North China who could be counted on to follow orders and use brute force. Thus, on June 4, the massacre of Tiananmen Square occurred, setting back for years the democracy movement in China.

This great tragedy was not necessarily the end of people power in China, however, any more than the Amritsar massacre of unarmed Indians by the British was the end of the Indian revolution nor the assassination of Benigno Aquino was the end of the people power movement in the Philippines. Both of those tragedies, in fact, proved to be beginnings rather than endings. Martin Luther King reminded us that "unearned suffering is redemptive." This can be true for a people as well as for an individual, though years, even decades may be required to rekindle such a movement.

China has also brutally sought to destroy the democratic rights of the people of Tibet. The Tibetans' exiled leader and 1989 Nobel Prize laureate, the Dalai Lama, bravely persists in calling his people not to flag in their nonviolent efforts to gain their freedom. He believes that these efforts will resonate with

China's democracy movement, which was so brutally setback at Tiananmen Square. The Dalai Lama maintains that following the course of nonviolent resistance will in time bring political concessions from China that seem unimaginable at present.

BURMA

Events remarkably parallel to China's occurred in Burma in 1988. In Rangoon, the capital, a students' nonviolent movement was launched in the summer of 1988 against the harshly repressive military rulers. Students began mass marches that increased week by week as professionals, middle-class, and working people joined in.

During this tumultuous period Aung San Suu Kyi quickly rose to prominence. The daughter of Aung San, the father of modern Burma, she married an Oxford professor and moved to England. She had returned to Rangoon from abroad because of her mother's illness. Suu Kyi was drawn into the democracy movement and fearlessly spoke at mass rallies, once walking through a contingent of soldiers ready to fire on her.

Finally, as would occur in China a year later, the threatened leaders ordered a bloody crackdown. Thousands of unarmed demonstrators were killed, with thousands more fleeing into the jungle. Nonetheless, in the May 1990 national elections the people voted overwhelmingly for Aung San Suu Kyi's National League for Democracy, even though she and the other NLD leaders had been placed under house arrest months earlier. The government refused to recognize the results of the election and continued to govern, keeping Suu Kyi under house arrest five years. Meanwhile she was awarded the Nobel Peace Prize in 1991. In one of her essays she wrote, "The wellspring of courage and endurance in the face of unbridled power is generally a firm belief in the sanctity of ethical principles, combined with a historical sense that despite all setbacks the condition of man is set on an ultimate course for both spiritual and material advancement." Her quiet determination and courage continue as a tower of strength to the Burmese in their quest for freedom.

OTHER ASIAN COUNTRIES

"Engaged Buddhism," as articulated by the Vietnamese monk, Thich Nhat Hanh, the Cambodian monk Maha Gosananda, and the Thai activist/intellectual Sulak Sivaraksa, has contributed to nonviolent struggles in many places in Asia. Thailand has evidenced ongoing nonviolent efforts against its military, including a successful student-led movement in 1973 that brought down the dictatorship. Recurring pro-democracy movements in the 1980s and 1990s have continued this long-term struggle. In the 1990s yearly Buddhist peace marches across the killing fields of a devastated Cambodia have promoted healing and the rebuilding of trust and hope among a war-weary people.

In Taiwan and South Korea pro-democracy efforts have won out over authoritarian regimes. The twentieth century ends with South Korea under the presidency of Kim Dae Jung, a human rights crusader who finally triumphed over those who tried repeatedly to kill him. His daunting effort to bring reconciliation between bitterly divided North and South Korea has been a hallmark of his presidency.

Pro-democracy students in Indonesia have been unrelenting in their struggle against dictatorship, corruption, and military involvement in politics. Unceasing rallies and protests—a democracy in the streets—finally brought down the authoritarian Suharto in May 1998, leading to a duly elected president in October 1999.

At the same time, however, unrest continued in East Timor, the former Portuguese colony taken over by Indonesia in 1975. In 1996 Bishop Carlos Belo and José Ramos-Horta received the Nobel Peace Prize for their nonviolent leadership in the freedom movement in East Timor. The post-Suharto government in Jakarta appeared more amenable to the possibility of freedom for East Timor, but in August 1999, when 78.5% of the East Timorese voted for independence, marauding militias backed by the Indonesian military attacked the population, killing thousands and driving hundreds of thousands into West Timor. The drive for independence nonetheless, with strong support in the UN and the world community, seems to be moving toward eventual success.

ISRAEL/PALESTINE

Prior to the start of the Peace Process in the Middle East, the predominant impression of the Palestinian/Israeli conflict, fed by media images, was one of rock-throwing Palestinian young men fighting the Israeli soldiers. But beginning in 1967 there were two parts of the Palestinian resistance movement, the paramilitary and the civil. The Intifada (Arabic for "to shake off") was from its inception a multidimensional movement containing many nonviolent aspects, such as:

- strikes by schools and businesses called to protest specific policies and actions of the occupying authorities;
- agricultural projects, e.g., the planting of victory gardens and trees planted on disputed lands;
- committees for visiting prisoners and families of those who have been killed;
- boycotts of Israeli-made products;
- tax refusal, as in the Palestinian village of Beit Sahour where the VAT (value added tax) and income taxes were not paid;

- when villagers were unjustly arrested, other residents went to police stations asking to be arrested as a way of showing their solidarity;
- the establishment of alternative institutions to build Palestinian self-sufficiency.

Commenting on such developments, Labor Party leader Schlomo Avineri observed, "An army can beat an army, but an army cannot beat a people. . . . Iron can smash iron, it cannot smash an unarmed fist." Nonetheless, the Palestinian resistance was met with brute force, from deliberately breaking the bones of demonstrators to demolishing the homes of suspects' families, from smashing the moveable goods of tax protestors to sealing off areas for months at a time, preventing people from going to their jobs or even going to the hospital.

The just demands and nonviolent actions of the Intifada strengthened the voices of Israelis working to find a just and peaceful resolution of the conflict. And, despite grave legal risks, covert meetings between Palestinians and Israelis slowly built growing areas of understanding. In March 1989 the chairman of the Palestine National Council's political committee told a New York audience how secret friendships with Jewish leaders helped Palestinian leaders to publicly adopt a two-state solution. In the fall of 1992 Norway began hosting fourteen secret meetings between Palestinians and Israelis out of which the Declaration of Principles was forged that provided the basis of the Israeli-PLO Accord signed on the White House lawn on September 13, 1993.

The accord was only a beginning on the long road to peace. Palestinian land was still being seized, settlements expanded, and arbitrary policies imposed upon the Palestinian people. Israelis still lived in fear of terrorist attacks. Extremists on both sides were unrelenting in their efforts to undermine the Peace Process. The assassination of Prime Minister Rabin and the electoral defeat of his government were immense setbacks to the cause of peace. Time will tell if both sides can once again build on the foundation that showed so much promise and yet faces such enormous obstacles. To those who say this is impossible, Gandhi reminds us, "Think of all the things that were thought impossible until they happened."

SOUTH AFRICA

Decades of resistance to apartheid and witness for a multiracial, democratic society slowly but surely wore away the stone of oppression in South Africa. The brutal policies of the government convinced many that apartheid would only end in a violent showdown, and to that end the African National Congress had an active military wing. Nonetheless, the heart of the resistance movement was classic nonviolent resistance: education, vigils, rallies, marches, petitions, boycotts, prayers, fasts, and civil disobedience. Governmental attempts to stop this resistance with massive detentions, bannings of organizations and individuals, intimidation and murder, as well as emergency rule could not, in the end, stop the movement.

In 1989 the churches responded to the draconian measures of emergency rule with a nationwide effort called "effective nonviolent action" that trained citizens for grassroots campaigns to break racial barriers in housing and transportation, defend conscientious objectors, visit prisoners across racial lines, and so on. Emergency rule, rather than strengthening the government, exposed its desperation and moral bankruptcy.

An unexpected breakthrough came when President deKlerk began instituting reforms. He eventually legalized the African National Congress and released Nelson Mandela, who had been in prison twenty-seven years. The dramatic changes demonstrate a concept from the civil rights movement in the United States, "top down/bottom up"; that is, pressure for change from the grassroots is met by reforms accepted by or initiated from the top, creating a dynamic tension that fosters change.

In the midst of these developments the government still carried out brutal policies. But the force for change was not to be denied. The first open elections in South Africa's history were held in an amazing manifestation of a whole nation peacefully voting for revolutionary change, moving from a white racist regime to multiracial democratic rule under the presidency of Nelson Mandela. His passion for freedom and justice for all was expressed in a greatness of spirit that reached out to his former enemies. Though he never forswore the ANC's recourse to violence, his approach has been remarkably nonviolent and reconciling. In his inaugural address he held before the people a unifying vision "in which all South Africans . . . will be able to walk tall, without any fear in their hearts, sure of their inalienable right to human dignity—a rainbow nation at peace with itself and the world."

THE FORMER SOVIET BLOC

The same "top down/bottom up" process occurred in the unraveling of the Soviet bloc that followed the policies of *glasnost, perestroika,* and *democratsatsiya* (openness, restructuring, and democracy) instituted by President Mikhail Gorbachev. Pressure from below—relentless persistence—helped to create a climate ripe for change. This ferment was long in building. On the one hand, there was a small but determined band of human rights advocates such as Andrei Sakharov and Yelena Bonner who were unrelenting in their demand for the observance of universally accepted standards of human rights. Others—religious, peace, and environmental groups, artists and poets—refused in varying ways to submit to totalitarian rule.

The crushing of Czechoslovakia's 1968 experiment to create "socialism with a human face" strengthened the widely held assumption that communism was incapable of peaceful change and democratic openness, that nonviolence might "work" in India or the United States but never with the communist regimes.

This added fuel to the Cold War and the nuclear arms race and the belief that World War III was a virtual certainty. Not many paid attention to those aspects of the Czech experiment that contained hints of the "people power" revolutions that were to flower in the 1980s, but they were highly significant.

The 1968 invasion by the Warsaw Pact armies had been expected to crush all resistance in a few days. It took eight months. Czechoslovakia's large and well-trained army was ordered to stay in its barracks while the populace responded in unexpectedly creative, nonviolent ways. The Czech news agency refused to report the disinformation that said Czech leaders had requested the invasion. Highway and street signs were turned around to confuse the invading forces. Students sat in the path of incoming tanks; others climbed on the tanks and talked to the crews. While they did not physically fight the invaders, the people refused to cooperate with them. Clandestine radio messages kept up the morale of the people, passing on vital information and instructions, such as the calling of one-hour general strikes. The Czech leaders were able to hold on to their offices and continue some of the reforms until the resistance finally began to erode, quite possibly through the work of agents provocateurs.

Twelve years later, in August 1980, neighboring Poland took up the fallen nonviolent banner as the Gdansk shipyard workers went on strike and, with prayers and rallies, Solidarity was born. Using strikes, sit-ins, and demonstrations, Solidarity gave laborers an independent voice and began a grassroots movement for change that spread rapidly across Poland.

The government responded with the imposition of martial law in December 1981. But instead of its destroying Solidarity, the people began the creation of an alternative society at the base, choosing to live "as if they were free." A new society was born in the shell of the old. When open elections finally were held, in 1989, Solidarity won by a landslide.

The Polish elections were aided by the breathtaking changes occurring in the Soviet Union. Gorbachev's reforms, beginning in 1985, opened the floodgates of pent-up longings for change that were eventually to sweep away even Gorbachev and the Soviet system. One by one totalitarian rule in the nations of Eastern Europe was overturned by people armed with truth and courage. A critical mass had been reached through the power of growing numbers of people emboldened by such things as the writings of Vaclav Havel from a Czech prison and prayer meetings and discussion groups in Leipzig, East Germany. The symbol of the vast changes was the peaceful breaching of the Berlin Wall on November 9, 1989, as the old order collapsed and its discredited regimes were swept aside with remarkably little violence or loss of life (the main exception to this being Romania).

The widespread assumption that totalitarian regimes could not be overturned by unarmed struggle was decisively shown to be wrong. Governments ultimately derive their strength from the consent—either passive or active—of the governed. Once that consent disappears and resistance spreads, governments find their power to rule weakened and, under the right circumstances, destroyed.

What happened in Eastern Europe happened in the U.S.S.R. as well. The reforms speeded up the stirrings for change, as thousands of grassroots groups sprang up to deal with a whole spectrum of social, economic, political, environmental, and cultural issues. In July 1990, one hundred thousand coal miners went out on a strike in Siberia that spread westward to Ukraine. Strongly disciplined, the miners policed themselves, closed down mining town liquor stores, and gathered for massive rallies.

From the local to the national level, elections became more democratic, bringing about the election of reform candidates. In the spring of 1989 two thousand persons, including Andrei Sakharov, were elected to the Congress of Peoples' Deputies in the freest election since the revolution. Popularly elected legislatures came into office throughout the U.S.S.R., breaking the monopoly of the Communist Party. The lead for these changes came from popular fronts established in republic after republic, beginning with Latvia (October 1988), Ukraine (September 1989), and in Lithuania where *Sajudis* won multi-party elections (February 1990). Respect for the language, history, and traditions of the various nationalities challenged the Russification that had undergirded Soviet power and control.

On March 11, 1990, the Baltic state of Lithuania became the first of the Soviet republics to proclaim outright independence. This most repressed of the republics started a "singing revolution," defying decades of cultural repression by reviving Lithuanian folk songs, festivals, religious practices, and traditions. The movie *Gandhi* was shown nationwide on television, enhancing the nonviolent resistance of the people. Trying to halt the dissolution of the Union, Moscow retaliated with a crippling blockade. The following January crack Red Army troops moved on the capital of Vilnius, killing fourteen unarmed demonstrators protecting the nation's TV tower. Instead of surrendering or issuing a call to arms, Lithuania called on the citizenry to "hold to principles of nonviolent insubordinate resistance and political and social noncooperation." The Lithuanians did just that, continuing their nonviolent and independent course. They protected their parliament with unarmed citizens and had nonviolence training for the volunteer militia they had established.

Then, in August 1991, elements of the Communist Party, the KGB, and the Army tried to stage a coup in Moscow. Despite the arrest of Gorbachev and his family, resistance was widespread. People poured into the streets to protect the Russian parliament. Women and students called on the soldiers to join the people. Religious people knelt in the streets in prayer. People trained in nonviolence passed out writings on the methods of nonviolent struggle. Closed newspapers and radio stations quickly set up alternative media. The mayor of Leningrad told the military there not to follow the orders of the plotters, and the head of the Russian Orthodox Church threatened excommunication to those who followed the coup. Even some members of the KGB refused orders, risking death for their defiance. Eventually the coup attempt collapsed, opening the way for Lithuania and the other republics to begin an independent course.

The breakup of the Soviet empire will doubtless be followed by years of upheaval as its constituent parts find their place in a world reaching for democracy but often lacking the experience, patience, and vision to implement the hope. The collapse of Soviet-style communism was followed by a predatory capitalism that in many places left the people with the worst of both systems. At this point in history we have learned a great deal about nonviolent resistance to evil and bringing down oppressors. We still have far to go in knowing how to take the next steps in fostering the democratic evolution of society that includes justice and peace, freedom and order.

Democracy is the institutionalization of nonviolent problem-solving in society.

Education, conflict resolution, the struggle for justice, organizing for special needs, voting on issues, adjudicating differences, framing laws for change and reform—these are all nonviolent in essence and help build what Martin Luther King Jr. called "the beloved community." Democratic nations are truest to their values when they deal with other nation states nonviolently, through diplomacy, treaties, mutual respect, and fairness.

The tragic warfare and ethnic cleansing that plagued the dissolution of the former Yugoslavia brought immense suffering to the region. Nonetheless, a stubborn and substantial nonviolent movement in Serbia has continued to struggle against the autocratic rule of Slobodan Milosevic. Through most of the 1990s a powerful nonviolent movement in Kosovo resisted Serbia's oppression of the majority Albanian population. Tragically, Kosovo was ignored until armed resistance started there against ethnic cleansing; then, in 1999, NATO came in with a heavy bombing campaign against the Serbs. Violent assistance to armed fighters seemed natural; nonviolent assistance to a nonviolent movement was not even attempted by nations schooled in the ways of war.

THE UNITED STATES

Nonviolent movements in the United States have a long and significant history, from the abolitionist struggle against slavery; the women's movement; the labor movement; the environmental movement; the peace movement; the movements for the rights of African Americans, gays and lesbians, as well as other minorities and oppressed groups. Peace studies in colleges, conflict resolution in schools and communities and similar developments in many areas of life give hope for the building of a culture of peace. Nonetheless, there is still far to go when one considers the degree of violence in the national life and in the foreign and domestic policies of the United States.

CONCLUSION

At the time of the Philippine overthrow of the Marcos dictatorship, a Filipino writer said that whereas the past one hundred years were dominated by

Karl Marx and the armed revolutionary, the next hundred years would be shaped by Gandhi and the unarmed *satyagrahi*, the votary of Truth. Gandhi said that "Truth is God" and that the Truth expressed in the unarmed struggle for justice, peace, and freedom is the greatest power in the world. During Gandhi's lifetime, many looked on him with contempt. Churchill dismissed him as a "half-naked fakir." Communists and other advocates of violent revolution branded his nonviolence as bourgeois and reactionary. King was arrested twenty-nine times; he was despised by many who were infuriated by his witness for justice and peace. Yet most advances in the human race have faced long years of ridicule and opposition. New insights of truth are often considered heresy. Prophets are driven out, their followers persecuted. But the influence of Gandhi and King, the martyred prophets, continues to grow as nonviolent movements spread around the world.

If a global, democratic civilization is to come into being and endure, our challenge is to continue developing nonviolent alternatives to war and all forms of oppression, from individuals to groups, from nation states to the peoples of the world. We must continue to challenge the age-old assumptions about the necessity of violence in overcoming injustice, resisting oppression, and establishing social well-being. In November 1998 the UN General Assembly unanimously proclaimed the first decade of the twenty-first century to be a Decade for a Culture of Peace and Nonviolence, a prescient recognition of the future that must be built if humanity is to endure.

What if in 1980 someone had predicted that unarmed Filipinos would overthrow the Marcos dictatorship in a four-day uprising? That military regimes across Latin America would be toppled by the relentless persistence of their unarmed opponents? That apartheid would end peacefully and that in a massive and peaceful plebiscite all races of South Africa would elect Nelson Mandela to the presidency? That the Berlin Wall would be nonviolently brought down?

Such a person would probably have been thought ridiculously naive and dismissed out of hand. And yet these things happened! Why do we so resist the potential of the not-yet stirring in the present moment? The sociologist Elise Boulding reminds us how deadly pessimism can be, for it can undermine our determination to work for a better tomorrow. Hope, on the other hand, infused in an apparently hopeless situation can create an unexpected potential for change. This is the faith that sings, in the face of police dogs and water cannons, "We Shall Overcome." Or, as Joan of Arc muses in Shaw's *St. Joan*, "Some people see things as they are and ask 'Why?' I dream of things that never were and ask, 'Why not?'"

Of Related Interest

The Vision of Peace
Faith and Hope in Northern Ireland
Mairead Corrigan Maguire
EDITED BY JOHN DEAR

ISBN 1-57075-251-6

The first ever collection of writings by Mairead Corrigan Maguire,
the 1976 Nobel Peace Prize Winner from Belfast.

"Points out the possibilities of faith, hope, and nonviolent love,
not only in Northern Ireland, but throughout the world.
Mairead Corrigan Maguire is a true prophet."

—*Martin Sheen*

The Nonviolent Coming of God
James W. Douglass
ISBN 0-88344-753-3

PAX CHRISTI AWARD WINNER

"This gripping and hopeful book not only declares God's
nonviolent coming. It helps to bring it about."

—*Walter Wink*

Martin Luther King
The Inconvenient Hero
Vincent Harding
ISBN 1-57075-06-5

In these eloquent essays, noted scholar and activist
Vincent Harding reflects on the forgotten legacy of
Martin Luther King, Jr., and the meaning of his life today.

Please support your local bookstore, or call 1-800-258-5838.

For a free catalogue, please write us at
Orbis Books, Box 308
Maryknoll NY 10545-0308
or visit our website at **www.orbisbooks.com**

Thank you for reading *Peace Is the Way.*
We hope you enjoyed it.